CREATING EXPERIENCE VALUE IN TOURISM

CREATING EXPERIENCE VALUE IN TOURISM

Edited by

Nina K. Prebensen

University of Tromsø, The Arctic University of Norway

Joseph S. Chen

Indiana University at Bloomington, USA

and

Muzaffer Uysal

Virginia Polytechnic Institute and State University, USA

www.cabi.org

CABI is a trading name of CAB International

CABI Head Office	CABI
Nosworthy Way	38 Chauncy Street
Wallingford	Suite 1002
Oxfordshire OX10 8DE	Boston, MA 02111
UK	USA
Tel: +44 (0)1491 832111	T: +1 800 552 3083 (toll free)
Fax: +44 (0)1491 833508	T: +1 (0)617 395 4051
Email: info@cabi.org	Email: cabi-nao@cabi.org
Website: www.cabi.org	

A catalogue record for this book is available from the British Library, London, UK.

Library of Congress Cataloging-in-Publication Data

Creating experience value in tourism / edited by Nina K. Prebensen, University of Tromsø, Norway, Joseph S. Chen, Indiana University at Bloomington, Muzaffer Uysal, Virginia Polytechnic Institute and State University.
       pages cm
  Includes bibliographical references and index.
  ISBN 978-1-78064-348-9 (alk. paper)
  1. Tourism--Psychological aspects. 2. Tourists--Attitudes. 3. Tourists--Psychology.
I. Prebensen, Nina K.

  G155.A1C735 2014
  338.4'791--dc23

                              2013042974

ISBN-13: 978 1 78064 348 9

Commissioning editor: Claire Parfitt
Editorial assistant: Alexandra Lainsbury
Production editor: Simon Hill

Typeset by Columns Design XML Ltd, Reading, UK.
Printed and bound in the UK by CPI Group (UK) Ltd, Croydon, CR0 4YY.

Contents

Contributors

Levent Altinay is Professor of Strategy and Entrepreneurship at Oxford Brookes University Business Faculty, UK. His research interests are entrepreneurship, strategic alliances and international business. Using primarily qualitative methods, as well as mixed methods, he is particularly interested in how entrepreneurs start up and develop their businesses and how firms establish partnerships internationally. Email: atilayuksel@gmail.com

Lidia Andrades is Assistant Professor of Marketing at the University of Extremadura in southwest Spain. Her research interests are tourist behaviour, destination competitiveness and multivariate analysis. Lidia is the Director of NETOUR (Network for excellence in tourism through organizations and universities in Russia). Email: andrades@unex.es

Peter Björk is Professor in Marketing at Hanken School of Economics in Finland. He is involved in research addressing various tourism-related issues, and he has had articles published in various tourism journals. His key areas of expertise are service design, branding consumer experience and ecotourism. Email: peter. bjork@hanken.fi

Eric S.W. Chan is Assistant Professor in the School of Hotel and Tourism Management at Hong Kong Polytechnic University. His research interests include hotel environmental management and tourist behaviour. In addition to conducting a range of training programmes for the hotel industry, he has served as Hotel Management Specialist, assisting the Hong Kong Quality Assurance Agency (HKQAA) audit team to assess the ISO 9000 quality management system of hotels. Email: eric.sw.chan@polyu.edu.hk

Prakash K. Chathoth is Associate Professor in the Department of Marketing, School of Business and Management, American University of Sharjah, UAE. His research interests include topics related to strategic and services management/marketing in the tourism/hospitality industry context. Email: pkchathoth@aus.edu

Joseph S. Chen is Associate Professor of Tourism, Hospitality and Event Management in the School of Public Health, Indiana University at Bloomington. His research interests include sustainable management, marketing and the social impact of tourism. Email: jochen@indiana.edu

Tove I. Dahl is an educational psychologist and Professor in the Department of Psychology at the University of Tromsø, Norway. Cross-cultural encounters have long been the focus of her academic work – most recently through the Norwegian Research Council's Northern InSights programme and her work at the Concordia Language Villages. Email: tove.dahl@uit.no

Graham M.S. Dann has been researching tourist motivation and such allied topics as tourism promotion for the past four decades. He has been recognized for his contribution to their understanding by the award of a higher doctorate. He is a founder member of the International Academy for the Study of Tourism and of the research committee on international tourism of the International Sociological Association. Email: dann_graham@yahoo.co.uk

Frédéric Dimanche is Professor of Marketing and Director of the Centre for Tourism Management at SKEMA Business School on the French Riviera. His research interests include tourist behaviour and destination/tourism organization management and marketing. Frédéric is a past President of the Travel and Tourism Research Association Europe. Email: frederic.dimanche@skema.edu

Monica Hanefors has more than 35 years' experience in teaching tourism and hospitality in Sweden and elsewhere. She has wide experience as a writer, educator and consultant and has published a range of articles and books on tourism and hospitality. Her research interests explore aspects of tourist behaviour, gourmet travel and tour employees' performance. Email: monica_hanefors@yahoo.se

Ann Heidi Hansen is a PhD Fellow at Bodø Graduate School of Business, University of Nordland, Norway. Her research interests are tourism experiences and consumer immersion. She has also been teaching a course in Experience Design at the University of Nordland. Email: ann.heidi.hansen@uin.no

Robert J. Harrington is the 21st Century Endowed Chair and Professor in Hospitality at the University of Arkansas, Fayetteville, USA. He is Editor-in-Chief for the *Journal of Culinary Science & Technology* and has published in the areas of hospitality strategic management, culinary innovation, culinary tourism, and food and wine. Email: rharring@uark.edu

Øystein Jensen is Professor in Marketing and Tourism at Bodø Graduate School of Business, University of Nordland and at Norwegian School of Hotel Management, University of Stavanger, Norway. He has a PhD in Marketing from Aalborg Business School in Denmark. He has been leader of the tourism research program Northern Insights, funded by the Norwegian Research Council, and been involved in several other projects on tourism, marketing and development. His main research interests involve exchange relationships, attraction development and local sustainable tourism development. Email: oje@uin.no

Tor Korneliussen is Professor of Marketing at Bodø Graduate School of Business, University of Nordland, Norway. His research interests are business performance, products and product perceptions and information search. He has published in journals such as *Industrial Marketing Management, International Journal of Advertising* and *Journal of Business Research*. Email: Tor.Korneliussen@uin.no

Young-Sook Lee is Senior Lecturer at the Department of Tourism, Sport and Hotel Management, Griffith University, Australia. Her research interests include East Asian tourism approached from cultural philosophies, sociological and literary perspectives. Email: young-sook.lee@griffith.edu.au

Vincent P. Magnini is Associate Professor and undergraduate program coordinator in the Department of Hospitality and Tourism Management at Virginia Tech University in the USA. Email: magnini@vt.edu

Line Mathisen is a PhD candidate in the Department of Business and Tourism, Finnmark University College, Norway with a specialization in tourism marketing. Her research interests include marketing and consumer behaviour. More specifically, her graduate work examines the effects of storytelling, and storytelling in interaction processes. Email: line.mathisen@hifm.no

Lena Mossberg is Professor of Marketing in the School of Business, Economics and Law at the University of Gothenburg, Sweden and also Professor II at the University of Nordland, Norway. Her interests include tourist behaviour and she has published several articles on guide performance. She has been involved in several international tourism and marketing programmes, not least in her capacity as tourism management expert for the UN and the EU. Email: lena.mossberg@handels.gu.se

Fevzi Okumus is Professor at the University of Central Florida, USA and the Editor of the *International Journal of Contemporary Hospitality Management* (*IJCHM*). His research areas include strategy implementation, competitive advantage, crisis management, experience marketing and destination marketing. He has published widely in top-tier journals and has over 160 publications (journal articles, books, book chapters, conference presentations and reports). Email: Fevzi.Okumus@ucf.edu

Nina K. Prebensen is Professor of Marketing at School of Business and Economics, UiT, Norway. Her research interests include consumer experience value, destination marketing and business strategy. She leads a work package of six projects in the research programme 'Service Innovation and Tourist Experiences in the High North: The Co-Creation of Values for Consumers, Firms and the Tourism Industry'. Email: nina.prebensen@uit.no

Bruce Prideaux is Professor of Marketing and Tourism Management at James Cook University, Australia. His current research interests include tourism transport, climatic change, agri-tourism, ecotourism and military heritage. He has published seven books, over 200 papers, chapters and conference papers on a range of tourism issues and currently supervises seven PhD students. Email: bruce.prideaux@jcu.edu.au

Haywantee Ramkissoon holds two doctoral degrees in Tourism and in Environmental Psychology. She is Senior Lecturer and currently a research fellow at Monash University, Australia. She has published in leading journals such as *Annals of Tourism Research, Tourism Management, Journal of Travel Research, Journal of Sustainable Tourism, Tourism Analysis*. Email: haywantee.ramkissoon@monash.edu

Kasey Roach was an undergraduate research assistant in the Department of Hospitality and Tourism Management at Virginia Tech University in the USA. Email: kmr2840@vt.edu

Zvi Schwartz is Professor and the J. Willard and Alice S. Marriott Senior Faculty Fellow for Hospitality Finance and Revenue Management in the Department of Hospitality and Tourism Management at Virginia Tech University, USA. His research aims to advance the forecasting, control and monitoring components of hotel revenue management systems. Email: zvi@vt.edu

M. Joseph Sirgy is a management psychologist and Professor of Marketing, and Virginia Real Estate Research Fellow at Virginia Polytechnic Institute and State University, USA. He has published extensively in the area of marketing, business ethics and quality of life. Email: sirgy@vt.edu

Gerardo R. Ungson is the Y.F. Chang Endowed Chair and Professor of International Business at San Francisco State University, USA. His teaching and research areas are global strategy, strategic alliances, poverty alleviation and Asian business, and he has co-authored six books. Email: bungson@sfsu.edu

Muzaffer Uysal is Professor of Tourism in the Department of Hospitality and Tourism Management – Pamplin College of Business, Virginia Tech, USA. His current research interests centre on tourism demand/supply interaction, tourism development and marketing, and QOL research in tourism. Email: samil@vt.edu

Akan Yanık graduated from the Communication Faculty of Ege University in 2007 and completed his master's degree at the same university. While studying in the faculty, he won nine awards including the IAA award in 2003, Golden Compass Awards of Turkey Public Relations Association in 2004 and 2005, Microsoft Imagine Cup in 2006 and other national awards. He became a Microsoft System Engineer (MCSE) and while studying worked in the Whirlpool (Vestel) Investigation & Development Laboratory. He has focused on information communication technologies and realized both theoretical publications and practical award-winning projects such as Holosbanking Project (Holographic VIP Customer Service) and TEMOC Project (Terrestrial Monitoring Central). Since 2009 he has been both a lecturer and PhD graduate student at the Adnan Menderes University, Turkey. Email: akanyanik@hotmail.com

Xiaojuan (Jady) Yu is Lecturer in the School of Tourism Management, Sun Yat-Sen University, China. She received her PhD in Recreation, Sport and Tourism from the University of Illinois at Urbana-Champaign, USA. Her current research interests include tourist behaviour and co-creation of experience. She has published in journals such as *Tourism Analysis* and *Tourism Review International*. Email: yuxiaojuan214@163.com

Atila Yüksel is Professor of Marketing at the University of Adnan Menderes, Turkey. He has published in the *Journal of Tourism Management*, *Journal of Hospitality and Tourism Research*, *Journal of Travel and Tourism Marketing*, *Cornell Quarterly*, *Annals of Tourism Research*, *Journal of Quality Assurance in Tourism and Hospitality* and *Journal of Vacation Marketing*. He has co-authored four books and is editor of the *Journal of Travel and Tourism Research*. Professor Yuksel's research interests are in tourism planning, destination management, services marketing, social web and customer relationships. Email: atilayuksel@gmail.com

Preface

The roles of hosts and guests are changing continuously. This is a consequence of technological innovations and developments, but also of people's changing mindsets: how and why tourists travel, what tourists value during a tourist journey, and how this value may be produced and consumed before, during and after a trip. Value creation as a theoretical construct, as well as a practical approach, is debated. This book attempts to outline value creation in tourist experiences, theoretically and practically, in order to obtain new understandings and models to help identify how value creation is changing within the tourism industry and demonstrate ways in which both tourists and settings can proactively take part in this change, thus becoming a vital element in its success.

The traditional view of value as something produced by one actor and consumed by another has been strongly debated in marketing and tourism literature over the last two decades. New logics supersede the traditional perspective of production and consumption as separate entities, and propose that the customer always partakes in value creation processes, and that without the customer no value is actually generated. This becomes even more relevant in the hedonic consumption of tourism goods and services. The fundamental idea is that various needs of consumers may lead to various degrees of participation in different phases of value creation. Tourist consumption is about travelling for personal enjoyment, which generates hedonic value for the customer. The customer participates in value creation because it is appealing and attractive.

Experience value can be created and/or co-created by the tourist alone, with fellow tourists, and/or with the service provider in a certain context or environment. However, in tourism, the tourist has to be present in the experience process for the value to be recognized. Current research provides a multitude of approaches to value creation and co-creation and these approaches may comprise a variety of characteristics, and imply others, in attempting to outline the essence of the concept. The wide variety of contributions in the present book, in terms of focus, scale and level of abstraction, has resulted in a complex setting of definitions, perspectives and interpretations of how tourists as customers create value alone, jointly with firms and with other actors. By including two major aspects of value creation, that is psychological and physiological aspects of a tourist journey, the book puts forward fundamental ideas on how to acknowledge and handle tourist experience as a value-based construct and personal narratives. The tourist's interest, involvement, motivation and partaking in value creation affect the tourist's value perceptions and future intentions. Furthermore, the tourist firm and service providers may enhance the firm value through developing a platform for enhanced experience value for the tourist.

The complex nature of the value creation concept may threaten its theoretical development. This book thus aims to provide an analytical and systematic clarification of the approaches and suggests a shared understanding of the differences, providing both tourism marketing scholars and practitioners with new and practical knowledge with which to increase the relevance of the concept to tourism firms and organizations. Furthermore, this book is an attempt to analyse the various factors affecting value creation in tourism from physiological and psychological perspectives. We hope that readers will find the text insightful and challenging.

Nina K. Prebensen
Joseph S. Chen
Muzaffer Uysal

1 Co-creation of Tourist Experience: Scope, Definition and Structure

Nina K. Prebensen,[1] Joseph S. Chen[2] and Muzaffer Uysal[3]

[1]School of Business and Economics, UiT, Norway; [2]Indiana University at Bloomington, USA; [3]Pamplin College of Business, Virginia Tech, Blacksburg, USA

Tourist Experience

A vacation trip is more often voluntarily and willingly performed to meet personal and hedonic needs; not because the tourists have to, but because they want to. Tourists participate in producing their vacation, before, during and after the journey, through their time, effort and money, because the process of doing so is highly valued, by themselves and relevant others. This simple but very important issue in tourist experience creation denotes a foundational difference compared with traditional products and services people buy in order to complete a task or for other instrumental reasons, i.e. to be transported, to have their apartment cleaned or to get medical help to get well from an illness. When tourists choose to spend money, time and effort to engage in activities of interest, they do so to produce an enjoyable moment of time, whatever their primary aims, motivation, interest, involvement, experiences and skills. This makes the hedonic side of tourist consumption of great importance, and so the focus on understanding tourist presence and participation in enjoying, playing and partaking relevant to the production of psychological well-being is essential. The tourism industry not only needs to focus on quality standards, but also needs to recognize and address the hedonic reasons for travelling in order to be able to facilitate and help tourists to fully enjoy and complete these motivations.

Experiences and their meanings usually appeal to tourists' high-order needs, such as novelty, excitement and enjoyment, prestige, socialization and learning, and contribute to the enhancement of a sense of well-being. Ongoing research in academia and the popular press indicates that today's travellers are gaining more power and control over what goes into the nature of tourism products as experience, with which travellers also construct their own narratives (Binkhorst and Dekker, 2009). The construction of narratives may be influenced by the extent to which the interaction takes place between tourists and the setting (or tangible place or the experience environment), as well as the interaction between local inhabitants and fellow tourists (Prebensen and Foss, 2011). The nature of this interaction provides the core of tourist experiences (Walls and Wang, 2011) and denotes enhanced experience value for the tourist handling various situations and people (Prebensen and Foss, 2011).

As implied, the experience environment, setting and/or sphere are more than the physical stage. It includes consumers, producers and the right to use amenities for a period of time (Bitner, 1992; Walls and Wang, 2011). Binkhorst and Dekker (2009) refer to this as a tourism experience network away from the home environment where the tourist as a participant is surrounded by a unique experience network of all stakeholders. This approach places the human being in the centre and considers tourism as an experience network in which various stakeholders co-create in order to engage in tourism experiences. This signifies the importance of the setting in which tourism activities take place to create value and produce experiences. Readiness of the individual, in terms of physical ability and capability, competency, willingness to work with others and the opportunity to participate, is also a significant variable that may affect the extent to which a prospective tourist as consumer may take part in creating value in the setting as much as the setting is conducive to facilitating and creating value (Mathis, 2013).

Tourist Experience and Co-creation

Creating value in tourism experiences is greatly focused on the role of tourist as consumer and the destination setting and the service company as the producer or provider in the co-creation process. Grönroos (2006, p. 324) stresses that it is not the tourists who get opportunities to engage themselves in the service provider's process, but the service provider who can create opportunities to engage itself with the tourists' value-generating process. Thus, the elements of the setting or experience dimensions should involve the tourist emotionally, physically, spiritually and intellectually (Mossberg, 2007). Another important point that needs to be mentioned is about how experiences appeal to higher order needs of satisfaction and motivation. If the setting and producer create an environment where the tourist becomes co-producer, then the perceived value that arises is likely to improve the quality of the vacation experiences, thus contributing to tourist well-being.

Tourists may perceive their vacation experiences differently based on a number of antecedents, as indicated above, and subsequent variations in their ability and desire to cope and co-create in the experience moment depending on situational aspects (Prebensen and Foss, 2011).

When discussing creating or co-creating value in tourism experiences, one may also like to see some brief discussion on definitional issues. We may start by using Frondizi's (1971) question: 'Are things valuable because we value them, or do we value them because they are valuable?' The simple reaction may be that things are valuable because we value them. This is because different people value different things.

The idea that value is something that someone produces for the consumer to buy and value afterwards is strongly debated by Vargo and Lusch (2004, 2006). Vargo and Lusch claim that 'The customer is always a co-creator of value. There is no value until an offering is used – experience and perception are essential to value determination' (2006, p. 44). Value is perceived as 'value-in-use', and consumer experiences are fundamental to the co-creation of value.

This perspective, delineated as the new service dominant logic of marketing (Vargo and Lusch, 2004, 2006, 2008; Grönroos, 2006), claims the consumer, i.e. the tourist role in creating experience value, is vital. This logic embraces the idea that in the process of co-creating value, the consumers, in addition to firms and organizations, act as resource integrators (Arnould *et al.*, 2006; Vargo and Lusch, 2006), and that value is centred in the experiences of consumers (Prahalad and Ramaswamy, 2004b). Consequently, the foundational idea in the service-dominant (S-D) logic is that the service encounter is an exchange process of value between the customer and the service provider. This perspective holds that the consumers and their skills and knowledge, depicted as operant resources, add to value creation by integrating physical, social and cultural resources (Arnould *et al.*, 2006).

Experience value becomes an integrated process between host and guests in a certain atmosphere where their respective meanings of value are shared and recognized. The meanings of value for different actors have been rooted in the foundations of economics and the study of market exchange; in particular, two broad meanings, 'value-in-exchange' and 'value-in-use', which reflect distinct ways of noting value and value creation. Vargo and Lusch (2004) describe these as the goods-dominant logic and service-dominant logic. The goods-dominant logic is based on the meaning of value-in-exchange and that value is produced by the firm in the market, usually by an exchange of goods and money (Vargo and Lusch, 2004; Vargo *et al.*, 2010). This perspective holds the roles of 'producers' and 'consumers' as separate and value creation is frequently thought of as a series of activities performed by the firm. The alternative view, S-D logic, relates to meaning of value-in-use (Vargo and Lusch, 2008). In the S-D logic the roles of producers and consumers are not separate, signifying that value is always co-created, jointly and reciprocally, in interactions among providers (including the setting) and customers or between customers through the integration of resources and application of competences.

The discussion points presented implicitly suggest that things have both exchange value and value-in-use. This distinction becomes more obvious in the context of hedonic consumption such as tourism goods and services. Exchange value measures the relative worth of something when compared with something else. This to a large extent is determined as a function of supply and demand forces. For example, the cost of a trip to London vs Tokyo from Oslo is determined by market factors. Or, a 24-carat gold bracelet is more expensive than a 14-carat bracelet when using cost or money to compare the two. The 24-carat bracelet is going to be significantly more expensive than the 14-carat bracelet simply because we as consumers believe that the higher the carat, the higher the cost of it, thus, more valuable. Value-in-use is essentially holding the sentimental value between the consumer and the consumed item. Value-in-use is the subjective and perceived benefit of an item that has been consumed. In this sense, use-in-value is created during usage, where value is socially constructed through experiences (Grönroos and Voima, 2013). For example, a week-long hike in the Norwegian mountains may be perceived differently in value by one person compared with another. If someone has 'value-in-use' for an object, it is a personal feeling or connection with that item that makes it important.

Vargo and Lusch (2008) eloquently put it that value creation refers to customers' creation of value-in-use; co-creation is a function of interaction. The degree to which interactions with spheres take place may also lead to different forms of value creation and co-creation. Tourism experience must be experienced and the customer has to be present. In this regard one can easily argue that value is subjective and determined by the consumer. Thus, co-creation is tied to usage, consumption and value-in-use; value that occurs at the time of use consumption or experience (Vargo and Lusch, 2008; Chathoth *et al.*, 2013).

Whatever name we use – the experience environment, servicescape, experience-scape, spheres or setting – on-site value creation processes are core foundations that the tourism industry must acknowledge in order to plan, develop, involve and accommodate tourists so that they are able to actively partake in such practices. The setting is also influenced by context, target, duration and goals of tourists. Tourists as consumers bring in various types of personal resources such as time, money, knowledge, past experience and learned skills. The setting and its characteristics also influence the interaction between provider sphere and customizer. The aesthetic of the setting or ambience and the functionality of the setting as a facilitator of experience creation are essential for the tourist to become part of the production system.

In order to understand value creation, antecedents of such processes should be recognized; these include the tourist's motivation, information provided, knowledge and skills, and the tourist's interest and involvement in the trip to come. Additionally, revealing the consequences and effects of value creation such as satisfaction, loyalty and subjective well-being should be acknowledged. During the journey and arriving back home, intentions concerning re-visitation and recommendation of the journey and the destination to others may be evoked. After the trip, the tourists may remember and tell others about their experiences, which all comprise value magnitudes for themselves as well as the service firms and destination visited. Therefore, understanding the value chain of tourist travel, before, during and after the trip, will help tourism businesses become competitive by enhancing tourist experience value.

The perception and valuation of an experience is relative (regarding cognitive images) and dynamic (changing within individuals over time) (Ulaga, 2003). Co-creation of value for tourists happens during the process of travelling in time and space, before, during and after the journey, and will subsequently affect tourism firms and destinations in various ways, in addition to the effects on the tourists' perception of experience value. Recent research reveals that a tourist more actively involved in the creation and co-creation of an experience evaluates that experience more positively (Arnould *et al.*, 2002; Prebensen and Foss, 2011). Studies have shown that consumers utilize personal resources actively in co-creating value (Bowen, 1986; Kelley *et al.*, 1990; Rodie and Kleine, 2000; Johnston and Jones, 2003). Researchers have suggested classifications of such resources, i.e. mental, physical and emotional (Rodie and Kleine, 2000), might vary in terms of the level of consumer involvement and role performance (Bitner *et al.*, 1997). The consumer literature has also put forward the importance of previous experience and knowledge in order to create value in various consumption situations and environments (McGrath and Otnes, 1995; Harris and Baron, 2004).

Despite an increased focus on value creation and co-creation in marketing literature (e.g. Holbrook, 1999, 2006; Prahalad and Ramaswamy, 2004a, 2004b; Vargo and Lusch, 2004) and in tourism research (Arnould *et al.*, 2002; Prebensen and Foss, 2011), there is a lack of understanding of the tourist as a resource provider and integrator, as mediator and moderator, in value co-creation processes.

Even though the subject of customer value has been addressed by a number of researchers (e.g. Holbrook, 1996; Woodruff, 1997; Sweeney and Soutar, 2001; Williams and Soutar, 2009), and further in the context of S-D logic (e.g. Berthon and Joby, 2006; Holbrook, 2006), the discussions on how and why tourists engage in co-creation are rather limited. Consequently, this book aims to explore and outline the concept of tourist experience value, and subsequently divulge important antecedents and consequences of the experience value construct. Specifically, the book strives to complement current theories regarding value co-creation in tourist experiences.

Phases of Tourist Experience Creation

It has been well documented that travellers usually go through different phases of a travel journey. Clawson and Knetsch (1971) provided five phases of a travel experience: pre-trip (planning and information gathering), travel to site, on-site activities, return trip and post-trip. Regardless of the number of phases, whether three (travel to site, onsite experience and return) or five, as put forward by Clawson and Knetsch (1971), the interaction between the tourist and the service provider (the industry) may occur with each phase of travel at the boundary of the tourist and provider spheres. Pre-trip activities may use personal resources to influence and create planning and finding motivation for the trip, and tourists use some form of transportation en route to the selected travel destination. Often tourists turn to travel and tourism service providers (e.g. airlines, bus companies) to help them reach their destination. Subsequently, when tourists reach their destinations they often rely on travel/tourism service providers to supply the accommodations, restaurants, entertainment and encounters of the traveller at the final destination. Then, tourists make their return trip, during which they may interact with travel carriers and personnel. After the travel experience is over and the travellers have returned to their homes, they often reflect on their trip experiences (Neal *et al.*, 1999). So, tourism consumption inherently possesses the unique capacity to create value as the tourists interact with each phase of the journey as the setting throughout the duration of the entire trip.

The different phases of a travel experience also imply that it is not only possible but also feasible to create value-added dimensions at any point of the process. It is important for providers and producers to know that the phases of the process can act both as sources of experience enhancement, satisfaction and dissonance. The simultaneous production and consumption of most of the tourism services adds a unique challenge to the creation of customer value. Creation of customer value in tourism can occur throughout the different phases of travel experience, ranging from the pre-trip planning and anticipation, to on-site experience, to post-trip reflection. The possible sources of value creation and co-creation may be context-based, target-oriented and/or goal-oriented. For example, Braithwaite (1992) discusses the importance of value creation in relation to information technology. He presents a framework called 'value chain' that stretches across the different subsectors of the travel and tourism industry. Each link on the value chain represents an experience point. The value each experience or travel phase creates may range from 'high' to 'moderate' to 'low'. Each point has the potential to produce value for the customer. However, this potential to create value may be influenced by the nature of the setting and its characteristics. Each offering of service-oriented technology may affect the value that a customer receives at one or more experience points.

The question is then, how do destinations and firms as providers and co-creators influence perceived value of the phases or processes of vacation experiences as the tourist moves into actual consumption of the offering? Marketing and research efforts of producers in different organizations, including partnerships between the public and private sectors, should be geared toward the creation of value to potential visitors at any point in the phases of vacation experience. Today, the use of information technology is one of the means available to make value creation easier, linking tourism product and consumer in real time and as a consequence limiting time devoted to planning and logistics and creating more time for relaxation and leisure.

Much of the cognitive and physical effort of the purchase occurs prior to actual buying behaviour. Therefore, the tourism industry should know how to constructively influence, motivate and involve customers in the pre-purchase stage. Perceived customer value has been found to be a powerful predictor of purchase intention (e.g. Zeithaml, 1988). Thus, identifying factors that are critical in acquiring new visitors and retaining old customers should be of great interest to marketers of tourist experiences and destinations.

Tourists interact with people and natural or man-made elements. Interaction traditionally has been seen a core characteristic of tourism as a result of simultaneous production and consumption, delineated as 'prosumption' by Toffler (1980). This is especially the case in experience production and consumption such as in tourist experiences.

Goffman (1967) focused on the intangible elements of experiences and the importance of the interactions between hosts and guests. The production, delivery and consumption of experiences are inextricably linked with the interpersonal interaction between service providers and consumers. The tourist interacts with a host often represented by the service worker, in addition to other guests and physical elements within a firm or as part of a destination. These interactions happen because it is valued or expected to provide future value (or hinder events, diminishing value) for the customer. All actors included in the service encounter, i.e. the participants in value creation, refer to all individuals, whether customers or workers are involved (Booms and Bitner, 1981). Research has repeatedly demonstrated that such an interaction is among the most significant determinants of consumer satisfaction with services (e.g. Bitner et al., 1997).

The impact of the physical surrounding of servicescapes for customers and employees, along with the service provided, involves people differently in terms of how they create and co-create their own and others' tourist experiences. Knowledge regarding the effect of the physical surroundings and the servicescapes is extremely important for the tourism industry in order to develop innovative and valued service experiences.

This knowledge will help tourist providers focus on the drivers of overall value for the tourist, and thus help firms enhance their overall value as well (Smith and Colgate, 2007). Both value for the customer and value for the firm includes the customer's perception of value. That being so, exploring the tourist value construct in an interaction framework would help tourist businesses identify how to tailor their businesses toward their customers and hence increase loyalty among their patrons.

Research demonstrates the advantage of acknowledging consumer behaviour through the perceived value construct (e.g. Woodruff and Gardial, 1996; Heskett *et al.*, 1997; Sweeney and Soutar, 2001). These authors, however, view value creation as something the service provider should deliver through acknowledging the consumer's needs and wants. Customers' perceived value is defined as the results or benefits customers receive in relation to the total costs (e.g. Zeithaml, 1988; Holbrook, 1994, 1996; Woodruff, 1997). Consequently, dimensions of value creation as part of an interaction process are lacking. Experience consumption (e.g. Arnould and Thompson, 2005) such as a tourist experience, deals with emotions and contextual, symbolic and non-utilitarian aspects of consumption. Value, then, is considered to reside in the experience and not in the object of consumption. A tourist visits destinations in order to enjoy valuable experiences, which signifies that partaking in the process or the journey is valuable in itself. That being so, a tourist spends money, time and effort to enjoy a journey, essentially to partake in co-creating preferred experiences, whatever the primary motivations may be (e.g. learning, socializing or indulging).

Structure of the Book

Over the past 25 years the field of tourism has witnessed a tremendous growth in the number of academic journals and books on the topic, and in the amount of information that has been generated on different aspects of tourist behaviour. As the field of tourism begins to display maturity and scientific sophistication, it is important that we as tourism researchers fully understand the breadth and depth of vacation experience value and how this experience is co-created as tourists engage in and go through different phases of a vacation experience. There have been a number of books in the scholarly literature on tourism and allied fields that have exclusively focused on tourist experiences or some aspects of experiences (e.g. Pine and Gilmore, 1999; Ryan, 2002; Wearing, 2002; Jennings and Nickerson, 2005; Morgan *et al.*, 2010; Pearce, 2012). However, there is no single book that focuses exclusively on creating value and co-creation in tourism experiences in the field of tourism and allied fields.

This book aims to serve as a reference from the unique perspective of co-creation of experience value and vacation experience in the field of tourism and allied fields such as leisure, recreation and service management. The book has brought together scholars from diverse areas to address the nature and types of tourist value and what factors affect value creation and co-creation in tourist experiences in particular from both the customers' participation and involvement point of view, and the business perspective of value creation. In other words, how does the tourist create and co-create experience value for him or herself, other tourists and the tourism firm by being more or less active throughout the duration of the consumption process? What is the role of the producer in the process of value-in-use consumption of tourism goods and services? Particularly, we attempted to structure the book in a way that provides a framework to distinguish key resources or antecedents of customer value that appear to validate consideration in the analysis of consumer behaviour. These antecedents of value co-creation refer to different aspects of consumption that have attracted the attention of various scholars in the field. Consequently, our contributors, who represent eleven countries in these areas of inquiry, discuss whether and how their concerns fit into the thematic framework, offering further insights into the applicability of the antecedents of customer value co-creation, consumption process and interaction in the experience environment across a broad range of research topics. By doing so, we believe that this book, with nineteen unique chapters, fills a gap that exists in our current tourism literature.

We think that this book will be of great interest to students of tourism and allied fields such as leisure, recreation and hospitality. In addition, tourism practitioners and researchers may find this book very useful in understanding how to best cater to, attract and increase tourists since it focuses on the merits and importance of co-creation value in tourist experiences and their associated management and marketing implications.

Acknowledgements

The book is part of a research programme 'Service Innovation and Tourist Experiences in the High North: The Co-Creation of Values for Consumers, Firms and the Tourism Industry', financed by the Norwegian Research Association, project no. 195306. The editors thank all the contributors to this book for their effort and skills in writing valuable chapters. Warm thanks also go to the publisher CABI and their highly skilled staff.

References

Arnould, E.J. and Thompson, C.J. (2005) Consumer culture theory (CCT): twenty years of research. *Journal of Consumer Research* 31, 868–882.
Arnould, E.J., Price, L.L., Malshe, A. and Zinkhan, G.L. (2002) *Consumers*, 2nd edn. McGraw-Hill/ Richard D. Irwin, New York.
Arnould, E.J., Price, L.L. and Malshe, A. (2006) Toward a cultural resource-based theory of the customer. In: Lusch, R.F. and Vargo, S.L. (eds) *The Service-Dominant Logic of Marketing: Dialog, Debate and Directions*. M.E. Sharpe, Armonk, New York, pp. 320–333.
Berthon, P. and Joby, J. (2006) From entities to interfaces: delineating value in customer–firm interactions. In: Lusch, R.F. and Vargo, S.L. (eds) *The Service-Dominant Logic of Marketing: Dialog, Debate and Directions*. M.E. Sharpe, Armonk, New York, pp. 196–207.
Binkhorst, E. and Dekker, T.D. (2009) Agenda for co-creation tourism experience research. *Journal of Hospitality Marketing and Management* 18, 311–327.
Bitner, M.J. (1992) Servicescapes: the impact of physical surroundings on customers and employees. *Journal of Marketing* 56, 57–71.
Bitner, M.J., Faranda, W.T., Hubbert, A.R. and Zeithaml, V.A. (1997) Customer contributions and roles in service delivery. *International Journal of Service Industry Management* 8(3), 193–205.

Booms, B.H. and Bitner, M.J. (1981) Marketing strategies and organizational structures service firms. In: Donnelly, J.H. and George, W.R. (eds) *Marketing of Services*. American Marketing Association, Chicago, Illinois, pp. 47–51.

Bowen, D.E. (1986) Managing customers as human resources in service organizations. *Human Resource Management* 25(3), 371–383.

Braithwaite, R. (1992) Value-chain assessment of the travel experience. *Cornell Quarterly* 33(5), 41–49.

Chathoth, P., Altinay, L., Harrington, R.J., Okumus, F. and Chan, E.S.W. (2013) Co-production versus co-creation: a process based continuum on the hotel service context. *International Journal of Hospitality Management* 32, 11–20.

Clawson, M. and Knetsch, J.J. (1971) *Economics of Outdoor Recreation*. Johns Hopkins Press, Baltimore, Maryland.

Frondizi, R. (1971) *What is Value?* Open Court, LaSalle, Illinois.

Goffman, E. (1967) *Interaction Ritual: Essays on Face-to-Face Behavior*. Anchor, Garden City, New York.

Grönroos, C. (2006) Adopting a service logic for marketing. *Marketing Theory* 6(3), 317–333.

Grönroos, C. and Voima, P. (2013) Critical service logic: making sense of value creation and co-creation. *Journal of Academy of Marketing Science* 41, 113–150.

Harris, K. and Baron, S. (2004) Consumer-to-consumer conversations in service settings. *Journal of Service Research* 6(3), 287–303.

Heskett, J.L., Sasser, W.E. and Schlesinger, L.A. (1997) *The Service Profit*. Free Press, New York.

Holbrook, M.B. (1994) The nature of consumer value: an axiology of services in the consumption experience. In: Rust, R.T. and Oliver, R.L. (eds) *Service Quality: New Directions in Theory and Practice*. Sage, Thousand Oaks, California, pp. 21–71.

Holbrook, M.B. (1996) Customer value: a framework for analysis and research. In: Corfman, K.P. and Lynch, J.G. Jr (eds) *Advances in Consumer Research* 23. Association for Consumer Research, Provo, Utah, pp. 138–142.

Holbrook, M.B. (1999) *Consumer Value: A Framework for Analysis and Research*. Routledge, London.

Holbrook, M.B. (2006) Consumption experience, customer value, and subjective personal introspection: an illustrative photographic essay. *Journal of Business Research* 59, 714–725.

Jennings, G. and Nickerson, N.P. (eds) (2005) *Quality Tourism Experiences*. Elsevier Butterworth-Heinemann, Oxford.

Johnston, R. and Jones, P. (2003) Service productivity: towards understanding the relationship between operational and customer productivity. *International Journal of Productivity and Performance Management* 53(3), 201–213.

Kelley, S.W., Donnelly, J.H. Jr and Skinner, S.J. (1990) Customer participation in service production and delivery. *Journal of Retailing* 66(3), 315–335.

Mathis, E. (2013) The effects of co-creation and satisfaction on subjective well-being. Master's thesis, Virginia Tech, Blacksburg, Virginia.

McGrath, M.A. and Otnes, C. (1995) Unacquainted influencers: when strangers interact in the retail setting. *Journal of Business Research* 32, 261–272.

Morgan, M., Lugosi, P. and Ritchie, J.R.B. (2010) *The Tourism and Leisure Experience*. Channel View, Bristol, UK.

Mossberg, L. (2007) A marketing approach to the tourist experience. *Scandinavian Journal of Hospitality and Tourism* 7(1), 59–74.

Neal, J., Sirgy, J. and Uysal, M. (1999) The role of satisfaction with leisure travel/tourism services and experience in satisfaction with leisure life and overall life. *Journal of Business Research* 44, 153–163.

Pearce, P. (2012) *Tourist Behavior and the Contemporary World*. Channel View, Bristol, UK.

Pine, J. and Gilmore, J. (1999) *The Experience Economy*. Harvard Business School Press, Boston, Massachusetts.

Prahalad, C.K. and Ramaswamy, V. (2004a) *The Future of Competition: Co-creating Unique Value with Customers*. Harvard Business School Press, Boston, Massachusetts.

Prahalad, C.K. and Ramaswamy, V. (2004b) Co-creation experiences: the next practice in value creation. *Journal of Interactive Marketing* 18(3), 5–14.

Prebensen, N.K. and Foss, L. (2011) Coping and co-creation in tourist experiences. *International Journal of Tourism Research* 13(1), 54–57.

Rodie, A. and Kleine, S. (2000) Consumer participation in services production and delivery. In: Swartz, T. and Iacobucci, D. (eds) *Handbook of Services Marketing and Management*. Sage, Thousand Oaks, California, pp. 111–125.

Ryan, C. (ed.) (2002) *The Tourist Experience: An Introduction*, 2nd edn. Thomson Learning, London.

Smith, J.B. and Colgate, M. (2007) Customer value creation: a practical framework. *Journal of Marketing Theory and Practice* 15(1), 7–23.

Sweeney, J. and Soutar, G. (2001) Consumer perceived value: the development of a multiple item scale. *Journal of Retailing* 77, 203–207.

Toffler, A. (1980) *The Third Wave*. Bantam Books, New York.

Ulaga, W. (2003) Capturing value creation in business relationships: a customer. *Industrial Marketing Management* 32(8), 677–693.

Vargo, S.L. and Lusch, R.F. (2004) Evolving to a new dominant logic of marketing. *Journal of Marketing* 68(1), 1–17.

Vargo, S.L. and Lusch, R.F. (2006) Service-dominant logic: what it is, what it is not, what it might be. In: Lusch, R.F. and Vargo, S.L. (eds) *The Service-Dominant Logic of Marketing: Dialog, Debate and Directions*. M.E. Sharpe, Armonk, New York, pp. 43–56.

Vargo, S.L. and Lusch, R.F. (2008) Service dominant logic: continuing the evolution. *Journal of the Academy of Marketing Science* 36, 42–53.

Vargo, S.L., Lusch, R.F., Akaka, M.A. and He, Y. (2010) The service dominant logic of marketing: a review and assessment. *Review of Marketing Research* 6, 125–167.

Walls, A.R. and Wang, Y. (2011) Experiential consumption and destination marketing. In: Wang, Y. and Pizam, A. (eds) *Destination Marketing and Management*. CAB International, Wallingford, UK, pp. 82–98.

Wearing, S. (2002) *Volunteer Tourism: Experiences that Make a Difference*. CAB International, Wallingford, UK.

Williams, P. and Soutar, G.N. (2009) Value, satisfaction and behavioral intentions in an adventure tourism context. *Annals of Tourism Research* 36(3), 413–438.

Woodruff, B.R. (1997) Customer value: the next source for competitive advantage. *Journal of the Academy of Marketing Science* 25(2), 139–153.

Woodruff, B.R. and Gardial, F.S. (1996) *Know Your Customer: New Approaches to Understanding Customer Value and Satisfaction*. Blackwell Business, Cambridge, Massachusetts.

Zeithaml, V.A. (1988) Consumer perceptions of price, quality, and value: a means–end model and synthesis of evidence. *Journal of Marketing* 52, 2–22.

2 Dynamic Drivers of Tourist Experiences

Joseph S. Chen,[1] Nina K. Prebensen[2] and Muzaffer Uysal[3]

[1]Indiana University at Bloomington, USA; [2]School of Business and Economics, UiT, Norway; [3]Pamplin College of Business, Virginia Tech, Blacksburg, USA

Introduction

In the face of a highly competitive market environment, tourism operators seek winning strategies capable of perpetuating their market share. The quality of service experience delivered to tourists has been considered as one of the highlights in market strategy development (Gunter, 1987; Taniguchi *et al.*, 2005; Obenour *et al.*, 2006; Larsen, 2007; Mossberg, 2007; Volo, 2010). Nevertheless, producing a satisfactory tourist experience seems to be a daunting task because tourist experiences can be rather subjective from person to person (Jackson and Marsh, 1996), complex due to the level of involvement (Fave and Massimini, 2003) and multifaceted in relation to the benefits sought (Prentice *et al.*, 1998). Consequently, how to fabricate and stage fulfilling trip experiences to create value for both tourists and service providers has become a prominent investigative theme (Uriely, 2005).

In an early stage of tourism research, several polemic tenets manifesting the phenomenon of tourism were proposed by sociologists (e.g. Boorstin, 1964; MacCannell, 1976; Cohen, 1979), who meanwhile attempted to delineate what constitutes tourist experiences. Afterwards, scholarly discussions on tourist experiences have largely touched on deterministic notions (e.g. Tussyadiah and Fesenmaier, 2009) that probe the relationship between certain behavioural elements, such as motivation (Gomez-Jacinto *et al.*, 1999; Dann and Jacobsen, 2003), and tourist experiences, embracing deductive and inductive ways of inquiry. Unarguably, understanding the causality relevant to the formation of tourist experiences could provide valuable insights in product development and service delivery. Although a variety of discourses of tourist experiences have been noted in the last three decades, a comprehensive model capturing the antecedents of these experiences while highlighting the nature of the experiences achieved has not been seen in research.

This chapter attempts to compose a conceptual framework that demonstrates the drivers influencing the creation of tourist experiences. In constructing this tourist experience model, three streams are offered. The first stream is to trace the past research of consumption experience in general and the tourist experience specifically while reviewing the concepts of the tourist experience, the determinants of the experience and the strategic frameworks utilizing the tourist experience as a facilitator in marketing management. The second attempts to explicate the relationships between the drivers and the formation of tourist experiences from a temporal consideration (e.g. before the trip, during the trip and after the trip). The last consideration intends to illustrate underlying challenges in incorporating the proposed model into business practices so as to infer possible directions for future research.

In contemporary management literature (Halbrook and Hirschmann, 1982), the focus of investigation effort has shifted from the consumption of goods to the consumption of experiences (e.g. Otto and Richie, 1995; Morgan, 2006), knowledge and services. In response to the emergence of experience-centric practices, Pine and Gilmore (1999) noted the phenomenon of the experience economy that means that the provision of quality consumption experiences is now a pivotal mission in businesses. Indeed, the travel industry is one of the largest service sectors in terms of the number of people employed and its contribution to the economy. Tourist experiences therefore necessitate critical debates and empirical undertakings among social-sciences scholars and social critics.

Boorstin (1964), for instance, denoted tourist experiences as contrived incidents owing to what is characterized as the trivial, superficial and frivolous nature of tourist pursuits, which in theory yield a pseudo-event. However, MacCannell's (1976) observation of tourist engagement contradicted Boorstin's theory and postulated tourist motives as a search for authenticity. However, Cohen (1979) questioned the validity of the two aforementioned schools of thought concerning tourist experiences in light of the narrowly selected study samples. He praised the contributions from Boorstin and MacCannell, stating 'each has contributed valuable insights into the motives, behaviors and experience of some tourists' (1979, p. 180), but that 'Different kinds of people may desire different modes of touristic experiences; hence, "the tourist" does not exist as a type' (1979, p. 180).

Moreover, in his bid to reconcile Boorstin and MacCannell's incompatible views of tourist experiences, Cohen (1979) derived a continuum of five modes of tourist experience (recreational, diversionary, experiential, experimental and existential), depending on the depth of seeking and escaping motives. Cohen implied that taking a leisure trip is a way of managing tension created by one's effort to conform to the social values of his/her society. Nevertheless, the magnitude of pressure created varies among the different groups of tourists. For example, those drawing on the recreational-mode experience are considered as the group of tourists who alienate themselves from their life space the least. On the other extreme of the experience continuum, tourists who aspire to existential experiences detach culturally and spiritually from their own society the most. Indeed, it is arguable that Cohen's phenomenological analysis erects a tourist experience theory from a holistic perspective, while laying a theoretical abstract influencing the development of market strategy.

Beyond the above ethnological contentions, researchers are overwhelmingly in accord with the proposition that tourist experiences are multidimensional, depending on the benefits sought (Prentice et al., 1998). The nature of tourist experiences is indeed deemed to be dynamic. Selstad viewed human behaviour as accommodative and argued that 'experiences anticipated by tourists do not always materialize, and unexpected events are integrated as a part of experience' (2007, p. 30). Further, it is likely that the desired experience may be shifted as the circumstances dictate. For example, in a given journey, tourists who are originally in search of existential experiences may switch their attention to recreational experiences when they no longer feel existential experiences can be fulfilled. The adaptive temptation is oriented by personal value and in conformity with personal goals. This may be best elucidated by the observation of Crick-Furman and Prentice, who drew their attention to tourism value in stating 'values do not remain constant but rather are adapted to different environments and contexts according to the immediate goals and objectives of the individual' (2000, p. 88). In other words, the motive to pursue a particular type of experience could be rather unstable and modified unexpectedly in certain situations.

Moreover, tourist experiences are generally derived either passively or proactively. This tendency to pursue desired experiences may be best described by Dilthey's concept of 'mere' experience and 'an' experience (Rickman, 1976). Turner and Bruner (1986) further enunciated the concept that mere experience is a reflection of the outcome from passive encountering, whereas an experience springs from an array of engagements which are undertaken in a constructive, goal-oriented fashion.

Empirical Undertakings Grounded on Experience Theories

When it comes to the conceptualization of experience stages, Csíkszentmihályi's (1975) flow theory, which relates to the feeling of spontaneous enjoyment in engagement of an activity, is considered as one of the most provocative and influential experience theories in psychology. Several tourism scholars (e.g. Vitterso *et al.*, 2000; Skadberg *et al.*, 2005) have utilized this concept as the theoretical foundation in empirical investigations to evaluate tourist optimal experiences.

In the domain of service management, the study of consumption experience has been prevalent. The thesis of Pine and Gilmore (1999) has also offered innovative directions for scholarly research on consumption experience. They described an emerging force called 'the experience economy', which will become the next economy following the service economy. Further, they emphasized that providers ought to orchestrate memorable experiences for their consumers. They divided consumption experiences into four functional zones: recreational, escapist, aesthetic and educational. Despite management thought frequently noted by tourism and hospitality scholars, no evidence-based investigation was presented until the work by Oh *et al.* (2007), who, mirroring the four domains of experience economy, constructed and validated a multi-trait and multi-dimensional tourism experience scale.

Another school of thought concerning consumption experience was presented by Schmitt (1999), who distinguished experiences using five dimensions or strategic experiential modules: sensory experience (sensing), emotional experience (feeling), thinking experience (thought), operational experience (action) and related experiences (belonging). Sensory experience is also tied to a person's intuition, and emotional and thinking experiences are the reflection of affective and cognitive quests. Operational experience springs from engagement in activity, while related experience is considered as personal attachment (belongingness) to certain social groups or cultures. Most recently, in their application to the five strategic experiential modules, Wang *et al.* (2012) evaluated the causal relationships among service quality, tourist experience and revisit intention concerning three popular wetland parks in Zhejiang, China. In their final analysis, however, they postulated that only sensory, emotional and operational experience could statistically describe the tourist experience of wetland parks under investigation. This may imply that experience dimensions may not all be necessarily valid and applicable.

Factors Influencing the Creation of Tourist Experiences

In conclusion, this chapter has traced the dynamic and evolutional nature of the tourist experience and postulates the tourist experience as an amalgam of cognitive and affective marks, caused by the bricolage of encounters occurring before, during and after the trip, reflecting in a passive or active state of mind.

In theory, tourist behaviour in relation to experience creation could be modified by a host of factors, which include but are not limited to: behavioural variances (e.g. expectation, perception and motivation), social-demographic traits (e.g. education, income), lifestyle (e.g. basic living, moderate living and extravagant living) and externalities (e.g. weather, regulations and the environment). This chapter does not discuss all possible antecedences influencing the creation of the tourist experience. Rather, it is an attempt to furnish a new perspective for examining the dynamic process of the creation of tourist experiences that may engender possible directions for further studies.

Consequently, the following section presents a conceptual framework called the Tourist Experience Driver Model (TEDM) that illustrates the formation of the tourist experience and the drivers facilitating the creation of the experience. The TEDM (see Table 2.1) presents two types of trip-related experience, differentiated by the time span of the trip. The experience received before and during the trip is labelled as the trip partaking experience. Once the trip is complete, the trip partaking experience becomes the trip reminiscing experience, which is in fact the recollection of various pieces of partaking experiences. In brief, as described above, the partaking experiences relate to different pieces of trip engagement (e.g. asking for one's recommendation for hotel booking and participating in a whale-watching activity), whereas the reminiscing experiences reflect one's recalling all partaking experiences at a certain point in time. It is suggested that trip reminiscing experiences may vary at different timeframes (e.g. one week after the trip vs one year after the trip) due to memory loss.

The trip partaking experience starts as early as the tourist shows a desire to take a trip. This arousing 'anxiety' motivates individuals to take further trip-related actions, such as making enquiries about the destinations of interest so as, at a certain point of time, to make trip decisions that involve diverse decision tasks (e.g. destination selection, airline booking and hotel reservation). The pre-trip engagements could produce a variety of memories in either a positive or negative fashion. It is suggested that positive memories yielded before the trip may help boost the tourist's other

Table 2.1. Tourist experience driver model.

	Trip partaking experiences		Trip reminiscing experiences
Before the trip	During the trip		After the trip
Personal driver	(Evolving influences) e.g. Modified involvement		Non-recallable
e.g. Age e.g. Motivation	e.g. Modified motivation		
Environmental driver			Recallable
e.g. Advertising	e.g. Modified perception		I. Disastrous
Interactive driver	e.g. Modified information search (Emerging influences)		II. Regretful
e.g. Information search	e.g. Encountering with travel partners e.g. Encountering with other guests e.g. Encountering with the service environment		III. Monotonous IV. Memorable V. Extraordinary

partaking experiences and vice versa. For example, individuals may be impressed by a friendly and quality-service attitude of a hotel reservation agent when making a room reservation before taking the trip. Afterwards, when staying in the hotel, the individuals may find that the hotel meets their original expectations. In such a situation, the two positive experiences toward service delivery occurring before and during the trip are likely to make the individuals believe that the hotel's service quality is consistently good. As a result, the individuals tend to possess a stronger belief toward the service quality of the hotel they visited. In the end, this helps secure a high level of customer satisfaction and increases the likelihood of achieving customer loyalty.

This chapter posits that three types of drivers collectively affect trip partaking experiences. The first is a personal driver that relates to an individual's characteristics. It is argued that the personal driver is comparatively profound. It is the most diverse and comprehensive driver whose profile consists of attributes ranging from socio-demographic traits to psychological elements such as personality. In a case of socio-demographic characteristics, some could be used as predictors and some could not. For example, elderly tourists prefer to read larger font-size printed documents; individuals travelling with small children may be happier if babysitting services or children's activities are provided at destinations. Retrospectively, individuals in an upper-income level may not necessarily want to stay at upscale hotels when taking a leisure trip. As for psychological traits, these could offer some valuable tips in predicting behavioural intention. One example is that people with a strong pro-environment attitude are likely to stay at a hotel implementing environmental management schemes, regardless of other service offerings.

The second is an environmental driver that deals with non-personal influences. For instance, appealing, informative promotion materials of the destination may give rise to an induced image, which could entice the trip demand from the tourist. It is true that the outcomes of marketing efforts by industry professionals could be foreseen at a certain point of time in regard to their effect on the tourist's decision making. Nevertheless, under some circumstances the environmental driver could rapidly emerge as a powerful stimulus on an individual's state of mind in either a positive or negative way. For example, when reading about news concerning an avalanche incident in the Alps, people who are scheduled to visit a winter resort surrounding the Sierra Nevada Mountains may have some concerns and apprehension for their winter trip. In a different vein, people's level of anxiety toward the trip will increase when they find out that they will have an opportunity to win an award of $10,000 as hotel guests. Therefore, the environmental driver is an essential property, manipulating individuals' perception as well as staging the partaking experience.

Finally, the interactive driver brings the destination to the tourists' attention through interactive and reciprocal channels of exchange. For example, during the information-search stage, tourists may consult with their friends or talk to service providers to obtain useful insights on the destination. At this trip stage, the interaction with people is of limited scope since it merely fulfils the cognitive gap of travel-related information. Through those interactions, tourists may, on the one hand, find their information needs fulfilled, yet on the other hand, become aware of new activities, amenities and attractions to explore. This newly acquired knowledge allows the tourists to instigate actions on new tourism services. The interactive driver therefore plays a viable role in assisting tourists to escalate their level of excitement and accordingly may result in a fulfilling trip experience.

The above three drivers may be further modified to reflect the different magnitude of effects on the partaking experience. For example, tourists who show no or low interest in reading the background literature on the points of interest and associated tourist activities rendered by the destination before taking their trip may be prompted to attain new knowledge when they find something interesting, or when they interaction with other tourists and service staff at the destination. Transition from this passive state of mind in acquiring trip information to the proactive attitude toward information search shows that the driver may be rapidly amplified in a different time span of the trip.

Nevertheless, when individuals are starting their trip, new attributes reinforcing the tourist experience may surface that are also considered as interactive drivers. For example, during the trip, generally the tourists will have many chances to interact with various kinds of people (e.g. tourists, service staff and locals) while experiencing the social, cultural, spiritual and aesthetic attributes along with the functional value of the service environment (e.g. the scenery, artefacts and architecture). Those interactions constitute some pieces of the puzzle in a tourist's memory map of their trip experience.

In mass tourism settings, the opportunity to mingle with the tourists, service staff and local people are abundantly supplied. Because socialization is one of the motivations of travel, it is expected that a certain degree of interaction with people other than travel partners will take place in a visitor centre or on a tour bus. In some situations, people may prefer to travel alone and express no desire to interact with anyone unnecessarily. Assuming that such people have little or no interaction with anyone during the trip, their trip experience could be altered by their perception of the environment as well as perceived tangible and intangible traits, such as a singular architecture style and the atmosphere of a destination. While taking the trip, people are able to expand their scope of interaction with others by including more service staff, other tourists and local people at destinations. In conclusion, individuals determine what people will be encountered and are largely in control of the interactive driver, contrary to the environmental driver, wherein the individuals have less or no power to avoid experiences such as an avalanche.

Above all, it is argued that the three types of drivers are linked and could thus affect each other. For example, a socialization motive (a personal driver) may push the tourists to initiate an interaction (an interactive driver) with local people; meanwhile, through conversation (an interactive driver) with other tourists at the destination the tourist may increase his/her involvement (a personal driver) in activity participation.

In summary, the trip partaking experience entails a host of different kinds of experiences evoked before and during the trip. Some experiences could be joyful, some could be regretful and some could be relatively monotonous or uneventful. To thoroughly recall those experiences seems to be a challenge for most individuals. It is likely that people may remember some parts of the partaking experience and completely forget something they have done on the trip. Hence, some partaking experiences are regarded as recallable and some as non-recallable. Above all, the quality of the past trip experience is judged by the two psychological consequences: recallable and non-recallable experiences. It is still unclear to what extent individuals can recall their trip engagement. In some situations, the majority of experiences are recallable and vice versa. Unquestionably, the likelihood of losing memories of a trip become higher as time progresses. Moreover, it is important to recognize that while the personal evaluation of partaking experiences may be unstable from time to time owing to the loss of trip memories, enhanced photographic possibilities and social media sharing of these experiences may give memories a longer existence, especially where reviewing travel images and experiences with friends and family is a well-established tradition.

It is common to see that individuals' evaluations of trip engagements differ from one trip to another. This can be because of many reasons, including service quality variation among the providers and consumers' expectations of service quality, which may change. Practitioners generally use customer satisfaction as a performance evaluation tool to understand the consumer's perception of service quality. To further operationalize post-trip evaluation by tourists, this chapter takes a similar concept, however with different descriptors, to present the tourist's assessment of the trip experience. It proposes five types of experience that can be illuminated by an experience spectrum entailing the (1) disastrous experience, (2) regretful experience, (3) monotonous experience, (4) memorable experience and (5) extraordinary experience. The first two reflect dissatisfactory experiences, whereas the last three present satisfactory ones. The disastrous experience, located at one end of the spectrum, epitomizes a highly unpleasant outcome. The regretful experience connotes a moderate level of dissatisfaction. Monotonous experience underlines a trip engagement resulting in marginal satisfaction. Memorable experience reflects personal enjoyment and accomplishment of the expectations/goals set by the tourist. Extraordinary experience highlights attainment of satisfaction in a colossal scale and may include a level of enjoyment that is unexpected where adventure may be sought by the tourist or a pleasant surprise.

Past studies have examined tourists' post-trip evaluation of their trip encounters using different expressions to portray the trip experience. For example, when conveying satisfactory outcomes, they include the memorable experience (e.g. Hudson and Ritchie, 2008; Kim *et al.*, 2011; Tung and Ritchie, 2011), optimal experience (e.g. Jackson and March, 1996; Fave and Massimini, 2003) and extraordinary experience (e.g. Liang and Crouch, 2005; Farber and Hall, 2007; Jefferies and Lepp, 2012). From a marketing perspective (Tung and Ritchie, 2011), creating a memorable experience is regarded as an effective way to achieve customer satisfaction. In his advocacy of creating memorable experiences, Pizam (2010) argued that for service delivery the intangible factor (e.g. ambience), not the tangible factor, is ultimately the key element in winning customer satisfaction. Moreover, recent literature (Pizam, 2010; Kim *et al.*, 2011; Tung and Ritchie, 2011) seems to suggest that a memorable experience may not be triggered until the tourist receives above-average satisfaction. Similar to memorable experience in terms of chance of occurrence, a flow experience occurs when the tourist's expectation is met owing to a match between the skill and challenge level. However, it is not clear which experience (e.g. memorable and optimal) represents a higher level of customer satisfaction. Jefferies and Lepp defined 'extraordinary experiences' as those that are 'highly memorable, very special, and emotionally charged' (2012, p. 37). Thus it is confirmed that the extraordinary experience is viewed as the experience above the memorable experience. The reason why this chapter excludes the optimal experience from the experience spectrum is that the optimal experience (which may meet expectations) is clearly an emotion above satisfaction, yet is not necessarily more than the extraordinary experience (which may exceed expectations). Perhaps the memorable and extraordinary experience may sufficiently denote the tourist's emotional outcomes arising from trip preparation and participation and resulting in a high level of satisfaction.

Incorporating the TEDM in Tourist Experience Creation

As for the TEDM framework discussed above, it is important to further review its application in advancing theory development and business practices in relation to tourist experience creation so as to recognize its associated challenges and limitations.

In facilitating experience creation, the three drivers reveal their strengths and weaknesses in creating and co-creating satisfactory experiences. The personal driver is regarded as having a stable and long-term influence on experience creation. For example, education level could not be changed in a short period of time. As extant literature has debated extensively, this driver widely serves as the foundation for service-strategy development. Conversely, the environmental driver could not only produce a long-term, latent influence on experience creation but also render a short-term effect to moderate tourist experiences. When browsing promotional flyers, for instance, tourists may alter their experiences if they discover something new and consequently engage in an unanticipated experience. As a result, the environmental driver, as a stimulus, may effectively enrich the tourist experience so as to facilitate the experience co-creation process spontaneously when additional information entices tourist demand. Lastly, the interactive driver could also be well utilized as an impetus in experience creation and co-creation. Nevertheless, the effect of the interactive driver on tourist experience creation may be instantaneous as long as it addresses the gap of service between tourists and service providers. For example, when a service fails to meet a tourist's expectations, the provider could exploit the interactive driver to recover the service inadequacy or failure effectively and quickly.

Indeed, past research has comprehensively evaluated the impacts of personal and environmental drivers on experience formation, but only occasionally covered the effects generated by the interactive driver. It is plausible to further examine the extent of impact created by the interactive driver relevant to experience creation and co-creation and subsequently to incorporate the driver into service delivery. Complementing the current literature, the TEDM overarches the three stages in experience creation moderated by the three drivers. Unfortunately, the interactive effects of the drivers remain unanswered. Broadly speaking, the interrelationships among the drivers at different stages should be explored.

It is important to note that interactive drivers may vary according to the settings of service due to the variations in engagements provided in different settings, as well as individual differences in tourists' personality, trip expectations and overall experience. For example, a tourist walking along a mountain trail may not interact with any people, only nature. A person staying in a beachfront resort, however, is likely to receive ample opportunity to interact with other people. The above argument may lead to a new direction for future research. Developing a typology of tourism service environments using the interactive driver as the standard could help practitioners and service professionals develop service strategies utilizing interactive drivers as the facilitators. For example, for typology development, a remote island without inhabitants could be classified as a non-habitant destination in which human interaction is highly limited; an oceanfront resort located in a wealthy district may be classified as a vibrant destination where ample interaction opportunities are available or likely. For different types of service environments, relevant service and product development strategies linking to the interactive driver may be developed.

It is critical to note that the three drivers may affect the experience formation at the three trip stages. In the spirit of the above proposition, a critical service implication emerges as follows. That is, the drivers may be exploited, in an individual or collective fashion, to transform unfulfilling experiences into memorable ones. Further, what warrants strong customer satisfaction is a memorable experience or beyond. The proposed experience spectrum thus divulges five kinds of experience outcomes that are suitable for market strategy development that can more easily target specific audiences. For future market research (e.g. positioning plot), integrating the suggested experience spectrum is highly recommended.

References

Boorstin, D.J. (1964) *The Image: A Guide to Pseudo-Events in America*. Harper and Row, New York.

Cohen, E. (1979) A phenomenology of tourist experience. *Sociology* 13, 179–201.

Crick-Furman, D. and Prentice, R. (2000) Modeling tourists' multiple value. *Annals of Tourism Research* 27, 69–92.

Csíkszentmihályi, M. (1975) *Beyond Boredom and Anxiety*. Jossey-Bass, San Francisco, California.

Dann, G. and Jacobsen, J. (2003) Tourism smellscapes. *Tourism Geography* 5, 3–25.

Farber, M.E. and Hall, T.E. (2007) Emotion and environment: visitors' extraordinary experiences along the Dalton Highway in Alaska. *Journal of Leisure Research* 39(2), 248–270.

Fave, A.D. and Massimini, F. (2003) Optimal experience in work and leisure among teachers and physicians: individual and bio-cultural implications. *Leisure Studies* 22, 323–342.

Gomez-Jacinto, L., Martin-Garcia, J.S. and Bertiche-Haud'Huyze, C. (1999) A model of tourism experience and attitude change. *Annals of Tourism Research* 26(4), 1024–1027.

Gunter, B.G. (1987) The leisure experience: selected properties. *Journal of Leisure Research* 19(2), 115–130.

Halbrook, M. and Hirschmann, E. (1982) The experiential aspects of consumption: consumer fantasies, feelings, and fun. *Journal of Consumer Research* 9, 132–140.

Hudson, S. and Ritchie, B.J.R. (2008) Branding a memorable destination experience: the case of brand Canada. *International Journal of Tourism Research* 11, 217–228.

Jackson, S.A. and Marsh, H.W. (1996) Development and validation of a scale to measure optimal experience: the flow state scale. *Journal of Sport and Exercise Psychology* 18, 17–35.

Jefferies, K. and Lepp, A. (2012) An investigation of extraordinary experiences. *Journal of Park and Recreation Administration* 30(3), 37–52.

Kim, J., Ritchie, B. and McCormick, B. (2012) Development of a scale to measure memorable tourism experience. *Journal of Travel Research* 51, 12–25.

Larsen, S. (2007) Some issues in the psychology of the tourist experience. *Scandinavian Journal of Hospitality and Tourism* 7(1), 7–8.

Liang, J. and Crouch, G. (2005) Extraordinary journeys: an exploratory cross-cultural study of tourists of the frontier. *Journal of Vacationing Marketing* 11, 209–223.

MacCannell, D. (1976) *The Tourist: A New Theory of the Leisure Class*. Schocken Books, New York.

Morgan, M. (2006) Making space for experiences. *Journal of Retail and Leisure Property* 5(4), 305–313.

Mossberg, L. (2007) A marketing approach to the tourist experience. *Scandinavian Journal of Hospitality and Tourism* 7(1), 59–74.

Obenour, W., Patterson, M., Pedersen, P. and Pearson, L. (2006) Conceptualization of a meaning-based research approach for tourism service experiences. *Tourism Management* 27, 34–41.

Oh, H., Fiore, A.M. and Jeoung, M. (2007) Measuring experience economy concepts: tourism applications. *Journal of Travel Research* 46, 119–132.

Otto, J. and Richie, J. (1995) Exploring the quality of the service experience: a theoretical and empirical analysis. *Advances in Services Marketing and Management* 4, 37–61.

Pine, J. and Gilmore, J. (1999) *The Experience Economy*. Harvard Business School Press, Boston, Massachusetts.

Pizam, A. (2010) Creating memorable experiences. *International Journal of Hospitality Management* 29, 243.

Prentice, R.C., Witt, S.F. and Hamer, C. (1998) Tourism as experience: the case of heritage parks. *Annals of Tourism Research* 25(1), 1–24.

Rickman, H.P. (ed.) (1976) *Dilthey: Selected Writings*. Cambridge University Press, Cambridge.

Schmitt, B.H. (1999) *Experiential Marketing: How to Get Customers to Sense, Feel, Think, Act and Relate to Your Company and Brands*. Free Press, New York.

Selstad, L. (2007) The social anthropology of the tourist experience: exploring the 'middle role'. *Scandinavian Journal of Hospitality and Tourism* 7, 19–33.

Taniguchi, S., Freeman, R. and Richards, A. (2005) Attributes of meaningful leaning experiences in an outdoor education program. *Journal of Adventure Education and Outdoor Learning* 5(2), 131–144.

Tung, V.W.N. and Ritchie, B. (2011) Exploring the essence of memorable experiences. *Annals of Tourism Research* 38, 1367–1386.

Turner, V.W. and Bruner, E.M. (1986) *The Anthropology of Experience.* University of Illinois Press, Urbana, Illinois.

Tussyadiah, I.P. and Fesenmaier, D.R. (2009) Mediating tourist experiences: access to places via shared videos. *Annals of Tourism Research* 36(1), 24–40.

Uriely, N. (2005) The tourist experience: conceptual development. *Annals of Tourism Research* 32(1), 199–216.

Vitterso, J., Vorkinn, M., Vistad, O.I. and Vaagland, J. (2000) Tourist experiences and attractions. *Annals of Tourism Research* 27(2), 432–450.

Volo, S. (2010) Bloggers' reported tourist experiences: their utility as a tourism data source and their effect on prospective tourists. *Journal of Vacation Marketing* 16(4), 297–311.

Wang, W., Chen, J.S., Fan, L. and Lu, J. (2012) Tourist experience and wetland parks: a case of Zhejiang, China. *Annals of Tourism Research* 39, 1763–1778.

3 Tourist Experience Value: Tourist Experience and Life Satisfaction

PETER BJÖRK

Hanken School of Economics, Vaasa, Finland

Introduction

The experience concept, which germinated into the discipline of tourism research in the 1970s (Quan and Wang, 2004), has created its own research traditions, attracting researchers from different disciplines (Ritchie *et al.*, 2011). In a social science approach, insight in and understanding of the concept has been sought by describing its structure, exploring its dimensionality and analysing influencing factors. The tourist experience concept has also been analysed from a marketing and management perspective, focusing on how the experience concept is linked to service quality, satisfaction and behaviour intention, management of customer interactions, and the phenomenon of 'scape' (service scape, experience scape). Experience from this perspective is regarded as a distinctive business offering to customers (Pine and Gilmore, 1998; Gilmore and Pine, 2002), a service of value.

The value concept has within a service-dominant logic approach (Vargo and Lusch, 2004; Grönroos, 2008) been positioned at the consumer end as value-in-use co-created in integrated processes with other stakeholders (Sfandla and Björk, 2012). Resource integration as a foundation for value creation has been discussed by tourism and destination marketing scholars (Flagestad and Hope, 2001; Ippolito, 2009), but not been explicitly linked to the experience concept, analysed out of a managerial perspective reflecting the transformation of the economy (Pine and Gilmore, 1999), and discussed by service marketing (Chen and Chen, 2010) and tourism researchers (Tung and Ritchie, 2011), who have focused on processes of co-creation. This line of research, in turn, has most often left the link between experience and value unexplored, a link that according to consumer behaviour researchers exists (Mitchell and Orwig, 2002; Holbrook, 2006; Meyer and Schwager, 2007).

It is commonly accepted that tourist experience is an individual perception generated in the context of interactions and resource integrations (Björk and Sfandla, 2009). Research on tourist experience is neither new nor novel. The experience

© CAB International 2014. *Creating Experience Value in Tourism*
(eds N.K. Prebensen *et al.*)

concept has been on the research agenda for more than 40 years (Cohen, 1979), and Ritchie *et al.* (2011), who documented the number of articles published in six leading tourism journals over a time period of ten years, 2000 to 2009, conclude that almost 10% were related to this concept. Notably, research on different types of experiences has been a priority, such as peak experience, and experience of flow. The essence of tourist experience, presented as definitions, has been explained by its characteristics. These definitions portray a concept in isolation, and the discourse has become repetitive and most unproductive. One can argue that the experience concept is equally elusive as, for example, the service concept, and is therefore hard to define. To merely add another dimension to existing definitions or reorganize existing knowledge into new definitions seems to be insufficient to take our understanding of the tourist experience concept one step further. Therefore we argue for an updated research agenda on the tourist experience concept.

Tung and Ritchie conclude, after having identified four dimensions driving memorable experiences, that future research should assume an evaluative standpoint and link experience to 'outcome variables such as level of satisfaction and/or future behavioral intentions' (2011, p. 1382). Walter *et al.* (2010, p. 255) also argue for a more holistic approach on 'customer experience'. Furthermore, Mason (2003) and Moscardo claim that most studies on tourism impacts have 'focused on the consequences of tourism for the destination and its residents' (2009, p. 159), and there are few studies focusing on the impact of tourism on tourists. We follow the lead and argue that further insight in the tourist experience concept can be gained by refocusing ongoing research in this area, and open up a discussion about how the tourist experience concept relates to concepts such as happiness, quality of life and life satisfaction. This implies a holistic approach on the human being, a focus on 'Overall Life' (Neal *et al.*, 1999), with no strict distinction between different types of times (leisure time, time at work, etc.) or isolated analysis of single events as most tourist quality and satisfaction researchers have practised (Sirgy, 2010).

Hence, the aim of this chapter is to enhance our understanding of the tourist experience concept by unravelling the tourist experience value concept, and based on that, present an updated research agenda. The future research directions proposed are based on a quality-of-life approach, here scaled down to a discussion of how tourist experience influences life satisfaction by means of happiness, quality of life and well-being, with increased value. Travel and tourism as an integrated part of other life-quality processes has been recognized in previous tourism research (McCabe, 2002), as well as tourism experience as a part of consumer experience (Quan and Wang, 2004). However, there is scant research focusing on how situation-specific experiences are embedded in experiences-of-life and are linked to perceived value and values. What seems to be needed is a model explaining the tourist experience value hierarchy.

The structure of the chapter is as follows. First, the dimensionality of the tourist experience concept is explored. Second, tourist experience value, or the value of tourist experience, is defined. Here input from the field of service marketing, consumer behaviour and quality-of-life studies is merged. Finally, urgent research questions still unanswered are discussed in the concluding section.

A Tripartite View on Tourist Experience

Tourist experience is a discourse about people, service and places (Westwood, 2006). It is a consumer experience with the same characteristics as service experience, being an individual, social and contextual construct. Tourist experiences happen as mental evaluations of consumption processes.

People, i.e. the tourists, are the ultimate creators of their own experiences. Perceived experience is an inner process, such as individual and subjective (Sfandla and Björk, 2012); 'subjective personal reactions and feelings that are felt by consumers when consuming or using a service' (Chen and Chen, 2010, p. 29). Tourist experiences are multidimensional (Fig. 3.1). Profane experiences are hardly remembered in comparison with sacred ones, which stand out in a mundane environment as peak experiences, something extraordinary, with both positive and negative connotations (Arnould and Price, 1993; Tumbat and Belk, 2011). Walter *et al.* (2010, p. 238) discuss, based on attitude theories, how external stimuli create memories about the experience based on customers' cognitive (utilitarian), emotional (hedonic) and behavioural (cognitive) responses. Tourist experiences emerge in relation to a tourist journey as a consequence of travelling, in sequences of events, of which some are defined as tourist service (Zouni and Kouremenos, 2008).

Service always comes with an experience (Carbone and Haeckel, 1994; Johnston and Kong, 2011) and tourist experience is created in service processes, in interactions with the service provider, other customers and actors. Kwortnik and Ross define experiential products as 'fusing tangible (sensory) and intangible (symbolic) attributes and co-produced by consumer and marketer to create an event that is pleasurable, meaningful, and memorable' (2007, p. 325). Following the service-dominant logic (Vargo and Lusch, 2004), perceived experience value is co-created in processes facilitated by the service system. Service experience can be direct, i.e. experienced in the process, or indirect, experienced as an outcome or outside the service process (Johnston and Clark, 2005). Kwortnik (2008) discusses how travel experiences differ from service (retail) experiences in that they are more likely to be hedonic- and

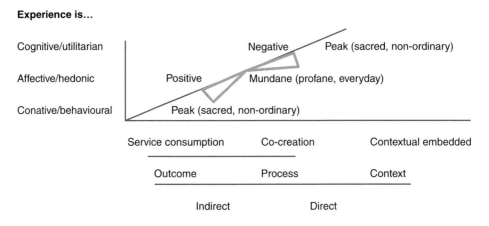

Fig. 3.1. The dimensionality of tourist experiences.

symbolic-oriented, sought for the setting and longer in duration. It seems reasonable to acknowledge that tourist experiences also can be created in no-service contexts, for example on beaches and streets, and in mountains and forests.

Places: tourist experience is contextual. Service experiences originate from: (i) complex interactions between the customers and the company's offerings and (ii) processes of co-creation (Prahalad and Ramaswamy, 2004), in which the company provides a servicescape (artefacts and contexts) (Bitner, 1992). This enables the consumer to shape his or her own experience (Carù and Cova, 2003) as personal contextual reflections. Mossberg (2007) describes the context in terms of an experiencescape based on a theatre metaphor (Goffman, 1959; Grove *et al.*, 1992). Tourist experiences are generated on a stage in interactions with other actors in an active or passive way. The tourist can be an active actor of the process or take a more distant approach (Pine and Gilmore, 1999). All services are taking place in a context, in a man-made physical surrounding, i.e. a servicescape (Bitner, 1992; Kwortnik, 2008), or a natural setting. Dimensions affecting tourist experience are ambient conditions (factors affecting the five senses), space and function (arrangement of details in the room), signs, symbols and artefacts (signals about the company that influence the customer), and social interactions (Edvardsson *et al.*, 2005). This includes interactions between customers and employees, as well as with other customers (Arnould and Price, 1993; Carù and Cova, 2003).

Tourist experiences are contextually embedded (Walls and Wang, 2011). Tourists' overall journey experience is a 'psychological outcome or emotional response' (Zouni and Kouremenos, 2008, p. 283), reflected on in context, en route and long after the trip has come to an end. Perspectives on the tourist experience concept have developed in the same way as the value concept, in an early phase defined as delivered by the service industry, to be positioned in a process of co-creating actors (Björk and Sfandla, 2009), now to be linked to a series of encounters en route embedded in a tourist domain of life. A journey experience is, by comparison, service experience boundary-open (Tumbat, 2011), and in combination with experiences from other life domains (McCabe, 2002), quality-of-life enhancing (Kruger, 2012).

Tourist Experience Value

The tourist experience value hierarchy presented in Fig. 3.2 explains the relationships that exist between tourist experience and life satisfaction mediated through quality of life, happiness and well-being in interactions. The basic premise is that tourism is one life domain contributing to life satisfaction. Neal *et al.* explain 'that overall life satisfaction is determined by satisfaction with major life domains. The affect within a life domain spills over vertically to the most superordinate domain (life in general), thus determining life satisfaction' (1995, p. 145; 1999). The logic of this reasoning is that tourist journey experiences are summed up in an overall leisure satisfaction measure, to be added to the satisfaction of other life domains, and valued in relation to its contribution to life satisfaction. This reasoning is in line with Graburn (1983), who declares that tourism is one of many 'institutions that humans use to embellish and add meaning to their lives' (1989, p. 22).

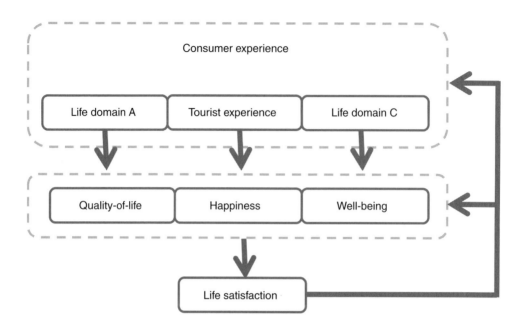

Fig. 3.2. The tourist experience value hierarchy.

Tourist experience value as a part of the consumer experience value system is temporal and dynamic, 'experienced before purchase, at the moment of purchase, at the time of use, and after use' (Sanchez *et al.*, 2006, p. 394).

Tourist experience and leisure satisfaction add to life satisfaction in many ways. Quality-of-life, happiness and well-being are presented in this section as mediating concepts by the argument that they are highly integrated and influence life satisfaction (Benckendorff *et al.*, 2009).

Happiness

Travel brings happiness to people 'no matter where they come from, how much money they have, how old they are, or whether they are male or female' (Nawijn, 2010, p. 287). In line with the theory of positive psychology (Seligman and Csíkszentmihályi, 2000), tourism enhances the feeling of happiness (Stebbins, 2007) linked to life satisfaction (Ryan, 1997). Happiness is defined by Martin as 'subjective well-being' (2008, p. 172), a response to meaningful activities valued for their own sake, a by-product, not an end itself. Happiness is about experiencing well-being as a 'subjective overall enjoyment of one's life as a whole' (Tsaur *et al.*, 2013). According to Waterman (1993), happiness can be understood as eudaimonia, i.e. the feeling that emerges in the process self-realization, or as hedonic enjoyment linked to consumption and satisfaction of needs (Waterman *et al.*, 2008). Consequently, the level of happiness is partially contextual, although it is an inherent characteristic, a personal trait and largely explained by genetic predispositions (Lykken and Tellegren, 1996). The influence of happiness on mood and service evaluation has been documented by Hellén and Sääksjärvi, who also position happiness 'first as an explaining variable' to life outcomes (2011, p. 321). It is here defined as life satisfaction.

Well-being

Well-being defined as 'an individual's sense that his/her life overall is going well' (Moscardo, 2009, p. 162), is a state of mind a holiday may influence (Gilbert and Abdullah, 2004). The positive effects of tourism on human well-being have long been known, and, in the last decade, has reached increased attention as a result of the emerging well-being tourism (Hjalager *et al.*, 2011). Human well-being today is more than the mere absence of illness, but is a positive dimension used to separate well-being tourism from health tourism, focusing on curing illness. Well-being is a personal, holistic state of mind including aspects of self-development in terms of life fulfilment. Well-being is an inner process, not 'out there', a personal experience to be lived throughout our daily life; work, leisure time, social relationships, achievements, growth, freedom etc. As a holistic phenomenon, it embraces the body, mind and soul – three separate but integrated dimensions, including physical, social, material, emotional and spiritual aspects. It is on the positive side of the 'Neutral point' in Travis and Ryan's (1988) life-quality continuum.

Quality of life

Quality of life, defined as 'one's satisfaction with life, and feelings of contentment or fulfillment with one's experience in the world' (Beckendorff *et al.*, 2009, p. 172), is often seen as equivalent to well-being and happiness. They share the same basic component in that they are all aspects of perceived life satisfaction. Happiness and well-being are more individual-oriented compared with quality of life, which is more comprehensive. Nuances can be recognized in the definition of quality of life presented by the OECD, 'the notion of human welfare (well-being) measured by social indicators rather than by "quantitative" measures of income and production' (2005, p. 1), and how some of the core dimensions of quality of life are defined, i.e. self-esteem, the ability and freedom to make choices; belongingness, opportunities to participate in social, cultural and political activities; security, opportunities to work and earn (Moscardo, 2009, p. 162). Furthermore, Moscardo (2009) suggests that quality of life should be used when analysing tourism impacts on four dimensions: the tourism-generating region, the transit region, individual tourist and destination region. The same structure can be found in the academic volume *Handbook of Tourism and Quality-of-Life Research*, edited by Uysal *et al.* (2012). Quality-of-life has also been discussed in terms of a goal theory to explain travel satisfaction (Sirgy, 2010). Here the basic principles are that fulfilled travel goals positively enhance the experiences of life satisfaction.

Life satisfaction

Life satisfaction is presented as an overall end that the tourism domain can influence. Ryan (1997) explains that good mood and happiness during a holiday add to life satisfaction as a whole; 'taking a holiday trip indeed increases life satisfaction afterwards' (Nawijn, 2010). Life satisfaction is, within the discipline of consumer behaviour research and a means–end chain structure (Gutman, 1982, 1984), defined as a terminal value (Rokeach, 1973). This implies that the pursuit of life satisfaction is the major aim of one's existence. Consequently, it is argued that tourism as a life domain adds to life satisfaction as an end state (Sirgy, 2008). A tourist's journey experience, considered a comprehensive overall experience, is composed of a sequence of encounters where some are within the domain of the service industry (Prahalad and Ramaswamy, 2004) and others are contextual (contextually embedded). One way to approach tourist experience value is to understand what is valued in an experience, i.e. how a tourist experience enhances life satisfaction. Life satisfaction is a comprehensive concept, which can be deconstructed and linked to concepts such as quality of life, happiness and well-being. These, in turn, have to be scaled down and analysed in detail to further approach the link between tourist experience and experience value. A reverse bottom-up spillover theory of subjective well-being theory (Neal et al., 1999; Kruger, 2012) is recommended for analysis. By this approach it seems possible to unravel the tourist experience value concept.

Summary

Seeking an updated research agenda for tourist experience value, this chapter suggests a closer examination of the tourist experience context and tourist experience should be considered as a process that enhances life satisfaction and that is of value.

The value concept, once made popular by Porter (1985), has been repeatedly redefined by service marketing scholars (Sfandla and Björk, 2012). Perceived value has been defined as an outcome of benefits to costs, as well as being embedded in the process of interactions between the and a variety of tourism firms (Gallarza and Gil, 2008). It is suggested here that the value-in-use concept needs to be further elaborated to also recognize all those value-creating processes that are not influenced by the service industry, i.e. the context, the tourist's 'overall experience is composed of numerous small encounters with a variety of tourism principals, such as taxi drivers, hoteliers, and waiters, as well as elements of local attractions such as museums, theatres, beaches, and theme parks' (Zouni and Kouremenos, 2008, p. 283).

Tourist experience, as a process and outcome, is embedded in individual value systems. Tourist experience value has been discussed on two levels. Contemporary academic research on the concept was first summed up in Fig. 3.1, illustrating that a majority of research has predominantly focused on the nature and characteristics of the experience concept. Hereby, a solid understanding of the essence of the concept is founded. Experience co-creation and value-in-use, two central fundaments in a service-dominant logic paradigm (Vargo and Lusch, 2004), have not been linked to quality of life, happiness and well-being in previous studies. Here, the experience value concept merges three research disciplines, at least. Quality-of-life research positions life satisfaction as a terminal value in the value-attainment constructs of consumer behaviour researchers, to be experienced as an outcome and in processes of value-in-use discussed by service marketing researchers.

The tourist experience concept is still much unexplored (Carù and Cova, 2003; Walter *et al.*, 2010), although Tung and Ritchie note that there is a 'wealth of literature on tourism experience' (2011, p. 1368). In particular, there seems to be a 'lack of conceptual models that offer a common terminology and a shared mindset' (Hosany and Witham, 2010, p. 352). This chapter offers the tourist experience value concept as a platform for merging knowledge generated in a number of adjoining research disciplines (e.g. service marketing, consumer behaviour, tourism and quality of life). Considering tourism as a domain with an influence on life satisfaction, a trip as a journey (Kruger, 2012) and a total travel experience consists of one's travel history, ongoing trips and those in the planning process, it is most evident that we need more research on: (i) how tourist experiences are remembered; (ii) how tourist experiences influence well-being, happiness, quality of life and life satisfaction, and their interaction; and (iii) the dimensionality of the tourist experience value concept.

This chapter has at least two major limitations. First, it does not present a thorough literature review, but sums up the identified and discussed dimensions of the tourist experience concept in Fig. 3.1. Antecedents to and consequences of the tourist experience, as well as all discussions about how experience quality is linked to service satisfaction and value in a service context, are left out. Researchers interested in this type of review are recommended to consult articles written by Ritchie and Hudson (2009) and Ritchie *et al.* (2011). Second, input to the discussion on tourist experience value was sought from a limited set of research disciplines, and could have been extended by input from cultural studies, for example, by the argument that tourist experience value seems to be culturally conditioned, still to be empirically tested.

Applying a service management perspective on the discussion would have enabled us to also discuss how the tourism industry could 'stage' for experience value (Mossberg, 2007; Björk and Sfandla, 2009). Consequently, more in-depth discussions about managerial issues pertaining to experience value are left out. However, this chapter identifies the importance of adding a non-managerial element, such as the public room, forests, silence and air to the list of important management issues. Tourist journeys are not discrete events, but complex sequences of activities in a chain of tourism-related processes, embedded in other life-satisfaction domains. This implies that it is essential for destination marketing managers, for example, to assess the portfolio of tourist well-being and value-enhancing service offerings, and guarantee quality assurance that resonates with the requirements of post- and transmodern travellers (Firat, 2001; Ateljevic, 2013).

References

Arnould, E. and Price, L. (1993) River magic: extraordinary experience and the extended service encounter. *Journal of Consumer Research* 20(1), 24–45.
Ateljevic, I. (2013) Transmodernity: integrating perspectives on social evolution. *Futures* 47(3), 38–48.
Benckendorff, P., Edwards, D., Jurowski, C., Liburd, J., Miller, G. and Moscardo, G. (2009) Exploring the future of tourism and quality of life. *Tourism and Hospitality Research* 9(2), 171–183.

Bitner, M.J. (1992) Servicescapes: the impact of physical surroundings on customers and employee responses. *Journal of Marketing* 54(2), 57–71.

Björk, P. and Sfandla, C. (2009) A tripartite model of tourist experience. *Finnish Journal of Tourism Research* 5(2), 5–18.

Carbone, L. and Haeckel, S. (1994) Engineering customer experience. *Marketing Management* 3(3), 8–19.

Carù, A. and Cova, B. (2003) Revisiting consumption experience: a more humble but complete view of the concept. *Marketing Theory* 3(2), 267–286.

Chen, C.F. and Chen, F.S. (2010) Experience quality, perceived value, satisfaction and behavioral intentions for heritage tourists. *Tourism Management* 3(1), 29–35.

Cohen, E. (1979) A phenomenology of tourism experiences. *Sociology* 13(2), 179–201.

Edvardsson, B., Enquist, B. and Johnston, R. (2005) Co-creating customer value through hyperreality in the prepurchase service experience. *Journal of Service Research* 8(2), 149–161.

Firat, F. (2001) The meanings and messages of Las Vegas: the present of our future. *Management* 4(3), 101–120.

Flagestad, A. and Hope, C. (2001) Strategic success in winter sports destinations: a sustainable value creation perspective. *Tourism Management* 22(5), 445–461.

Gallarza, M. and Gil, I. (2008) The concept of value and its dimensions: a tool for analyzing tourism experiences. *Tourism Review* 63(3), 4–20.

Gilbert, D. and Abdullah, J. (2004) Holiday-taking and the sense of well-being. *Annals of Tourism Research* 31(1), 103–121.

Gilmore, J. and Pine, I. (2002) Customer experience places: the new offering frontier. *Strategy & Leadership* 30(4), 4–11.

Goffman, E. (1959) *The Presentation of Self in Everyday Life*. Doubleday, New York.

Graburn, H. (1983) The anthropology of tourism. *Annals of Tourism Research* 10(1), 9–33.

Graburn, H. (1989) The sacred journey. In: Smith, V. (ed.) *Hosts and Guests: The Anthropology of Tourism*. University of Pennsylvania Press, Philadelphia, Pennsylvania, pp. 21–36.

Grönroos, C. (2008) Service logic revisited: who creates value? And who co-creates? *European Business Review* 20(4), 298–314.

Grove, S., Fisk, R. and Berry, L. (1992) Dramatizing the service experience: a managerial approach. In: Swartz, T., Bowen, D. and Brown, S. (eds) *Advances in Services Marketing and Management*. JAI Press, Greenwich, Connecticut, pp. 91–121.

Gutman, J. (1982) A means-end chain model based on consumer categorization processes. *Journal of Marketing* 46, 60–72.

Gutman, J. (1984) Analyzing consumer orientations toward beverages through means-end chain analysis. *Psychology and Marketing* 1(3/4), 23–43.

Hellén, K. and Sääksjärvi, M. (2011) Happy people manage better in adverse services. *International Journal of Quality and Service Science* 3(3), 319–336.

Hjalager, A.M., Konu, H., Huijbens, E., Björk, P., Flagestad, A., Nordin, S. and Tuohino, A. (2011) *Innovating and Re-Branding Nordic Wellbeing Tourism*. Final Report. Nordic Innovation Centre, Norway.

Holbrook, M. (2006) ROSEPEKICECIVECI versus CCV: the resource-operant, skills-exchanging, performance-experiencing, knowledge-informed, competence-enacting, co-producer-involved, value-emerging, customer-interactive view of marketing versus the concept of customer value: 'I can get it for you wholesale'. In: Lush, R. and Vargo, S. (eds) *The Service-Dominant Logic of Marketing. Dialog, Debate and Directions*. M.E. Sharpe, Armonk, New York, pp. 208–223.

Hosany, S. and Witham, M. (2010) Dimensions of cruisers' experiences, satisfaction and intention to recommend. *Journal of Travel Research* 49(3), 351–364.

Ippolito, A. (2009) Creating value in multiple cooperative relationships. *International Journal of Quality and Service Science* 1(3), 255–270.

Johnston, R. and Clark, G. (2005) *Service Operations Management: Improving Service Delivery*. Pearson Education, Harlow, UK.

Johnston, R. and Kong, X. (2011) The customer experience: a road-map for improvement. *Managing Service Quality* 21(1), 5–24.

Kruger, P. (2012) Perceptions of tourism impacts and satisfaction with particular life domains. In: Uysal, M., Perdue, R. and Sirgy, J. (eds) *Handbook of Tourism and Quality-of-Life Research. Enhancing the Lives of Tourists and Residents of Host Communities*. Springer Media, London, pp. 279–292.

Kwortnik, R. (2008) Shipscape influence on the leisure cruise experience. *International Journal of Culture, Tourism and Hospitality Research* 2(4), 289–311.

Kwortnik, R. and Ross, W. (2007) The role of positive emotions in experiential decisions. *International Journal of Research in Marketing* 24(4), 324–335.

Lykken, D. and Tellegren, A. (1996) Happiness is a stochastic phenomenon. *Psychological Science* 7(3), 186–189.

Martin, M. (2008) Paradoxes of happiness. *Journal of Happiness Studies* 9(2), 171–184.

Mason, P. (2003) *Tourism Impact*. Butterworth-Heinemann, London.

McCabe, S. (2002) The tourist experience and everyday life. In: Dann, G. (ed.) *The Tourist as a Metaphor of the Social World*. CAB International, Wallingford, UK, pp. 61–75.

Meyer, C. and Schwager, A. (2007) Understanding customer experience. *Harvard Business Review* 85, 116–128.

Mitchell, M. and Orwig, R. (2002) Consumer experience tourism and brand bonding. *Journal of Product and Brand Management* 11(1), 30–41.

Moscardo, G. (2009) Tourism and quality of life: towards a more critical approach. *Tourism and Hospitality Research* 9(2), 159–170.

Mossberg, L. (2007) A marketing approach to tourist experience. *Scandinavian Journal of Hospitality and Tourism* 7(1), 59–74.

Nawijn, J. (2010) The holiday happiness curve: a preliminary investigation into mood during a holiday abroad. *International Journal of Tourism Research* 12(3), 281–290.

Neal, J., Uysal, M. and Sirgy, J. (1995) Developing a macro measure of quality of life/leisure satisfaction with travel/tourism services: stage one (conceptualization). In: Lee, J. *et al.* (eds) *Development in Quality of Life Studies in Marketing*. Academic Science, Blacksburg, Virginia, pp. 145–151.

Neal, J., Sirgy, J. and Uysal, M. (1999) The role of satisfaction with leisure travel/tourism services and experiences in satisfaction with leisure life and overall life. *Journal of Business Research* 44(3), 153–163.

OECD (2005) *Glossary of Statistical Terms*. Available at: http://www.stats.oecd.org/glossary (accessed 4 January 2013).

Pine, J. and Gilmore, J. (1998) Welcome to the experience economy. *Harvard Business Review* 76, 97–105.

Pine, J. and Gilmore, J. (1999) *The Experience Economy*. Harvard Business School Press, Boston, Massachusetts.

Porter, M. (1985) *Competitive Advantage: Creating and Sustaining Superior Performance*. Free Press, New York.

Prahalad, C. and Ramaswamy, V. (2004) Co-creation experiences: the next practice in value creation. *Journal of Interactive Marketing* 18(3), 5–14.

Quan, S. and Wang, N. (2004) Towards a structural model of the tourist experience: an illustration from food experiences in tourism. *Tourism Management* 25(3), 297–305.

Ritchie, B. and Hudson, S. (2009) Understanding and meeting the challenges of consumer/tourist experience research. *International Journal of Tourism Research* 11, 111–126.

Ritchie, B., Tung, V. and Ritchie, R. (2011) Tourism experience management research. Emergence, evolution and future directions. *International Journal of Contemporary Hospitality Management* 23(4), 419–438.

Rokeach, M. (1973) *The Nature of Human Values*. Free Press, New York.

Ryan, C. (1997) *The Tourist Experience: A New Introduction*. Cassell, London.

Sanchez, J., Callarisa, L., Rodriguez, R. and Moliner, M. (2006) Perceived value of the purchase of a tourism product. *Tourism Management* 27(3), 394–409.

Seligman, M. and Csíkszentmihályi, M. (2000) Positive psychology: an introduction. *American Psychologist* 55(1), 5–14.

Sfandla, C. and Björk, P. (2012) Tourism experience network: co-creation of experiences in interactive processes. *International Journal of Tourism Research* 15, 495–506.

Sirgy, J. (2008) Ethics and public policy implications of consumer well-being (CWB) research. *Journal of Public Policy and Marketing* 27(2), 207–212.

Sirgy, J. (2010) Towards a quality-of-life theory of leisure travel satisfaction. *Journal of Travel Research* 49(2), 246–260.

Stebbins, R. (2007) *Serious Leisure: A Perspective for Our Time*. Transaction, London.

Travis, J. and Ryan, R.S. (1988) *The Wellness Workbook*. Ten Speed Press, Berkeley, California.

Tsaur, S.H., Yen, C.H. and Hsiao, S.L. (2013) Transcendent experience, flow and happiness for mountain climbers. *International Journal of Tourism Research* 15, 360–374.

Tumbat, G. (2011) Co-constructing the service experience: exploring the role of customer emotion management. *Marketing Theory* 11(2), 187–206.

Tumbat, G. and Belk, R. (2011) Marketplace tension in extraordinary experiences. *Journal of Consumer Research* 38(1), 42–61.

Tung, V. and Ritchie, B. (2011) Exploring the essence of memorable tourism experiences. *Annals of Tourism Research* 38(4), 1367–1386.

Uysal, M., Perdue, R. and Sirgy, J. (2012) *Handbook of Tourism and Quality-of-Life Research. Enhancing the Lives of Tourists and Residents of Host Communities*. Springer, London.

Vargo, S. and Lusch, R. (2004) Evolving to a new dominant logic for marketing. *Journal of Marketing* 68(1), 1–17.

Walls, A. and Wang, Y. (2011) Experiential consumption and destination marketing. In: Wang, Y. and Pizam, A. (eds) *Destination Marketing and Management: Theories and Applications*. CABI International, Wallingford, UK, pp. 82–98.

Walter, U., Edvardsson, B. and Öström, Å. (2010) Drivers of customers' service experiences: a study in the restaurant industry. *Managing Service Quality* 20(3), 236–258.

Waterman, A. (1993) Two conceptions of happiness: contrasts of personal expressiveness (eudaimonia) and hedonic enjoyment. *Journal of Personality and Social Psychology* 64(4), 678–691.

Waterman, A., Schwartz, S. and Conti, R. (2008) The implications of two conceptions of happiness (hedonic enjoyment and eudaimonia) for the understanding of intrinsic motivation. *Journal of Happiness Studies* 9(1), 41–79.

Westwood, S. (2006) Shopping in sanitized and un-sanitized spaces: adding value to tourist experiences. *Journal of Retail & Leisure Property* 5(4), 281–291.

Zouni, G. and Kouremenos, A. (2008) Do tourist providers know their visitors? An investigation of tourism experience at a destination. *Tourism and Hospitality Research* 8(4), 282–297.

4 Conceptualization of Value Co-creation in the Tourism Context

Prakash K. Chathoth,[1] Gerardo R. Ungson,[2] Robert J. Harrington,[3] Levent Altinay,[4] Fevzi Okumus[5] and Eric S.W. Chan[6]

[1]American University of Sharjah, UAE; [2]San Francisco State University, USA; [3]University of Arkansas, Fayetteville, USA; [4]Oxford Brookes University Business Faculty, UK; [5]University of Central Florida, USA; [6]Hong Kong Polytechnic University

Introduction

Value-creation in today's ever-changing service landscape requires not only a deeper consumer engagement, but also an increased focus on the experiences that are created during the interaction between the firm and the customer (as per Pine and Gilmore, 1998). The historic production-centric modalities steeped in the goods-dominant logic (Vargo and Lusch, 2004) have given way to a customer-centric philosophy (individualization), resulting in the transformation of the twentieth-century business model (Ramaswamy and Gouillart, 2010). Specifically, evolving consumer attitudes (better awareness, expectations and technology know-how) and new informational technologies (Humphreys and Grayson, 2008) have impelled more responsive firms to adopt the service-dominant logic (Vargo and Lusch, 2004). With the escalation of these two trends, the 'rules-of-the-game' for the service sector have undergone a significant shift and introduced a new mantra for customer engagement. It is quite conceivable that the ability to meet increased consumer requirements will differentiate the performance of service firms in the future (Prahalad and Ramaswamy, 2004a).

In the context of tourism, more organizations (albeit embryonic) have responded by exploring ways to enhance unique and memorable positive experiences for their customers (Walls *et al.*, 2011). For example, luxury hotels have specialized services, from a mini-bar, a bed, to a wardrobe, which are tailored to meet the specific needs and expectations of the guest. 'Informed, connected, empowered, and active consumers are increasingly learning that they too can extract value at the traditional point of exchange' (Prahalad and Ramaswamy, 2004a, p. 6), which has led to the evolution of the co-production service paradigm into its modern variant, co-creation. From a tourism context, as the tourist interacts with the destination's product and services, the emergence of co-creative processes leads to a higher level of engagement and customer experiences that transcends the traditional concepts underlying tourist–destination interactions. These interactions range from travel agents, tour operators, travel guides to hospitality services entailing concierge, front desk, housekeeping and restaurant products and services. Holistically, these interactions at the micro level lead to a macro-level destination orientation in co-creating the visitor/tourism experience (e.g. Binkhorst and Den Dekker, 2009; Shaw *et al.*, 2011).

In its complete realization, co-creation systematically and strategically purports close engagement with customers (Prahalad and Ramaswamy, 2004a, 2004b) using the foundations of the service-dominant logic (Vargo and Lusch, 2004), and enhancing the experiences of the consumer in the actual interaction. Unlike the production-centric modality, however, it will not be simply a sequestered process of adding value at each stage, and then marking up the price at the final stage of the value chain. To fully capitalize on co-creation, the focus on anticipated engagement of customers occurs at every stage of the value creation process (Ramaswamy and Gouillart, 2010). As such, the need to directly engage consumers in a pre-exchange dialogue with the firm (with co-creative processes in place) is a prerequisite to altering this traditional mindset and to have various components of product-service offerings in place designed to meet their specific needs (Ramaswamy and Gouillart, 2010). Accordingly, this chapter builds on previous studies by incorporating the customer-centric co-creation paradigm within a tourism context. Specifically, it extends the co-production–co-creation matrix developed by Chathoth *et al.* (2013) by proposing a co-production–co-creation continuum framework. In doing so, the authors incorporate findings from previous studies that attend to benefits and barriers to a superior level of service orientation, and build the case of higher levels of customer engagement.

The chapter is organized as follows. It first uncovers the definitions pertaining to co-production, co-creation and other related concepts. This is followed by theoretical perspectives on co-production/co-creation and the co-production–co-creation matrix as they apply to the tourism context. A review of the literature on barriers to a superior level of customer orientation (including co-creation) is then introduced, followed by the co-production–co-creation continuum framework. The chapter concludes with implications of moving along the continuum framework and future directions towards co-creative modalities of service orientation in the tourism context.

Theoretical Perspectives and Definitions

Historically, the service literature has emphasized the term co-production (Lovelock and Young, 1979; Mills, 1986) as relating to a higher degree of involvement of customers during the exchange process (Bitner *et al.*, 1997). In such transactions, the simultaneity associated with production and consumption of services is the focal point of the process. To some extent, co-production is used to refer to the 'interactive nature of services', including high customer participation (e.g. haircuts, medical consultations, higher education) that require a higher level of customer information input for the effective delivery of the service (Yen *et al.*, 2004). Despite the inclusion/ involvement of the customer in the production process, co-production as an approach is steeped in the goods-dominant logic (Vargo and Lusch, 2006) because it involves a firm's own viewpoint of how the customer–firm interaction should take place (Payne *et al.*, 2008).

In the tourism context, destinations and organizations that simply thrust their conceptualization of the service experience on to customers are indulging in the goods-dominant logic of experience creation. Note that customers in such inter-actions have essentially very little choice and leverage in defining the experience emanating from the consumption of the various elements of the product/service bundle. In such instances, for example in hospitality services, 'the producer pre-dominantly predefines both the tangible and intangible aspects of various product/service bundles within the hotel service environment, before the customer becomes involved in the process. Be it a pillow or a meal, the customer, for the most part, is only a bystander in the production process even if the hotel provides a variety, as in the case of pillow and food menus' (Chathoth *et al.*, 2013, p. 15). In such service interactions, the role of the customer is to choose the best available option that relates to his/her need.

Contrarily, co-creation requires 'collaboration with customers for the purpose of innovation' (Kristensson *et al.*, 2008, p. 475) in order to create unique experiences for customers (Prahalad and Ramaswamy, 2004a, 2004b). For this to materialize, co-creation emphasizes interactive processes involving the customer's and firm's idiosyncratic resources that create value for both parties involved. The contact between the customer and the firm is managed in such a way as to encourage customer engagement. The essence of co-creation is defined by Payne *et al.* who describe the 'relationship between the provider and the customer as a longitudinal, dynamic, interactive set of experiences and activities performed by the provider and the customer, within a context, using tools and practices that are partly overt and deliberate, and partly based on routine and unconscious behavior' (2008, p. 85).

In the tourism context, the essence of interaction between the tourist and the destination is dependent on how the primary stakeholder of the tourism firm, i.e. the tourist, is involved in the process. To move towards a higher level of customer involvement as per Vargo and Lusch (2004, 2006, 2008) requires a dialogue between the parties involved during co-creation of services. Customer experience therefore is the focal point of such interactions and the outcome of such a process is value creation. Note that 'co-creation' differs from 'customization' in that 'the customer plays a less active role in customisation than in co-creation' (Kristensson *et al.*, 2008, p. 475). In customization, value creation occurs during the production process, whereas in co-creation it happens during the 'consumption, usage process' (Lusch *et al.*, 2007; Kristensson *et al.*, 2008; Michel *et al.*, 2008).

Therefore, following Vargo and Lusch (2004), for value to emerge in tourism transactions it is imperative that the experiential component of the product-service bundle be emphasized by the producer and consumer alike. The level of involvement of customers leads to a higher level of engagement and dialogue, which is the primary source of information for the firm. Through this, tourism firms ranging from travel agents and tour operators to travel guides are able to 'reorganize its current portfolio of products and services' (Kristensson *et al.*, 2008, p. 476) in order to build a dynamic and emergent co-creative platform rather than one that is static and historical in nature. Sharing of customer experiences with the firm leads to a shift in the role of the customer from a passive to an active partner, while being a productive resource during the creation of services (Plé and Cáceres, 2010). Table 4.1 highlights the major differences between co-production and co-creation.

Friesen suggests that the customer and the firm should indulge in a cooperative arrangement that leads to an ongoing dialogue, resulting in a 'win–win dynamic' (2001, p. 30). This is the outcome when firms and customers build trust in their relationship. Trust building leading to co-creation cannot simply result when customers are provided the leverage to participate or interact in the production process. In such a situation, the firm is still in charge of 'the overall orchestration of the experience. What we need to create is an experience environment within which individual … consumers can create their own unique personalized experience'. Personalized co-creation reflects how the individual chooses to interact with the experience environment that the firm facilitates. It involves more than a company's 'à la carte menu' (Prahalad and Ramaswamy, 2004a, pp. 8, 10).

The underlying benefit in co-creating experiences with customers is that it enables the firm and the customer to use each other as a productive resource to 'co-shape' the expectations of the latter. For this to happen, it is imperative that firms provide leverage to the customer while engaging them in such an exchange; 'the consumer is empowered to co-construct a personalized experience around herself' (Prahalad and Ramaswamy, 2004a, p. 12). Therefore, the essence of co-creation lies

Table 4.1. Differentiating between co-production and co-creation. (Adapted from Chathoth *et al.*, 2013.)

	Co-production	Co-creation
1.	Customer participates in creating the core offering through shared inventiveness and co-design	The focus is on usage, consumption, value-in-use (i.e. value that occurs at the time of use, consumption or experience)
2.	The role of the customer is relatively passive	Customers are regarded as active partners in the production process
3.	The customer is regarded as a source of information for customization to result but has negligible control over the production process after relevant information has been shared	The customer is an operant resource defined as people's knowledge, skills, expertise, capacity and time
4.	Firm-centricity is inherent in this approach	Customer- and experience-centricity are the foci of this orientation
5.	Customers have less control over the production process and the product/ service itself	Customers have more control over the production process and are involved in design and development of the product-service features and attributes
6.	Co-production is less transparent when it comes to communication and dialogue with the customer	A two-way dialogue between the firm and its customers (and other stakeholders) is at the crux of this process
7.	Customer needs are not always met	Customer needs are addressed through a higher degree of customer engagement – customer/ experience centricity is based on the level of engagement

in the level of decentralization of the power firms have in controlling the brand and product experience (Collins and Murphy, 2009). This is embedded in the service-dominant logic put forward by scholars such as Vargo and Lusch (2004) and others, which focuses on transparency, access and dialogue (Prahalad and Ramaswamy, 2004a) in allowing customers to engage at a 'deeper level' while creating an experience environment centred on co-creation. The engagement platform that integrates the firm's resources (material, labour and technology) with the customer is the essence of co-creation.

The literature suggests that there are two ways in which collaboration between the firm and customers could result: (i) value-in-use (Kristensson *et al.*, 2008; Payne *et al.*, 2008) and (ii) shared inventiveness, co-design or shared production (Lusch *et al.*, 2007). As per the literature, value-in-use is exemplified through Qbic Design Hotels in how this firm allows its customers to get involved in changing the colour schemes of their rooms depending on their mood. On the other hand, shared inventiveness, co-design or shared production is reflected in how Starwood Hotels used the 'virtual Aloft' platform in Second Life to co-create the design of the hotel using a virtual setting (Chathoth *et al.*, 2013).

Using the conceptualizations of both Prahalad and Ramaswamy (2004a, 2004b) and Vargo and Lusch (2004), it needs to be underscored that the traditional value chain that is centred around production and consumption as two separate activities may not be effective in building the experience environment described earlier. It is imperative that 'consumers are not recipients of a completed output but are involved in the whole value creation process' (Shaw *et al.*, 2011, p. 128). This, in the tourism context, may emerge if the production process is integrated with the consumption process and when the resources are linked to the product–service requirements of the customers.

A Co-production/Co-creation Matrix

As noted earlier, a firm is able to transition from a co-production to a co-creation modality if it is able to shift from a production-oriented process to a consumption-driven process. The transition from co-production to co-creation could be achieved if the focus is more on the customer than on the firm in building key resources and in the development of products and services. In so doing, it is imperative that communication platforms are built around the former whose involvement in such processes needs to be at a much higher level than subsumed within the co-production process. In other words, among the key differences between co-production and co-creation are whether value creation is derived through a production or consumption process, whether involvement and communication between the firm and customer is predominantly firm- or customer-driven, and whether that involvement/communication is sporadic or continuous (Chathoth *et al.*, 2013). Chathoth *et al.* identify four ideal types ranging from firm centric to customer-centric modalities, i.e. co-production, customer-driven customization, firm-driven service innovation and co-creation. This typology outlines the two key elements, i.e. value creation and involvement/dialogue, and the relationship to co-production, customization, service innovation and co-creation.

Chathoth *et al.*'s (2013) framework identifies co-production and customer-driven customization as similar in terms of the production modality for value creation. In other words, they are production-centric. However, these two types differ in terms of the level of involvement of the customer, i.e. sporadic or continuous, with the firm's production platform. Note that in the case of co-production, the involvement/dialogue type is sporadic, whereas in customer-driven customization, the involvement/dialogue type is continuous. Regardless of the type of involvement/dialogue, both involve production-centric modalities using a value chain process steeped in traditional supply chain characteristics. The role of the customer in such a process is suited for the production–consumption process defined by the firm using the firm-centric resource attributes.

Examples of such processes are seen in the case of hospitality and tourism firms, wherein the firms' resources define the type of menu in a restaurant or for that matter when tourism destinations have an array of restaurants that simply use the idiosyncratic nature of their resources to define certain cuisines or themes. The latter is seen in the case of destinations wherein the host country's indigenous cuisine(s) take(s) centre stage to attract tourists. The focus on developing target market preferences of cuisines to attract and retain these customers is not part of the tourism destination development framework. For instance, Hong Kong, until recently, was not positioned to cater to the Middle East travel market, whose needs were unmet owing to host country attributes dominating specific (i.e. the Middle East) target market-related needs and wants. This is despite the fact that Hong Kong had purposefully targeted the emerging Middle East market for future growth. The Mainland Chinese market has had a similar orientation too, wherein travellers from the Middle East found food and other services not suited for stays that spanned a longer duration.[1] Certain attributes that suited the Middle East traveller were considered, but only to make cosmetic improvements to the product/service. Note that in production-centric modalities, the destination's resource commitments define customer centricity and the alterations made to the firm's or destination's offerings are mainly to customize the products and services at the final stage of throughput – hence the production centricity inherent in such an approach. Therefore, it could be said that the orientation of Hong Kong and Mainland China to markets such as the Middle East was previously of a 'co-production' orientation.

On the other hand, in the case of firm-derived service innovation and co-creation, as per the literature, the modality shifts towards the consumption/usage process to create value for the incumbents. Note that in such orientations, the firms' resources are centred on customers so as to engage them in the creation of outputs. In the case of service innovation, customer engagement and access are of the essence (Kristensson *et al.*, 2008), which incorporates value-in-use into the production process. This is also the underlying process for co-creation. However, note that in the context of co-creation, the involvement/dialogue is continuous, whereas in service innovation it is sporadic so as to only engage the customer from the point of view of reviewing and testing prospective/potential service innovations.

The example provided above on Hong Kong and Mainland China could be further expanded to build on customer centricity. These destinations have now developed various services and product attributes that include key characteristics based on Middle East customers' needs and wants. For instance, among various other requirements, for the most part travellers from the Middle East expect meat to be processed in a particular way, while preferring destinations that allow them to observe certain religious practices during travel. These specific attributes have now been integrated into the destination attributes within the Hong Kong/Chinese context. Likewise, many travellers from South Asia prefer vegetarian food with specific requirements, which they do not easily find during their travels within China. Note that within the Chinese context, it is not standard practice for vegetarian stock to be used to address the food-related needs of vegetarians. If a customer-centric approach is to be developed to attract the South Asian traveller, it is imperative that tourism development authorities take into account the needs and wants of the traveller while incorporating them into the service production process.

It should be noted that recent developments have suggested that a more market-oriented approach has emerged within the Chinese destination resource offerings vis-à-vis the Middle East and South Asian markets, given their strategic importance in developing inbound tourism to China. For instance, hotels in Hong Kong have targeted the South Asian market by incorporating idiosyncratic requirements of the traveller. This is reflected in the various improvements made to hotel products/services such as buffets or à la carte menus that are tailored to suit specific requirement of the Middle East[2] and South Asian travel markets.[3] Moreover, Hong Kong International Airport now includes prayer rooms for Middle East travellers who observe religious practices during travel.[4] The inclusion of such idiosyncratic target market requirements in the production of services is essential to move towards more customer-centric modalities within the aforementioned tourism context.

The underlying conceptualization of a co-production and co-creation continuum by Chathoth *et al.* (2013) underscores how the degree of involvement defines customization and co-creation. The higher the degree of involvement of the customer (from sporadic to continuous), the further the system orientates from a co-production to a co-creation type. Moreover, a shift from production to consumption in the value creation process will accordingly define the orientation of the system. Using the example of the service environment within a hotel context, Chathoth *et al.* state that 'the firm defines a honeymoon package from what it determines as the requirements that would meet the needs and wants of a honeymoon couple based on previous transactions. While defining the package, the hotel's customisation of the product-service bundle to suit a honeymoon couple would be based on such previous exchanges with the market, leading to a firm centric approach to customisation' (2013, p. 16). The term 'customer-driven customisation' (Kristensson *et al.*, 2008) underscores the essence of customer centricity in the customization of services. In the tourism context, such customizations are evidenced when travel agents become more market-oriented by building linkages with suppliers in order to meet the specific needs of customers centred around the latter's idiosyncratic needs and wants. In the case of the honeymoon couple, travel agents could use technology-based customer engagement platforms to build specific linkages with suppliers (e.g. resorts) in order to further involve the customer during the production of services.

The co-production–co-creation continuum is depicted in Fig. 4.1. This continuum identifies co-production and co-creation as two ends of a continuum rather than as a dichotomy. Within the two ends of this continuum lie 'firm-driven service innovation' and 'customer-driven customization'. Therefore, tourism firms need to move along the continuum towards co-creative modalities through which they are able to benefit from customer centricity. To move along the continuum requires firms to focus on operant resources that build customer engagement platforms for co-creative processes to emerge. Note that these customer engagement platforms require customer- and firm-specific resources, which take time to develop.

There are various benefits of moving from co-production to co-creation. As firms move along the continuum, feedback and learning loops to build on historic processes emerge, which allow them to become more of a learning organization. Given that a learning organization is served by a resource base that includes competent employees, this resource becomes the building block of customer centricity. Such 'competency-driven' firms foster employee loyalty that has a two-pronged impact, i.e. customer service orientation at the transaction level and at the organizational level. Needless to say, higher customer satisfaction and loyalty result from such an orientation, which in turn impacts the firm's overall profitability in the long term. Note that positive employee and customer experiences are at the crux of such an evolution that drive firms towards customer-centric modalities of service orientation.

Examples of such orientations are found in firms in the global luxury hotel market segment such as the Ritz Carlton and Four Seasons that are more customer-centric. For example, Ritz Carlton's emphasis on their service culture and empowerment has had a positive impact on employee loyalty, customer loyalty and firm performance (Michelli, 2008). Furthermore, a very unique and memorable hotel experience can also be achieved through customer involvement/engagement as seen in the case of the Hong Kong Disneyland Hotel. The hotel achieves this by getting the kids of their guests to 'stage' the registration process through which a memorable moment is co-created for both the kids and parents alike in a resort atmosphere. Likewise, tourism destinations that are more customer-centric have been able to attract and retain tourists to a large extent, as seen in the case of destinations such as Thailand where the level of customer service is high.

The literature provides support for the synergistic effects of operant knowledge resources as a foundation for developing a competitive advantage in service organizations. The knowledge developed before, during and after the co-creation process will provide more adaptive competence to address the changing needs of customers that is likely to be derived from feedback and learning loops in tourism firms. However, moving along the continuum requires that firms develop systems and processes that overcome key barriers, which firms such as Ritz Carlton have been able to do. Through this the firm will be able to evolve from co-production to co-creative platforms. Regardless, it is imperative that firms identify these barriers at the outset, which are addressed in the following section.

Barriers to Moving Along the Co-production–Co-creation Continuum

Barriers to a superior service orientation (including co-creation) according to the literature are identifying the obstacles to building a service-oriented platform and problems encountered after such a strategy is initiated. Customers' involvement is central to the co-creation approach and 'co-creation requires certain qualifications from its participants' (Füller *et al.*, 2009, p. 93), because in terms of their social resources and intellectual capabilities, only when they are qualified would participants feel empowered and a sense of self-determination. More creative consumers with higher lead-user characteristics possess higher needs and empowerment to transfer their knowledge to the organization. Also, it is crucial for the organization to develop and design interactive tools as a means of co-creation, because only when the tools are well-designed will consumers feel empowered and willing to share their vision. Moreover, good 'co-creation tools that lower the level of qualifications required for participation or that enable less skilled consumers to make valuable contributions can be considered as empowering tools' (Füller *et al.*, 2009, p. 93), thus a less-favourable tool might hinder the effectiveness, hence efficiency, of a co-creation strategy.

Plé and Cáceres (2010) have likewise raised concerns that if the co-creation process is not managed properly after implementation, it might lead to a disaster, which they coined 'value co-destruction'. According to them, 'misuse of resources is at the heart of value co-destruction' (Plé and Cáceres, 2010, p. 435). Be it 'accidental misuse' or 'intentional misuse', this wrongdoing would create discrepancies on the expectations of the two parties, and could bring about adverse effects on brand image. Therefore, it is important for managers, or empowered frontline employees, to precisely communicate their expectations as well as to share the willingness to apply resources for co-creation through all possible means. A premature adoption of customer input could also lead to barriers to co-creation (Hoonhout, 2007). Therefore, an alignment between customer and firms and the timely adoption of customer inputs are essential for knowledge sharing and co-creation to materialize.

More general barriers and resistance to change include financial difficulties, priority of other businesses, cost of the change, lack of co-operation and skills, lack of resources, insecurity, fear of losing the existing customer, fear of losing something valuable, internal politics and time limitations (Okumus and Hemmington, 1998). It should be noted that resistance to change on the part of customers and employees are the main barriers to implementing any system/process-related improvements. Okumus and Hemmington (1998) use the example of change in service style/menu offerings from the hospitality context to elucidate this. When the change itself is radical, the resistance is that much greater.

A lack of communication has been identified as a generic barrier leading to employee uncertainty (Okumus, 2001; Bordia *et al.*, 2004) and psychological strain, feelings of job insecurity and turnover intentions. Poor change management history has been shown to affect the employees' perception of organizational change management practices, which in turn influence employees' trust in the organization and turnover intentions (Bordia *et al.*, 2004). Barriers related to the firm's ability to engage in innovation have been attributed to emotional blocks (such as habits, fear of making mistakes), inexperience and certain misconceptions (Calish and Gamache, 1981; Okumus, 2003).

Employees' attitude to change has been considered as a major internal barrier, which includes readiness to change, commitment to change, openness to change and cynicism about change (Choi, 2011). Coping with change has been identified as a mediator in the relationship between affective commitment to change and organizational turnover intentions (Cunningham, 2006). When employees believed in the value of the change, they would have a sense of obligation to support and take responsibility for the change (Jennings, 2004). Individual resistance, none the less, showed a non-significant relationship with commitment to change (Foster, 2010).

Internal barriers to customer orientation practices have also been linked to time needed for change (Halliday, 2002; Jennings, 2004). The change itself can bring about negative emotions in employees, including perceptions of: an insecure future, unfavourable working conditions and unjust treatment from the organization. As a result, a lack of trust in the organization can emerge, leading to withdrawal from the organization (Kiefer, 2005). Employees' participation in the process of change has been considered as important for the adoption of change (Lines, 2004). A perceived 'low quality' change-related decision led to negative emotions and mistrust (Lines *et al.*, 2005). Poor performance has been perceived as the antecedent to organizational change leading to a destruction of trust between the employee and the organization (Lo and Aryee, 2003).

A lack of resources (including technological support) has been regarded a barrier to change (Nielsen *et al.*, 2000). While supporting this notion, Rafferty and Simons (2006) suggested that for 'fine-tuning change', trust in peers, participation and logistics played a role. However, for corporate transformational change to occur, flexible policies and procedures and perceived organizational support as well as trust in leadership are essential. An organization open towards its stakeholders is also more open to change compared with one that is internally focused (i.e. self-interest) (Raza and Standing, 2011). Cross-functional integration, training, communication, technology, organizational culture and facilitative leadership are considered to affect employees' affective commitment to change in the context of customer relationship management (Shum *et al.*, 2008; Okumus *et al.*, 2010). Insufficient technology and low level of customer involvement have been considered as barriers to customization, among other factors (Yeung and Choi, 2011).

The Co-production–Co-creation Continuum Framework

Based on the literature on barriers to co-creation, the model depicted in Fig. 4.1 was further developed and adapted to build on the continuum suggested by the authors. The continuum concept reflects the proposition that the four ideal types shown in the earlier typology of Chathoth *et al.* (2013) can be represented in a linear continuum ranging from co-production to firm-driven service innovation, customer-driven customization and, finally, to co-creation. This continuum relationship is implicitly described in the synthesis of earlier studies that explain factors of differentiation between co-production, the innovation process, customization and co-creation. These differentiating factors (see Table 4.1) represent several continua in their own right and range from: (i) a passive role of the consumer to an active one; (ii) use as the primary value creation to consumption as the source of primary value; (iii) a firm-centric view to a customer- or experience-centric view; and (iv) the customer's individual needs not always being met to the customer's individual needs met to a higher degree.

This modified framework is depicted in Fig. 4.1, which is more holistic because it includes the barriers that need to be overcome for firms to move along the continuum as well as the potential benefits that accrue to firms that overcome these

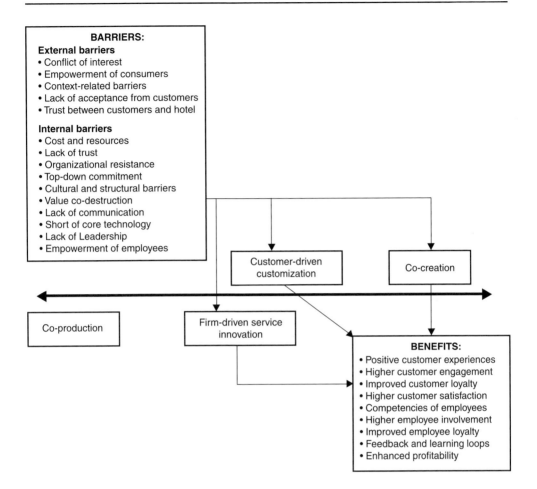

BARRIERS:

External barriers
• Conflict of interest
• Empowerment of consumers
• Context-related barriers
• Lack of acceptance from customers
• Trust between customers and hotel

Internal barriers
• Cost and resources
• Lack of trust
• Organizational resistance
• Top-down commitment
• Cultural and structural barriers
• Value co-destruction
• Lack of communication
• Short of core technology
• Lack of Leadership
• Empowerment of employees

Customer-driven customization

Co-creation

Co-production

Firm-driven service innovation

BENEFITS:
• Positive customer experiences
• Higher customer engagement
• Improved customer loyalty
• Higher customer satisfaction
• Competencies of employees
• Higher employee involvement
• Improved employee loyalty
• Feedback and learning loops
• Enhanced profitability

Fig. 4.1. Co-production and co-creation continuum framework.

barriers. At the left side of Fig. 4.1, the continuum includes contingent factors that are barriers to co-creation, which need to be considered in order for firms to move from co-production to co-creative modalities of value creation. It is imperative for firms to consider these barriers right at the outset, given that a strategic approach to building resources needs to be at the crux of moving along the co-production–co-creation continuum. Weighing the cons of each of these barriers is integral to the achievement of competitive advantage in the long-term because firms need to invest in key resources that are able to address the firm's posture towards co-creative processes. These barriers include both external and internal barriers to move along the continuum from strictly co-production to other more customer-driven and involved approaches.

External barriers are externalities that limit the firm from moving away from co-production approaches to customer service. The basis of many barriers appears to be determined by the culture of the consumer and a lack of trust with the organization.

In the tourism example, consumers may have preconceived ideas on the service process based on tradition and previous experiences. For example, in hotel settings, the processes of check-in or check-out are fairly standard, and empowering the consumer to deviate from these service processes can be a barrier if it creates uncertainty, confusion or sensory overload in the mind of the customer. Therefore, the tourism entity's ability to gain trust and acceptance of a change in service procedures in which customers are more engaged, can create a formidable barrier.

Similarly, internal barriers are dependent on the motivation and capabilities of staff and leadership of the tourism organization. In many cases, the ability to minimize these internal barriers requires a cultural shift in thought and action of (i) what the firm is providing; (ii) understanding what is valued by the consumer; (iii) how these changes may create competitive advantage; and (iv) how success will be assessed. To make this shift, tourism industry leaders will need to address resistance to change, provide a top-down commitment, break down internal structural barriers, and (once again) empower employees to find innovative ways to be able to consistently address the heterogeneous needs of individual consumers throughout the service process.

Once these processes are designed, a systematic process-driven approach to co-creation should be developed. The result should be substantial benefits in the form of enhanced customer and employee experiences, engagement, loyalty and satisfaction, as well as ongoing organizational learning and, ultimately, enhanced profitability.

Implications, Conclusions and Future Directions

This chapter suggests that a continuum from co-production to co-creation may be a better way of capturing the position of organizations in the tourism sector. The degree of customer involvement in terms of the role during the value creation process and the modality, i.e. production/consumption, influences where these firms will lie on this continuum and how they could move within it. Product-centric characteristics would be the foci of the firm if it is steeped in co-production-oriented modalities. On the other hand, co-creation would emerge if firms move from sporadic to continuous involvement of their customers during the production process, leading to customer centricity.

It is imperative that tourism destinations move towards a co-creation modality to attract and satisfy customer needs. In order for such firms to be able to move towards the co-creation end of the spectrum, the service-dominant logic could be used as the underlying philosophy to develop the firm's strategic orientation towards its markets. Therefore, tourism firms would have to consciously include systems and processes that move from the goods-dominant to the service-dominant logic while overcoming the barriers to co-creation. As indicated in Fig. 4.1, the benefits of customer centricity should be juxtaposed with relevant barriers, while developing and implementing co-creative processes in tourism firms. It must be noted that unless the benefits outweigh the barriers, value co-creation will not emerge.

Based on the above, engaging customers at a higher level is essential for tourism firms to move towards the co-creation end of the spectrum. For this to happen, tourism organizations and destinations should be customer-centric with the objective of developing resources that are targeted to meet (or even exceed) specific needs of customers on an ongoing basis. Historically, tourism destinations have been able to sustain a higher level of competitiveness using attractions to draw customers, activities to engage them and facilities to meet certain travel-related needs. However, the advent of technological platforms to engage customers at a superior level prior to travel and during/post-travel phases has led to the emergence of co-creative tourism processes and modalities. Attractions, facilities and activities need to be linked to the customers during the various phases of the travel experience through engagement platforms.

It is this that tourism organizations and destinations would need to exploit in order to move towards a higher level of customer engagement while focusing on tourists' experiences (e.g. Ritchie *et al.*, 2011), rather than satisfaction alone. The implementation of service-dominant logic and the co-creation framework in the tourism context will also provide the required impetus in further developing the experiential elements of the tourism product. For this to happen, further research is required that focuses on the development of technology/other resources so as to build customer engagement platforms from the perspective of the tourism destination/firm. This would in turn enable these destinations/firms to move from the co-production to the co-creation end of the continuum framework.

Notes

[1] These facts are based on the first author's own observations within the Chinese context and from feedback received from Middle East and South Asian travellers to mainland China and Hong Kong.

[2] Source: http://mikahaziq.blogspot.com/2012/09/halal-food-disneyland-hong-kong.html

[3] This fact was extracted from an interview with the General Manager of one of the five-star hotels in Hong Kong that participated in a study on co-creation in 2010.

[4] Source: http://www.hongkongairport.com/eng/passenger/arrival/t1/airport-services-facilities/prayer-room.html

References

Binkhorst, E. and Den Dekker, T. (2009) Agenda for co-creation tourism experience research. *Journal of Hospitality Marketing & Management* 18(2/3), 311–327.

Bitner, M.J., Faranda, W.T., Hubbert, A.R. and Zeithaml, V.A. (1997) Customer contributions and roles in service delivery. *International Journal of Service Industry Management* 8(3), 193–205.

Bordia, P., Hunt, E., Paulsen, N., Tourish, D. and DiFonzo, N. (2004) Uncertainty during organizational change: is it all about control? *European Journal of Work and Organizational Psychology* 13(3), 345–365.

Calish, I.G. and Gamache, D.R. (1981) How to overcome organizational resistance to change. *Management Review* 70(10), 21–28.

Chathoth, P.K., Altinay, L., Harrington, R.J., Okumus, F. and Chan, E.S.W. (2013) Co-production versus co-creation: a process based continuum in the hotel service context. *International Journal of Hospitality Management* 32(1), 11–20.

Choi, M. (2011) Employees' attitudes toward organizational change: a literature review. *Human Resource Management* 50(4), 479–500.

Collins, N. and Murphy, J. (2009) Operationalising co-creation: service dominant logic and the infinite game. *Proceedings of the Australian and New Zealand Marketing Academy* (ANZMAC 2009), Melbourne, Australia. Available at: http://www.duplication.net.au/ANZMAC09/papers/ANZMAC2009-299.pdf (accessed 28 November 2012).

Cunningham, G.B. (2006) The relationships among commitment to change, coping with change, and turnover intentions. *European Journal of Work and Organizational Psychology* 15(1), 29–45.

Foster, R.D. (2010) Resistance, justice and commitment to change. *Human Resource Development Quarterly* 21(1), 3–39.

Friesen, G. (2001) Co-creation: when 1 and 1 make 11. *Consulting to Management* 12(1), 28–31.

Füller, J., Mühlbacher, H., Matzler, K. and Jawecki, G. (2009) Consumer empowerment through Internet-based co-creation. *Journal of Management Information Systems* 26(3), 71–102.

Halliday, S.V. (2002) Barriers to customer-orientation: a case applied and explained. *European Journal of Marketing* 36(1/2), 136–158.

Hoonhout, H.C.M. (2007) Setting the stage for developing innovative concepts: people and climate. *CoDesign* 31, 19–33.

Humphreys, A. and Grayson, K. (2008) The intersecting roles of consumer and producer: a critical perspective on co-production, co-creation and prosumption. *Sociology Compass* 2(3), 963–980.

Jennings, D.A. (2004) Myths about change. *CPA Journal* 74(4), 12.

Kiefer, T. (2005) Feeling bad: antecedents and consequences of negative emotions in ongoing change. *Journal of Organizational Behavior* 26(8), 875–897.

Kristensson, P., Matthing, J. and Johansson, N. (2008) Key strategies for the successful involvement of customers in the co-creation of new technology-based services. *International Journal of Service Industry Management* 19(4), 474–491.

Lines, R. (2004) Influence of participation in strategic change: resistance, organizational commitment and change goal achievement. *Journal of Change Management* 4(3), 193–215.

Lines, R., Selart, M., Espedal, B. and Johansen, S.T. (2005) The production of trust during organizational change. *Journal of Change Management* 5(2), 221–245.

Lo, S. and Aryee, S. (2003) Psychological contract breach in a Chinese context: an integrative approach. *Journal of Management Studies* 40(4), 1005–1020.

Lovelock, C.H. and Young, R.F. (1979) Look to consumers to increase productivity. *Harvard Business Review* 57(3), 168–178.

Lusch, R.F. and Vargo, S.L. (2006) Service-dominant logic: reactions, reflections and refinements. *Marketing Theory* 6(3), 281–288.

Lusch, R.F., Vargo, S.L. and O'Brien, M. (2007) Competing through service: insights from service-dominant logic. *Journal of Retailing* 83(1), 5–18.

Michel, S., Brown, S.W. and Gallan, A.S. (2008) An expanded and strategic view of discontinuous innovations: deploying a service-dominant logic. *Journal of the Academy of Marketing Science* 36(1), 54–66.

Michelli, J.A. (2008) *The New Gold Standard: 5 Leadership Principles for Creating a Legendary Customer Experience Courtesy of The Ritz-Carlton Hotel Company*. McGraw-Hill, New York.

Mills, P.K. (1986) *Managing Service Industries: Organizational Practices in a Postindustrial Economy*. Ballinger, Cambridge, Massachusetts.

Nielsen, J.F., Bukh, P.N.D. and Mols, N.P. (2000) Barriers to customer-oriented management accounting in financial services. *International Journal of Service Industry Management* 11(3), 269–386.

Okumus, F. (2001) Towards a strategy implementation framework. *International Journal of Contemporary Hospitality Management* 13(7), 327–338.

Okumus, F. (2003) A framework to implement strategies in organizations. *Management Decision* 41(9), 871–883.

Okumus, F. and Hemmington, N. (1998) Barriers and resistance to change in hotel firms: an investigation at unit level. *International Journal of Contemporary Hospitality Management* 10(7), 283–288.

Okumus, F., Altinay, L. and Chathoth, P. (2010) *Strategic Management for Hospitality and Tourism.* Elsevier/Butterworth-Heinemann, Oxford.

Payne, A.F., Storbacka, K. and Frow, P. (2008) Managing the co-creation of value. *Journal of the Academy of Marketing Science* 36(1), 83–96.

Pine, J.B. and Gilmore, J. (1998) *The Experience Economy.* Harvard Business School Press, Boston, Massachusetts.

Plé, L. and Cáceres, R.C. (2010) Not always co-creation: introducing interactional co-destruction of value in service-dominant logic. *Journal of Services Marketing* 24(6), 430–437.

Prahalad, C.K. and Ramaswamy, V. (2004a) *The Future of Competition: Co-Creating Unique Value with Customers.* Harvard Business School Press, Boston, Massachusetts.

Prahalad, C.K. and Ramaswamy, V. (2004b) Co-creation experiences: the next practice in value creation. *Journal of Interactive Marketing* 18(3), 5–14.

Rafferty, A.E. and Simons, R.H. (2006) An examination of the antecedents of readiness for fine-tuning and corporate transformation changes. *Journal of Business and Psychology* 20(3), 325–350.

Ramaswamy, V. and Gouillart, F. (2010) *The Power of Co-creation: Build it with them to Boost Growth, Productivity, and Profits.* Free Press, New York.

Raza, S.A. and Standing, C. (2011) A systemic model for managing and evaluating conflicts in organizational change. *Systemic Practice and Action Research* 24(3), 187–210.

Ritchie, B., Tung, V. and Ritchie, R. (2011) Tourism experience management research: emergence, evolution and future directions. *International Journal of Contemporary Hospitality Management* 23(4), 419–438.

Shaw, G., Bailey, A. and Williams, A. (2011) Aspects of service-dominant logic and its implications for tourism management: examples from the hotel industry. *Tourism Management* 32(2), 207–214.

Shum, P., Bove, L. and Auh, S. (2008) Employees' affective commitment to change: the key to successful CRM implementation. *European Journal of Marketing* 42(11/12), 1346–1371.

Vargo, S.L. and Lusch, R.F. (2004) Evolving to a new dominant logic for marketing. *Journal of Marketing* 68(1), 1–17.

Vargo, S.L. and Lusch, R.F. (2006) Service-dominant logic: what it is, what it is not, what it might be. In: Lusch, R.F. and Vargo, S.L. (eds) *The Service-Dominant Logic of Marketing: Dialog, Debate, and Directions.* M.E. Sharpe, Armonk, New York, pp. 43–56.

Vargo, S.L. and Lusch, R.F. (2008) Why 'service'? *Journal of the Academy of Marketing Science* 36(1), 25–38.

Walls, A.R., Okumus, F., Wang, Y.R. and Kwun, D.J. (2011) An epistemological view of consumer experiences. *International Journal of Hospitality Management* 30(1), 10–21.

Yen, H.R., Gwinner, K.P. and Su, W. (2004) The impact of customer participation and service expectation on locus attributions following service failure. *International Journal of Service Industry Management* 15(1), 7–26.

Yeung, H.T. and Choi, T.M. (2011) Mass customisation in the Hong Kong apparel industry. *Production Planning and Control* 22(3), 298–307.

5 Why, Oh Why, Oh Why, Do People Travel Abroad?

GRAHAM M.S. DANN

Finnmark University College, Alta, Norway

Introduction

Motivation is derived from the Latin *movēre*, to move. In English this 'mobility word' possesses a variety of meanings that are grounded conceptually in the mind and behaviourally in experience, as for example, 'get a move on', or 'she was moved to tears'. A motive may also establish a connection between the responsibility and justification for actions. Nevertheless, and in spite of this broad, and sometimes ambivalent, brushstroke of signification, many of its quotidian experiential understandings can be extended to the specific realm of international tourism. In this regard, there are expressions that indicate a transition through space from one place to another, either temporarily as in 'he was on the move' (e.g. on the road), or more permanently as a form of expatriate migration, e.g. 'he decided to move' (overseas). Thus, because of the richness and depth of the concept, it is appropriate that the study of tourist motivation should be equally multi-vocal. Some instances of its associated different methods are briefly outlined in order that additional light can be thrown on the link between motive and experience. They can be broadly described as ways of researching the 'why factor'.

In a state-of-the-art paper, Jamal and Lee (2003) make a fundamental distinction between micro and macro approaches to the study of tourist motivation. The former, they say, are closely identified with (social) psychology and focus on disequilibrium in the need system, the use of approach/avoidance models, and so on. Their protagonists include such tourism scholars as Crompton (1979), Iso-Ahola (1982) and Pearce and Caltabiano (1983). In turn, they rely on classical authorities in their discipline, though outside their field, like Maslow (1954), who claim that the satisfaction of lower needs necessarily precedes the satisfaction of higher needs until the pinnacle of self-actualization is reached. These psychology-oriented tourism academics also apply the useful distinction in their discipline between intrinsic and extrinsic motivation, although some, like Iso-Ahola, even go so far as believing that his is consequently the unique discipline for researching tourist motivation. Jamal and Lee, however, beg to differ on this last point since they feel that many of his accompanying assertions and related hypotheses have been inadequately tested. They, along with psychologist Moscardo (forthcoming), who cites later more developed works of Maslow (Maslow, 1971; Maslow and Lowery, 1998), also challenge the assumption that only tourism can provide correlated need satisfaction, when equally a factor such as religion could perform that task. For this reason they maintain that a social dimension is necessary in order to gain an understanding of why people travel and that this fundamental goal can only be achieved within tourism research by recourse to socially grounded disciplines that go beyond the limited individual-focused explanations of psychology.

The latter observation is demonstrated by recourse to sociologists such as Cohen, Dann, MacCannell and Wang, all of whom offer theoretical insights into tourist motivation that are grounded in a corresponding experiential environment of social interaction. Nevertheless, Jamal and Lee (2003) argue that most of these more nuanced conceptual frameworks often lack an adequate empirical dimension and that, while the justifiable addition of the social can compensate for the deficiencies of an individual orientation, the two approaches still require integration if scholars are to fully understand the linkages between the experiential worlds of home and away. Only in this manner can tourism as production (macro) be united with tourism as consumption (micro). Jamal and Lee illustrate their point by referring to such classical thinkers as Veblen on conspicuous consumption (see Dann (1977) on ego-enhancement as motivation) and by calling for more multidisciplinary research.

Different Approaches to Researching Tourist Motivation

One approach to the study of tourist motivation is via typology, as for example in the classical works of Plog (1974) and Cohen (1972, 1979). More recent contributions have additionally been made by the likes of Hvengaard (2002), Prentice (2004) and Uriely (2009). Sometimes these motivational types are purely conceptual and derived from the ivory tower rather than the field. On other occasions they may be the result of complex factor analyses whose input data are *a priori* statements that invite respondents to supply varying degrees of agreement or disagreement. That said, the use of typologies is still limited, since they are heuristic devices that describe, rather than explain or predict, and hence do not and cannot adequately answer the all-important 'why' question.

On the other hand, motivation that is studied from tourist narratives can employ such personal information sources as interviews and diaries, by adopting a grounded theory approach (Mehmetoglu *et al.*, 2001). When the data are content analysed, categories emerge that are uniquely founded on the *ipsissima verba* of the subjects. To this end, computer programs such as Atlas-ti can be of assistance, thereby usefully combining quantitative (content) with qualitative (semiotic) analyses.

Sometimes pictures act as stimuli for projective tests that can reveal latent motivation. Here a study of tourist motivation in Barbados comes to mind (Dann, 1995). The case in point involved four photographs that displayed increasing levels of strangerhood. These photos were taken from the island's Board of Tourism catalogue and simply asked the respondents to describe what they saw in relation to the time immediately prior to their visit (pre-trip) and now that they were experiencing the holiday (on-trip). These pictorial images evoked a variety of expressions that contained many insights into the tourists' motivations which originated from their own minds and experiences rather than from the prompting of the researcher. They also yielded a whole vocabulary of motives that could be used in subsequent interviews with a different sample of subjects.

On other occasions, motives can be imputed. This technique has been found worthwhile in understanding situations of a delicate nature. In examining the interaction between foreign white tourists and black beach-boys in Barbados, Karch and Dann (1981), for instance, found the dramaturgical perspective of Goffman (1959) useful in comprehending the imputation of experiential roles (and hence motives) between *ego* and *alter*, along with the dynamics of alter-casting consequent upon such interaction. According to this symbolic-interactionist view, the key to understanding motivation is how given situations are defined, since if they are defined as real, they are real in their experiential consequences.

Further Theoretical and Methodological Issues

From the iterative and rhetorical title of this account it would seem that unresolved issues concerning international tourist motivation must necessarily include the hitherto most fundamental and unsatisfactorily treated of them all, namely 'why do people travel [abroad]?'(Lundberg, 1972). Indeed, such a crucial question requiring a combined yield of integrated understandings (Harrill and Potts, 2002), that has so far eluded generations of researchers, needs to be asked serially and exhaustively before it can ultimately provide complete dialogical responses that are mutually and meaningfully acceptable to both the investigator and the investigated. Yet, strangely, few analysts, in attempting to peel back the layers of surface and manifest tourist motivation in their interviewees, in order to reveal the in-depth latent variety below, rarely see the necessity for a corresponding continuation and persistence in their interrogational discussions. True, some experts have reached the happy stage where they routinely and successfully apply *a posteriori* open-ended qualitative techniques, and can thus legitimately justify the valid data they generate in terms of the vocabulary of motive employed by their subjects. Even so, and by contrast, the authors of most alternative enquiries tend to adopt a less than justifiable *a priori* checklist approach, which at best can only elicit reliable replies to close-ended items on so-called objective scales. Indeed, these positivistic measuring devices are designed either by themselves or the industry in words that typically and solely reflect their own backgrounds rather than the subjectively motivated experiences of their respondents and the language these subjects use to communicate them.

Another reason for the question 'why' requiring adequate answers at the level of meaning (Weber, 1968) is because the delicate probing exercise of unearthing motivation represents a revelatory attempt to discover the causality underpinning a personally defined chain of cognitive and experiential events. This attainable cumulative reply to the *why* is not the same as finding out the way in which something works, i.e. *how* it functionally performs in terms of its described *modus operandi* (Aramberri, 2010). Instead, the former response seeks meaningful explanations that lie behind and beneath experiences (McCabe, 2001). These ethnomethodological rationalizations in turn are not couched in terms of pure reason (since, according to Pareto (1935), very few human actors are entirely rational). Rather they employ auto-defined acts of self-justification in terms of the degree of reasonableness for a given like-minded individual or group (Mehmetoglu *et al.*, 2001). In other words, and as Schutz (1972) rightly observes, such people imaginatively construct their personal projects in terms of their mentally projected courses of action. Indeed, it is only by being aware of these reflective conscious states, articulated in the future-perfect tense (as if they had already been experienced), that the ultimate goal of in-order-to-motivation (and hence explanation) becomes possible.

Social scientists in their attempt to identify specific independent variables that operate in logical and temporal sequences, while simultaneously taking into account other associated predictor variables at successive levels, often do so via path models. Here the strength and valence of normalized regression coefficients are calculated and placed in a theoretical structure that explains change in a series of dependent variables (that, with the exception of the last one in the series, are also independent). The direction of causality in any such path model thus proceeds from left to right.

In terms of tourist motivation, the relevant offered path model[1] is as follows:

Push Motive(s) → Pull Motive(s) → Decision where to go → Experience(s) → Satisfaction → New Motive(s) (promotion to potential tourists) (see also Uysal Li and Sirakaya-Turk, 2008, p. 413)

Following this framework, one or more hypothetically identified push motives (e.g. a situation of anomic meaninglessness, normlessness and lack of belonging in the society of tourist generation (Dann, 1977)) can lead in turn to the quest for one or more compensatory pull motives in the host people and their society (e.g. a happy and carefree, *joie de vivre* population liberated from the experiential constraints of anomie (Cazes, 1976)). A shortlist of destinations with this motivational match between demand and supply is then drawn up by the tourists-to-be before being reduced to a single unity by the introduction of complementary push (e.g. status enhancement through taking vacations (e.g. Dann, 1977)) and pull factors (e.g. the presence of celebrities whose names can be correspondingly 'trip-dropped' (Dann, 1994)). In such a manner, a decision is taken where to go as a result of a response to the promotional blend of push and pull. This pre-trip exercise of choice is subsequently transferred to the holiday location where on-trip touristic experiences are evaluated in terms of the earlier deliberation at the cognitive and affective levels. Where this assessment is positive, the tourist is said to be satisfied; where it is neutral or negative various degrees of equilibrium or dissatisfaction are respectively attained. In some (more complex) models (Dann, 2012a; Dann and Berg Nordstrand, 2009), quality of life (or well-being) is introduced at this stage of the proceedings as an intermediate dependent/independent variable lying between domain (dis)satisfaction (e.g. an intervening variable such as health (Moscardo, 2011)) and an ensuing (new) motivation. Whether or not quality of life and domain (dis)satisfaction are contained in the framework, a post-trip stage sees the reformulation of pre-trip motives in light of the tourist's new role as promoter to self and/or others. In so doing, different contexts may be introduced, as for example in Moscardo's (2011) analysis at the levels of the family and the natural environment.

However, in terms of explanation, the model travels from right to left. From the 'why' of the new motive, further 'why' questions are asked regressively about satisfaction, experience, decision, pull and push. Moreover, it is only by the constant questioning of the final stage of the push motives that the researcher can begin to capture the fullness of meaning for any individual or type of individual. In such a manner, a tourist may be asked, for instance, whether she would like to return to Barbados for a holiday (repeater status being predicated on satisfaction). If the answer is negative, then further questioning seeks to discover the corresponding degrees of dissatisfaction, low evaluation of experiences, and the mismatch between pull and push motives. A series of whys hence continue at each stage until saturation point is reached and the researcher can then proceed to the next lower level. On the other hand, if the response is positive, a similar process ensues, though now the accent is on the equally favourable dimensions of each regressive step. Thus, for example, if the tourist says that she would like to come back because of the lovely weather, a succession of whys may ensue so as to test the assertion for critical coherence, particularly if it is raining at the time or the level of humidity approaching 100% is practically unbearable when the interview takes place. Even if the sun is shining from a cloudless blue sky, the questioning may well continue until a more mutually satisfying new motive is articulated that transcends the all-too-frequent utterances of meaningless cliché. Once this cliché-free meaningful situation is attained, attention turns to the next level to the left, and so on, until the initial push motive is reached. In other words, the whole process involves the dialogical confrontation of contradictories, or if not contradictories, then at least contraries.

It should also be evident from the model that, in spite of the realization that 'to consume tourism is to consume experiences' (Sharpley and Stone, 2010), or that it is possible to speak of the 'poetics of the tourist experience' as a form of auto-ethnography (Noy, 2008) that we encounter, for example, in travel blogs (Pudliner, 2007), the tourist experience is no more or less than an intermediate variable between old and new motives.

Additionally, it is worth noting that, if researchers wish to understand motives that are adequate at the level of meaning (where motivation is classically defined 'a complex of subjective meaning which seems to the actor himself (sic) and to the observer an adequate ground for the conduct in question' (Weber, 1968, p. 11)), then the fullness of response to why questions and the corresponding *erklären Verstehen* can only be achieved if there are no further anomalies, paradoxes, ambivalences or contradictions remaining; in other words, if there are no unresolved whys that still need to be asked and answered.

Besides the previously mentioned case of Barbados and its weather, another example of an unresolved why is the following behavioural issue: why do tourists, in seeking to 'get away from it all', spend such a great deal of their experiential time mixing with fellow nationals abroad, especially since part of the 'it all' from which they wish to escape comprises people who, to all intents and purposes, appear to be virtually the same as themselves? By contrast, though equally problematic, is the question of why some tourists seek to avoid the company of their compatriots, on a cruise ship for instance, even to the point where they refuse to talk to them, preferring instead to sit for every meal at a pre-assigned restaurant table with their family and friends to the exclusion of their fellow passengers. Again, and supposing that the foregoing dilemmas are resolved, it still needs to be asked why some tourists ('as child' (Dann, 1996)) travel abroad to meet and interact with the destinational 'other' ('the other as mother'), even to the point of shedding tears of joy as a result of being treated with a friendliness that is typically absent in their daily lives, when in that same home society they routinely seek to avoid contact with immigrants, non-nationals and other strangers who ironically and by extension form part of this pre-vacation 'other' ('the other as brother') (Dann, 1999).

And, if it is not so much a matter of *tourists*, but of a particular type of *tourism*, religious tourism, for instance, why do some vacationers abroad devote so much of their experiential sightseeing to visiting cathedrals and churches when they rarely darken the doors of such spiritual edifices in their domestic environment, let alone profess any institutionalized belief in a deity? Is it that they are motivated by the sacred while away and by the secular when at home and, if so, should not this unexplained cognitive dissonance be confronted in order to make greater motivational and experiential sense? Isn't this what Crompton (1979) means when he speaks of psychological disequilibrium being an important motive for travel?

Another motivationally driven behavioural anomaly is the whole question of why tourists supposedly seeking change [illogically?] return to the same destination year after year, while at the other end of the spectrum there are increasingly unresolved difficulties concerning those tourists who have been everywhere. Indeed, it may legitimately be asked why people should continue being tourists when they have lost the very *raison d'être* of travel – the quest for novelty. Have they simply changed their identities and become 'post tourists', replacing the active experience of real travel with the passive substitute of virtual travel as they watch the flickering images of faraway locales on their home televisions, mobile phones and computer screens?

However, perhaps the greatest motivational paradox of all can be seen in the apparent contradiction between the push motive of tourists 'getting away from it all' abroad and the sometimes equally strong desire to spend holidays in their own country. Such motivational tension is quite evident in recent publicity advocating the respective foregoing positions. The former is illustrated by Princess Cruise Line (2012) under the imperative strap-line 'Escape Completely'. Its website continues the ambitious theme by explaining that people are 'inspired to cruise' by a 'year of reasons to get away from the everyday'. It then provides excerpts from passenger blogs to support this claim once a week over a period of 12 months. Included among these 'reasons' for cruising one finds such responses as 'to fulfil my husband's bucket list', 'to see my wife smile again', 'to bridge a generation gap', 'to get married by surprise', 'to spoil the grandkids' and 'to visit the family far away'. Many of these examples are family oriented, thus facilitating self-identification by a plethora of anonymous blog commentators who, in response, place themselves in a similar position to the blogger. But what makes this type of promotion so different is that it is the relevant arm of the tourism industry which enters the already established dialogue between the blog compilers and their readers and attempts to convert the communication into a trialogue (Dann, 2012b) by asking its hitherto uninvolved customers, 'What's your reason to cruise?' before answering in their client-appropriated words, 'Perhaps to celebrate a milestone occasion, to re-connect with friends and family, or mark a special accomplishment. Our passengers regularly tell us inspiring stories about why they've cruised, and each week throughout 2012 we're going to share one of them. We hope these reasons will inspire your own!'

Thus, so far, the ostensibly persuasive argument is relatively simple: in order to escape everyday tedium, and thereby put life back into a familial relationship, it is necessary to travel abroad and enjoy multiple new experiences together. A cruise ship can provide this novelty on a daily basis. But only a cruise line, such as Princess, or those adopting a similar strategy, can carry out this task effectively because only they have deliberately entered a three-way form of communication in the language of tourism promotion (Dann, 1996, 2012b). Even so, and in the absence of a convincing answer, it must still be asked why this escape can be accurately described as 'complete'. Does Princess really mean that rupture with the home society must be total and that such a situation is desirable or even possible? Surely more questions need to be posed before the difference between promotional myth and experiential reality can be successfully exposed and thus better understood.

The contrasting point of view is exemplified by the proponents of 'staycation' (a recent hybrid term combining a 'stay-(at-home)' with a '(va)-cation' (Staycation, 2012)). Such was the message of Visit England (2012) during the early summer of 2012. Its appeal to 'make it a great 2012' was based on the asserted premise that 'holidays at home are great'. The organization's website also included a short explanatory video. This pictorial and aural communication featured a young couple intent on taking a holiday abroad, the first disadvantage of which was the apparent need for them to get up at 4.15 am in order to catch an (unacceptably early) no-frills aircraft from an (inconveniently) distant airport. In the meantime, and by contrast, popular television presenter Stephen Fry stood by bemusedly and comfortably in the garb of a country squire clasping an iconic cup of English tea in the aristocratic surrounds of a stately home. Fry's mellifluous, upper middle class, public school and Oxbridge accent was complemented by the more proletarian tones of actress Julie Walters (of *Billy Elliott* and *Mamma Mia* fame). Their combined narrative continued by praising the delights of experiencing such home-grown sights as the Giant's Causeway, a Scottish loch, a typical Cotswold village, a pastoral scene complete with gambolling lambs, Buckingham Palace and a nostalgic street party in honour of Queen Elizabeth II's diamond jubilee. The covert message was that pride in one's country bore its own rewards, at least in so far as the domestic tourism industry was concerned.

However, both of these home and away promotions can be faulted. The pro-abroad position adopted by Princess makes the mistake of confusing motivation with reason, thereby assuming (incorrectly) that the former is the logical outcome of the latter. It also tends to assume that most consenting adults are in monogamous marital relationships which, statistically speaking, in the West, seems rather unlikely, even for a Princess passenger profile. One thus reaches the conclusion that further probing may be necessary in order that really real motivation be attained.

A similar verdict is reached from the stay-at-home advertisement. Although it may be logical to suggest that, in times of austerity, a precarious national balance of payments position, deteriorating significantly by tourism expenditure overseas, can be rescued by alternative domestic spending, it is nevertheless one-sided to remove the potential non-monetary benefits of foreign travel and more importantly to threaten the freedom to enjoy them. At the same time, the two ambassadors for 'staycations' are individuals who have already enjoyed considerable overseas travel, and given that even in the UK social stratification is predicated on wealth, there is always the danger that such inherent class bias may detract from the motivation itself. Thus there is surely the need for an additional analysis along the lines of the inversionist perspective advocated by Gottlieb (1982). Here experiential roles are reversed to the point where members of the working class seek compensation by becoming 'king or queen for a day' while the more highly stratified attempt to become 'peasants for a day'. In other words, what we have here, as also with the pro-abroad position, is an incomplete picture of motivation, and hence of understanding.

Examples of Some Empirical Studies of Tourism Motivation

At this juncture it is necessary to confront the earlier charge that, whereas there are several theoretically robust studies of tourist motivation, they often lack an adequate empirical basis. Since they typically take a number of years before they are independently tested and their results disseminated (analogous perhaps to medical trials), the relationship between tourist motivation and experience is likely to be similarly disadvantaged. With that proviso, we can examine variations in motivation, from single and dual to multiple (three or more).

Testing/Critique of Single Motivation Hypotheses

- MacCannell (1976): Tourism as a quest for authenticity. *Inter alia* theoretically critiqued by Cohen (1979, 2007), Wang (1999), Lengkeek (2001), Olsen (2002), Bruner (2005), Reisinger and Steiner (2006). Empirically tested, for example, by Pearce and Moscardo (1986) and Mantecón and Huete (2007).
- Dann (1976) (cf. Cohen (2011, p. 17): 'Fantasy is becoming one of the leading motives for travel.' But why did it take 35 years for this situation to be acknowledged?
- Graburn (1977): Tourism as a quest for the sacred. Tested by Wickens (2002).

What these three examples have in common is the reliance on a single factor. This shortfall is carried over to the experiential stage, where it is extremely unlikely that 100% of the variance can be explained.

Testing/Critique of Dual Motivational Hypotheses

Here the motivational typologies of Plog and Cohen (see below) have been described as binaries and identified as 'paradigms' by Chen *et al.* (2011), as indeed has the multi-motivational framework of Pearce (see next sub-section). However, the appropriate use of such a term in this context is debatable, given that typologies are heuristic devices rather than theoretical frameworks, and that paradigms comprise two or more theories (Dann, 2011). That said, the principal dual motivational typologies include such instances as:

- Cohen's (1972) 'institutionalised/non-institutionalised' tourist, based on Simmel's (1908) 'familiarity/stranger-hood' binary distinction. Tested by Snepenger (1987).
- Plog's (1974) 'psychocentric'/'allocentric' (two ends of a continuum similar to Cohen's that yield the corresponding personality types of 'authentics' (comfort zoners) and 'venturers' (novelty seekers) and two variants of each in between 'mid' and 'centric'). An online attitudinal quiz ('carried out over four decades then matches personality type with domestic and international destinations'). Tested by Smith (1990) and rejected. Plog subsequently modifies his position in a rejoinder (1990). Even so, one cannot help feeling that his meaning of authentic is quite different from the polysemic offerings of other scholars (e.g. Cohen, 2007) and that it too can contain an element of risk taking. In other words, the distinction between authentic and venture is not mutually exclusive.
- Gray's (1970) distinction between 'sunlust' and 'wanderlust' has been described as 'crude' by Wood (1980); the latter subsequently goes on to examine typologies that he maintains are more discriminating.
- Iso-Ahola (1980, 1982) 'escape and seeking' (personal/interpersonal). Critiqued by Dann (1983) and Jamal and Lee (2003). Jamal and Lee argue that Iso-Ahola over-relies on Deci's theory of intrinsic motivation, which is too tied to psychology at the micro-level as to permit the necessary inclusion of a macro-sociological analysis (Dann, 1983). Insufficient testing also fails to answer the basic question as to why people should want to escape. Tested by Snepenger *et al.* (2006) and Uysal *et al.* (1993), and partially confirmed. The familiar trope of escape also appears commercially, for example, in the strap-line of Princess Cruise Line (2012) (see earlier). Its sociological dimension has been treated by Rojek (1993, p. 199), where he links it to the novelty seeking of curiosity, one of the strongest tourist motives of all.
- Gottlieb (1982) 'king or queen for a day'/'peasant for a day'. Tested by Stein (2011).
- Wang (2000) 'love' side and 'dark' side of tourism as modernity. Included by Jamal and Lee (2003) as an example of a sociological, macro approach to motivation.
- Dann (1977, 1981) 'push/pull'. Tested, for example, by Bello and Etzel (1985), Oh *et al.* (1995), Bagoglu and Uysal (1996), Uysal *et al.* (2008) and Prayag (2010) and confirmed as the major existing model. According to Dolnicar *et al.*, 'The "push-pull factor" theory of tourism motivation by Dann (1977) is perhaps the most recognized theory within the realm of tourism research' (2012, p. 298) to provide an understanding of consumption. This positive evaluation was written some 35 years after the theory had been initially articulated in relation to tourism (i.e. it has stood the test of time). It is reinforced by Uysal *et al.*, who claim that 'the literature on tourist motivation indicates that the examination of motivations based on the push and pull factors has been generally accepted' (2008, p. 414). Indeed, to the best of one's knowledge, there has been no widely acknowledged empirical study that has rejected this framework. An additional advantage is that it is also applicable to the domain of leisure (Prentice, 2004). Even so, maybe now is as good a time as any to question the structural world of binaries and its adequacy in providing motivational understanding of experiential reality.

Testing/Critique of Multi-motivational Hypotheses

- Cohen's (1979) 'Phenomenology of tourist experiences'. Critiqued by Lengkeek (2001). Tested by Uriely (2009) and partially upheld. However, according to the latter, a tourist type relates to motivation and meaning, whereas its form refers to travel arrangements and touristic practices.
- Pearce's (career ladder model (1993, 2005) based on Maslow (1954)). Rejected by Ryan (1995, 1998). Tested by Mansfeld (1992) and found to be limited with respect to adequate predictability, one of the essential criteria of theory.
- Crompton (1979). Referred to by Dolnicar *et al.* as a 'foundational study' (2012, p. 300).

Even here the question must be asked as to the comprehensiveness of multivariable models. Surely it is not just an exercise in increasing the numbers.

Conclusion: Some Unresolved Issues of Tourism Motivation

From what has been stated earlier it would appear that the phenomenon of tourism is based on the notion of human incompleteness and lack of closure. Whether we travel in order to escape or to satisfy our sense of curiosity, for example, there is still something missing in the human psyche that requires experiential fulfilment in 'the-centre-out-there' (Cohen, 1979). Because this vital ingredient awaits us *there*, rather than being present *here*, travel or spatial movement is required in order to attain it. Yet how many tourism researchers have studied this unique condition and how many have received satisfactory answers that have been subsequently debated among their academic colleagues? True, some scholars associate such an experiential situation with the alienation of modernity (Rojek, 1993; Wang, 2000), where this type of estrangement is described in push factor terms, as escape from the developing world's 'hard' evils of poverty, suffering and persecution and the developed world's 'soft' evils of monotony and stress (Wang, 2000, p. 19). Such commentators also speak in terms of a false demand that is the result of manipulation, seduction and control by the tourism industry (Wang, 2000, p. 15). Whether or not we share this point of view, there is nevertheless a prevailing distinction between eros-motivated tourists (emotion, freedom, difference) and a logos-motivated industry (reason, control, homogeneity) (Wang, 2000, pp. 32–33).

It thus follows that the idea of human incompleteness must refer to something beyond the physical. It is suggested here that this missing element, which somehow straddles the individual and the social, the micro and the macro (Jamal and Lee, 2003), is a lack of belonging consequent upon degrees of anomie in the home society (Dann, 1977, 1981). According to this view, what makes tourism possible is the realization that a tourist owns virtually nothing in the touristic environment and very little in the home environment. S(he) rents a seat on a plane, a seat in a taxi, a seat on the beach, a seat in a restaurant, several seats and a bed in the chosen accommodation and a good number of other items and experiences that make up the tourist's repertoire of identity through appropriation. In other words, the tourist is a cultural tenant, participating in a game of rental that is a necessary condition for being a tourist, a situation that is linked to an absence of ownership in the environment of origin (Dann, 2013). The tourist therefore temporarily exchanges one lack of belonging for another. To do otherwise would be to detract from the essence of being a tourist, the domain not of the physical but of the metaphysical.

The desire to complete what is missing can additionally assume more than one form. It has been relatedly argued, for instance, that there is an important difference between warm and cold water islands (Dann, 2006). The former are often portrayed as paradises patronized by the rich and famous. The motivational pull of these exotic and erotic destinations is a make-believe fantasy of blue skies, palm trees and white sandy beaches (conveniently omitting the Third World realities of vermin, disease, poverty, hurricanes, etc.), while emphasising the associated elevation in status of being in the company of celebrities (push factor). Cold water islands, by contrast, appeal to a different sort of clientele, people who may have the financial means in order to be able to afford travel to peripheral destinations, but who have no further need to flaunt their wealth via their attire and possessions in a freely chosen surrounding lacking in comfort. There is even an appeal to aestheticism in some of these remote and sacred locales since they are often associated with a history of saintly figures and their holy burial grounds. The warm island paradises, by contrast, have no such supernatural connection. Theirs is a world of instant here-and-now riches that are paraded rather than surrendered.

Yet in spite of these various scholarly insights, there still seems to be lack of consensus as to the precise nature of push and pull factors followed by a questioning of the identity of the former and whether they really are what they claim to be. According to Uysal *et al.* (2008, p. 414), for instance, push factors relate to the internal forces of the subject of travel, while pull factors refer to the external forces constituting the object of travel; the former comprise the end, the latter the means. It is therefore rather surprising that, having itemized several push factors correctly (e.g. escape from everyday routine), some of the other typical push factors that they identify (e.g. nature, adventure) seem closer to being pull factors, and some of the pull factors that they cite (e.g. religion) are arguably nearer to being push factors. However, and even though the same could be said of Crompton's (1979) listing of multiple push and pull factors, the difference between him and Uysal *et al.* is the latter's conviction that 'the challenge is not or should not be what push and pull factors are but the challenge is to capture the extent to which these factors interact' (2008, p. 429). This statement, then, in spite of the unaddressed terminological confusion, nevertheless highlights a worthy goal in its own right.

Yet there is still one proviso that introduces a further notion of caution into the acceptance of the foregoing position, and it is the possibility that a given motive can be simultaneously considered as *both* a push factor and a pull factor. Take the earlier consideration of the weather, for example. If it is interpreted as a pull factor, as in the case of the repeat visitor to Barbados, then, even if the sun is not actually shining, it can still be articulated as a motive for going there time and again. Since it is based on past experience, and that in turn can be interpreted in terms of average expectation or probability, it falls into Schutz's (1972) category of 'because-of-motivation'. However, and as we have seen in relation to that previously cited philosophical sociologist, if it is projected into the future, it then assumes the qualities of 'in-order-to motivation'. The second scenario is the 'really real' motive, while the first one is a 'pseudo in-order-to' motive. It is thus the latter that requires further probing.

On the other hand the weather could act as a push factor, since it relates to conditions in the home society. Here the dreary grey skies, the incessant rain and the long cold winters cumulatively act as an impetus for getting the potential tourist out of the armchair and on to the plane. When these conditions of home are contrasted with the real or imaginary conditions of away, then we have an attempted matching of push and pull factors, a situation much sought after by promoters of destinations. A similar scenario can be found in the publicity surrounding television game shows. Even if the prize is not a holiday for two in an exotic destination, when successful contestants are asked what they would like to do with the money they have just won, they often reply in terms of taking a holiday. Indeed their response has become so typical and unthinking that it has reached the level of cliché; and cliché, it should be noted, is a figure of speech that ordinarily proscribes further questions.

And so we, like the phenomenon of tourism itself, have travelled full circle and are now back at the beginning. Initially we asked 'why, oh why, oh why do people travel abroad?' (where the iterative threefold question theoretically knows no numerical limit). Consequently we should now be able to see that unless the response is framed as an adequate, meaningful and genuine 'in-order-to motivation', then we need to repeat the question again and again until both ourselves as researchers and our subjects as tourists receive satisfactory answers. Only then will we have the full links between motivation and experience, between personal drive and what drives experiential value.

Note

[1] An interesting alternative model has been put forward by Prebensen *et al.* (2012, 2013). According to them, motivation acts as an antecedent in creating the perceived value of a destination, and this in turn is linked as an antecedent to satisfaction and loyalty (which become the consequences that influence the positive intention of taking future trips). By appealing to the higher needs of motivation, the quality of the vacation is enhanced, thereby additionally enriching subjective well-being. However, at the same explanatory level as motivation are two co-variables of involvement/relevance and knowledge. The former refers to the tourist's internal state comprising the factors of interest, arousal and drive, together with their intensity, direction and persistence, and extending to such considerations as interest, pleasure, signs and the importance and probability of risk. Nevertheless, Prebensen *et al.* (2013) argue that, for a more complete model, variables like norms, past experiences, expectations and demographics should be added, a conclusion that also applies to the path model of the current presentation. The two frameworks share further similarities in the variables they identify, along with their logical and temporal sequencing (antecedents/consequences).

References

Aramberri, J. (2010) *Modern Mass Tourism*. Emerald, Bradford, UK.

Baloglu, S. and Uysal, M. (1996) Market segments of push and pull motivations: a canonical correlation approach. *International Journal of Contemporary Hospitality Management* 8(3), 32–38.

Bello, D. and Etzel, M. (1985) The role of novelty in the pleasure travel experience. *Journal of Travel Research* 24(1), 20–26.

Bruner, E. (2005) *Culture on Tour: Ethnographies of Travel*. Chicago University Press, Chicago, Illinois.

Cazes, G. (1976) Le tiers-monde vu par les publicités touristiques: une image mystifiante. [The third world seen by tourism advertising: a mystifying image]. *Cahiers du Tourisme, série C* 33.

Chen, Y., Mak, B. and McKercher, B. (2011) What drives people to travel: integrating the tourist motivation paradigm. *Journal of China Tourism Research* 7(2), 120–136.

Cohen, E. (1972) Towards a sociology of international tourism. *Social Research* 39(1), 164–182.

Cohen, E. (1979) A phenomenology of tourist experiences. *Sociology* 13(2), 179–201.

Cohen, E. (2007) Authenticity in tourism studies: après la lutte. *Tourism Recreation Research* 32(2), 75–82.

Cohen, E. (2011) The changing faces of contemporary tourism. *Folia Turistica* 25(1), 13–19.

Crompton, J. (1979) Motivations for pleasure vacation. *Annals of Tourism Research* 6(4), 408–424.

Dann, G. (1976) The holiday was simply fantastic. *Tourist Review* 31(3), 19–23.

Dann, G. (1977) Anomie, ego-enhancement and tourism. *Annals of Tourism Research* 4(4), 184–194.

Dann, G. (1981) Tourist motivation: an appraisal. *Annals of Tourism Research* 8(2), 187–219.

Dann, G. (1983) Comment on Iso-Ahola's 'Toward a social psychological theory of tourism motivation'. *Annals of Tourism Research* 10(2), 273–276.

Dann, G. (1994) Hyping the destination through the rich and (in)-famous: the boundaries of name dropping. *Cahiers du Tourisme, série C* 187.

Dann, G. (1995) A sociolinguistic approach towards changing tourist imagery. In: Butler, R. and Pearce, D. (eds) *Change in Tourism: People, Places, Processes*. Routledge, London, pp. 114–136.

Dann, G. (1996) *The Language of Tourism: A Sociolinguistic Perspective*. CAB International, Wallingford, UK.

Dann, G. (1999) 'Den andre' i turismens språk ('The Other' in the language of tourism). In: Jacobsen, J. and Viken, A. (eds) *Turisme. Stedet i en Bevegelig Verden (Tourism: Place in a Moving World)*. Universitetsforlaget, Oslo, pp. 96–108.

Dann, G. (2006) Promotional issues. In: Baldacchino, G. (ed.) *Extreme Tourism: Lessons from the World's Cold Water Islands*. Elsevier, Oxford, pp. 15–29.

Dann, G. (2011) Take me to the Hilton: the language of tourism paradigm. *Folia Turistica* 25(1), 23–40.

Dann, G. (2012a) Tourist motivation and quality of life: in search of the missing link. In: Uysal, M., Perdue, R. and Sirgy, M.J. (eds) *Handbook of Tourism and Quality-of-Life Research: Enhancing the Lives of Tourists and Residents of Host Communities.*, Springer, New York, pp. 233–247.

Dann, G. (2012b) Re-modelling a changing language of tourism: from monologue to dialogue and trialogue. *PASOS: Revista de Turismo y Patrimonio Cultural* 10(4), 59–70.

Dann, G. (2013) Rooms for rent. Editor's choice. *Tourism, Recreation Research* 38(2), 203–212.

Dann, G. and Berg-Nordstrand, K. (2009) Promoting well being via multisensory tourism. In: Bushell, R. and Sheldon, P. (eds) *Wellness and Tourism: Mind, Body, Spirit, Place*. Cognizant Communication Corporation, New York, pp. 125–137.

Dolnicar, S., Lazarevski, K. and Yanamandram, V. (2012) Quality-of-life and travel motivations: integrating the two concepts in the Grevillea model. In: Uysal, M., Perdue, R. and Sirgy, M.J. (eds) *Handbook of Tourism and Quality-of-Life Research: Enhancing the Lives of Tourists and Residents of Host Communities*. Springer, New York, pp. 293–308.

Goffman, I. (1959) *The Presentation of Self in Everyday Life*. Doubleday, New York.

Gottlieb, A. (1982) Americans' vacations. *Annals of Tourism Research* 9, 165–187.

Graburn, N. (1977) Tourism, the sacred journey. In: Smith, V. (ed.) *Hosts and Guests: The Anthropology of Tourism*. University of Pennsylvania Press, Philadelphia, Pennsylvania, pp. 21–36.

Gray, J. (1970) *International Travel – International Trade*. Lexington Books, Lexington, Massachusetts.

Harrill, R. and Potts, T. (2002) Social psychological theories of tourist motivation: exploration, debate and transition. *Tourism Analysis* 7(2), 105–114.

Hvenegaard, G. (2002) Using tourist typologies for ecotourism research. *Journal of Ecotourism* 1(1), 7–18.

Iso-Ahola, S. (1980) *The Social Psychology of Leisure and Recreation*. William Brown, Dubuque, Iowa.

Iso-Ahola, S. (1982) Toward a social-psychological theory of tourist motivation: a rejoinder. *Annals of Tourism Research* 9, 256–262.

Jamal, T. and Lee, J. (2003) Integrating micro and macro approaches to tourist motivations: toward an interdisciplinary theory. *Tourism Analysis* 8(1), 47–59.

Karch, C. and Dann, G. (1981) Close encounters of the Third World. *Human Relations* 34(4), 249–268.

Lengkeek, J. (2001) Leisure experience and imagination: rethinking Cohen's modes of tourist experience. *International Sociology* 16(2), 173–184.

Lundberg, D. (1972) *The Tourist Business*. Institutions/Volume Feeding Management Magazine, Chicago, Illinois.

MacCannell, D. (1976) *The Tourist: A New Theory of the Leisure Class*. Schocken Books, New York.

Mansfeld, Y. (1992) From motivation to actual travel. *Annals of Tourism Research* 19(3), 399–419.

Mantecón, A. and Huete, R. (2007) The role of authenticity in tourism planning: empirical findings from southeast Spain. *Tourism Review* 55(3), 323–333.

Maslow, A. (1954) *Motivation and Personality*. Harper, New York.

Maslow, A. (1971) *The Further Reaches of Human Nature*. Viking Press, New York.

Maslow, A. and Lowery, R. (1998) *Toward a Psychology of Being*, 3rd edn. Wiley, New York

McCabe, S. (2001) Worlds of reason – the praxis of accounting for 'day visitor' behaviour in the Peak National Park: a qualitative investigation. Unpublished PhD thesis, University of Derby, Derby, UK.

Mehmetoglu, M., Dann, G. and Larsen, S. (2001) Solitary travellers in the Norwegian Lofoten islands: why do people travel on their own? *Scandinavian Journal of Hospitality and Tourism* 1(1), 19–37.

Moscardo, G. (2011) Searching for well-being. Exploring change in tourist motivation. *Tourism, Recreation Research* 36(1), 15–26.

Moscardo, G. (forthcoming) Do tourists travel for the discovery of 'Self' or to search for the 'Other?' (Research Probe) *Tourism, Recreation Research*.

Noy, C. (2008) The poetics of tourist experience: an autoethnography of a family trip to Eilat. *Journal of Tourism and Culture Change* 5(3), 141–157.

Oh, H.-Chu, Uysal, M. and Weaver, P. (1995) Product bundles and market segments based on travel motivations: a canonical correlation approach. *International Journal of Hospitality* 14(2), 123–137.

Olsen, K. (2002) Authenticity as a concept in tourism research: the social organization of the experience of authenticity. *Tourist Studies* 2(2), 159–182.

Pareto, V. (1935) *Mind and Society*. Harcourt, Brace, New York.

Pearce, P. (1993) Fundamentals of tourist motivation. In: Butler, R. and Pearce, D. (eds) *Tourism Research: Critiques and Challenges*. Routledge, London, pp. 113–134.

Pearce, P. (2005) Developing the travel career approach to tourist motivation. *Journal of Travel Research* 43(3), 226–237.

Pearce, P. and Caltabiano, M. (1983) Inferring travel motivation from travellers' experiences. *Journal of Travel Research* 22(2), 16–20.

Pearce, P. and Moscardo, G. (1986) The concept of authenticity in tourists' experiences. *Australian and New Zealand Journal of Sociology* 22(1), 121–132.

Plog, S. (1974) Why destination areas rise and fall in popularity. *Cornell Hotel and Restaurant Administration Quarterly* 14(4), 55–58.

Plog, S. (1990) A carpenter's tools: an answer to Stephen L.J. Smith's review of psychocentrism/allocentrism. *Journal of Travel Research* 28(4), 43–45.

Prayag, G. (2010) Images as pull factors of a tourist destination: a factor-cluster segmentation analysis. *Tourism Analysis* 15(2), 213–226.

Prebensen, N., Woo, E., Chen, J. and Uysal, M. (2012) Motivation and involvement as antecedents of the perceived value of the destination experience. *Journal of Travel Research* 52(2), 253–264.

Prebensen, N., Woo, E. and Uysal, M. (2013) Experience value: antecedents and consequences. *Current Issues in Tourism*. Available at: http://www.tandfonline.com/loi/rcit20 (accessed 5 March 2013).

Prentice, R. (2004) Tourist motivation and typologies. In: Lew, A., Hall, C.M. and Williams, A. (eds) *A Companion to Tourism*. Blackwell, Oxford, pp. 261–279.

Princess Cruise Line (2012) Online advertisement. Available at: http://www.princess.com (accessed 2 May 2013).

Pudliner, B. (2007) Alternative literature to tourist experience, travel and tourist weblogs. *Journal of Tourism and Cultural Change* 5(1), 46–59.

Reisinger, Y. and Steiner, C. (2006) Reconceptualising object authenticity. *Annals of Tourism Research* 33(1), 65–86.

Rojek, C. (1993) *Ways of Escape: Modern Transformations in Leisure and Travel*. Macmillan, London.

Ryan, C. (1995) *Researching Tourist Satisfaction: Issues, Concepts, Problems*. Routledge, London.

Ryan, C. (1998) The travel career ladder: an appraisal. *Annals of Tourism Research* 25(4), 936–957.

Schutz, A. (1972) *The Phenomenology of the Social World*. Heinemann, London.

Sharpley, S. and Stone, P. (2010) *Tourist Experience: Contemporary Perspectives*. Routledge, London.

Simmel, G. (1908) Exkurs uber den Fremden [Excursus on the Stranger]. In: Rammstedt, O. (ed.) *Soziologie [Sociology], Gesamtausgabe* (complete edn). Suhrkamp, Frankfurt, pp. 764–771.

Smith, S. (1990) A test of Plog's allocentric/psychocentric model: evidence from seven nations. *Journal of Travel Research* 28(4), 40–43.

Snepenger, D. (1987) Segmenting the tourist market by novelty-seeking role. *Journal of Travel Research* 26(2), 8–14.

Snepenger, D., King, J., Marshall, E. and Uysal, M. (2006) Modeling Iso Ahola's motivation theory in the tourism context. *Journal of Travel Research* 45(2), 140–149.

Staycation (2012) Available at: http://www.staycation.org.uk (accessed 4 June 2013).

Stein, K. (2011) Getting away from it all: the construction and management of temporary identities on vacation. *Symbolic Interaction* 34(2), 290–308.

Uriely, N. (2009) Deconstructing tourist typologies: the case of backpacking. *International Journal of Culture, Tourism and Hospitality Research* 3(4), 306–312.

Uysal, M., Gahan, L. and Martin, B. (1993) An examination of event motivations: a case study. *Festival Management and Event Tourism* 1(1), 5–10.

Uysal, M., Li, X. and Sirakaya-Turk, E. (2008) Push–pull dynamics in travel decisions. In: Haemoon, O. (ed.) *Handbook of Hospitality Marketing Management*. Butterworth-Heinemann, Oxford, pp. 412–439.

Visit England (2012) Available at: http://www.enjoyengland.com (accessed 4 June 2013).

Wang, N. (1999) Rethinking authenticity in tourism experience. *Annals of Tourism Research* 26(2), 349–370.

Wang, N. (2000) *Tourism and Modernity: A Sociological Analysis*. Pergamon, Oxford.

Weber, M. (1968) *The Theory of Social and Economic Organization*, trans. A. Henderson and T. Parsons. Free Press, New York.

Wickens, E. (2002) The sacred and profane: a tourist typology. *Annals of Tourism Research* 29(3), 834–851.

Wood, R. (1980) International tourism and cultural change in Southeast Asia. *Economic Development and Cultural Change* 28(3), 561–581.

6 Revisiting Self-congruity Theory in Travel and Tourism

M. Joseph Sirgy

Virginia Polytechnic Institute and State University, Blacksburg, USA

Introduction

Over the last 30+ years, this author has done much research on self-congruity theory in consumer behaviour and marketing. For literature reviews, see Sirgy (1982, 1985a, 1985b, 1986), Claiborne and Sirgy (1990), Johar and Sirgy (1991), Sirgy *et al.* (1991, 2000) and more recently a meta-analysis by Rodriguez *et al.* (2012). In 2000, Sirgy and Su developed an integrated model of self-congruity in travel and tourism. The model was designed to capture the current state of the science in travel and tourism regarding self-congruity theory with specific theoretical propositions designed to spur future research. This chapter reviews the research to date related to the Sirgy and Su (2000) integrated model in the travel and tourism literature, and in doing so this author makes an attempt to refine the model and offer further guidance and suggestions for additional future research.

It is important to note from the onset that self-congruity is an important construct in value creation. This is due to the fact that much research has linked motivational constructs such as tourists' pre-travel behavioural phenomena (e.g. tourists' attitude toward the destination, preference to the destination and choice of the destination) and post-travel phenomena (e.g. tourists' satisfaction with the destination, their loyalty and commitment to the destination, and word-of-mouth related to the destination) are all directly related to tourists' perceived value (e.g. Holloway and Plant, 1988; Moliner *et al.*, 2007). Self-congruity plays an important role in all these behavioural constructs through perceived value. That is, increased self-congruity serves to increase the perception of value, which in turn plays a positive role in tourists' destination attitude, preference, choice, satisfaction, loyalty and word-of-mouth communication.

The Original Model

The Sirgy and Su (2000) self-congruity model of travel and tourism is shown in Fig. 6.1. The model posits that various aspects of the destination and its atmosphere are related to the destination visitor image. The destination visitor image is then evaluated in light of specific dimensions of the tourist's self-concept to determine the degree of self-congruity. Self-congruity motivates travel behaviour and the self-congruity is moderated by a number of situational and tourist characteristics (see Fig. 6.1). Selected constructs and relationships in the model are briefly described below. Also, new evidence related to the relationships identified in the model will be highlighted.

The model identified four aspects of the self-concept to explain and predict travel behaviour. These are the actual self-image, the ideal self-image, the social self-image and the ideal social self-image. The actual self-image is defined as how tourists see themselves. The ideal self-image is defined as how tourists would like to see themselves. The social self-image is defined as how tourists believe they are seen by significant others. The ideal social self-image is defined as how tourists would like to be seen by significant others.

Self-congruity in a tourism context involves a process of matching (some dimension of) a tourist's self-concept with the destination visitor image. The greater the match between self-concept and the destination visitor image, the greater the likelihood that tourists feel motivated to travel to that destination. Research in tourism has identified a significant relationship between tourists' satisfaction/

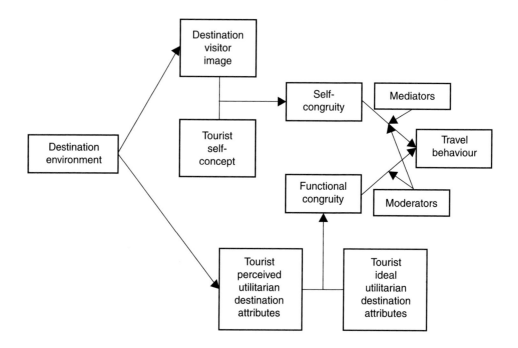

Fig. 6.1. An integrated model of self-congruity and functional congruity in explaining and practicing travel behaviour (based on Sirgy and Su, 2000).

dissatisfaction and tourists' self-image/destination-image congruity (Chon, 1990, 1992). Specifically, the greater the congruity between the tourists' self-image and the destination image, the greater the satisfaction. Thus, Sirgy and Su (2000) formally proposed that travel behaviour is positively influenced by self-congruity. That is, the greater the match between the destination visitor image and the tourist's self-concept (actual, ideal, social and/or ideal social self-image), the more likely that this tourist will be motivated to visit that destination. Recent evidence provides additional support to this proposition (e.g. Litvin and Goh, 2002; Kastenholz, 2004; Beerli *et al.*, 2007; Boksberger *et al.*, 2011; Hung and Petrick, 2011; Hosany, 2012).

The Sirgy and Su (2000) model articulated four self-concept motives (self-consistency, self-esteem, social consistency and social approval) corresponding to the four self-concept dimensions (actual, ideal, social and ideal social self-image) and the resulting self-congruities: actual-, ideal-, social-, and ideal social-self-congruity. Evidence of the predictiveness of actual self-congruity and the self-consistency motive on travel behaviour comes from studies that identify socio-demographic and psychographic factors related to destination choice show that ideal self-congruity is a strong predictor of destination choice (e.g. Pizam and Calantone, 1987; Sheldon and Mark, 1987; Witt and Martin, 1987; Klenosky *et al.*, 1993; Beerli *et al.*, 2007; Hung and Petrick, 2011). For example, several studies found that tourists choose destinations whose images match their personal values (Jackson, 1973; Ascher, 1985; Hsieh and O'Leary, 1994). Thus, Sirgy and Su (2000) proposed that actual self-congruity affects travel behaviour. That is, tourists who experience a match between the visitor image of a destination and their actual self-image will be motivated to visit that destination. Consider the study by Prentice *et al.* (1998) that revealed that a cultural destination plays an important role in maintaining the tourist's cultural identity or actual self. In this case, tourists are motivated to visit destination sites that reinforce their conceptions of who they are, culturally-speaking. The work of the need for self-consistency is evident here.

With respect to ideal self-congruity, tourists' ideal self motivates their travel behaviour through the need for self-esteem. In other words, tourists have ideal images of themselves, and realizing these images (through visiting destinations and resorts that are consistent with their ideal self-image) boosts their self-esteem (e.g. Amin, 1979; Ascher, 1985). Thus, Sirgy and Su (2000) proposed that ideal self-congruity affects travel behaviour. That is, tourists who experience a match between the visitor image of a destination and their ideal self-image will be motivated to visit that destination. Recent evidence provided by Beerli *et al.* (2007) shows that ideal self-congruity is a strong predictor of destination choice. Similarly, Ekinci *et al.* (2008) show that ideal self-congruity is a strong predictor of consumer satisfaction with hotels and restaurants. Their study was based on a large-scale adult sample in the UK. Hung and Petrick (2011) were able to demonstrate that ideal self-congruity is a significant predictor of tourists' cruising intentions.

Social self-congruity refers to the fit between how tourists believe they are seen by others in relation to the destination patron image. The social self-image influences behaviour through the social consistency motive in that tourists are motivated to maintain an image others have of them. They feel uncomfortable taking action inconsistent with how they believe others see them. Suggestive evidence of this phenomenon in tourism comes from studies linking tourists' reference group influence with destination choice (e.g. Robinson, 1979; Pearce, 1989; Mansfeld, 1992). Tourists conform to the norms of their reference groups. Thus, Sirgy and Su (2000) proposed that social self-congruity affects travel behaviour. That is, tourists who experience a match between the visitor image of a destination and their social self-image will be motivated to visit that destination. Recently, Hung and Petrick (2011) were able to demonstrate that social self-congruity is a significant predictor of tourists' cruising intentions, providing some support for the theoretical proposition.

Ideal social self-congruity refers to the fit between how tourists would like to be seen by others in relation to the destination visitor image. The ideal social self-image affects tourists' travel behaviour through the social approval motive. In other words, tourists are motivated to do things that would cause others to think highly of them. They believe that acting in ways that realize the ideal social self-image is likely to earn approval from others. Actions inconsistent with the ideal social self-image may lead to social disapproval. Several studies have found that going on a fashionable trip bestows honour and social recognition to the traveller (e.g. Crompton, 1979; Coleman, 1983; Graburn, 1983; Moeran, 1983; Matra, 1984; Reimer, 1991; Riley, 1995). Thus, Sirgy and Su (2000) proposed that ideal social self-congruity affects travel behaviour. That is, tourists who experience a match between the visitor image of a destination and their ideal social self-image will be motivated to visit that destination. Hung and Petrick's (2011) study provided evidence in support of the proposition. Ideal social self-congruity was found to be a significant predictor of tourists' cruising intentions.

Factors Affecting the Activation of Self-concept Dimensions

The Sirgy and Su (2000) model also identified factors that enhance the activation of particular dimensions of tourists' self concept that ultimately may influence travel behaviour. That is, under what conditions do private self constructs (actual- and ideal-self-congruity) predict destination patronage better than public self constructs (social- and ideal social-self-congruity)? Much of this discussion is covered in the Sirgy and Su (2000) article, and the propositions will not be reiterated here. It is enough to indicate that the model identified several factors: characteristics related to destination visibility (or destination conspicuousness), touring with others (or co-touring) and characteristics related to the individual tourist, such as age and response mode.

Ekinci et al. (2008) conducted a study testing the predictiveness of actual vs ideal self-congruity on consumer satisfaction with hotels and restaurants using a large-scale adult sample in the UK. The study findings showed that ideal self-congruity was a stronger predictor of consumer satisfaction than actual self-congruity. One may argue that consumer satisfaction judgements are essentially affective, and as such may be more influenced by the need for self-esteem (the underlying motive for the ideal self-congruity effect) than the need for self-consistency (the underlying motive for the actual self-congruity effect).

The Interrelationship between Self-congruity and Functional Congruity

As described throughout the preceding discussion, self-congruity is tourists' comparison between their destination visitor image and their own self-image. Functional congruity, on the other hand, is based on the perceived utilitarian aspects of the destination in reference to some ideal aspects. For example, a tourist may consider the proximity of the resort from his residence, the price range of alternative resort facilities, the quality of the services the resort carries, the variety of activities and/or the possible use of credit cards. These criteria used in decision-making are utilitarian or functional in nature, compared with symbolic criteria such as destination visitor image.

Both functional and self-congruity have been suggested to influence tourism motivation and destination travel (e.g. Dann, 1981; Blank, 1989; Chon and Olsen, 1991; Riley, 1995; Chiang *et al.*, 2012). The relative weights given to each may depend on a number of situational- and tourist-related characteristics. Sirgy and Su (2000) proposed that self-congruity influences functional congruity, and the predictive effects of self-congruity vs functional congruity are moderated by tourists' knowledge, prior experience, involvement with site selection and time pressure. The reader should refer back to the Sirgy and Su (2000) article for a complete explanation of these moderator effects.

With respect to the moderating effect of knowledge/prior experience, recent evidence of this proposition during the last decade or so includes a study conducted on a sample of experienced international travellers from the USA who evaluated the functional attributes of Turkey as a tourist destination (Sonmez and Sirakaya, 2002). Those who rated Turkey highly on attributes (e.g. safety, the hospitality environment, the general mood and vacation atmosphere, travel experience, relaxing effect, local attractions, authenticity of experience, social and personal communication channels, comfort, and tourist facilitation facilities) expressed higher intentions to travel to Turkey. Furthermore, a study conducted by Beerli *et al.* (2007) has provided evidence suggesting that the predictive effect of both actual and ideal self-congruity on destination choice diminishes significantly for tourists who have previously visited the considered destination.

Concerning the moderating effects of involvement, a recent study by Beerli *et al.* (2007) made an attempt to test this proposition by focusing on the strength of destination choice prediction of self-congruity (actual and ideal congruity) for different countries when tourists had varying degrees of involvement (Kenya, Paris and the Dominican Republic). The results showed exactly the opposite pattern. That is, self-congruity was more predictive of destination choice when tourists were more involved than less involved.

Here is an attempt to explain this anomaly. We should distinguish between two types of involvement, involvement in travel decision-making (i.e. selecting the destination site) vs involvement with the destination site. Involvement with the destination site typically occurs post-travel, whereas involvement in travel decision-making is essentially a pre-travel phenomenon. These two psychological constructs are expected to play very different roles in moderating the self-congruity effect on travel behaviour. When a tourist is not involved in travel decision-making (e.g. a wife who does not really care where she goes as long as she travels to some exotic destination with her husband), her motivation to visit a specific destination is likely to be more affected by self-congruity than functional congruity. In other words, she is not likely to spend much time and effort evaluating the various functional attributes of the possible destination sites that perhaps her husband may propose. She sees herself as a classy middle-aged married woman. She sees a brochure about a destination site that shows other tourists who are classy, middle-aged married women providing a testimonial about that site. She experiences high self-congruity with the person providing the testimonial making her feel that this particular destination site is attractive. Previously we proposed that the effect of self-congruity on site selection is likely to be stronger for tourists who are not involved with site selection than for those who are very involved. However, this proposition is not likely to be true in a post-travel context. After the site visit, tourists are likely to feel more strongly about the destination visitor image having experienced the destination first hand. As such, they are likely to experience matches and mismatches between the destination image and their various dimensions of their self-concept (actual self, ideal self, social self, etc.). Those who experience high levels of self-congruity are likely to experience greater involvement, attractiveness, commitment and attachment to the site than those who experience low levels of self-congruity (Hou *et al.*, 2005; Prayag and Ryan, 2012). In other words, the self-congruity experience post-travel is said to induce a high level of site involvement, commitment and attachment. Formally stated, self-congruity with the destination following the actual visit is likely to heighten tourists' involvement with the destination, which in turn may contribute to other post-travel behavioural constructs such as consumer satisfaction and well-being, destination loyalty/commitment/attachment and positive word-of-mouth.

With respect to the self-congruity bias, research in travel and tourism has provided evidence suggesting that functional congruity explains consumer satisfaction better than self-congruity in a tourism context (Chon and Olsen, 1991). However, the evidence also suggests that self-congruity is correlated with functional congruity. Tourists who experience high self-congruity tend to favourably process the utilitarian attributes, and vice versa. Tourists who perceive a destination to match their actual, ideal, social and/or ideal social self-image may form an initial favourable attitude toward the destination. This is essentially what is commonly known as 'first impression'. First impressions bias further information processing. If the first impression is positive, then it is likely that further information processing may be biased in the positive direction. The converse is also true. As such, Sirgy and Su (2000) proposed that self-congruity biases functional congruity. That is, tourists who experience a match between the destination visitor image and their self-concept are likely to process the utilitarian attributes in a favourable light, thus increasing the likelihood of forming an overall favourable attitude toward the destination. Those who experience a mismatch are likely to process the utilitarian attributes in an unfavourable light, thus increasing the likelihood of forming an unfavourable attitude. Hung and Petrick (2011) conducted a study that tested the self-congruity bias directly in relation to cruising intentions. The study showed that self-congruity successfully predicted functional congruity (0.156 for actual self-congruity, 0.284 for ideal self-congruity, 0.143 for social self-congruity and 0.250 for ideal self-congruity). That self-congruity predicted cruising intentions (range between 0.448 and 0.215). Also, functional congruity predicted cruising intentions (range between 0.254 and 0.158).

Broadening the Scope of the Travel Behaviour Construct

Much of the theorizing in the original Sirgy and Su (2000) model involved pre-travel decision-making as in site selection. Evidence has accumulated in the tourism literature indicating that the self-congruity effect extends to a variety of pre-travel and post-travel behavioural constructs (e.g. destination attractiveness, destination preference decisions, destination site selection, actual visits, tourists' expression of positive emotions following the visit, tourists' satisfaction with the destination following the visit, feelings of loyalty and commitment to a destination, intention to revisit the destination, attachment to the destination, positive word-of-mouth, tourist sense of well-being). For example, Litvin and Kar (2003) found that self-congruity is a significant predictor of destination satisfaction (cf. Chon, 1992; Murphy *et al.*, 2007b). Similarly, Wilkins *et al.* (2006) were able to document a similar effect in relation to customer satisfaction in hotels. Beerli *et al.* (2007) found the greater the match between a destination's image and one's self-concept, the greater the tendency for tourists to actually visit that destination. Ekinci *et al.* (2008) showed that ideal self-congruity is a strong predictor of consumer satisfaction with hotels and restaurants. Hosany (2012) employed 'internal self-compatibility' (a construct highly akin to various forms of self-congruity and defined as the tourist's perception of the degree to which the experience is consistent with one's self-concept) in a study to predict tourist emotional responses. The study results indicate that when tourists perceive the destination experience as compatible with their internal self, they experience positive emotions such as joy, love and positive surprise. Formally stated, travel behaviour is positively influenced by self-congruity. That is, the greater the match between the destination visitor image and the tourist's self-concept (actual, ideal, social and/or ideal social self-image), the more likely that this tourist will feel attracted toward the destination, feel motivated to visit that destination, prefer that destination over others, actually visit the destination, feel satisfied with the destination during and after the visit, feel a sense of loyalty and commitment to the destination, experience positive feelings toward the destination and gain a greater sense of well-being, as well as harbour positive feelings of attachment. The converse may be true too. That is, the more tourists feel attracted toward the destination (and feel motivated to visit that destination, prefer that destination over others, actually visit the destination, feel satisfied with the destination during and after the visit, feel a sense of loyalty and commitment to the destination, experience positive feelings toward the destination and gain a greater sense of well-being, as well as harbour positive feelings of attachment), the more likely they will experience self-congruity with the destination visitor image.

Distinguishing Between Destination Visitor Image and Destination Personality

In contrast to the destination visitor image, new research has identified the concept of destination personality (e.g. Ekinci, 2003; Ekinci and Hosany, 2006; Murphy *et al.*, 2007a, 2007b). Ekinici (2003) proposed that destination brands should establish a brand personality and make links to the tourist's self-image through their travel motives. Destination personality is based on the concept of brand personality propagated by Aaker and Fournier (1995; Aaker, 1997). The idea is that consumers perceive brands as having personalities in terms of sincerity, excitement, competence, sophistication and ruggedness. The concept of destination personality has been applied successfully in tourism to predict travel behaviour in various countries such as Spain (Gilmore, 2002), Wales (Pride, 2002), Turkey (Ekinci *et al.*, 2007), Australia (Murphy *et al.*, 2007a, 2007b) and Singapore (Henderson, 2000). Of course, some of the brand personality dimensions seem to be more predictive of travel behaviour than others and may be moderated by a host of destination and tourists' characteristics (cf. Ekinci and Hosnay, 2006).

As such, a new proposition concerning the relationship between destination personality and pre/post-travel behaviour is introduced here. The first proposition deals with the reciprocal influence between destination personality and pre-/post-travel behaviour. Destination personality attributes, such as sincerity, excitement, competence, sophistication and ruggedness, are personal characteristics that are highly valued by most cultures. Therefore, they have positive connotations, and therefore carry positive valence. When tourists perceive a certain destination in terms of positive personality attributes, they are likely to express a favourable attitude toward that destination (i.e. destination attractiveness). This may occur in the context of pre- or post-travel, or both. Also, reciprocal causation may be inferred. Tourists who have already formed a positive attitude toward a given destination (i.e. destination attractiveness) are likely to infer positive personality attributes associated with that destination, and vice versa. This may be due to cognitive consistency. There is a plethora of research in social-personality psychology that has documented the effects of cognitive consistency in social behaviour (e.g. Abelson *et al.*, 1968). Formally stated, destination personality is likely to influence the formation of destination attractiveness. Conversely, destination attractiveness, once determined by sources other than destination personality, is likely to prompt tourists to infer consistent personality attributes (i.e. high destination attractiveness is likely to prompt tourists to infer a destination personality involving positive personal characteristics, whereas low destination attractiveness should prompt the formation of a destination image involving negative personal characteristics).

Furthermore, there should be a relationship between destination personality and destination visitor image, as well as perceived destination environment. More specifically, many of the same cues related to the destination environment that are used to infer the destination visitor image can equally prompt the formation of destination personality, and the destination visitor personality once formed can prompt the formation of destination personality. The converse could also be equally applicable in the sense that destination personality, once formed, can prompt the formation of the destination visitor image. Again, this may be due to cognitive consistency (e.g. Abelson *et al.*, 1968). Formally stated, destination personality is positively associated with destination user image, and the same destination environmental cues that influence the formation of destination visitor image are likely to influence the formation of destination personality.

If we accept the notion that destination visitor image is positively associated with destination personality, then it is reasonable to infer that tourists are likely to experience self-congruity with destination personality as well as personality visitor image. And if so, self-congruity with destination personality should be a strong predictor of pre- and post-travel behaviour. This notion of self-congruity with destination personality (rather than with destination visitor image) was supported empirically by research conducted by Ekinci and Riley (2003), Murphy *et al.* (2007a, 2007b) and Boksberger *et al.* (2011). Formally stated, self-congruity with destination personality is likely to influence pre-travel and post-travel behaviour in that high self-congruity should predict high levels of pre- and post-travel constructs.

Additional Moderators Distinguishing the Differential Effects of the Various Forms of Self-congruity

Under what conditions does actual self-congruity predict travel behaviour more strongly than, let's say, ideal self-congruity, or social or ideal-social self-congruity? The original Sirgy and Su (2000) model identified the following moderators: (i) destination conspicuousness; (ii) co-touring; (iii) age; and (iv) response mode. Recent evidence points to individualism vs collectivism as a possible additional moderator. Specifically, Litvin and Kar (2003) hypothesized that the self-congruity effect, at large (without making any distinctions among its varied dimensions), is a phenomenon that may be more evident among tourists from individualistic rather than collectivistic countries. People in individualistic countries tend to focus on one's self-interest and possibly their immediate family. Conversely, people in collectivistic countries have tightly knit social networks (i.e. relatives, clan and other in-groups) in which members of the network are expected to look after each other and in which group loyalty is viewed as essential to social harmony (see Hofsteade, 2001). The authors collected data from tourists in an airport in Singapore and found that destination satisfaction was significantly correlated with self-congruity (range between 0.358 and 0.314). Higher correlations were found among tourists from individualistic countries (0.347–0.416) compared with tourists from collectivistic countries (0.286–0.313). Furthermore, this difference between the two groups seemed more evident in relation to ideal self-congruity (0.416 for tourists from individualistic countries compared with 0.313 for tourists from collectivistic countries) than actual self-congruity (0.347 for tourists from individualistic countries compared with 0.286 for tourists from collectivistic countries). This makes sense, theoretically speaking. One can argue that self-congruity focuses on the individual, not the collective. Therefore, tourists from individualistic countries are more likely to experience self-congruity more readily than tourists from collectivistic countries, and the effect of self-congruity on travel behaviour is likely to be more evident. It is also reasonable to expect that the moderating effect of individualism vs collectivism would be more pronounced in relation to ideal-self-congruity than actual self-congruity. Tourists from individualistic countries are likely to place much emphasis on how destination travels could realize their ideal self. In contrast, tourists from collectivistic societies are less likely to express the ideal selves because doing so is not socially condoned – the emphasis on the family, the community, the employer and the country at large. Formally stated, destination satisfaction among tourists from individualistic countries is likely to be influenced more by ideal self-congruity than tourists from collectivistic countries. This pattern is not as evident in relation to actual self-congruity.

Distinguishing Between Self-congruity and Identity Salience

Identity salience is a concept originating from identity theory (Stryker, 1968; McCall and Simmons, 1978; Turner, 1978; Burke, 1980; Callero, 1985; Reed et al., 2012). Tourists tend to define themselves in terms of certain places. For example, local residents of a tourism community are likely to identify themselves with their community much more so than tourists visiting from the outside. These local residents are likely to engage in positive word-of-mouth communication about the destination site because their identity is directly related to the destination site. In other words, identity salience is place identity, the extent to which the place is an important part of the self-concept (Simpson and Siguaw, 2008). Recent research has shown that place identity is highly correlated with place involvement (e.g. Kyle and Mowen, 2005), place attachment (e.g. Hou et al., 2005) and positive word-of-mouth communications (e.g. Simpson and Siguaw, 2008). Example measurement items of identity salience related to place include '[Name of Place] is an important part of who I am'; '[Name of Place] means more to me than just a place or tourist destination' (cf. Callero, 1985; Stachow and Hart, 2010).

The concept of identity salience has much affinity with self-congruity, especially actual self-congruity. Actual self-congruity focuses on the match between the destination visitor image (or destination personality) and the actual self-image of the tourist, whereas identity salience focuses on the extent to which the destination is perceived by the tourist as important to their identity (how they actually see themselves). As such, identity salience is likely to be associated with self-congruity and travel behavioural phenomena such as place satisfaction, place attachment, place loyalty and positive word-of-mouth.

Identity salience may also be a significant moderator between self-congruity and travel behavioural phenomena (travel motivation to destination, destination satisfaction, destination loyalty, destination attachment and positive word-of-mouth communication). Specifically, when a tourist experiences congruity between a particular destination visitor image (or personality image), the tourist is likely to respond to the destination with heightened emotional intensity, given that the person experiences high identity salience with that particular image. For example, suppose that a tourist may experience high self-congruity with a place like Acapulco (Mexico) by thinking that Acapulco is a party place and that he is a 'party animal'. Although he may perceive himself as a party animal, how salient is this identity to him *vis-à-vis* other possible identities that he has (e.g. 'I am a responsible person', 'My family is very important to me', 'I am the adventurous type'). Some of these identities are more or less important to him, and some may conflict with the identity of 'I am a party animal', while others may be highly consistent with the identity in question. Thus, self-congruity is likely to play a stronger role predicting pre- and post-travel behavioural constructs given that the self-congruity experienced with a destination site is also accompanied with high identity salience.

Distinguishing Between Self-congruity and Destination Identification

Uner and Armutulu (2012) argued that self-congruity leads to destination identification through tourist satisfaction and perceived quality of life (i.e. life satisfaction). Destination identification is akin to brand identification in the sense that tourists perceived that the destination (or place) is part of their social identity. Thus, one can make a distinction between two interrelated concepts: self-congruity and destination identification. Based on the literature in travel and tourism, self-congruity can take two forms: (i) match between the tourist's self-concept (actual, ideal, social and ideal social self) and the stereotypical image of the type of person who is likely to visit the destination and (ii) match between the tourist's self-concept and destination personality. These two definitions of self-congruity are different from destination identification, which can be defined as the match between the tourist's self-concept and the type of people who are residents of the destination site. Destination identification is likely to strongly influence destination attachment, but not self-congruity *per se*. For example, a Palestinian American travelling to the Holy Land may feel an attachment to the Holy Land because he identifies with the people who live there. However, an American who is Christian travelling to the Holy Land with other devout Christians may experience self-congruity, which may influence his level of motivation and satisfaction visiting the Holy Land, but not contribute to a sense of 'place attachment'.

Based on this discussion, another theoretical proposition can be formalized. Self-congruity with destination personality (or visitor image) is likely to influence motivation to travel to the destination (and satisfaction having travelled to the destination), but not destination attachment. Conversely, destination identification is likely to influence pre-travel and post-travel behaviour as well as attachment to the destination.

Does Self-congruity Influence Travel Behaviour? Or Does Travel Behaviour Influence Self-congruity?

Recent evidence also points to the possibility of reverse causation. That is, actual travel behaviour tends to produce a self-congruity experience. Consider the study conducted by Yarnal and Kerstetter (2005) that focused on tourists' experience on a cruise ship. The study underscored the notion that tourists tend to gravitate and interact with other tourists who are similar to them and like-minded. Doing so is likely to occur in tourist-type facilities such as a cruise ship in which tourists are confined together in space and time. In time, they develop a self-congruity experience, which further reinforces their attitude toward the tourist event, their intention for a repeat experience and positive word-of-mouth. Formally stated: not only does self-congruity influence travel behaviour but also travel behaviour influences self-congruity.

Self-congruity Effects Over Time

Research by Lee (2001) indicates that children travelling with family members become attached to a destination and they tend to return to it as adults. It could be that as children visit a destination site, they incorporate the destination image into their social self-concept (their social and ideal social self) (Belk, 1988). In other words, the destination becomes part of the social and ideal social self-concept. In time, the social and ideal social self (the public self) influence the development of the actual and ideal self (the private self). In adulthood, these tourists are likely to experience higher levels of self-congruity (all forms) with the same destination when considering a set of destination sites in travel decision-making. Hence, the model can be expanded by offering this new theoretical proposition: Adult tourists who have developed a place attachment to a destination site because they visited that site in childhood are likely to experience higher levels of self-congruity with the same destination site in the context of site selection decision-making, which, in turn, would influence site selection.

The Differential Effects of Self-congruity vs Functional Congruity in Relation to Pre-travel vs Post-travel Behavioural Constructs

Does self-congruity play a stronger role in post-travel behaviour than functional congruity? One can argue that this may be the case. In post-travel, self-congruity is likely to trump functional congruity in influencing place involvement, attractiveness, commitment and attachment. This may be so because self-congruity involves hot cognitions, whereas functional congruity involves cold cognitions. In personality-social psychology there is a long history documenting the effects of cognitive appraisals on emotions (e.g. Lazarus, 1991). However, subsequent evidence was provided documenting the effects of emotions on cognitive appraisals (e.g. Smith *et al.*, 1993). The phenomenon of emotions influencing cognitive appraisals has come to be known as 'hot cognitions'. Specifically, hot cognitions are cognitive appraisals directly related to personal well-being. Moreover, they are self-related cognitions (e.g. 'What does this have to do with me?' 'Is it good or bad for me?'). Hot cognitions take precedence over cold cognitions (non-self beliefs and inferences) in decision-making (e.g. Janis, 1977; Hogarth and Reder, 1987; Kahneman *et al.*, 1987; Frank, 1988; Dietz and Stern, 1995). As such, self-congruity is considered to be a hot cognition, whereas functional congruity is a cold one; and therefore the self-congruity effect on place involvement, attractiveness, commitment and attachment is likely to trump the functional congruity effect. Thus, the following is proposed: tourists are likely to experience greater involvement, attractiveness, commitment and attachment with the destination site given high levels of self-congruity and functional congruity with the destination image. Furthermore, self-congruity is likely to play a stronger role in influencing place involvement, commitment and attachment than functional congruity.

Conclusion

This chapter was designed to review the research literature on self-congruity in travel and tourism and refine the theoretical model that Sirgy and Su proposed in 2000. The goal is to revisit the theoretical propositions in light of the recent evidence and to propose new theoretical propositions to further guide this programme of research. The goal may have been accomplished. Researchers in travel and tourism may find the theoretical propositions helpful in further building this programme of research in travel and tourism.

References

Aaker, J. (1997) Dimensions of brand personality. *Journal of Marketing Research* 34, 347–356.

Aaker, J. and Fournier, S. (1995) A brand as a character, a partner and a person: three perspectives on the question of brand personality. *Advances in Consumer Research* 22, 391–395.

Abelson, R.P. (1968) *Theories of Cognitive Consistency: A Sourcebook*. Rand McNally, Chicago, Illinois.

Amin, S. (1979) *Classe et Nation*. Editions de Minuit, Paris.

Ascher, F. (1985) *Tourism: Transnational Corporations and Cultural Identities*. CAB International, Wallingford, UK.

Beerli, A., Meneses, G.D. and Gil, S.M. (2007) Self-congruity and destination choice. *Annals of Tourism Research* 34, 571–587.

Belk, R.W. (1988) Possessions and the extended self. *Journal of Consumer Research* 15, 139–168.

Blank, U. (1989) *The Community Tourism Industry Imperative: the Necessity, the Opportunities, its Potential*. Venture, State College, Pennsylvania.

Boksberger, P., Dolnicar, S., Laesser, C. and Randle, M. (2011) Self-congruity theory: to what extent does it hold in tourism? *Journal of Travel Research* 50, 454–464.

Burke, P.J. (1980) The self: measurement requirements from an interactionist perspective. *Social Psychology Quarterly* 43, 18–29.

Callero, P.L. (1985) Role-identity salience. *Social Psychology Quarterly* 48, 203–215.

Chiang, C.C., Chen, Y.C., Huang, L.F. and Hsueh, K.F. (2012) Destination image and marketing strategy: an investigation of MICE travelers to Taiwan. *Journal of American Academy of Business* 18, 224–231.

Chon, K. (1990) The role of destination image in tourism: a review and discussion. *Tourist Review* 45, 2–9.

Chon, K. (1992) Self-image/destination-image congruity. *Annals of Tourism Research* 19, 360–363.

Chon, K. and Olsen, M.D. (1991) Functional and symbolic congruity approaches to consumer satisfaction/dissatisfaction in tourism. *Journal of the International Academy of Hospitality Research* 3, 2–22.

Claiborne, C.B. and Sirgy, M.J. (1990) Self-congruity as a model of attitude formation and change: conceptual review and guide for future research. In: B.J. Dunlap (ed.) *Developments in Marketing Science*. Academy of Marketing Science, Cullowhee, North Carolina, 1–7.

Coleman, R. (1983) The continuing significance of social class to marketing. *Journal of Consumer Research* 10, 265–280.

Crompton, J. (1979) Motivations for pleasure vacation. *Annals of Tourism Research* 6, 404–424.

Dann, G. (1981) Tourism motivation: an appraisal. *Annals of Tourism Research* 9, 87–219.

Dietz, T. and Stern, P.C. (1995) Toward a theory of choice: socially embedded preference construction. *Journal of Socio-Economics* 24, 261–279.

Ekinci, Y. (2003) From destination image to destination branding: an emerging area of research. *e-Review of Tourism Research* 1(2), 21–24.

Ekinci, Y. and Hosany, S. (2006) Destination personality: an application of brand personality to tourism destinations. *Journal of Travel Research* 45, 127–139.

Ekinici, Y. and Riley, M. (2003) An investigation of self-concept: actual and ideal self-congruence in the context of service evaluation. *Journal of Retailing and Consumer Services* 10, 201–214.

Ekinci, Y., Sirakaya-Turk, E. and Baloglu, E. (2007) Host image and destination personality. *Tourism Analysis* 12, 433–446.

Ekinci, Y., Dawes, P.L. and Massey, G.R. (2008) An extended model of the antecedents and consequences of consumer satisfaction for hospitality services. *European Journal of Marketing* 42, 35–68.

Frank, R.H. (1988) *Within Reason: The Strategic Role of Emotions.* Norton, New York.

Gilmore, F. (2002) A country: can it be repositioned? Spain: the success story of country branding. *Journal of Brand Management* 9, 218–284.

Graburn, N. (1983) The anthropology of tourism. *Annals of Tourism Research* 10, 9–13.

Henderson, J. (2000) Selling places: the new Asia-Singapore brand. *Journal of Tourism Studies* 11, 36–44.

Hofsteade, G. (2001) *Cultural Consequences.* Sage, Thousand Oaks, California.

Hogarth, R.M. and Reder, M.W. (1987) *Rational Choice: The Contrast between Economics and Psychology.* University of Chicago Press, Chicago, Illinois.

Holloway, J.C. and Plant, R.V. (1988) *Marketing for Tourism.* Pitman, Southport, UK.

Hosany, S. (2012) Appraisal determinants of tourist emotional responses. *Journal of Travel Research* 51, 303–314.

Hou, J.S., Lin, C.H. and Morias, D.B. (2005) Antecedents of attachment to a cultural tourism destination: the case of Hakka and Non-Hakka Taiwanese Visitors to Pie-Pu, Taiwan. *Journal of Travel Research* 44, 221–231.

Hsieh, S. and O'Leary, J.T. (1994) A travel decision model for Japanese pleasure travel. In: Hsieh, S. and O'Leary, J.T. (eds) *Tourism: The Economy's Silver Lining.* Travel and Tourism Research Association, Wheat Ridge, Colorado, pp. 94–104.

Hung, K. and Petrick, J.F. (2011) The role of self- and functional-congruity in cruising intentions. *Journal of Travel Research* 50, 100–112.

Jackson, G. (1973) A preliminary bicultural study of value orientations and leisure attitudes. *Journal of Leisure Research* 5, 10–20.

Janis, L.M. (1977) *Decision Making: A Psychological Analysis of Conflict, Choice and Commitment.* Free Press, New York.

Johar, J.S. and Sirgy, M.J. (1991) Value expressive versus utilitarian appeals: when and why to use which appeal. *Journal of Advertising* 20, 23–34.

Kahneman, D., Slovic, P. and Tversky, A. (1982) *Judgment Under Uncertainty: Heuristics and Biases.* Cambridge University Press, Cambridge.

Kastenholz, E. (2004) Assessment and role of destination-self-congruity. *Annals of Tourism Research* 31, 719–723.

Klenosky, D.B., Charles, E.G. and Michael, M. (1993) Understanding the factors influencing ski destination choice: a means–end analytic approach. *Journal of Leisure Research* 24, 362–379.

Kyle, G. and Mowen, A.J. (2005) An examination of the leisure involvement-agency commitment relationship. *Journal of Leisure Research* 37, 342–363.

Lazarus, R.S. (1991) *Emotion and Adaptation.* Oxford University Press, New York.

Lee, C.C. (2001) Predicting tourist attachment to destinations. *Annals of Tourism Research* 28, 229–232.

Litvin, S.W. and Goh, H. (2002) Self-image congruity: a valid tourism theory? *Tourism Management* 23, 81–83.

Litvin, S.W. and Kar, G.H. (2003) Individualism/collectivism as a moderating factor to the self-image congruity concept. *Journal of Vacation Marketing* 10, 23–32.

Mansfeld, Y. (1992) *Tourism: Toward a Behavioural Approach.* Pergamon Press, Oxford.

Matra, J. (1984) *Social Inequality, Stratification, and Mobility.* Prentice Hall, Englewood Cliffs, New Jersey.

McCall, G. and Simmons, J. (1978) *Identities and Interactions,* revised edition. Free Press, New York.

Moeran, B. (1983) The language of Japanese tourism. *Annals of Tourism Research* 10, 93–108.

Moliner, M.A., Sánchez, J., Rodríguez, R.M. and Callarisa, L. (2007) Perceived relationship quality and post-purchase perceived value: an integrative framework. *European Journal of Marketing* 41, 1392–1422.

Murphy, L., Benckendorff, P. and Moscardo, G. (2007a) Destination brand personality: visitor perceptions of a regional tourism destination. *Tourism Analysis* 12, 419–432.

Murphy, L., Benckendorff, P. and Moscardo, G. (2007b) Linking travel motivation, tourist self-image and destination brand personality. *Journal of Travel and Tourism Marketing* 22, 45–59.

Pearce, G.D. (1989) *Tourist Development.* Longman, Harlow, UK.

Pizam, A. and Calantone, R. (1987) Beyond psychographics: values as determinants of tourist behavior. *International Journal of Hospitality Management* 6, 177–181.

Prayag, G. and Ryan, C. (2012) Antecedents of tourists' loyalty to Mauritius: the role and influence of destination image, place attachment, personal involvement, and satisfaction. *Journal of Travel Research* 51, 342–356.

Prentice, R.C., Guerin, S. and McGugan, S. (1998) Visitor learning at a heritage attraction: a case study of discovery as a media product. *Tourism Management* 19, 5–23.

Pride, R. (2002) Brand Wales: 'natural revival'. In: Morgan, N., Pritchard, A. and Pride, R. (eds) *Destination Branding: Creating the Unique Destination Proposition.* Butterworth-Heinemann, Oxford, pp. 109–123.

Reed II, A., Forehand, M.R., Puntoni, S. and Warlop, L. (2012) Identity-based consumer behavior. *International Journal of Research in Marketing* 29, 310–321.

Reimer, G. (1991) Packaging dreams: Canadian tour operators at work. *Annals of Tourism Research* 18, 501–512.

Riley, R.W. (1995) Prestige worthy tourist behavior. *Annals of Tourism Research* 22, 630–649.

Robinson, H. (1979) *A Geography of Tourism.* Macdonald and Evans, Plymouth, UK.

Rodriguez, A., Bosnjak, M. and Sirgy, M.J. (2012) Moderators of the self-congruity effect on consumer decision-making: a meta-analysis. *Journal of Business Research* 65, 1179–1188.

Sheldon, P.J. and Mark, J. (1987) The demand for package tours: a mode choice model. *Journal of Travel Research* 24, 16–23.

Simpson, P.M. and Siguaw, J.A. (2008) The role of traveler type, residents, and identity salience. *Journal of Travel Research* 47, 167–182.

Sirgy, M.J. (1982) Self-concept in consumer behavior: a critical review. *Journal of Consumer Research* 9, 287–300.

Sirgy, M.J. (1985a) Self-image/product-image congruity and consumer decision making. *International Journal of Management* 2, 49–63.

Sirgy, M.J. (1985b) Using self-congruity and ideal congruity to predict purchase motivation. *Journal of Business Research* 13, 195–206.

Sirgy, M.J. (1986) *Self-Congruity: Toward a Theory of Personality and Cybernetics.* Praeger, New York.

Sirgy, M.J. and Su, C. (2000) Destination image, self-congruity, and travel behavior: toward an integrative model. *Journal of Travel Research* 38, 340–352.

Sirgy, M.J., Johar, J.S., Samli, A.C. and Claiborne, C.B. (1991) Self-congruity versus functional congruity: predictors of consumer behavior. *Journal of the Academy of Marketing Science* 19, 363–375.

Sirgy, M.J., Grewal, D. and Mangelburg, T. (2000) Retail environment, self-congruity, and retail patronage: an integrative model and a research agenda. *Journal of Business Research* 49, 127–138.

Smith, C.A., Haynes, K.H., Lazarus, R.S. and Pope, L.K. (1993) In search of the 'hot' cognitions: attributions, appraisals, and their relation to emotion. *Journal of Personality and Social Psychology* 65, 916–929.

Sonmez, S. and Sirakaya, E. (2002) A distorted destination image? The case of Turkey. *Journal of Travel Research* 41, 185–196.

Stachow, G. and Hart, C. (2010) Exploring place image: formation and measurement. *Place Branding and Public Diplomacy* 6, 145–155.

Stryker, S. (1968) Identity salience and role performance: the relevance of symbolic interaction theory for family research. *Journal of Marriage and Family* 30, 558–564.

Turner, R.H. (1978) The role and the person. *American Journal of Sociology* 84, 1–23.

Uner, M.M. and Armutulu, C. (2012) Understanding the antecedents of destination identification: linkage between perceived quality-of-life, self-congruity, and destination identification. In: Uysal, M., Perdue, R. and Sirgy, M.J. (eds) *Handbook of Tourism and Quality-of-Life Research*. Springer, New York, pp. 251–261.

Wilkins, H., Merrilees, B. and Herington, C. (2006) How self-image congruence impacts customer satisfaction in hotels. *Tourism Analysis* 11, 311–318.

Witt, S.F. and Martin, C.A. (1987) Econometric models for forecasting international tourism demand. *Journal of Travel Research* 25, 23–30.

Yarnal, C.M. and Kerstetter, D. (2005) Casting off: an exploration of cruise ship space, group tour behavior, and social interaction. *Journal of Travel Research* 43, 368–379.

7 Moving People: A Conceptual Framework for Understanding How Visitor Experiences can be Enhanced by Mindful Attention to Interest

Tove I. Dahl

UiT The Arctic University of Norway

Introduction

You know that feeling you get when you have looked forward to something for a long time and you finally get to experience it? Like finally seeing the rich display of coloured fabrics at a Bangkok textile market, catching a whiff of the chilled, sulphur-laced Iceland air or feeling the ache in your legs as you hike up the Inca Trail to Machu Picchu? Those are the kinds of experiences you expect, hope for and are grateful for. When you experience them, you feel fulfilled and deeply satisfied. That's what happens when we let our personal interests guide our travel.

You know that feeling, though, when you experience something during your travels that you didn't expect – something that might not have even crossed your mind as a potential experience along the way? When we were preparing this book, the authors gathered at a sea resort at Sommarøy, Norway for a writing seminar. While there, our host had arranged for us to take the small Skåskjær ferry to a nearby lighthouse. The ferry captain surprised us, though, taking us in the opposite of the originally planned direction. An uncanny number of herring had made their way into the fjords around us, along with scores of humpback and orca whales hot on the herrings' heels. The gathering of marine life was unlike anything seen before in this area's recent history. Thousands of gulls filled the sky around us, and the herring dimpled the water with their jumps. The whales spouted, breached and thrilled us with their playful displays. These creatures filled the fjord, and we were in the middle of it all. The captain and his first mate couldn't stop talking about it with wonder, telling us about what they knew about these animals, their travel patterns, how they eat. After the seminar ended, we all returned to our respective corners of the world, one experience richer and, for at least some of us, that experience has had a long life since that fateful hour in November.

Contrary to the first experiences, the second experience was unexpected and led to, among many other things, content for this chapter. That's the kind of thing that can happen when we get sufficiently interested in things we don't expect.

And that's the power of interest – moving people psychologically. That's also the power of stealth tourism – creating experiences that not only fuel visitors' existing personal interests, but that can arouse and help them sustain new interests that are so robust that visitors want to continue pursuing them even when they return home. That matters to people, and hosts can influence that.

In this chapter, a tourist is referred to as a visitor travelling in an arena of interest-generating or interest–sustaining opportunities that can be scaffolded by experiences with or through others in that place. Value for the visitor is defined in terms of interest enhancement – a state that focuses attention and fuels our desire to explore and discover new things in ways that we ultimately enjoy in the end. Accordingly, value creation is about the facilitation of these interest outcomes through the meeting of a host's (i.e. experience provider's) management of experiences imbued with opportunities for learning, positive affect and meaningfulness through visitor participation. Hosts and visitors play different roles at different times in this process. Hosts are especially important for facilitating things that visitors know less about but that have value for a region and potentially for visitors as well. Visitors are especially important for enhancing their participation in experiences that touch on topics in which they have strong personal interests from before.

With this as a basis, research should be designed to help us (i) create measures of positive value creation that capture increases in the amount, intensity and/or correlation of the component parts of a visitor's interest-provoking experience and (ii) determine which learning principles and activities, used when, facilitate that movement best.

Interest enhancement is not a given in any situation, though; during an experience, any involved party (hosts or visitors) may experience either an increase, a decrease or no change in their experience-relevant interest. The key to assuring positive change is to understand what interest is, its value, the mechanisms behind its development and how hosts may manage these mechanisms effectively.

Interest

Interest is a fascination we feel towards something else (Krapp, 2002; Hidi and Renninger, 2006; Krapp and Prenzel, 2011). It is a general feeling that is comprised of both physiological and psychological parts (Krapp, 2007; Krapp and Prenzel, 2011; Renninger and Hidi, 2011). Interest serves us well by helping us focus our attention (Silvia, 2006) and involving us cognitively and affectively (Krapp, 2007). Interest can be fleeting; what's here today may well be gone tomorrow. Likewise, we tend to develop relatively few stable interests in life, so transforming a newly aroused interest into something lasting and personal is a big task.

Learning is an important component of this task. Learning is essentially about harnessing the knowledge and feelings associated with novel, fleeting experiences and making them last. We make things last by making them interesting, coherent, relevant, personally meaningful and valued (e.g. Schraw et al., 1995; Dahl, 2009).

What we learn becomes a part of our knowledge base about negative things to watch out for and avoid in the future (Baumeister *et al.*, 2001), or positive things that guide us to repeatedly pursue endeavours on our own accord (Hidi, 2006).

Falk *et al.* defined learning quite broadly to include 'changes in cognition, affect, attitudes and behavior' (2007, p. xix) based on definitions gleaned from both formal and non-formal learning environments. In more formal environments, learning is typically motivated by the pursuit of achievement goals. In these achievement settings, learning is often formally measured as some form of knowledge demonstration that is affirmed in summative forms of feedback like grades and diplomas. Learning is thus defined by the grade or educational level achieved. In informal, free-choice settings, on the other hand, other aspects of the learning process are at play. In free-choice settings (where we live a large chunk of our lives, really – perhaps especially when we are on vacation), we tend to act more based on our personal interests, prior experiences, our preferences and expectations. We self-select how to spend our time and which fleeting experiences to invest in. Progress is not a formal process, so any feedback sought or given is typically for fuelling personal mastery.

Given how driven free-choice activities are by what we know and like, when given the choice, we often take the easy route to learning, gravitating more towards opportunities to reinforce, consolidate, strengthen or extend our established feelings, knowledge and skills, or beliefs (Falk *et al.*, 2007). This is less cognitively demanding than learning something entirely new. If we want to enrich people's experiences by sending them 'home with more', hosts have to understand how to share the cognitive load of the task.

The range of interesting and meaningful experiences hosts can create is vast. The beauty of tourism is that hosts have a rich palette of possibilities to draw from to create experiences that influence what people know (knowledge), what they like or dislike (attitudes), what they believe to be true, beautiful or good (beliefs) or people's basic life values related to ways of being (such as helpful, courageous or independent) or to people's life goals (such as security, happiness, accomplishment or a world of beauty) (Rokeach, 1973; Robinson *et al.*, 1991).

When at Sommarøy, for example, we also visited a fish factory where several hundred tons of fish were being unloaded from the spiffy red-and-white ship *Storeknut* to be processed into fillets for shipping. The wet, slippery dock, the briny smell of ocean mixed with the smell of fish, the deafening sounds of the equipment and the sight of the huge hoses sucking the shiny blue fish from the bowels of the ship and transporting them onto conveyor belts inside all set the stage for our understanding of the work being done. When our local host then appeared with a tray of just-filleted fish and offered us a taste of it, several volunteered to bite into the raw, white meat and taste the herring's distinctive but mild flavour. Those who chose not to try watched the expressions of those who did with great curiosity.

We recognized that the fish on the one hand was both sustenance for the whales we'd already seen and the livelihood of the small seaside community we were visiting. We knew, too, that these very fish would provide delicious, healthy meals in homes all around Europe, Russia and Japan. And there we stood, in the brightly lit hall where it was all happening – many showing great interest in this place they had never before been, eating a fish they had never before tasted uncooked, so freshly caught in the waters just beyond.

What Does It Take to Help People Develop Situational and Personal Interest?

In the four-phase model of interest proposed by Suzanne Hidi and Ann Renninger (2006), the key ingredients for developing both situationally aroused and personally pursued interests are defined as knowledge, positive affect and meaningfulness. Each phase in their model is distinguished by how much we know about and value something. It is also distinguished by how positively we feel about it.

The first two phases (triggered and maintained) are about situational interest – interest for which we are dependent on people, resources or opportunities in a situation we find ourselves in in order to arouse or nurture our interest for it. At this level of interest, tasks that help trigger (catch) and subsequently sustain (hold) our interest are important, as are opportunities to connect the new experience with something meaningful to us (Krapp, 2002). Also, though the initial emotions associated with the experience ought to have a certain intensity, they can range from sadness and disgust to pleasure and enjoyment. Any continued pursuit of an interest, however, must be accompanied at some point with positive emotions in order for us to stick with it (Turner and Silvia, 2006). Given the fledgling nature of these phases, situational interest is more dependent on situational support than the subsequent, more personal phases of the model.

The second two phases (emerging and well-developed) are about individual (or personal) interest – interest we begin pursuing independently and for our own purposes (Hidi and Renninger, 2006). The more we do, the more we come to know about it, associate positive feelings with it and value it. Individual interest is characterized by focused attention, considerable prior knowledge, a desire to learn more, positive feelings, perceptions of value and curiosity-driven engagement. At this level of interest, we become increasingly resourceful in pursuing the interest independently, managing challenges fairly well and knowing when and how to seek out help if needed.

Our Northern InSights research group has taken Hidi and Renninger's 2006 model one step further and operationalized its variables in a way summarized in Fig. 7.1. In each phase of this model, the three key variables of knowledge, positive affect and meaningfulness vary. It is hypothesized that we cross the thresholds of each phase of interest development after sufficiently boosting the development of each of the interest qualities that distinguish each phase (various amounts, intensity/integration and intercorrelations).

In terms of amount, positive affect is especially important in the triggered phase and is hypothesized to grow over the next three phases only slightly, whereas meaningfulness is not particularly important in the triggered phase but is hypothesized to grow with a steep slope over the remaining three phases. Meanwhile, knowledge is hypothesized to be relatively important in the triggered phase (we at least have to know enough to have some sense of what we are experiencing) and it continues to grow, though less sharply than meaningfulness, as interest develops.

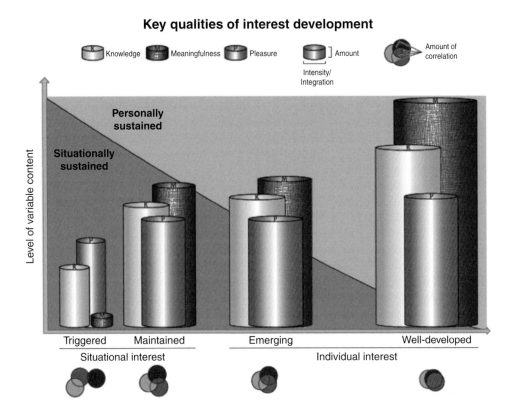

Fig. 7.1. A proposed operationalization of Hidi and Renninger's 2006 four-phase model of interest development.

In terms of intensity and integration, they are hypothesized to increase steadily for all three variables, though least for positive affect and most for meaningfulness. In the case of knowledge, integration is about linking new knowledge or skills (competencies) with other things we know or can do, and in the case of meaningfulness, the integration is with our attitudes, beliefs and values.

In terms of correlations, it is hypothesized that in the triggered phase of situational interest, meaningfulness is hardly correlated with knowledge and affect at all, though knowledge and affect are correlated with each other to a small degree. Those correlations grow to be more equal in the phases of maintained situational and emerging individual interest and much higher in the final phase of well-developed individual interest.

Finally, the greater distance between each phase from triggered situational interest to well-developed individual interest is simply a reminder that it is increasingly hard to move from one phase of interest to the next. How much harder it is to move from one phase to the next, however, is not specified.

The differences between each of the four phases, based on our operationalizations, are theoretically valid, though these relationships are currently being tested empirically.

How Can Hosts Facilitate Interest Development?

Given this model, the logical conclusion for how hosts can facilitate interest development has three main components:

- Competence. Facilitate visitor learning. This can be done by moderately increasing experience-relevant competencies (what visitors know or are able to do), increasing their integration with other things a visitor knows or is able to do, and helping visitors make appraisals that increasingly correlate their competencies with their feelings of pleasure while at the same time recognizing their meaningfulness.
- Pleasure. Help visitors feel good. Use the experience to achieve feelings of pleasure, increase the intensity of those feelings, and help visitors make appraisals that increasingly correlate their feelings with experience-relevant competencies and meaningfulness.
- Meaningfulness. Feature aspects of the experience that visitors find meaningful, i.e. that have personal relevance and are associated with things that matter to them. Increase the intensity of this feeling by linking it with visitor attitudes, beliefs and values, and help visitors make appraisals that increasingly correlate these feelings with their sense of competence and feelings of pleasure.

In some sense, you could say that satisfying people's expectations is about attending to their individual interests – an already quite developed level of interest in something. Visitors travel with an idea of what they would like to experience, and given the self-selected nature of how they spend their time, a good deal of the experiences they choose to participate in are likely driven by things they already (i) know, enjoy, are able to do and find meaningful and (ii) want to pursue more. By doing things they expect to do, they feel satisfied (Chen and Chen, 2010).

However, a study of Hong Kong visitors indicated that only ca. 10% of the visitors were purposeful tourists who processed their cultural experiences deeply (McKercher, 2002). The actual number of tourists who specifically seek deep experiences in other places may well differ from the number who seek deep Hong Kong experiences. Still, by primarily focusing on offering experiences to people we assume are ready to deeply engage in the experience, we miss a sizeable section of visitors who may be the most important segment for the further development of any tourism market. Offering people more than they bargained for while travelling, then, requires hosts to design their experiences in such a way that they arouse visitor interest for something new or unexpected that helps give a visit greater purpose.

To develop a situational interest through this kind of encounter, visitors typically need external help for catching and keeping their attention (Hidi and Renninger, 2006). Though arousing situational interest is necessary to get the ball rolling, it is still not sufficient for enabling long-term, independent interest pursuit. It definitely gets a host or region's foot in the interest door, but unless visitors (i) find pleasure in pursuing the interest; (ii) are convinced of the new interest's personal relevance and value; and (iii) see outlets for where they could pursue it more with help of others or other readily available resources, the situationally interested visitors are far less likely to continue pursuing the new interest on the trip or later on their own. Hosts must therefore set in motion a series of experiences in the right ways at the right times to support the development of new personal interests if they want to increase their chances of success at interest-based value creation.

Success for this approach, then, is related to the experiences visitors are offered and the ways they are scaffolded to help visitors develop new interests that have value for them, the hosts and, ideally, for the region. Providing the right boosts at the right time can yield interest-related ways of thinking, feeling or acting with broad ripple effects for visitors, hosts and the regions where they meet.

Does Interest-related Learning Really Benefit Visitors and Business?

Getting *more* than what we expected at a destination definitely matters for our sense of trip value – particularly when we *don't* get what we expected (Dahl *et al.*, 2010). Therefore, creating experiences that match people's expectations and prior interests will address their sense of satisfaction. However, it will not necessarily move people, or move people as far, interest-wise. The learning aspect of interest is a critical factor for visitors' overall sense of value in both best and worst experiences, though particularly in the face of adversity.

Meeting visitor expectations and facilitating learning of the unexpected is therefore a worthy prospect for experience designers. This is different from accommodating market segmentations or niches that identify experiences as particular kinds of services or groups as representing particular kinds of motives (e.g. MacKay *et al.*, 2002). Though segmented approaches do have value in helping predict appropriate categories of experiences to provide, so does attending to interest-based differences among individuals and understanding how to mindfully adapt or differentiate any experience on interest-based terms (Stamboulis and Skayannis, 2003).

The remainder of this chapter will introduce educational and psychological principles that are known to 'move' people through the learning opportunities we create. Special emphasis is given to the arousal of interest and mastery learning – particularly as they pertain to experiences that visitors may have had little or no prior interest in in order to better reach sceptics or the otherwise unengaged, since it is for this group that hosts arguably have the greatest potential to increase interest-based value creation.

Using the Model for Identifying Value Creation Principles

Our operationalization of Hidi and Renninger's model points to which variables need attention when we strive to move people from one phase of interest to the next. A host doesn't have time to assess the details of each visitor's interest phase, but if they understand general principles that can be applied when they get a sense that a visitor's interest is sagging or moving forward, they can adjust their experience in more general ways to meet the visitors where they are at and move them along in a good direction. Research still needs to be done to tidily link these principles and activities to particular steps in the interest development process facilitated by hosts with visitors, but it builds on a substantial literature from multiple learning environments where these principles have been shown to be viable.

Prime the pump by awakening curiosity

Arousing a new interest entails focusing our attention on a task and rendering it both cognitively and emotionally engaging. In any situation like this, there are at least three key variables at play: (i) the degree of curiosity and/or prior interest with which we meet a situation with (Ainley, 2007); (ii) the natural degree of interestingness characteristic of targeted experiences (Schank, 1979); and (iii) the kinds of tasks created for us related to the targeted elements (Schraw and Lehman, 2001).

Even though experience success is affected by the match between visitor interest levels and the content and structure of their experience (Ballantyne and Packer, 2011), hosts tend to seek and find out very little about individual visitors who partake in their experiences (Ballantyne *et al.*, 2009). Hosts who are keen to create interest-based value use individuals' prior level of interest to adapt the content and structure of visitor experiences for: (i) beginners/sceptics; (ii) visitors with some but not yet much personal interest or prior knowledge and/or skill; and (iii) seasoned visitors with well-developed personal interests, prior knowledge and/or skill.

If visitors enter an experience with little to no interest from before, they are dependent upon the structure and content of the experience in order to become interested. The host's first job in this case is to catch people's attention (Krapp, 2002), and, if successful, trigger situational interest. This entails awakening a certain degree of curiosity, some feeling of emotional intensity (related to any range of emotions) and building on the inherent interestingness of the experience itself through surprise, novelty or other personally relevant or extreme but manageable experience qualities (Schank, 1979; Hidi and Renninger, 2006). Offering outside support for getting and staying engaged is also central (Hidi and Renninger, 2006). When we authors boarded the Skåskjær ferry, for example, the captain aroused curiosity by greeting us and telling that there was a change in plans. Describing the unusualness of the fjord activity, he incited excitement (that felt good), and knowing that we were entering the whale-infested waters in the safety of his boat gave us comfort (that felt good, too). That whales are exotic and seldom seen by the likes of us, and knowing that we were both safe and about to see something unusual and grand drew us easily into a state of situational interest.

Moving visitors to the second maintained situational interest phase involves holding people's interest (Krapp, 2002) and helping them develop an increasingly robust relationship with the targeted interest. This second phase is reached by helping master new content or skills, feel positive emotions and develop an awareness of how the experience is personally relevant and meaningful. Though visitors may show greater personal involvement in the maintained situational interest phase than in the triggered situational interest phase, they are still reliant on the help of others or situational opportunities to keep their interest up. After seeing the first whale in the far distance, for example, our attention was focused. With the occasional sighting reinforcing our activity, our eyes remained fixed on the waters, fervently scanning the surface for the next appearance. Our interest was held.

Facilitate pleasurable experiences through interest-relevant mastery learning

Once interest is aroused, the chance of learning something new increases, though the kind of learning possible depends on the clarity of what hosts wish for visitors to learn, how much the visitors already know about it and how the learning experience is crafted. At the fish factory, for example, we novices could appreciate the extreme cleanliness of the facility, the ingenuity of the equipment design that transformed the gleaming fish into sterile, vacuum-packed, tasty fillets in a matter of minutes.

Know what visitors can walk away with from the experience

As Paul Silvia summarizes, 'Finding something understandable is the hinge between interest and confusion' (2008, p. 58). The more coherently a message is conveyed during an experience, the more likely it will be understood, learned and correctly recalled later. This is also the case for influencing the development or refinement of knowledge, skills, attitudes, beliefs and values (Dahl, 2009). Therefore, it is important for a host to be clear about what new learning they wish to send their visitors home with and to mindfully design experiences to facilitate that.

Interpreting experiences for visitors within pre-chosen themes offers a powerful starting point for the learning process (Ballantyne *et al.*, 2011b). In recent research on wildlife experiences in Australia, for example, researchers studied hosts who had designed learning experiences related to respect and appreciation of natural surroundings, the promotion of ecologically sound attitudes and actions, and how people can incorporate environmentally friendly activities in their everyday lives. Through such intentional programming, the researchers found that visitors could, indeed, be nudged to alter their behaviour later – helping finance ecological activity by making contributions to other ecological causes at home (Ballantyne *et al.*, 2011b). Visitors can be nudged in other ways, too: to pursue information-seeking, adopt new patterns in their everyday habits, change purchasing practices and/or include new topics of discussion with others. Hosts that keep these kinds of goals in mind can collect and share the necessary resources for encouraging these kinds of outcomes. If not, the likelihood of such experience legacies are, by lack of design, reduced.

Set the stage for mastery

Hosts should assure that their visitors have the relevant knowledge and/or skills to meet their experience with success. Whereas some people walk into new experiences confidently, ready to take on whatever the experience brings them (scoring high on curiosity, self-efficacy for and/or compatibility with the targeted experience, for example), others do not (Schunk, 1989; Hartig *et al.*, 1997; Laumann *et al.*, 2001; Norling *et al.*, 2008; Zimmerman and Schunk, 2011). Extensive self-efficacy research reminds us that even if we actually possess the requisite knowledge, feelings or skill to successfully learn something, we will perform at a lower level if we do not believe that. Efforts to appropriately set expectations that visitors believe they can manage can considerably ease the success of the next steps.

Turn people on

Hands-on activities tend not to be as effective in fostering deep learning as activities that are hands-on *and* 'minds-on' (engaging learner minds). Turning people on therefore involves activating relevant prior knowledge, interests and/or emotions that are relevant for the task at hand (Alvermann *et al.*, 1985; Silvia, 2006) as well as getting people involved.

Engage and involve

Experiences that meet our cognition needs (by structuring the task in a way that is reasonably feasible for people to understand and/or master) and or emotional needs (by making the task enjoyable) increase our desire to pursue interest-related learning (Schraw and Lehman, 2001; Hidi and Renninger, 2006). This is particularly the case when the experiences are vivid (clear, distinct, attention-catching, arousing wonder, awe and/or excitement) (Schraw *et al.*, 1995; Ballantyne *et al.*, 2011b), sensorily rich (Ballantyne *et al.*, 2011b) and concrete (Sadoski *et al.*, 2000). This, in turn, helps us remember and believe in what we are learning (Wang, 2006).

Visitors engage more when attention is paid to the cognitive and emotional climate of the task, the nature of the interactions among the people present, and the sense of control people feel and are able to practise (Zaichkowsky, 1994; Handelsman *et al.*, 2005; Appleton *et al.*, 2006; Pearce and Larson, 2006). Engaging activities include puzzles and group tasks, and, as interest grows, one-on-one work, collaborative group work and project-based learning (Hidi and Renninger, 2006). Opportunities for exploration have been shown to engage people, too, as has trust and belief in the credibility of the guides, providing focus and intuitive structures around the main task (as well as removing distractions, and fine-tuning aspects of it that are not intuitive), multiple representations of key parts of the experience, playfulness and fun, appropriate challenge and repetition where necessary (Adams *et al.*, 2008). Other important social factors include peer support (friendly, collaborative and enjoyable) and leader support (welcoming, with a clear focus, offering connection-building learning opportunities and appropriate challenges and offering instrumental support as needed) (Pearce and Larson, 2006).

As the captain of our small ferry steered us into waters teeming with whales, we were first treated to distant views of the fine arcs of whales' backs and fins breaking the ocean surface that were at first hard to distinguish from waves. The captain and crew member clarified what we were seeing so that we knew what to look for as the whales intermittently appeared. By working together to scan the horizon and point to and discuss what we were seeing, we were eventually able to distinguish the humpback whale from the orcas, we were able to imagine their trajectories, and we were able to focus our attention on where they would likely appear next. By so doing, we notably increased our success at seeing the whales around us with greater frequency and delight.

Visitors may experience different kinds of engagement during their experiences. Experiential engagement involves feelings of having enough to do, a sense of wonder and engagement with the experience. Reflective engagement, on the other hand, involves visitors' cognitive and affective processing of the experience. In one study, more than twice as many visitors (85%) reported experiential engagement as a salient aspect of their experience, while only 38% reported reflective engagement as salient (Ballantyne *et al.*, 2011a). Both are valuable, and hosts can influence this.

Relevance

Designing experiences that link content to people's interests, prior knowledge or skills or current events and enable people to pose and answer their own questions can be especially powerful (Hidi, 2006; Adams *et al.*, 2008). When it is not immediately evident how to do that, highlighting activity relevance that at least provides rationales for doing the activity helps (Jang, 2008).

Coherence

Identify the defining message of the experience and then prepares visitors for what's to come. Scaffolding the experience with advanced organizers to help visitors know what lies ahead helps them understand and recall things later (Ausubel, 1960; Luiten *et al.*, 1980). Fill those expectations with clear, concrete content (Sadoski *et al.*, 2000; van Dijk and Kintsch, 1983). Clarity and coherence help visitors identify the point of an experience (Seidel *et al.*, 2005) and later remember what they learned (van Dijk and Kintsch, 1983; Lehman and Schraw, 2002; Seufert, 2003). Other helpful tools include repetition to clarify or reinforce people's understandings relevant to the experience (Dahl, 2009), review to show people how all the pieces of the experience form a coherent whole, and reflection to help people make the connections as to how their experience is relevant for other things they know or are able to do, what they feel, what they believe in and/or what they value (Kolb, 1984; Dahl, 2009; Ballantyne and Packer, 2011).

Appropriate challenge

It is ideal to create learning experiences that are at a level within visitors' grasp – or, even better, just beyond (Wertsch, 1984). Complement those experiences with sufficient, concrete feedback to affirm visitors' beliefs that they are capable of the task (Silvia, 2005; Axelsson, 2007; Durik and Harackiewicz, 2007).

Make learning last through mastery and feedback

Visitors' prior level of interest for a topic matters for the kinds of challenges that motivate them. For example, newcomers to an interest, by definition, do not yet have sufficient motivation for the task to invest in working through any substantial obstacles (Hidi and Renninger, 2006). For that reason, those with situational interest are particularly susceptible to checking out if the task is overly challenging for them (Silvia, 2010). On the other hand, those with more developed interests are more susceptible to assuming too much about what they know and may miss important experience information when they believe its content is too simple for them (McNamara *et al.*, 1996). Learn where visitors are at and attend to the level of the challenge accordingly.

To make learning last, it is important that visitors have fully mastered some relevant aspect of its content well enough to manage it on their own before they leave an experience. Feedback about what people have mastered is crucial for this process. Build into the experience opportunities for feedback on what visitors are learning (Nicol and Macfarlane-Dick, 2007), like conversations with others and high-quality, concrete information about how visitors are doing. As our whale viewing experience illustrates, interaction with the boat crew enabled us to understand when we 'got' how to distinguish between the humpback whales and the orcas in terms of their appearances and behaviours. We were then able to start recognizing whales and their somewhat predictable behaviours on our own with a reasonable degree of task-specific self-efficacy. The movement from guided to self-directed activity is important for moving people from situational to individual interest, and here differences in the group began to emerge as some of the members felt satisfied with what they had seen as it got cold and sought the warmth of the cabin to sort through their photographs (reflecting on their whale experience so far) and/or engage in other conversations (feeling ready to move on to other things). Meanwhile, others remained outside on deck, compelled to pursue their interest in the whales even more.

Meaningfulness and reflection

It is through the process of making sense of experiences that lasting meaning-making occurs and leaves a lasting impact (Kolb, 1984; Ballantyne et al., 2011b). Building opportunities for people to reflect on what they have experienced also helps them integrate it into their repertoire of related thoughts and skills. People's sensory impressions (including what they saw and heard, but also other impressions), the degree of emotional affinity they feel with an experience and the way they are able to process it with others later also significantly impact meaning-making (Ballantyne et al., 2011b).

Ballantyne et al. (2011a) discovered when they asked visitors about their experiences four months afterwards, the biggest predictor of the learning that lasted was what visitors learned at the time, though the only (and very strong) predictor of what they learned at the time was people's reflective engagement.

Other ways to facilitate powerful memories include involving multiple senses during experiences, making comments and signage to support the theme of the experience interpretation, providing people with doable tasks they can do again on their own, setting aside time for reflection during and after the experience, meeting visitors with knowledgeable guides to answer questions, encouraging visitors to talk with others about their experiences when they get home, and providing visitors with resources that help them stay connected, help them develop their interest further or even motivate them to act in experience-relevant ways (Ballantyne et al., 2011b). Online resources and social media can be quite useful for this.

Next Steps

Although this chapter has operationalized a model and linked it to general educational principles that have been shown in other contexts to advance people's competence, feelings of pleasure and sense of meaningfulness, research has yet to systematically assert these links through evidence-based tourism research. To take this on, the first thing the field has to recognize is that interest is more than just a general outcome. It is a complex state that is co-created by visitors and their hosts, and it can have both direct and indirect value for individuals, businesses and regions. It is worth exploring to determine exactly how interest works, how it can be developed mindfully, and how it can be used to the benefit of the tourism industry and its guests.

Secondly, this work is ripe for programmatic research where particular aspects of the model and their relationship with particular learning principles and outcomes are explored in depth. We are doing that in our Northern InSights project, but the range of questions we can pose is vast. To summarize their range very simply, four central questions worthy of pursuit are:

1. Do knowledge, positive affect and meaningfulness develop in the ways posited by the model?
2. Do the learning principles presented in this chapter influence movement between each of the four phases in predictable and/or phase-specific ways?
3. In which ways do opportunities created by others influence the trajectories?
4. In which ways does visitor interest development benefit visitors, hosts and regions – directly and indirectly?

Finally, though culture has not been given particular attention in this chapter, it (like age, expertise and other collective variables) is relevant for consideration in terms of what kinds of prior knowledge or interest people from different cultures bring with them to an experience and in which ways people with different cultural backgrounds feel comfortable engaging with others.

Closing Remarks

Tourism offers an opportunity for unleashing regional learning potentials. These theoretical, empirical and anecdotal reflections were collected to frame a particular way of looking at potential contents, structures and outcomes for tourist experiences – a way to understand how hosts can take visitors beyond times that are 'nice', 'fun' or 'good enough'.

As research shows and as tales from our fjord adventure and fish factory visit illustrate, there is value in designing experiences with content that visitors can delightfully engage in, master and remember through the process of co-creation. If we want them to care about continuing with experience-relevant activities later, making the experience content personally meaningful to them ought to be central. This has value, and it can be central to a broader kind of value creation that can have substantial ripple effects – both in the regions people visit and their everyday lives at home. It is not just about providing experiences that people expect, but moving them beyond those for the inspirations inherent in stealth tourism.

Remember the 90% of Hong Kong visitors who were not purposeful tourists (McKercher, 2002)? If the size of this finding is even remotely relevant for other regions as well, then we have considerable room to grow in delighting visitors – by meeting their expectations, and by helping them develop new interests in region-relevant ways by delighting them with experiences they hadn't even imagined. If hosts co-create experiences with newcomers and sceptics so successfully that they move visitors towards new interests that they wish to continue pursuing on their own, then the range of visitors we can entice back to our region increases substantially, as do the reasons why they want to return.

The details of these claims are currently being tested in the context of High North experiences and are yielding promising results. Research will tell if, how much and in which ways the model we have operationalized is viable and how much and in which ways mindful facilitation of value through co-created, interest-enhanced experiences works. Our bottom line is that we want to move people who visit our region. We start with interest.

References

Adams, W.K., Reid, S., Lemaster, R., McKagan, S.B., Perkins, K.K., Dubson, M. and Wieman, C.E. (2008) A study of educational simulations part I – engagement and learning. *Journal of Interactive Learning Research* 19, 397–419.

Ainley, M. (2007) Being and feeling interested: transient state, mood and disposition. In: Schutz, P.A. and Pekrun, R. (eds) *Emotion in Education*. Academic Press, Burlington, Massachusetts, pp. 147–163.

Alvermann, D.E., Smith, L.C. and Readence, J.E. (1985) Prior knowledge activation and the comprehension of compatible and incompatible text. *Reading Research Quarterly* 20, 420–436.

Appleton, J.J., Christenson, S.L., Kim, D. and Reschly, A.L. (2006) Measuring cognitive and psychological engagement: validation of the Student Engagement Instrument. *Journal of School Psychology* 44, 427–445.

Ausubel, D.P. (1960) The use of advance organizers in the learning and retention of meaningful verbal material. *Journal of Educational Psychology* 51, 267–272.

Axelsson, O. (2007) Individual differences in preferences to photographs. *Psychology of Aesthetics, Creativity, and the Arts* 1, 61–72.

Ballantyne, R. and Packer, J. (2011) Using tourism free-choice learning experiences to promote environmentally sustainable behaviour: the role of post-visit 'Action resources'. *Environmental Education Research* 17, 201–215.

Ballantyne, R., Packer, J. and Hughes, K. (2009) Tourists' support for conversation messages and sustainable management practices in wildlife tourism experiences. *Tourism Management* 30, 658–664.

Ballantyne, R., Packer, J. and Falk, J. (2011a) Visitors' learning for environmental sustainability: testing short- and long-term impacts of wildlife tourism experiences using structural equation modelling. *Tourism Management* 32, 1243–1252.

Ballantyne, R., Packer, J. and Sutherland, L.A. (2011b) Visitors' memories of wildlife tourism: implications for the design of powerful interpretive experiences. *Tourism Management* 32, 770–779.

Baumeister, R.F., Bratslavsky, E., Finkenauer, C. and Vohs, K.D. (2001) Bad is stronger than good. *Review of General Psychology* 5, 323–370.

Chen, C.F. and Chen, F.S. (2010) Experience quality, perceived value, satisfaction and behavioral intentions for heritage tourists. *Tourism Management* 31, 29–35.

Dahl, T.I. (2009) The importance of place for learning about peace: residential summer camps as transformative thinking spaces. *Journal of Peace Education* 6, 225–245.

Dahl, T.I., Vittersø, J., Prebensen, N.K. and Hetland, A. (2010) Lessons from the top of the world: the nature of learning from best and worst experiences on land and sea. *Opplevelser i Nord [Northern InSights] Annual Meeting*, Tromsø, Norway.

Durik, A.M. and Harackiewicz, J.M. (2007) Different strokes for different folks: how individual interest moderates the effects of situational factors on task interest. *Journal of Educational Psychology* 99, 597–610.

Falk, J.H., Dierking, L.D. and Foutz, S. (2007) *In Principle, in Practice: Museums as Learning Institutions*. AltaMira Press, Lanham, Maryland.

Handelsman, M.M., Briggs, W.L., Sullivan, N. and Towler, A. (2005) A measure of college student course engagement. *Journal of Educational Research* 93, 184–192.

Hartig, T., Korpela, K., Evans, G.W. and Gärling, T. (1997) A measure of restorative quality in environments. *Scandinavian Housing and Planning Research* 17, 175–194.

Hidi, S. (2006) Interest: a unique motivational variable. *Educational Research Review* 1, 69–82.

Hidi, S. and Renninger, K.A. (2006) The four-phase model of interest development. *Educational Psychologist* 41, 111–127.

Jang, H. (2008) Supporting students' motivation, engagement, and learning during an uninteresting activity. *Journal of Educational Psychology* 100, 798–811.

Kolb, D.A. (1984) *Experiential Learning: Experience as the Source of Learning and Development*. Prentice-Hall, Englewood Cliffs, New Jersey.

Krapp, A. (2002) Structural and dynamic aspects of interest development: theoretical considerations from an ontogenetic perspective. *Learning and Instruction* 12, 383–409.

Krapp, A. (2007) An educational–psychological conceptualisation of interest. *International Journal for Educational and Vocational Guidance* 7, 5–21.

Krapp, A. and Prenzel, M. (2011) Research on interest in science: theories, methods, and findings. *International Journal of Science Education* 33, 27–50.

Laumann, K., Gärling, T. and Stormark, K.M. (2001) Rating scale measures of restorative components of environments. *Journal of Environmental Psychology* 21, 31–44.

Lehman, S. and Schraw, G. (2002) Effects of coherence and relevance on shallow and deep text processing. *Journal of Educational Psychology* 94, 738–750.

Luiten, J., Ames, W. and Ackerson, G. (1980) A meta-analysis of the effects of advance organizers on learning and retention. *American Educational Research Journal* 17, 211–218.

MacKay, K.J., Andereck, K.L. and Vogt, C.A. (2002) Understanding vacationing motorist niche markets. *Journal of Travel Research* 40, 356–363.

McKercher, B. (2002) Towards a classification of cultural tourists. *International Journal of Tourism Research* 4, 29–38.

McNamara, D.S., Kintsch, E., Songer, N.B. and Kintsch, W. (1996) Are good texts always better? Interactions of text coherence, background knowledge, and levels of understanding in learning from text. *Cognition and Instruction* 14, 1–43.

Nicol, D.J. and Macfarlane-Dick, D. (2007) Formative assessment and self-regulated learning: a model and seven principles of good feedback practice. *Studies in Higher Education* 31, 199–218.

Norling, J.C., Sibthorp, J. and Ruddell, E. (2008) Perceived restorativeness of activities scale (PRAS): development and validation. *Journal of Physical Activity and Health* 5, 184–195.

Pearce, N.J. and Larson, R.W. (2006) How teens become engaged in youth development programs: the process of motivational change in a civic activism organization. *Applied Developmental Science* 10, 121–131.

Renninger, K.A. and Hidi, S. (2011) Revisiting the conceptualization, measurement and generation of interest. *Educational Psychologist* 46, 168–184.

Robinson, J.P., Shaver, P.R. and Wrightsman, L.S. (eds) (1991) *Measures of Personality and Social Psychological Attitudes*. Academic Press, San Diego, California.

Rokeach, M. (1973) *The Nature of Human Values*. Free Press, New York.

Sadoski, M., Goetz, E.T. and Rodriguez, M. (2000) Engaging texts: effects of concreteness on comprehensibility, interest and recall in four text types. *Journal of Educational Psychology* 92, 85–95.

Schank, R.C. (1979) Interestingness: controlling inferences. *Artificial Intelligence* 12, 273–297.

Schraw, G. and Lehman, S. (2001) Situational interest: a review of the literature and directions for future research. *Educational Psychology Review* 13(1), 23–52.

Schraw, G., Bruning, R. and Svoboda, C. (1995) Sources of situational interest. *Journal of Reading Behavior* 27, 1–17.

Schunk, D.H. (1989) Self-efficacy and achievement behaviors. *Educational Psychology Review* 1, 173–208.

Seidel, T., Rimmele, R. and Prenzel, M. (2005) Clarity and coherence of lesson goals as a scaffold for student learning. *Learning and Instruction* 15, 539–556.

Seufert, T. (2003) Supporting coherence formation in learning from multiple representations. *Learning and Instruction* 13, 227–237.

Silvia, P.J. (2005) Cognitive appraisals and interest in visual art: exploring an appraisal theory of aesthetic emotions. *Empirical Studies of the Arts* 23, 119–133.

Silvia, P.J. (2006) *Exploring the Psychology of Interest.* Oxford University Press, Oxford.

Silvia, P.J. (2008) Interest: the curious emotion. *Current Directions in Psychological Science* 17, 57–60.

Silvia, P.J. (2010) Confusion and interest: the role of knowledge emotions in aesthetic experience. *Psychology of Aesthetics, Creativity and the Arts* 4, 75–80.

Stamboulis, Y. and Skayannis, P. (2003) Innovation strategies and technology for experience-based tourism. *Tourism Management* 24, 35–43.

Turner, S.A. and Silvia, P.J. (2006) Must interesting things be pleasant? A test of competing appraisal structures. *Emotion* 6, 670–674.

Van Dijk, T.A. and Kintsch, W. (1983) *Strategies of Discourse Comprehension.* Academic Press, New York.

Wang, A. (2006) Advertising engagement: a driver of message involvement on message effects. *Journal of Advertising Research* 46, 355–368.

Wertsch, J.V. (1984) The zone of proximal development: some conceptual issues. *New Directions for Child and Adolescent Development* 23, 7–18.

Zaichkowsky, J.L. (1994) The personal involvement inventory: reduction, revision and application to advertising. *Journal of Advertising* 23, 59–70.

Zimmerman, B.J. and Schunk, D.H. (2011) *Handbook of Self-Regulation of Learning and Performance.* Routledge, New York.

8 Co-creation of Experience Value: A Tourist Behaviour Approach

Lidia Andrades[1] and Frederic Dimanche[2]

[1]University of Extremadura, Badajoz, Spain; [2]SKEMA Business School, France

Introduction

As discussed earlier in this book, the need to move from a classical conception of tourism services towards designing and offering tourism experiences has been addressed by researchers since the late 1990s. This new management paradigm highlighted the necessary transition from service delivery to experience creation (Pine and Gilmore, 1999). From a managerial perspective, tourism destinations and the providers of tourism services are increasingly recognizing that providing satisfactory experiences to their customers represents the best way to provide their target markets with a differentiated image, enhance their brand equity and consolidate an advantageous position. Therefore, destination management organizations have begun to consider the delivery of memorable experiences as essential to competitiveness and sustainability (Ritchie and Crouch, 2003; Tung and Ritchie, 2011).

The central idea of this approach to reinforce tourism destinations' and firms' competitiveness is to involve the visitor in taking an active role and, together with service providers, create rewarding, authentic, unique, peak and ultimately memorable experiences (Gnoth and Knobloch, 2012). But, to be able to provide unforgettable experiences, the visitor's participation and involvement in the consumption process is required. Subsequently, the role of the tourism managers should be to favour tourists' state of feeling physically, mentally, emotionally, socially or spiritually engaged with the tourism event, so their experience would be memorable (O'Sullivan and Spangler, 1998).

Involvement plays a central role over the quality of the tourist experience and, consequently, it has a direct effect over tourists' satisfaction. Meyer and Schwager described the 'customer experience' as 'the internal and subjective reactions and feelings experienced by consumers when they have any direct or indirect contact with the company' and, as a result, 'customer satisfaction' is the outcome of 'a series of customer experiences or, one could say, the result of the good ones minus the bad ones' (2007, p. 2). So, to understand how to achieve customers' satisfaction, tourism managers must deconstruct it into its component experiences. And, as will be shown in this chapter, one of these components is the tourist's level of involvement with the leisure activity. Hence, for tourism managers, creating the right psychological environment and facilitating tourist involvement represents the real challenge in order to boost the competitiveness of their destinations and businesses (Otto and Ritchie, 1996).

Since tourism destinations and firms must involve tourists in order to be able to provide them with satisfactory experiences, the implementation of adequate strategies to obtain visitors' cooperation in the co-creation of experiences becomes essential. Consequently, involvement appears to be a key factor in the tourist experience management context. But what does involvement really mean? How is it defined from a tourist behaviour perspective?

To answer these questions, this chapter will first describe what is and what constitutes a memorable experience and will address afterwards the issue of how to engage tourists to collaborate in the co-creation of such experiences. The chapter considers involvement in tourist experiences as a mediator and moderator variable in value co-creation.

In particular, after defining the involvement construct, discussing its measurement, and presenting the different research methodologies that have been used to investigate it, the chapter will discuss the main implications and consequences of tourists' involvement in the delivery of tourism experiences. Strategies that could be adopted in order to encourage tourists' engagement with the tourism firms and destinations are provided at the end of the chapter. Together with these managerial and marketing implications for tourism managers, future lines of research that may be identified from gaps identified in the literature are also discussed.

Theoretical Framework for Involvement in the Context of Experience Co-creation

The definition of involvement

In behavioural terms, Engel and Blackwell (1982) explained how consumers' purchase involvement can be measured with variables such as time spent in product search, the energy spent, the number of alternatives examined or the extent of the decision process. Accordingly, purchase decision involvement was defined by Zaichkowsky (1985) as the perceived relevance of the object based on people's inherent needs, values and interests. Laurent and Kapferer (1985) concluded that enduring involvement derives from the perception that the product is related to central values, those defining one's singularity, and identity, one's ego. Beatty *et al.* (1988) distinguished between ego involvement and purchase involvement. Ego involvement is described as the importance of a product to the individual and to the individual's self-concept, values and ego, while purchase involvement is related to the level of concern for, or interest in, the purchase process triggered by the need to consider a particular purchase.

In the same line of thought, Celsi and Olson (1988, p. 211) explained involvement as the extent to which an object, situation or action is considered personally relevant. The personal relevance of a product, as in the previous definitions, is represented by the perceived linkage between an individual self knowledge (i.e. needs, values, goals) and the product attributes (Kyle *et al.*, 2006, p. 471). This definition implies that through the activation of personally relevant knowledge, 'a motivational state' may be created, driving or energizing consumers' overt behaviours. Consequently, there is a close relationship between motivation and involvement, and what is more, if the relevant attributes of a product for a consumer can be identified, it would be possible to use them as a gimmick to get their interest, motivation and willingness to buy it. Therefore, involvement toward an activity can be seen as a predictor of consumer behaviour, and is considered a motivational variable reflecting the extent of personal relevance of the decision to the individual in terms of basic goals, values and self concept (e.g. Richins and Bloch, 1986; Kyle *et al.*, 2006; Prebensen *et al.*, 2013c).

In leisure, recreation and tourist behaviour contexts, involvement has been defined and operationalized as a salient concept (Bloch and Bruce, 1984): an unobservable state of motivation, arousal or interest toward a recreational activity or associated product (e.g. Rothschild, 1984; Havitz and Dimanche, 1997, 1999). Additionally, it is the consequence of the state of identification existing between an individual and a recreational activity, at one point in time, characterized by some level of enjoyment and self-expression being achieved through the activity (Selin and Howard, 1988; Ferns and Walls, 2012). Although some authors (e.g. Kim *et al.*, 1997) proposed behavioural proxies for involvement such as frequency of participation, money spent, miles travelled, ability or skill, ownership of equipment and number of memberships, there is agreement in the literature that these are consequences of involvement and that involvement is best understood and measured as a multidimensional construct. As a result, several scales have been proposed over the years, such as the Personal Involvement Inventory (PII) by Zaichkowsky (1985), revised by McQuarrie and Munson in 1987, or the Consumer Involvement Profile (CIP) scale (Laurent and Kapferer, 1985), translated and adapted to tourism and leisure contexts by Dimanche *et al.* (1991). Laurent and Kapferer (1985) conceptualized involvement as a five-dimensions scale, the Consumer Involvement Profile (CIP), and described the concept as resulting from the degree of: (i) interest, which depends on the centrality of ego importance of the product class for the consumer; (ii) pleasure experienced during the consumption, as a hedonic and rewarding value of the product class; (iii) sign, related to the perceived symbolic value of the product class; (iv) risk importance, referring to the perceived importance of the negative consequences of a mispurchase; and (v) risk probability, which represents the subjective probability of making the wrong purchase. The scale, tested in tourism and leisure contexts, often resulted in four dimensions following the merging of importance/interest and pleasure (Havitz and Dimanche, 1997).

Other authors (e.g. Gahwiler and Havitz, 1998; Bricker and Kerstetter, 2000; Kyle *et al.*, 2003) adopted the conceptualization of involvement developed by McIntyre (1989) and McIntyre and Pigram (1992) as a construct consisting of three facets: attraction, centrality and self-expression. Attraction is the facet composed of items measuring the importance and pleasure of the activity to the recreationist; centrality includes items referring to the lifestyle choices recreationists make that bind them to the activity; and self-expression consists of items designed to examine the expressive elements associated with the activity. Later on, Kyle and Chick (2004) outlined involvement as a construct composed of five dimensions: attraction, centrality, identity affirmation, identity expression and social bonding. They extended the tripartite construct, splitting self-expression into identity affirmation and identity expression facets, and adding the social bonding facet. Self-expression was divided into identity affirmation and expression, since leisure activities afford recreationists opportunities to both affirm their identities to themselves as well as to express these identities to those around them (Haggard and Williams, 1992; Dimanche and Samdahl, 1994; Kyle *et al.*, 2006). Lastly, social bonding denotes the extent to which involvement is driven by the consumers' social ties. This scale was reviewed by Kyle *et al.* in 2007, who presented a Modified Involvement Scale (MIS), with the same dimensions but alternative items for measuring them.

Finally, to end this brief review of involvement discussions, it must be noted that most leisure involvement research has focused on enduring aspects of involvement instead of situational ones. Many authors have considered involvement as enduring because the level of importance an individual ascribes to an activity is dependent on his or her personal values, which are less susceptible to variations induced by situational stimuli (Kyle and Chick, 2004). However, although the relationship between involvement and length of participation in the leisure activity has been proven, several authors noted that there are still too few longitudinal pieces of research that would prove the stability of leisure involvement over time (Havitz and Dimanche, 1999). None the less, it is generally accepted that involvement consists of situational and enduring components (Richins *et al.*, 1992), and as the situational sources of personal relevance emanate from stimuli most often encountered in the immediate environment (e.g. merchandising, price promotions, suggestive selling by employees), for the situational involvement, the motivational properties are dynamic, changeable and transitory. In contrast, for enduring involvement, these motivational properties are intrinsic and relatively stable (Kyle *et al.*, 2007).

The effects of involvement on tourist consumption

Tourists' involvement can be understood as their attitudes toward an activity, and their behaviour with respect to the activity and decision-making, and is considered a motivational variable that mediates purchase, usage and participation. Accordingly, the effects of enduring involvement across search, planning, purchase and recollection consumption phases have been widely analysed (Havitz and Dimanche, 1997; Iwasaki and Havitz, 1998). In this section, the main results obtained about how involvement affects tourist consumption are presented.

Concerning the searching and planning phase of consumption, involvement influences search behaviour, ability to differentiate between activity and programme options, and leisure behaviour itself. Havitz and Dimanche (1999) found that leisure and tourist search behaviour patterns are affected by involvement profile scores. So, highly involved participants are expected to acquire information from more different sources than would less-involved participants, or to keep recreation programme brochures longer than would less-involved participants. Even receptiveness to information concerning travel products and the destination differs according to tourists' involvement profiles. Jamrozy *et al.* (1996) noted that highly involved nature-oriented travellers tend to be more receptive to information about travel products or destinations and spread that information willingly. Also, various activity-specific reading behaviours were found for more involved consumers, finding differences between the types of information needs they exhibit. Likewise, tourists with low involvement profiles scores responded best to high repetition, entertaining forms of promotion, while those with high involvement profile scores responded best to persuasive forms of promotion based on rational arguments. Consequently, when persuasive communication strategies are designed, differing strategies will probably be needed to reach people with various involvement levels.

Another consequence of tourists' involvement profiles is that the number of options in tourists' awareness sets diverges (Celsi and Olson, 1988; Bloch *et al.*, 1989; Cai *et al.*, 2004). Therefore, tourists with high involvement profiles have smaller evoked sets in proportion to the size of their awareness sets.

Regarding leadership dynamics and how leaders' opinions affect tourists' choices, it has been found that the level of involvement is positively related to opinion leadership: highly involved people influence other people's choices.

From the reviewed studies, it can be stated that developing segmentation strategies specifically during the pre-trip stage of the tourist decision-making process would be effective in boosting tourism destinations' and firms' competitiveness, due to the fact that highly involved tourists will demand a different treatment than less-involved ones. With regard to the purchase consumption phase, many studies support the relationship between enduring travel involvement and travellers' visitor intentions, as well as the frequency of the trips (Clements and Josiam, 1995; Havitz and Dimanche, 1999; Kyle and Mowen, 2005; Lee and Beeler, 2009; Ferns and Walls, 2012). So enduring involvement can be considered as a predictor of travel decision and destination selection, but it can also be seen as an influencer of destinations' brand equity. For example, tourists with a high involvement profile score have a greater probability of travelling abroad. Moreover, the ability to differentiate between facilities, equipment and destinations was found to be positively related to high involvement scores. Neophytes with high involvement profiles will tend toward aspirational overbuying (Havitz and Dimanche, 1999). A relationship between tourists' leisure involvement and place attachment has also been demonstrated (Williams *et al.*, 1992; Moore and Graefe, 1994; Bricker and Kerstetter, 2000; Jorgensen and Stedman, 2001; Cai *et al.*, 2004; Kyle *et al.*, 2006; Raymond *et al.*, 2010).

Literature has also paid special attention to the relationship between commitment and involvement, and how this relationship may moderate behavioural loyalty (Iwasaki and Havitz, 2004). Commitment is understood as a result of leisure involvement (Iwasaki and Havitz, 1998), and can be defined as 'those personal and behavioral mechanisms that bind individuals to consistent patterns of leisure behavior' (Kim *et al.*, 1997, p. 323).

During the purchase consumption phase, people who reported high involvement with a particular activity also tended to report strong levels of psychological commitment to a favoured service provider (Gahwiler and Havitz, 1998). As commitment implies consistent patterns of leisure behaviour, individuals initially develop involvement(s) with an activity, and then gradually develop psychological commitment to brands (Iwasaki and Havitz, 1998). Accordingly, involvement has been mainly analysed at product level, while commitment has usually been studied at brand level (Kyle and Chick, 2004).

Kyle and Mowen (2005) examined the relationship between involvement and agency commitment, concluding that consumers advance through a developmental process where involvement with a leisure activity leads to the development of specific service preferences. Also, involvement has a social extension that influences involvement: the 'expectations among socially relevant others that favour the individuals' continuance in their participation' at the leisure activity. Thus, 'socially relevant others may also become sources of meaning', and as will be explained below, social bonding and attachment constitute an essential ingredient of memorable experiences and at the same time explain people's involvement (Kyle and Chick, 2004, p. 261).

As part of social interactions, another relevant aspect in understanding tourist experiences is the tourist resources that are available at the tourism destination, which undoubtedly determine its competitiveness (Ritchie and Crouch, 2003; Dwyer et al., 2004). Prebensen et al. (2013a, 2013b) analysed how individual tourist resources influence the overall value of tourist experiences, and the role of involvement in modulating this relationship. They found that the level of involvement explains significant variance in overall experience value, and that this level of involvement is affected by tourist resources. Consequently, tourist resources represent a tool to influence tourist involvement.

Regarding the risk that may be perceived during purchase, it has been observed that loyal consumers who have experience with the consumption of a leisure product might be less involved (they perceive a lower risk) than would novice buyers.

Ultimately, the implications of involvement over pricing and distribution strategies have not been addressed sufficiently in the literature, representing a gap in the theory, which requires further analysis.

To close the consumption cycle, the effect of involvement during the recollection phase of consumption is analysed. Several authors have identified a direct relationship between involvement and perceived value, satisfaction and loyalty (Cronin et al., 2000; Chen and Tsai, 2008; Lee and Beeler, 2009; Prebensen et al., 2013b, 2013c). However, some other studies do not support that enduring travel involvement leads to brand loyalty (Ferns and Walls, 2012). The finding that the more involved consumers report more satisfaction with the leisure activity than the lower involved ones appears to have been accepted by most authors (Havitz and Dimanche, 1999). So involvement can be thought of as a very relevant constituent of the tourists' experience.

The role of involvement as moderator in the tourist experience: engineering/co-creating leisure and tourism experiences

Smith (1994) took a holistic view of the tourism product, summarizing previous demand- and supply-side perspectives, and breaking it down into five elements: the physical plant, service, hospitality, freedom of choice and involvement. From this approach, tourist involvement is considered as an essential part of the tourism product, and tourists are consequently expected to participate in its delivery. Pine and Gilmore (1999) highlighted how tourism companies and destinations should move away from the classical conception of delivering tourism products toward designing and providing experiences. Richards (1999) forecast that in new developed societies, quality of life will be measured in terms of the accessibility that their citizens have to experiencing. This idea has now gained validity and many researchers have addressed this issue. Moreover, from a tourism management standpoint, competitiveness demands innovativeness, which for tourism companies means being able to provide experiences that connect with the latent needs of the human being (Prahalad and Ramaswamy, 2003, 2004). So, it is essential to understand what a real memorable experience is for tourists (Obenour et al., 2006), what its basic elements are (Quan and Wang, 2004), how tourists construe them (Colton, 1987; Hsu et al., 2009; Xu, 2010) and how to propose them to very different customer profiles, with diverse motivations, expectations, needs, past experiences, knowledge, etc. (Ballantyne et al., 2004). In this context, it is obvious that tourists play a central role as active participants in the tourism service delivery. Consequently, understanding their motivations and what factors may facilitate their involvement represent fundamental information for those companies and destinations who wish to increase their competitiveness in the experience economy. This issue is addressed in the present section, which discusses how involvement moderates tourists' experiences, and how involvement could be managed to garner tourists' cooperation in creating their tourism experiences.

The tourism experience may be explained as the result of a set of physical, emotional, spiritual and/or intellectual impressions (Pine and Gilmore, 1999), subjectively perceived by the tourists (Otto and Ritchie, 1996), since they start planning their trip, while they enjoy it and until they are back home. Thereby, the tourism experience may be interpreted as a ritual process, an individual search for inner meaning that could be even close to a religious experience, in the sense that it may become a source of personal development (MacCannell 1976; Cohen 1979; Mannell and Iso-Ahola, 1987; Sharpley and Jepson, 2011). Havitz and Dimanche (1999) highlighted that leisure contexts often provide meaningful experiences and afford individuals opportunities to reveal their true selves. Nash and Smith (1991) described tourism as a 'quest', and defined the tourism experience as a rite of passage, comprising the three stages of separation from the community, liminality or transition, and reintegration. Every memorable experience is characterized by rupture with routines, and for providing tourists with the chance to escape from everyday stressors, a sense of separation from the everyday world, feelings of intense pleasure, freedom of choice, spontaneity, timelessness, fantasy, adventure and sense of self-realization (Unger and Kernan, 1983; Celsi et al., 1993). For Cary, the memorability of a tourist experience is determined by the unexpected, fortuitous, surprising and serendipitous moments, which 'simultaneously produces and erases the "tourist" as a subject' (2004, p. 63). From a psychological point of view, these sorts of experience combine personal growth and the feeling of renewal of self (Arnould and Price, 1993), the interpersonal enjoyment derived from the communion with nature, with friends, family and even with strangers (Redfoot, 1984) together with the feeling of external achievement (Csíkszentmihályi, 1990; Hoffman et al., 2012). There are affective, cognitive and conative elements that are linked to those experiences that are recognized as remarkable by tourists (Coghlan and Pearce, 2010; Uysal and Noe, 2003).

Tung and Ritchie (2011), when exploring the essence of memorable tourism experiences, identified four dimensions: affect, expectations, consequentiality and recollection. While 'affect' and 'expectations' are intuitively understood, 'consequentiality' may not be that obvious. This dimension refers to tourists' perceived relevance of the outcome of the trip, and it includes four main sub-dimensions: enhancing social relationships, intellectual development, self-discovery and overcoming physical challenges. Finally, 'recollection' is related to the efforts made and actions taken by tourists to remember the tourism experience and/or to reflect back on the trip. Recently, Kim *et al.* (2012) proposed a seven-dimension scale to assist in understanding the concept of memorable experiences and in improving their effective management: hedonism, refreshment, local culture, meaningfulness, knowledge, involvement and novelty.

Again, involvement is recognized as a part of every outstanding experience. Moreover, as shown in the previous section, involvement is considered to be a motivational variable, which means that to connect with visitors and to engage them, it is necessary to know about their interests, goals, values, expectations in life, personal needs, etc. Quinlan-Cutler and Carmichael (2012) suggested that the fundamental motivations for leisure seekers are: escape, adventure, novelty, recreation, regression, interpersonal interactions, enhancement of relationships, exploration of self, relaxation, health, prestige, education and/or mastery. And these different motivations for travelling vary across a wide range of variables related to tourists' personality, their life style, life cycle, reference groups, previous knowledge and experiences, culture, interests, self-perceptions, identity, etc. Thus, it is quite a complex task to design a tourism product that meets tourists' expectations and needs. None the less, tourists' involvement would be easy to obtain if destinations and firms were able to catch their attention, offering them a tourism product that they perceive as real value proposition. The question is what is 'a proper value proposition' for them? How and where could we get the knowledge about tourists' longings? Havitz and Dimanche (1999) affirmed that socio-demographic variables were not good predictors of tourists' involvement in leisure activities. Consequently, to understand what tourists long for, it would be advisable to draw tourism segments characterized by similar values, opinions, interests, life-cycle stage, social status, culture, hobbies and activities, risk tolerance, or preferences based on their previous destination choices and experiences.

To achieve this, traditional research techniques may seem unsuitable and insufficient. Since the late 1980s, scholars have expressed frustration at the lack of methodological developments in tourism research and have called for a more critical assessment of traditional research approaches (Dann *et al.*, 1988; Tung and Ritchie, 2011). Traditionally, tourism research has been developed by longitudinal and cross-sectional structured surveys (Havitz and Dimanche, 1999), travel diaries, structured or unstructured interviews (Sharpley and Jepson, 2011) and observant participation (Volo, 2010). However, more recently, experience research has also used the experience sampling method (Mannell and Iso-Ahola, 1987; Csíkszentmihályi and LeFevre, 1989) and memory-work (Small, 1999). Other techniques that have proved useful are those that elicit memories related to certain stimuli (Kyle and Chick, 2004), like storytelling, that shape memories and impressions of events over time (McGregor and Holmes, 1999; Hsu *et al.*, 2009); narrative analysis (Giddens, 1990, 1991; Reissman, 1993); or ethnographic research (Bueno and Rameckers, 2003; Hsu *et al.*,

2009). These techniques embody alternatives that may assist with surpassing the practical difficulties of discovering and understanding tourist segments from the tourism experience management perspective.

Considering what consumer information would be valuable for companies who wish to provide their customers with true satisfactory experiences, Meyer and Schwager (2007) analysed the procedures through which companies systematically collect information about their customers. After examining information collected by customer relationship management systems, they concluded that managers learn about what the company knows about customers, but not about what customers think about the company. However, if a customer experience encompasses every aspect of a company offer – the quality of customer care, of course, but also advertising, packaging, product and service features, ease of use and reliability – it would be necessary to review the way companies gather information to capture customers' subjective thoughts about their experience with the company. As a solution, they proposed the implementation of customer experience management systems, intended to capture the immediate response of the customer to its encounters with the company at every 'touch point'. These systems would monitor the past, present and potential patterns of customers' behaviours. According to the literature, new methodologies and procedures to collect, analyse and report on tourist expectations, needs and longings should be adopted by tourism destinations and companies to tackle the challenge of exploring what is a memorable experience for different tourism segments and how involvement modulates the individuals' interpretation of their experiences.

Strategies

Once tourism destinations and tourism companies have adequate information to co-design and co-create with their customers the experiences they are longing for, which strategies would be best for using this knowledge and to deliver remarkable tourism experiences? Satisfaction has been commonly understood as the outcome of tourism experiences (Tung and Ritchie, 2011). A satisfactory experience can be perceived as 'the congruence of need and performance', while dissatisfaction may be expressed as 'the gap between expectation and experience' (Ryan, 1997). Although customer satisfaction and service quality are not synonymous, service quality affects the tourist experience (Prebensen et al., 2013c). Wang et al. (2012) examined the causal relationships between service quality at tourism nature destinations, the tourists' experiences and the post-trip behavioural intentions. Their analysis revealed that tourist experience is a mediator between service quality and intention to revisit. In the framework of the service quality theory, the service gap model describes how service quality perceived by consumers is dependent on how companies understand their customers' needs and expectations, together with how companies design and deliver the service to them, accordingly to these needs (Parasuraman et al., 1998). Consequently, understanding and managing tourists' expectations is an essential aspect of experience management.

At this point, the key questions are first to understand which elements of the tourist experiences can be controlled by companies in order to get their customers involved in co-creating the tourism experience; and second, to determine how specific aspects of a destination may be linked to memorable experience dimensions. Considering the relevance of the performance presentation strategies, Pine and Gilmore (1999) suggested that for involving tourists and getting their cooperation in co-creating the tourism experience, the theme of the experience as well as the mix in memorabilia must be carefully designed to engage all five tourists' senses. So tourists' engagement is obtained through appealing to their interests while getting their mindful attention and, subsequently, invoking the pleasure dimension of involvement. Harmonizing tourists' impressions with positive cues will be also appropriate. Morgan (2006) emphasized the advisability of providing abundant choices linked to local distinctiveness, as well as providing moments of amazement. Again the reference to the attraction/pleasure dimension of tourist involvement is evident. Additionally, the whole experience should be designed to reinforce positive values that connect with tourists' values and goals in life, an aspect that once more is related to another of the identified dimensions of involvement, 'centrality'.

When the Canadian Tourism Commission (2004) drafted a report for tourism planners and managers, it aimed at offering some cues to enhance country competitiveness as a tourism destination. In this report the relevance of managing service encounters and touch points at the destination – for example, the role played by tour guides or local specialists who connect tourists with the local community – was emphasized. This becomes meaningful since social bonding was identified in the involvement theory as another relevant dimension (see Kyle et al.'s (2006) place bonding model). So to succeed in delivering memorable experiences, it is necessary to plan and control customers' interactions with service providers, in facilitating tourists' development of feelings of attachment toward the place and to the local communities. Also, providing them with free time and the flexibility to allow for self-discoveries and interactions with others was also advised, thereby connecting with the social dimension of involvement and the individual's need for identity affirmation and expression.

In addition, regarding tourists' perceptions of risk probability and importance, both identified as dimensions of involvement (Kyle et al., 2006), Havitz and Dimanche (1999) stated that perceived risk is lower for tourists who present a high involvement profile. None the less, 'tourism planners must moderate the level of risk at a destination through risk avoidance or enhancement policies in an attempt to satisfy tourists' motivations' (Ryan, 1997, cited in Tung and Ritchie, 2011, p. 1370).

Finally, following Csíkszentmihályi's 'flow' theory (1998), getting tourists involved with leisure activities would be easier if destinations and companies were able to design affordable challenges for the tourists, providing them with opportunities to reinforce their self-esteem and to accomplish personal growth. To manage efficiently these challenging experiences for tourists, an essential prerequisite is to provide tourists with adequate skills, and constant positive feedback, so they experience a feeling of fulfilment. Hamilton-Smith (1987) described tourism as a personal quest characterized by two dimensions: existential reality and structural reality. On the one hand, existential reality is defined as the extent to which one feels 'high levels of satisfaction, freedom, involvement and (intrinsic) reward' (p. 334). On the other hand, structural reality entails 'the extent to which the activity is task oriented and wherein completion is externally reinforced' (Otto and Ritchie, 1996, p. 166). This last definition of tourism as a quest for existential and structural reality matches Csíkszentmihályi's 'flow' theory. His description of what individuals experience when 'flowing' is what Hamilton-Smith described as existential reality, while the process through which individuals reach the 'flow state' matches the activities that lead to experience the structural reality as described by Hamilton-Smith. So if the chance to freely select between a range of leisure activities that match their interests is provided to tourists, and at the same time, those activities represent a manageable challenge for them, this would be the way to involve them in experience co-creation. Accordingly, such experience could be described as a quest through which tourists learn about themselves, about their skills, if they are getting positive feedback from the supplier.

To sum up, experience management at tourism destinations and firms implies several things in order to generate memorable experiences: (i) managing the technical background, operant resources, as well as the business background; (ii) relating all the providers to design the environment where the tourism experience will be delivered; and (iii) facilitating a tourism environment that encourages tourists' willingness to co-create and cooperate with tourism service providers.

Cases as Illustration

Consumers will thrive on experiences that are intelligently proposed to them. The end goal of a tourist experience is to create lasting memories that a visitor will reminisce about and will share in their social networks. The experience must be felt as unique, or at least customized; it must differentiate itself from those experiences provided by the competition; and often, it will involve some level of innovation, thereby creating novelty. There are a number of examples in the literature as well as in tourism destinations that illustrate the need for and the benefits resulting from involving customers in creating unique experiences. The following section presents two such examples.

As a first example, in a hospitality context, Neuhofer et al. (2013) relate how Hotel Lugano Dante used technology to create customer involvement before the trip, during the stay and after the trip to create customized and satisfying experiences. The hotel proposes the use of a web platform called 'Happy Guest Relationship Management' to bring together all interactions between guests and staff throughout the customer service journey. The company tries to identify each touch point of the experience and encourages guests to communicate with staff to voice their needs and preferences so as to improve the quality of each touch point. Guests log on to a dedicated page called 'my page' (Hotel Lugano, https://mypage.hotel-luganodante.com/mypage) where they can, for example, state, before arrival or during a stay, preferences regarding dietary needs, activities, type of pillow, etc. This leads to a personalized relationship with staff members that not only heightens the level of service but also increases the involvement of the guest with the service provider to achieve experience co-creation and higher perceived quality. Value is created for the guest, but also for the hotel, which reserves this service to clients who book directly through the hotel, without going through an intermediary (as a result, the hotel saves on expensive commissions paid to intermediaries). After the trip, 'my page' can be used by the hotel to maintain an ongoing relationship with their loyal guests. In this example, the company found a strategy, through technology, to engage and involve guests in a way that allows for the co-creation of experience value on both ends of the counter. This can also be seen as a good example of planning service design in tourism to create experiences for a new generation of technology-savvy customers (Dimanche, 2010; Prayag *et al.*, 2012).

A second example of how a service provider can involve customers to create experience value refers to a business event experience in Canada that one of the chapter's authors participated in. Business events, particularly with tourism professionals, often involve leisure activities and side trips. In fact, other than to entertain and give the business event participants a breather, a side tourist activity is designed to add value to a meeting. It allows people to meet others in a more relaxed and open context; it may even allow for participants to have experiences that become the highlight of the event, the one aspect they remember, years later. The event I am referring to took place in 2010 in Nova Scotia; it was in fact a professional conference whose aim was to help tourism professionals understand tourist motivations and needs for unique experiences. After a few hours of meeting room work, all delegates were invited to a short trip to a nearby forest. They were first treated to a cup of hot cider that had been prepared by a host: a tasting and smelling experience. Recipes were shared, forest-related stories were told and delegates were slowly increasingly involved with a story-teller who was there to share his passion for nature and the forest. Although there was no obligation to participate and listen to stories, we could feel how people's interest quickly grew around this man who enthusiastically talked about his passion. The man then took us away to a clearing in the forest where traditional logging tools were lying: an axe, saw and other specialty tools. He continued to tell his story and that of his ancestors: all loggers in the Canadian forest and contributors to the development and history of a country. By then, people could not help but listen and join in the conversation from various perspectives. He involved the attendees in his discussion of nature and the forest, but also in the history of their country, in forgotten ways of living, in the heydays of the wood shipbuilding industry.... The logger then went on to demonstrate his ability in cutting or carving logs with his tools. We then learned that he was a lumberjack world champion, specializing in log rolling (you can visit http://www.lumberjackworldchampionships. com/ for more information about this sport)! After involving people socially, historically, culturally and intellectually, he gave us opportunities to act and try the tools in a game format.

As a participant observer and contributor to this conference, I grew increasingly conscious of the power of the experience that was designed according to Schmitt's (1999) experience framework: sense, feel, think, act and relate. The organizers had identified a way to simply engage and involve people in an experience that became the highlight of the trip, the memorable experience that they would talk about many times and use as a reference example in their own professional lives. Value was created, once again on both sides of the counter, for the visitor but also for the organizer who communicated very effectively their message.

Implications

As may be deduced from the above-discussed theories, the effectiveness of tourist involvement at all of the levels will impact tourism destinations, firms' productivity, and ultimately quality and tourist satisfaction (Bitner *et al.*, 1997). In practice, the strategies and actions designed to manage tourists' involvement in the co-creation of experiences will differ, depending on the type of segment we are working with, and also depending on whether we are working at a destination level or at a tourism firm level. But in any case, thinking in terms of 'experience co-creation' constitutes a new institutional culture gaze based on serving, excellence and openness.

At destination level, destination planning, policy and development should contemplate resource conditions, recreational activities, tourism facilities and related personnel as well as its integrated management (Wang *et al.*, 2012) in order to propose a scenario where tourism companies may design and deliver, together with their customers, peak, unique, singular and remarkable experiences. From the perspective of the tourism business, getting into the culture of delivering experiences, instead of tourism services, must be reflected in developing marketing plans. That means thinking about how to introduce 'co-creation' in the objectives of the firm, how to redefine strategies and actions accordingly, and how to identify the relevant indicators to monitor the implementation of marketing strategies. Mills and Morris (1986) developed a model of 'client involvement stages' guided by the idea that customers should be viewed as partial employees of service organizations. In the present chapter, the concept of tourist involvement has been deconstructed to show how it moderates the tourist experience, and how its dimensions can be managed to encourage tourists to engage with the experience delivery process.

Finally, it is important that introducing the experiencing paradigm for tourism businesses and destinations is done in a sustainable way. This means doing it so that its implementation will lead destinations and businesses to become more competitive in economic, environmental, social and institutional terms (Ritchie and Crouch, 2003). Due to this, tourism managers must keep in mind the need for analysing the delivery of experiences in terms of return on investment. One must think about cost–benefit analyses in appraising the cost of training and hiring qualified employees required for this new context, in implementing flexibility for an organization to be really able to provide freedom of choice to its customers, etc. On the other hand, tourism planners and managers should be aware that benefits may not be easily measured quantitatively in the short term: the effects of introducing such a new organizational culture will lead to organizational competitiveness in the long term. So, possibly, instead of 'return of investment', tourism destinations and organizations should start thinking in terms of 'return on experience', thereby defining a new methodological approach to measure tourism business success, one that implies adopting a new culture built around tourists as part of the tourism product.

Concluding Remarks

As discussed above, to create experience value in tourism, it is necessary to design the whole experience by focusing on the tourist. But tourists are individuals; they display complex and varied behaviours. The root of all behaviours has been determined to be motivation. Tourists' motivations and interests determine their involvement in leisure activities, and explain the efforts they are willing to make in order to satisfy their needs. Consequently, involvement becomes a relevant moderator of tourist experience. As a result, creating experience value for tourists should be easily achieved if tourism destinations and organizations succeed in involving tourists. Toward this aim, it becomes essential to get a deep understanding of potential customers' needs and expectations. Although many efforts have been made by researchers in tourism and leisure fields, there are still questions left unanswered regarding the topic of this chapter. The first questions are how to segment tourist markets according to experiences sought? Which variables would reveal themselves useful in discriminating between various tourist segments? And once distinctive segments are identified, where should tourists be intercepted and presented with tourism experience propositions by businesses or the destination? To answer these questions, additional empirical marketing studies on distribution, communication and pricing strategies are necessary. A second issue to be addressed is about how to introduce in tourism management efficient indicators to help monitor the effectiveness of an organization in providing tourism experiences. Finally, additional longitudinal quantitative studies would allow researchers to track tourist needs and expectations across their life cycles. This would help with the analysis of the effects of factors such as previous tourism experiences or changes experienced in leisure preferences between the alternative leisure value propositions on motivations and levels of involvement. Such studies would also make possible the increased generalizability of the results of previous research, increasing our understanding of what constitutes a really memorable experience for tourists, at various points of their lives, in various countries, with diverse skills, interests, values and goals in life.... Leisure and tourism researchers have made much progress in the past 25 years, but consumer involvement and interest remain, in many ways, complex concepts. We can certainly suggest that they are central to tourist behaviour and to the creation of quality experiences, but much is yet to be tested and understood about their application and professional contributions.

References

Arnould, E. and Price, L. (1993) River magic: extraordinary experience and the extended service encounter. *Journal of Consumer Research* 20(1), 24–45.

Ballantyne, R., Packer, J. and Sutherland, L.A. (2011) Visitors' memories of wildlife tourism: implications for the design of powerful interpretive experiences. *Tourism Management* 32, 770–779.

Beatty, S.E., Kahle, L.R. and Homer, P. (1988) The involvement-commitment model: theory and implications. *Journal of Business Research* 16(2), 149–167.

Bitner, M.J, Faranda, W.T., Hubbert, A.R. and Zeithaml, V.A. (1997) Customer contributions and roles in service delivery. *International Journal of Service Industry Management* 8(3), 193–205.

Bloch, P. and Bruce, G. (1984) Product involvement as leisure behavior. *Advances in Consumer Research* 11, 197–202.

Bloch, P.H., Black, W.C. and Lichtenstein, D. (1989) Involvement with the equipment component of sport: links to recreational commitment. *Leisure Sciences* 11, 187–200.

Bricker, K.S. and Kerstetter, D.L. (2000) Level of specialization and place attachment: an exploratory study of white water recreationists. *Leisure Sciences* 22, 233–257.

Bueno, M. and Rameckers, L. (2003) Understanding people in new ways – personas in context: forging a stronger link between research and its application in design. *Proceedings of the Esomar Conference*, Venice, Italy, pp. 1–15.

Cai, L.A., Feng, R. and Breiter, D. (2004) Tourist purchase decision involvement and information preferences. *Journal of Vacation Marketing* 10(2), 138–148.

Canadian Tourism Commission (2004) *Defining Tomorrow's Tourism Product: Packaging Experiences.* Research report, 2004–2007. Canadian Tourism Commission, Ottawa, pp. 1–41.

Cary, S.H. (2004) The tourist moment. *Annals of Tourism Research* 31(1), 61–77.

Celsi, R.L. and Olson, J.C. (1988) The role of involvement in attention and comprehension processes. *Journal of Consumer Research* 15, 210–224.

Celsi, R.L., Rose, R. and Leigh, T. (1993) An exploration of high-risk leisure consumption through skydiving. *Journal of Consumer Research* 20(1), 1–23.

Chen, C.F. and Tsai, M. (2008) Perceived value, satisfaction and loyalty of TV travel product shopping: involvement as a moderator. *Tourism Management* 29(6), 1166–1171.

Clements, C. and Josiam, B. (1995) Role of involvement in the travel decision. *Journal of Vacation Marketing* 1(4), 337–348.

Coghlan, A. and Pearce, P. (2010) Tracking affective components of satisfaction. *Tourism and Hospitality Research* 10(1), 42–58.

Cohen, E. (1979) A phenomenology of tourist experiences. *Sociology* 13(2), 179–201.

Colton, C.W. (1987) Leisure, recreation, tourism. A symbolic interactionism view. *Annals of Tourism Research* 14, 545–560.

Cronin, J., Brady, M.K. and Hult, G. (2000) Assessing the effects of quality, value, and customer satisfaction on consumer behavioral intentions in service environments. *Journal of Retailing* 76(2), 193–218.

Csíkszentmihályi, M. (1990) *Flow: The Psychology of Optimal Experience.* Harper and Row, New York.

Csíkszentmihályi, M. (1998) *Finding Flow: The Psychology of Engagement with Everyday Life.* HarperCollins, New York.

Csíkszentmihályi, M. and LeFevre, J. (1989) Optimal experience in work and leisure. *Journal of Personality and Social Psychology* 56(5), 815.

Dann, G., Nash, D. and Pearce, P. (1988) Methodology in tourism research. *Annals of Tourism Research* 15(1), 1–28.

Dimanche, F. (2010) En quête de la génération 'C': pour un nouvel agenda de recherche marketing et tourisme [The quest for the 'C' generation: a new tourism marketing research agenda]. *Mondes du Tourisme* 1(1), 30–38.

Dimanche, F. and Samdahl, D. (1994) Leisure as symbolic consumption: a conceptualization and prospectus for future research. *Leisure Sciences* 16(2), 119–129.

Dimanche, F., Havitz, M.E. and Howard, D.R. (1991) Testing the Involvement Profile (IP) scale in the context of selected recreational and touristic activities. *Journal of Leisure Research* 23(1), 51–66.

Dwyer, L., Mellor, R., Livaic, Z., Edwards, D. and Kim, C. (2004) Attributes of destination competitiveness: a factor analysis. *Tourism Analysis* 9(1/2), 91–102.

Engel, J.F. and Blackwell, R.D. (1982) *Consumer Behavior*, 4th edn. Dryden Press, New York.

Ferns, B. and Walls, A. (2012) Enduring travel involvement, destination brand equity, and travelers' visit intentions: a structural model analysis. *Journal of Destination Marketing and Management* 1(1/2), 27–35.

Gahwiler, P. and Havitz, M.E. (1998) Toward a relational understanding of leisure social worlds, involvement, psychological commitment, and behavioral loyalty. *Leisure Sciences* 20(1), 1–23.

Giddens, A. (1990) *The Consequences of Modernity.* Polity Press, Cambridge.

Giddens, A. (1991) *Modernity and Self-Identity. Self and Society in the Late Modern Age.* Polity Press, Cambridge.

Gnoth, J. and Knobloch, U. (2012) Segmenting tourism markets by experiences. *Proceedings of the 2nd Interdisciplinary Tourism Research Conference*, 24–29 April, Fethiye, Turkey, pp. 385–398.

Haggard, L.M. and Williams, D.R. (1992) Identity affirmation through leisure activities: leisure symbols of the self. *Journal of Leisure Research* 24, 1–18.

Hamilton-Smith, E. (1987) Four kinds of tourism. *Annals of Tourism Research* 14(3), 332–344.

Havitz, M. and Dimanche, F. (1997) Leisure involvement revisited: conceptual conundrums and measurement advances. *Journal of Leisure Research* 29(3), 245–278.

Havitz, M.E. and Dimanche, F. (1999) Leisure involvement revisited: drive properties and paradoxes. *Journal of Leisure Research* 31(2), 122–149.

Hoffman, E., Kaneshiro, S. and Compton, W.C. (2012) Peak-experiences among Americans in midlife. *Journal of Humanistic Psychology* 52(4), 479–503.

Hotel Lugano (nd) Available at: https://mypage.hotel-luganodante.com/mypage

Hsu, S.Y., Dehuang, N. and Woodside, A. (2009) Storytelling research of consumers' self-reports of urban tourism experiences in China. *Journal of Business Research* 62(12), 1223–1254.

Iwasaki, Y. and Havitz, M.E. (1998) A path analytic model of the relationships between involvement, psychological commitment and loyalty. *Journal of Leisure Research* 30(2), 256–280.

Iwasaki, Y. and Havitz, M.E. (2004) Examining relationships between leisure involvement, psychological commitment and loyalty to a recreation agency. *Journal of Leisure Research* 36(1), 45–72.

Jamrozy, U., Backman, S.J. and Backman, K.F. (1996) Involvement and opinion leadership in tourism. *Annals of Tourism Research* 23(4), 908–924.

Jorgensen, B. and Stedman, R. (2001) Sense of place as an attitude: lakeshore owners' attitudes toward their properties. *Journal of Environmental Psychology* 21(3), 233–248.

Kim, J.H., Ritchie, J.R.B. and McCormick, B. (2012) Development of a scale to measure memorable tourism experiences. *Journal of Travel Research* 51(1), 12–25.

Kim, S.S., Scott, D. and Crompton, J.L. (1997) An exploration of the relationships among social psychological involvement, behavioral involvement, commitment, and future intentions in the context of bird-watching. *Journal of Leisure Research* 29(3), 320–339.

Kyle, G. and Chick, G. (2004) Enduring leisure involvement: the importance of relationships. *Leisure Studies* 23(3), 243–266.

Kyle, G. and Mowen, A. (2005) An examination of the leisure involvement–agency commitment relationship. *Journal of Leisure Research* 37(3), 342–363.

Kyle, G., Graefe, A., Manning, R. and Bacon, J. (2003) An examination of the relationship between leisure activity involvement and place attachment among hikers along the Appalachian Trail. *Journal of Leisure Research* 35(3), 249–273.

Kyle, G., Absher, J.D., Hammitt, W.E. and Cavin, J. (2006) An examination of the motivation–involvement relationship. *Leisure Sciences* 28(5), 467–485.

Kyle, G., Absher, J., Norman, W., Hammitt, W. and Jodice, L. (2007) A modified involvement scale. *Leisure Studies* 26(4), 399–427.

Laurent, G. and Kapferer, J.N. (1985) Measuring consumer involvement profiles. *Journal of Marketing Research* 22, 41–53.

Lee, J. and Beeler, C. (2009) An investigation of predictors of satisfaction and future intention: links to motivation, involvement, and service quality in a local festival. *Event Management* 13(1), 17–29.

Lumberjack World Championships (nd) Available at: http://www.lumberjackworldchampionships.com/

MacCannell, D. (1976) *The Tourist: A New Theory of the Leisure Class*. Schocken Books, New York.

Mannell, R. and Iso-Ahola, S. (1987) Psychological nature of leisure and tourist experience. *Annals of Tourism Research* 14(3), 314–331.

McGregor, I. and Holmes, J.G. (1999) How storytelling shapes memory and impressions of relationship events over time. *Journal of Personality and Social Psychology* 76(3), 403–419.

McIntyre, N. (1989) The personal meaning of participation: enduring involvement. *Journal of Leisure Research* 21(2), 167–179.

McIntyre, N. and Pigram, J.J. (1992) Recreation specialization re-examined: the case of vehicle-based campers. *Leisure Sciences* 14(1), 3–15.

McQuarrie, E. and Munson, M. (1987) The Zaichkowsky Personal Involvement Inventory: modification and extension. In: Anderson, P. and Wallendorf, M. (eds) *Advances in Consumer Research* 14. Association for Consumer Research, Ann Arbor, Michigan, pp. 36–40.

Meyer, C. and Schwager, A. (2007) Understanding customer experience. *Harvard Business Review* 85(2), 116–126.

Mills, P.K. and Morris, J.H. (1986) Clients as 'partial' employees: role development in client participation. *Academy of Management Review* 11(4), 726–735.

Moore, R.L. and Graefe, A. (1994) Attachments to recreation settings: the case of rail-trail users. *Leisure Sciences* 16(1), 17–31.

Morgan, M. (2006) Making space for experiences. *Journal of Retail and Leisure Property* 5(4), 305–313.

Nash, D. and Smith, V. (1991) Anthropology and tourism. *Annals of Tourism Research* 18(1), 12–25.

Neuhofer, B., Buhalis, D. and Ladkin, A. (2013) High tech for high touch experiences: a case study from the hospitality industry. Paper presented at *The ENTER Conference*, Innsbruck.

Obenour, W., Patterson, M., Pedersen, P. and Pearson, L. (2006) Conceptualization of a meaning-based research approach for tourism service experiences. *Tourism Management* 27(1), 34–41.

O'Sullivan, E.L. and Spangler, K.J. (1998) *Experience Marketing: Strategies for the New Millennium*. Venture, State College, Pennsylvania.

Otto, J. and Ritchie, J.R.B. (1996) The service experience in tourism. *Tourism Management* 17(3), 165–174.

Parasuraman, A., Zeithaml, V.A. and Berry, L.L. (1998) SERVQUAL: a multiple-item scale for measuring consumer perceptions of service quality. *Journal of Retailing* 64(1), 12–40.

Pine, B.J. and Gilmore, J.H. (1999) *The Experience Economy: Work is Theater and Every Business a Stage*. Harvard Business School Press, Boston, Massachusetts.

Prahalad, C.K. and Ramaswamy, V. (2003) The new frontier of experience innovation. *MIT Sloan Management Review* 44(4), 12–18.

Prahalad, C.K. and Ramaswamy, V. (2004) *The Future of Competition: Co-creating Unique Value with Customers*. Harvard Business School Press, Boston, Massachusetts.

Prayag, G., Dimanche, F. and Keup, M. (2012) Designing tourism services. In: Stickdorn, M. and Birgit, F. (eds) *Service Design and Tourism*. Books on Demand, Norderstedt, Germany, pp. 35–47.

Prebensen, N.K., Vitterso, J. and Dahl, T.I. (2013a) Value co-creation significance of tourist resources. *Annals of Tourism Research* 42, 240–261.

Prebensen, N.K., Woo, E., Chen, J.S. and Uysal, M. (2013b) Motivation and involvement as antecedents of the perceived value of the destination experience. *Journal of Travel Research* 52(2), 253–264.

Prebensen, N.K., Woo, E. and Uysal, M. (2013c) Experience value: antecedents and consequences. *Current Issues in Tourism* (in press).

Quan, S. and Wang, N. (2004) Towards a structural model of the tourist experience: an illustration from food experiences in tourism. *Tourism Management* 25(3), 297–305.

Quinlan-Cutler, S. and Carmichael, B. (2012) The dimensions of the tourist experience. In: Morgan, M., Lugosi, P. and Ritchie, J.R.B. (eds) *The Tourism and Leisure Experience: Consumer and Managerial Perspectives*. Channel View, Bristol, UK, pp. 3–26.

Raymond, C.M., Brown, G. and Weber, D. (2010) The measurement of place attachment: personal, community, and environmental connections. *Journal of Environmental Psychology* 30(4), 422–434.

Redfoot, D.L. (1984) Touristic authenticity, touristic angst and modern reality. *Qualitative Sociology* 7, 291–309.

Reissman, C.K. (1993) *Narrative Analysis*. Sage, Newbury Park, California.

Richards, G. (1999) Vacations and quality of life: patterns and structures. *Journal of Business Research* 44, 189–198.

Richins, M.L. and Bloch, P.H. (1986) After the new wears off: the temporal context of product involvement. *Journal of Consumer Research* 13, 280–285.

Richins, M.L., Bloch, P.H. and McQuarrie, E.F. (1992) How enduring and situational involvement combine to create involvement responses. *Journal of Consumer Psychology* 1(2), 143–153.

Ritchie, J.R.B. and Crouch, G. (2003) *The Competitive Destination: A Sustainable Tourism Perspective.* CAB International, Wallingford, UK.

Rothschild, M.L. (1984) Perspectives on involvement: current problems and future directions. *Advances in Consumer Research* 11, 216–217.

Ryan, C. (1997) *The Tourist Experience: A New Introduction.* Cassell, London.

Schmitt, B. (1999) Experiential marketing. *Journal of Marketing Management* 15, 53–67.

Selin, S.W. and Howard, D.R. (1988) Ego involvement and leisure behavior: a conceptual specification. *Journal of Leisure Research* 20(3), 237–244.

Sharpley, R. and Jepson, D. (2011) Rural tourism: a spiritual experience? *Annals of Tourism Research* 38(1), 52–71.

Small, J. (1999) Memory-work: a method for researching women's tourist experiences. *Tourism Management* 20(1), 25–35.

Smith, S.L.J. (1994) The tourism product. *Annals of Tourism Research* 21(3), 582–595.

Tung, V. and Ritchie, J.R.B. (2011) Exploring the essence of memorable tourism experiences. *Annals of Tourism Research* 38(4), 1367–1386.

Unger, L. and Kernan, J. (1983) On the meaning of leisure: an investigation of some determinants of the subjective experience. *Journal of Consumer Research* 9(4), 381–392.

Uysal, M. and Noe, F. (2003) Satisfaction in outdoor recreation and tourism settings. In: Laws, E. (ed.) *Case Studies in Tourism Marketing.* Continuum, London, pp. 140–158.

Volo, S. (2010) Bloggers' reported tourist experiences: their utility as a tourism data source and their effect on prospective tourists. *Journal of Vacation Marketing* 16(4), 297–311.

Wang, W., Chen, J.S., Fan, L. and Lu, J. (2012) Tourist experience and wetland parks: a case of Zhejiang, China. *Annals of Tourism Research* 39(4), 1763–1778.

Williams, D.R., Patterson, M.E., Roggenbuck, J.W. and Watson, A.E. (1992) Beyond the commodity metaphor: examining emotional and symbolic attachment to place. *Leisure Sciences* 14, 29–46.

Xu, J.B. (2010) Perceptions of tourism products. *Tourism Management* 31(5), 607–610.

Zaichkowsky, J.L. (1985) Measuring the involvement construct. *Journal of Consumer Research* 12(3), 341–352.

9 Authenticity as a Value Co-creator of Tourism Experiences

HAYWANTEE RAMKISSOON[1] AND MUZAFFER UYSAL[2]

[1]Monash University, Melbourne, Australia; [2]Pamplin College of Business, Virginia Tech, Blacksburg, USA

Introduction

Authenticity is a term that has long been discussed in the literature, resulting in a number of studies on its differing conceptualizations and usage. Introduced by MacCannell (1973) to sociological studies of tourist motivations and experiences, the term has since been widely used in tourism studies. Recent decades have witnessed increasing demand from tourism for new and authentic experiences. The modern and sophisticated tourist expresses increasing interest in learning, exploring and experiencing tourist attractions (Ramkissoon and Uysal, 2010; Chhabra, 2012; Mkono, 2012; Zhu, 2012) and interestingly seeks to co-create valuable tourist experiences (Prebensen and Foss, 2011). The creation of authenticity remains important in tourism and prompts the desire to create and add value to the experience (Taylor, 2001). The experience of the tourism product (both tangible and intangible) however is unique to the consumer (Jewell and Crotts, 2002). Authenticity is embraced in the consumption process to add value to the tourist's experience.

The tourism industry can only project authenticity but cannot determine whether the tourist is having a real experience (Prentice, 2001). It is therefore important to create platforms where the tourist explores, engages, participates and co-creates authentic experiences. The authentic experience arguably is not an end in itself but a means to allow the tourist to enhance the quality of his/her experience. The interaction between the tourist and object may become the site where value is generated (Taylor, 2001). Authenticity as a co-creator of value is important to the tourist in that it generates a sense of well-being. Neff and Suizzo (2006) argue that authenticity is strongly associated with a sense of well-being. It is equally important to the tourism industry in that it provides a pathway to add value to the tourism product. As the basis of the economy changes (Pine and Gilmore, 1999), the consumer taking for granted the tourism product (Richards, 2001) demands engaging, absorbing experiences. Creating such experiences necessitates an understanding of authenticity perceived by the 'self'. As put eloquently forward by

Cohen, 'the question here is not whether the individual does or does not really have an authentic experience in MacCannell's (1973) sense, but rather what endows his experience with authenticity in his own view' (1988, p. 378). In this sense, authenticity may not be simply treated as a socially constructed concept (as suggested MacCannell, 1973) but a concept that is 'negotiable' in terms of its meanings and the extent to which tourism experiences are perceived to be authentic, scaled on a continuum from complete authenticity, through various stages of partial authenticity, to complete falseness (Cohen, 1988). This point implies that authenticity, however it may be perceived, has the inherent potency to contribute to one's quality of vacation experience in the setting, thus creating value in tourism experiences and enhancing the subjective well-being of tourists and their expressive consumption of tourism goods such as arts and culture. However, the impact of perceived authenticity on consumption has received very limited empirical investigation. One such study was recently carried out by Casteran and Roederer (2013), who examined how the perception of authenticity is constructed and how authenticity can explain behaviour based on the dimensions of authenticity, namely originality and artificiality as articulated by Camus (2010). Their work revealed that the market that is perceived to be an 'original' (a lack of artificial components) explained differences in visiting frequency in the selected market, Strasbourg Christmas Market. This signals the fact that creating such experiences necessitates an understanding of authenticity perceived by the 'self' as tourists and the perceived value of such experiences. This implication of authenticity also reveals some support for the notion of existential authenticity of experiences, thus adopting an authentic attitude (Brown, 2013). Indeed, only a few studies have investigated authenticity and its role as a value co-creator of tourist experiences. Yet, the experience of tourism sites cannot be complete without the engagement with the self (Breathnach, 2006).

This chapter attempts to analyse how tourists' self-interpretive meanings of their 'authentic' cultural heritage experience contribute to construct their own definitions of the term enhancing the value of consumption experience. It deals with tourists' co-created experiences at cultural sites and landscape in the island of Mauritius, highlighting future opportunities for its tourism industry. This is essential for the development of appropriate cultural heritage marketing strategies for the island. It opens doors for additional research avenues exploring authenticity as a value co-creator of tourism experiences.

Literature Review

Authenticity has for a long time been acknowledged as a driving force motivating tourists to consume cultural heritage (Kolar and Zabkar, 2010; Ramkissoon and Uysal, 2010; Chhabra, 2012) and remains an important area of research in cultural heritage marketing and management (Asplet and Cooper, 2000; Lynch et al., 2011). Tourists often seek authentic experiences as a result of the increasing fragmentation caused by modernity (MacCannell, 1976). However, the meaning and value of authentic experience have become rather elusive and it is more defined by the self and the nature of the interaction with the setting in which tourism experiences are produced and consumed with different goal orientations towards cultural tourism consumption. While Hewison (1989) and Urry (1990) do share MacCannell's view that authenticity should be measured in an objective way, Wang (1999) suggests what is important is to clarify its meaning in tourist experiences. Indeed in today's travel market, what has changed is the meaning and interpretation of authenticity; once contrived and inauthentic cultural products may, in the course of time, be recognized as authentic (Cohen, 1988). With cultural heritage becoming the focus of tourism business (Hughes and Carlsen, 2010), the question that arises is what the concept represents in cultural tourism consumption. Is it a property of the toured object, the tourist's state of mind or perception, and/or tourist experiences co-created at the cultural offerings?

Tourists' motivations or experiences cannot be explained in terms of the conventional concepts of authenticity. It has given rise to much criticism and demands substantive investigation (Wang, 1999). The tourism industry can only project authenticity but cannot determine whether the tourists are having a real experience (Prentice, 2001). Hence, it becomes important to understand the relationship between object and self (Wang, 1999). A number of studies have delved into the co-creation of valuable vacation experiences for tourists (e.g. Volo, 2009; Prebensen and Foss, 2011). The tourist object often plays an important role in creating the atmosphere which influences the tourist experience (Reisinger and Steiner, 2006). The tourists relate to these objects, build the experience (Pine and Gilmore, 1999; Morgan et al., 2009) and may hence influence their interpretation of authenticity. The perceived authenticity of the object hence could be a manifestation of the tourist's participation, engagement, learning and reflection (Stebbins, 1996; McKercher and du Cros, 2002) at tourist attractions. Broadening notions of authenticity reflect the term as an instrument for co-creation of tourist experiences.

Thrilling argued that authenticity in tourism was first applied to museums where experts wanted to determine 'whether objects of art are what they appear to be or are claimed to be, and therefore worth the price that is asked for them or … worth the admiration they are being given' (1972, p. 93). Tourists, tourism marketers and academics extended this museum-linked usage to products such as gastronomy, festivals, dress, rituals or housing (Reisinger and Steiner, 2006). Adams (1996) argued culture and authenticity are but products constructed by tourists and hosts themselves. Sharpley (1994) referred to authenticity in tourism as traditional culture and its origin, in the sense of the real, genuine and unique product. It has to do not only with genuineness and the reliability of face value, but with tourists' desire and their interpretation of genuineness (Spooner, 1986, 2000). McIntosh and Prentice (1999) further concluded that what is presumed to be authentic, whether applied to a museum or a retail shop, depends not only on the interpretation provided for the displays but also on the viewer. Wang (1999) shared a similar view showing that things appear to be authentic not because they are inherently so, but because their genuineness is perceived by the viewers. Congruent with Wang's view, Bruner (1994) also argued that authenticity is dependent on interpretation of history or time and is not inherently found in the object.

Wang (1999) proposed two kinds of authenticity, authenticity of the toured object and existential authenticity, arguing that both terms can co-exist. Existential authenticity, being subjective in nature (Poria et al., 2003), has more power to explain tourist experiences, referring to one's state of mind, perceptions and feelings of being in touch with oneself (Reisinger and Steiner, 2006). Tourists search for their authentic selves with the aid of toured objects rather than searching for the authenticity of these objects (Wang, 1999). Selwyn (1996) conceptualized authenticity as 'hot' and 'cool'. Toured objects, for instance cultural sites, provide tourists with 'hot' authenticity as they provide a more real experience as compared to one's everyday life. The 'hot' authenticity concept focuses on the authentic self as opposed to the authentic object. Object authenticity, on the other hand, reflects the genuineness of artefacts and events (Reisinger and Steiner, 2006), advocating pure, original and local versions of heritage (Chhabra, 2012). The theoplacity discourse is yet another prominent view of authenticity (Belhassen *et al.*, 2008), reflecting the merging of existential and objective seeking to integrate social and cultural meanings with physical objects (Chhabra, 2010).

With the quest for authenticity sought by the modern, sophisticated tourist of today (Kolar and Zabkar, 2010; Ramkissoon and Uysal, 2010; Casteran and Roederer, 2013), there is in fact an emerging need to explore how tourists' emotions and state of mind (hot or existential) are entwined with the objective (e.g. tourist sites) to co-create and add value to the authentic experiences. It is argued that existential and objective authenticity formations do not sufficiently explain the full gamut of tourist experiences. Understanding what is considered to be authentic in tourism consumption presents a challenge for destination marketers. The preceding discussion and points mentioned suggest that the perceived value and importance of the object to the self is a better measure of authenticity than a philosophical approach to objective authenticity.

The next section attempts to fill this gap in the literature, using the island of Mauritius as a case study. It investigates tourists' engagement and consumption of the cultural and natural heritage sites of the island, fuelling a discussion on how the authenticity of the self may be experienced through the representations at the sites and engagement and participation of the respondents.

The Case Study

Mauritius, an island with a land area of around 1860 square kilometres, is situated in the western Indian Ocean, off the south-east coast of Africa. Over the past 30 years, the Mauritian economy has diversified from a sugar cane-based mono-crop economy to one based on sugar, textiles, financial services and tourism. The island currently receives around 982,000 visitors annually (Central Statistical Office, 2011). In light of the structural changes occurring in the island, the tourism industry has been called to play a very important role in the economic and social development of the island. This is evidenced by the government's renewed interest in the tourism industry, with a policy objective of achieving two million tourist arrivals by 2020. Consequently, a number of policy measures have been taken in this direction, part of which is the development of cultural and heritage assets of the destination. The sun, sand and sea remain the main tourism products. However, the government is seeking to develop and promote cultural tourism in an attempt to diversify the existing tourism product and attract high spending and low impact tourists. The island hosts a number of natural and cultural attractions, which are now being increasingly marketed by the

Mauritius Tourism Promotion Authority. Examples of natural and cultural sites of the island include botanical gardens, waterfalls, natural landscape and scenic heritage, museums, religious sites and historical monuments, amongst others.

Through an analysis of previous studies on the selection of cultural tourism sites, the present study sought to identify a series of natural and cultural heritage sites across the island. A total of ten sites were identified and site inspection visits were arranged in June 2009 to assess their suitability for conducting fieldwork. The respective sites were further categorized into site types, namely: religious sites, museums, markets, industrial heritage sites, built heritage sites, commercial redevelopment, gardens and natural heritage sites. The site inspection allowed a detailed analysis of each site, thus enabling the researcher to reflect and comment on their suitability for the purpose of this study. Table 9.1 presents a description of the ten sites retained for the study. Given the importance of the authenticity construct for this piece of research, the site characteristics also helped in understanding how authenticity relates to the various attractions.

The exploratory study employs a qualitative research approach to investigate authenticity as a co-creator of the cultural tourism experience. The fieldwork for this

Table 9.1. Cultural and natural heritage sites.

Site name	Site type	Site characteristics
Grand Bassin	Religious site	Symbolic site. Natural lake within the crater of an extinct volcano hosting the second world's largest statue of the Hindu deity, Lord Shiva. It is an important pilgrimage site for Hindus.
Mahebourg Museum	Museum	Traditional museum with artefacts of Mauritian history.
Blue Penny Museum	Museum	Contemporary museum focusing on the history of Mauritius, principally maritime and communication.
Mahebourg Market	Market	Market selling local crafts, vegetables, fruits, spices and savouries. Experiential attraction.
L'Aventure du Sucre	Industrial heritage	The sugar factory is interpreted by displays and is preceded by a mass of written material presented on display boards.
Domaine les Pailles	Industrial heritage	The sugar mill involves people in period costumes with an ox turning a mill. However, the wider site is principally a restaurant and conference complex. Tourists also visit natural heritage with jeep tours from the site.
SSR Botanical garden	Garden	Both natural and cultural site. Garden with native plants. It also holds cultural monuments.
Chamarel 7-coloured earth	Natural heritage	Natural scenic landscape with colourful mounds of earth resulting from erosion of volcanic ash.
Le Gorges viewpoint	Natural heritage	Spectacular natural and cultural landscape with native plants and species of birds.
Ile-aux-Aigrettes	Natural heritage	Coastal forest with native plants and species, once the home of the Dodo. The site is interpreted to tourists by personal guides.

study was conducted in June–July 2009. Tourists at the selected sites were approached on a next-to-pass basis and the aim of the research was explained. The study sought to examine tourists' personal experiences of object (cultural sites) authenticity and its role as a value co-creator of tourism experiences in a cultural tourism context. They were further asked if they would be willing to participate. A total of 40 in-depth interviews were conducted with tourists. If one respondent refused to participate, the next available person was approached. The interviews were tape recorded with the consent of the participants. The length of the interviews varied from 30 to 45 minutes each. The recorded information was transcribed into keyword written notes on the same day of the interview to ensure that all the conversational data were captured while the interview sessions were still fresh in the mind of the interviewer. Each interview was individually tailored to elicit the rich information where respondents freely expressed their ideas and opinions. Further to completing the semi-structured interviews, individual transcripts of all interviews were read several times, the similarities and differences were grouped, and the important emerging themes were identified (Miles and Hubermann, 1994). Manual coding of the data was effected with the 40 transcribed interview notes. Overall, a number of common themes emerged from the visitor survey and, as argued by Ryan and Cave (2005), this is particularly true when a common structure is used for the questioning. Codes and categories derived from the emerging important themes allowed the analyst to spot quickly, draw out and cluster (Miles and Hubermann, 1994) all the particular segments relating to the particular question, concept or theme. Relevant literature was consulted for a more theoretically informed examination of the emerging themes and categories. This allowed an in-depth and exploratory analysis of the data sets. Respondents consisted of 16 (40%) females and 24 (60%) males. The vast majority (87.5%) were from Europe, aged 18–65 years, with more than half being aged 25–34 years. They were essentially white-collar workers (80%), with the remaining being skilled workers (2.5%), students (7.5%) and unemployed (10%). Most respondents (80%) were on their first visit to the island. The visitor profile is comparable to statistics collected by the Central Statistical Office (2011).

Discussion and Implications

An analysis of the emergent themes allowed the researchers to unravel the meanings and interpretations of authenticity by the consumers of the cultural offerings, providing insights into how authenticity can help co-create cultural tourism experiences. An important finding that emerges from the data analysis is that the authenticity of the cultural heritage sites is a value or judgement brought forward by the consumer. The tourist is viewed as part of the authentication process rather than as a passive observer. Findings attest that the tourists' self-interpretation and meanings, combined with the experiences derived from the objects being consumed, served as a basis for their evaluation of authenticity. The respondents' experiences relate well to Wang (1999) and Cohen's (1979) existentialist view of authenticity. The existential tourist lives in two worlds, the world devoid of meaning where one considers himself/herself to be living in exile and the real world where one experiences his/her real self. In the present context, the cultural and natural sites allowed the participants to be away from their routine activities, providing an opportunity to reflect on one's sense of self. Consistent with the views of Ferrara (1998), findings show that existential authenticity is a key issue of contention for cultural and natural heritage sites. Consumers of heritage necessitate reflection on these objects during the consumption process and often the experience involves feelings and emotions (Domenico and Miller, 2012).

Some of the participants emphasized the intangible experiential factor, although they claim that the tangible elements play an important role in their overall evaluation of their experience as being authentic. These emerging findings suggest tourists tend to prefer a merging of existential, objective and experiential elements. This supports Chhabra's (2012) contention that authenticity can be traced to the objective, which she describes as genuine versions of heritage, and existential, the subjective version of the term reflecting one's perception, self discovery and truth of the moment (Poria *et al.*, 2003; Reisinger and Steiner, 2006). Findings further support the experiential characteristic of authenticity defined as trueness to oneself (Thrilling, 1974). Our findings corroborate with Chang *et al.*'s (2011) study of the travel dining experience. These three elements may constitute the totality of the participants' interpretation of authenticity. This is reflected in the interview excerpts.

> the garden is amazing giving me a sense of psychological restorativeness. It has been so long since I have had such a beautiful experience and the trees and lake of the SSR botanical garden make me feel fresh and rejuvenated. I feel that I have reconnected with nature and with myself and I am experiencing a deep sense of well-being here …

> I had an amazing experience at Le Gorges Viewpoint. The spectacular views of the mountain ranges allowed me to reconnect with nature, something that I always seek for when I go on holiday …

> I will want to visit a second time. Ile-aux-Aigrettes has such scenic views and the history was well elaborated by our tour guide. The indigenous nature and wildlife and past history created the magic of the experience. Only when I travel can I afford these luxuries …

From the present research it is evident that tourists made frequent reference to authenticity of the experience and place. This is consistent with Brown's (2013) view, suggesting that place and experience play a significant role in conceptualizing tourism as a catalyst for existential authenticity. Not only did the visit to the cultural and natural heritage sites allowed a break from the routine, as Wang (1999) would suggest, it also made the consumers of place realize their authentic self. Individuals with more experience with natural environments may express stronger emotional connections than those with less experience (Hinds and Sparks, 2008). This particularly shows how the tourist co-creates authenticity and adds value to his/her experience through emotional connections with the surroundings, allowing reflection on one's sense of self.

In a tourism/leisure context, tourists' engagement with the cultural and natural settings gives rise to a sense of emotional well-being (Ramkissoon *et al.*, 2012). Such settings tend to further increase positive emotions in individuals about the cultural/natural object (Ulrich, 1979; Hartig *et al.*, 1996), hence generating a sense of psychological well-being for tourists (Kaplan and Talbot, 1983; Korpela *et al.*, 2009). Our findings suggest that these natural and cultural settings allow the authentic self to emerge (Brown, 2013), offering an opportunity for self-exploration and wellness (Brown 2009; Lean, 2009). This embodies the co-creation of the 'authentic' between the cultural tourist and the surroundings. This interaction allows the co-creation of value in the tourist's experience. However, tourists may not always seek to self reflect while they are on holiday. Nevertheless, visits to cultural and natural attractions allow one to be away from his/her familiar environment. Such settings may serve as a catalyst for existential authenticity (Wang, 1999; Brown, 2013) and contribute to wellness. Iso-Ahola (1982) further suggests that tourists desire to break from their routine environment to pursue personal/interpersonal rewards and achieve optimal experiences.

Another attribute participants emphasized was past history. The market has now changed with experienced and sophisticated tourists being more aware of the past history (Chhabra, 2012) and in quest of a rich heritage experience. People want to relive old ways of life through tourism, even if it is for a brief moment (Chhabra et al., 2003). The 'fake' hence acts as a vehicle into the past, showing representations of old traditions, events and ways of life (e.g. Donaldson, 1986). Replication is not intrinsically bad and can be the only way in which visitors can experience the original to some extent (Hall, 2007). Further, what is staged is not necessarily superficial as it contains elements of the original traditions, though it does involve displacement of cultural production from one place to another and modifications to fit into new conditions of time and place (Chhabra et al., 2003). Our findings support the literature and are exemplified in the participants' views:

> I loved seeing the ox turning the mill and this actually showed a representation of the past. This was an authentic feeling of being in the past days. It gave me a feeling of nostalgia with the past when sugarcane was being crushed using the ox-driven machinery …

> I felt that I had gone back in the past and am reliving it again. My experience at L'aventure du Sucre is unique and the old machinery is well in place. The displays clearly present how sugar is manufactured and besides I have acquired a lot of information on the history of the island …

> We consume sugar and this sugar museum provides a great insight into its manufacturing process. The old mill and machinery, the audio guides and visual displays make me feel it is an authentic museum. For me personally, I could connect to these objects satisfying my quest for knowledge on the manufacturing of sugar. I am living the experience and my visit to the factory museum is very worthwhile …

These quotes suggest that authenticity enhanced the quality of tourist experiences through engagement with the objects depicting past history and industrial heritage. These allowed reflections into the past, emotional connections and learning processes. By observing and identifying themselves with the surroundings, the cultural tourists co-create and enhance the value of their authentic experiences, generating a sense of well-being. This finding corroborates other studies (e.g. Morgan et al., 2009; Prebensen and Foss, 2011) and reinforces the premise that authenticity is not an end in itself but a means to enhance the tourism value of the sites and experience.

Conclusion

This chapter addresses a particular view of authenticity as a co-creator of value in cultural tourism experiences. This study outlines the findings from an empirical investigation of tourists consuming cultural and natural heritage sites on the island of Mauritius. By using the views and self meanings and interpretations of authenticity by the consumers of place, this research has allowed a deeper understanding of the term from the tourist's perspective. This allows reflection on how the experiential authentic experience can merge with the objective, hence adding value to the tourist experience. The findings offer a number of insights into the understanding of how tourists can authentically present their experiences in cultural tourism consumption by being part of the authentication process in contrast to being a passive observer. This implies that existential, objective and experiential authenticity may play significant roles in the co-creation of the authentic tourist experience. This is a noteworthy observation destination marketers may wish to focus on in developing and promoting their cultural tourism offerings. It could also be part of the destination branding strategies (Ahmad, 2013). For instance, the Mauritius Tourism Promotion Authority responsible for destination branding may liaise with the site managers and conduct further research into the objective and experiential elements of authenticity. This will be valuable in developing and formulating effective promotion strategies, ensuring that the products marketed are congruent with tourists' projections of authenticity.

This study has contributed to the theoretical discourses on the search for self (Cohen, 1979, 2010), objective authenticity (Reisinger and Steiner, 2006) and experiential authenticity (Thrilling, 1974; Prentice, 2001). While there is a growing body of work on these differing conceptualizations of authenticity, few studies explain how authenticity can be a value co-creator of tourism experiences leading to the tourist's sense of well-being. Implicit in these conceptualizations of authenticity is the notion that what tourists experience in consumption of culture and heritage is as authentic as they perceive authenticity to be, suggesting that authenticity is conceived in different degrees of strictness (Cohen, 1979). One then can make the argument that what tourists derive from the consumption of culture and heritage is likely to appeal to high-order needs of satisfaction and motivation, such as novelty seeking, prestige and learning. These higher-order needs certainly appeal more to subjective well-being of tourists as tourists engage in consumption. The setting also allows the participant to be part of the process of consumption, thus not only enabling the participant to co-create the nature of his/her experience but also add differing levels of value to his/her experience. Notwithstanding these issues, this chapter delivers valuable theoretical and practical outcomes. Attention in this chapter is directed towards the personal experiences of tourists at cultural and natural heritage sites, yielding valuable insights on how authenticity assists in tourists' engagement, participation and reflection of the self in the consumption process. It is expected that the findings would provide rich potential research avenues on authenticity as a value-added component in tourism experiences.

References

Adams, V. (1996) *Tigers of the Snow and Other Virtual Sherpas: An Ethnography of Himalayan Encounters.* Princeton University Press, Princeton, New Jersey.

Ahmad, A. (2013) The constraints of tourism development for a cultural heritage destination: the case of Kampong Ayer (water village) in Brunei, Darussalam. *Tourism Management Perspectives* 8, 106–113.

Asplet, M. and Cooper, M. (2000) Cultural designs in New Zealand souvenir clothing: the question of authenticity. *Tourism Management* 21(3), 307–312.

Belhassen, Y., Caton, K. and Stewart, W. (2008) The search for authenticity in the pilgrim experience. *Annals of Tourism Research* 35(3), 668–689.

Breathnach, T. (2006) Looking for the real me: looking for the self in heritage tourism. *Journal of Heritage Tourism* 1(2), 100–120.

Brown, L. (2009) The transformative power of the international sojourn: an ethnographic study of the international student experience. *Annals of Tourism Research* 36(3), 502–521.

Brown, L. (2013) Tourism, a catalyst for existential authenticity. *Annals of Tourism Research* 40, 176–190.

Bruner, E. (1994) Abraham Lincoln as authentic reproduction: a critique of postmodernism. *American Anthropologist* 96, 397–415.

Camus, S. (2010) L'authenticité d'un site touristique, ses antecedents et ses influences sur le touriste. *Gestion 2000* 27(1), 101–117.

Casteran, H. and Roederer, C. (2013) Does authenticity really affect behaviour? The case of Strasbourg Christmas market. *Tourism Management* 36, 153–163.

Central Statistical Office (2011) *Economic and Social Indicators: International Travel and Tourism.* Ministry of Finance and Economic Development, Port Louis, Mauritius.

Chang, R., Kivela, J. and Mak, A. (2011) Attributes that influence the evaluation of travel dining experience: when East meets West. *Tourism Management* 32, 307–316.

Chhabra, D. (2010) Back to the past: a sub-segment of Generation Y's perceptions of authenticity. *Journal of Sustainable Tourism* 18(6), 793–809.

Chhabra, D. (2012) A present-centred dissonant heritage management model. *Annals of Tourism Research* 39(3), 1701–1705.

Chhabra, D., Healy, R. and Sills, E. (2003) Staged authenticity and heritage tourism. *Annals of Tourism Research* 30(3), 702–719.

Cohen, E. (1979) A phenomenology of tourist experiences. *Sociology* 13, 179–201.

Cohen, E. (1988) Authenticity and commoditization in tourism. *Annals of Tourism Research* 15, 371–386.

Cohen, E. (2010) Chasing a myth? Searching for 'Self' through lifestyle travel. *Tourist Studies* 10(2), 117–133.

Domenico, M. and Miller, G. (2012) Farming and tourism enterprise: experiential authenticity in the diversification of independent small scale family farming. *Tourism Management* 33(2), 285–294.

Donaldson, E. (1986) *The Scottish Highlands Games in America.* Pelican, Los Angeles, California.

Ferrara, A. (1998) *Reflective Authenticity: Rethinking the Project of Authenticity.* Routledge, New York.

Hall, C.M. (2007) Response to Yeoman et al: the fakery of the authentic tourist. *Tourism Management* 28, 1139–1140.

Hartig, T., Book, A., Garvill, J., Olsson, T. and Garling, T. (1996) Environmental influences on psychological restoration. *Scandinavian Journal of Psychology* 37, 378–393.

Hewison, R. (1989) Heritage: an interpretation. In: Uzzell, D. (ed.) *Heritage Interpretation.* Belhaven, London, pp. 15–23.

Hinds, J. and Sparks, P. (2008) Engaging with the natural environment: the role of affective connection and identity. *Journal of Environmental Psychology* 28(2), 109–120.

Hughes, M. and Carlsen, J. (2010) The business of cultural heritage tourism: critical success factors. *Journal of Heritage Tourism* 5(1), 17–32.

Iso-Ahola, S.E. (1982) Toward a social psychological theory of tourism motivation: a rejoinder. *Annals of Tourism Research* 9(2), 256–262.

Jewell, B. and Crotts, J. (2002) Adding psychological value to heritage tourism experiences. *Journal of Travel and Tourism Marketing* 11(4), 13–28.

Kaplan, S. and Talbot, J.F. (1983) Psychological benefits of a wilderness experience. In: Altman, I. and Wohlwill, J.F. (eds) *Human Behavior and the Environment: Advances in Theory and Research: Behavior and the Natural Environment*. Plenum Press, New York, pp. 163–203.

Kolar, T. and Zabkar, V. (2010) A consumer-based model of authenticity: an oxymoron or the foundation of cultural heritage marketing? *Tourism Management* 31(5), 652–664.

Korpela, K., Ylen, M., Tyrvainen, L. and Silvennoinen, H. (2009) Stability of self-reported favourite places and place attachment over a 10-month period. *Journal of Environmental Psychology* 29, 95–100.

Lean, G. (2009) Transforming travel: inspiring sustainability. In: Bushell, R. and Sheldon, P. (eds) *Wellness and Tourism: Mind, Body, Spirit, Place*. Cognizant, New York, pp. 191–205.

Lynch, M., Duinker, P., Sheehan, L. and Chute, J. (2011) The demand for Mi'kmaw cultural tourism: tourist perspectives. *Tourism Management* 32(5), 977–986.

MacCannell, D. (1973) Staged authenticity: arrangements of social space in tourist settings. *American Journal of Sociology* 79, 589–603.

MacCannell, D. (1976) *The Tourist: A New Theory of the Leisure Class*. Macmillan, London.

McIntosh, A. and Prentice, R. (1999) Affirming authenticity: consuming cultural heritage. *Annals of Tourism Research* 26, 589–612.

McKercher, B. and Du Cros, H. (2002) *Cultural Tourism: The Partnership Between Tourism and Cultural Heritage Management*. Haworth Hospitality Press, New York.

Miles, M. and Hubermann, M. (1994) *Qualitative Data Analysis: A Sourcebook of New Methods*. Sage, London.

Mkono, M. (2012) Authenticity does matter. *Annals of Tourism Research* 39(1), 480–483.

Morgan, M., Elbe, J. and de Esteban Curiel, J. (2009) Has the experience economy arrived? The views of destination managers in three visitor-dependent areas. *International Journal of Tourism Research* 11, 201–216.

Neff, K. and Suizzo, M. (2006) Culture, power, authenticity and psychological well-being within romantic relationships: a comparison of European American and Mexican Americans. *Cognitive Development* 21, 441–457.

Pine, B. and Gilmore, J. (1999) *The Experience Economy: Work is Theater and Every Business a Stage*. Strategic Horizon, Aurora, Ohio.

Poria, Y., Butler, R. and Airey, D. (2003) The core of heritage tourism. *Annals of Tourism Research* 30(1), 238–254.

Prebensen, N. and Foss, L. (2011) Coping and co-creating in tourist experiences. *International Journal of Tourism Research* 13, 54–67.

Prentice, R. (2001) Experiential cultural tourism: museums and the marketing of the new romanticism of evoked authenticity. *Museum Management and Curatorship* 19(1), 5–26.

Ramkissoon, H. and Uysal, M. (2010) Testing the role of authenticity in cultural tourism consumption. *Tourism Analysis* 15(5), 571–583.

Ramkissoon, H., Smith, L. and Weiler, B. (2012) Relationships between place attachment, place satisfaction, and pro-environmental behaviour in an Australian national park. *Journal of Sustainable Tourism* 21(3), 434–457.

Reisinger, Y. and Steiner, C. (2006) Reconceptualizing object authenticity. *Annals of Tourism Research* 33(1), 65–86.

Richards, G. (2001) Gastronomy: an essential ingredient in tourism production and consumption. In: Hjalager, A.E. and Richards, G. (eds) *Tourism and Gastronomy*. Routledge, London, pp. 3–20.

Ryan, C. and Cave, J. (2005) Structuring destination image: a qualitative approach. *Journal of Travel Research* 44(2), 144–150.

Selwyn, T. (1996) Introduction. In: Selwyn, T. (ed.) *The Tourist Image: Myths and Myth-Making in Tourism.* Wiley, Chichester, UK, pp. 1–32.

Sharpley, R. (1994) *Tourism, Tourists and the Society.* ELM, Huntingdon, UK.

Spooner, B. (1986) Weavers and dealers: the authenticity of an oriental carpet. In: Appadurai, A. (ed.) *The Social Life of Things.* Cambridge University Press, Cambridge, pp. 195–235.

Spooner, D. (2000) Reflections on the place of Larkin. *Area* 32(2), 209–216.

Stebbins, R. (1997) Identity and cultural tourism. *Annals of Tourism Research* 24, 450–452.

Taylor, J. (2001) Authenticity and sincerity in tourism. *Annals of Tourism Research* 28(1), 7–26.

Thrilling, L. (1972) *Sincerity and Authenticity.* Oxford University Press, Oxford.

Thrilling, L. (1974) *Sincerity and Authenticity.* Harvard University Press, Cambridge, Massachusetts.

Ulrich, R.S. (1979) Visual landscape and psychological well-being. *Landscape Research* 4(1), 17–23.

Urry, J. (1990) *The Tourist Gaze: Leisure and Travel in Contemporary Societies.* Sage, London.

Volo, S. (2009) Conceptualizing tourist experience: a tourist based approach. *Journal of Hospitality Marketing and Management* 18(2/3), 111–126.

Wang, N. (1999) Rethinking authenticity in tourism experience. *Annals of Tourism Research* 26(2), 349–370.

Zhu, Y. (2012) Performing heritage: rethinking authenticity in tourism. *Annals of Tourism Research* 39(3), 1495–1513.

10 Experience Co-creation Depends on Rapport-building: Training Implications for the Service Frontline

VINCENT P. MAGNINI AND KASEY ROACH

Virginia Tech University, Blacksburg, USA

Introduction

Co-creation is characterized as the transformation of visitors from 'passive audiences' to 'active players' (Prahalad and Ramaswamy, 2000). As detailed in a value co-creation framework developed by Payne *et al.* (2008), such co-creation is centred on the relationship experience between the frontline provider and the customer. This relationship experience involves emotion, cognition and behaviour (Payne *et al.*, 2008). In fact, experiential consumption research and consumer culture theory (Arnould and Thompson, 2005) stress the vital role of emotions in the co-creation process. Within the context of co-creation, emotions can be used as a term to describe moods, feelings and affect-based personality traits (Payne *et al.*, 2008). Such moods, feelings and affect-based personality traits play a central part in the co-creation.

Because co-creation is often an emotion-centric process surrounding a series of interactions, 'rapport' is a construct that deserves attention in the co-creation literature. Rapport is a construct that is difficult to precisely define (Gremler and Gwinner, 2000), but we all know rapport when we feel it. Tickle-Degnen and Rosenthal state that individuals 'experience rapport when "they click" with each other or [feel] that the good interaction is due to "chemistry"' (1990, p. 286). Nearly a century ago, Park and Burgess stated, 'Rapport implies the existence of a mutual responsiveness, such that every member of the group reacts immediately, spontaneously, and sympathetically to the sentiments and attitudes of every other member' (1924, p. 893).

Despite the fact that rapport is a key element in the co-creation process, the co-creation literature has offered the topic little to no attention. This gap in the current literature is surprising given that value co-creation relies on the overlap between the provider sphere and the customer sphere (Grönroos and Voima, 2013). The purpose of this chapter, therefore, is to review and synthesize literature from disparate disciplines to offer a series of propositions regarding how firms can develop and offer a rapport-building training programme for its frontline providers. Such a review is useful because co-creation and rapport go hand-in-hand. Co-creation is stimulated by a sense of rapport between the frontline provider and visitor. As called for by Bolton (2006), firms must develop best practices for fostering co-creation. Calls such as this provide motivation for this chapter on rapport-building training design.

To achieve the desired intent of this chapter, the content proceeds as follows: First, as depicted in Fig. 10.1, a series of propositions are offered that address what training content should be included in a programme designed to teach frontline providers how to foster rapport. Second, several propositions are detailed describing how such training should be delivered in order to maximize its effectiveness. Next, propositions are extended that relate to how training transfer can be maximized when teaching rapport-building. Finally, the chapter concludes with a discussion of possibilities for future research extensions.

Rapport-building Training: A Content Perspective

Rapport-building can be bolstered in a service setting if the dramaturgical metaphor is stressed at the frontline. Specifically, it should be stressed in the service training that actors (the employees), an audience (the customers) and a stage exist in the service environment. As in a theatrical performance, therefore, the actor is considered to be on-stage when the audience can see or hear him or her. This dramaturgical metaphor serves as a powerful metaphor that guides norms of conduct in social

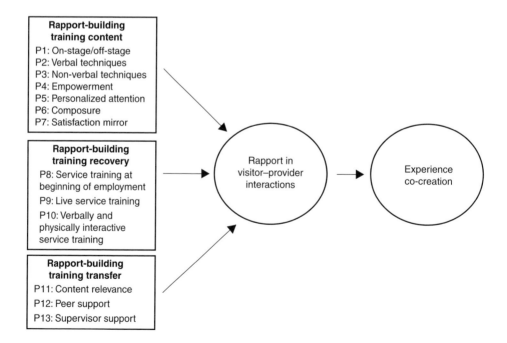

Fig. 10.1. Drivers of rapport-building training success.

interactions (Goffman, 1959) and in service environments (Grove and Fiske, 1983; Deighton, 1994). Service workers who internalize this metaphor are less likely to engage in off-stage acts and/or conversations while on-stage than workers who do not grasp the concept. This concept is important in co-creation because visitors expect that the provider plays a certain part in the exchange and feel uncomfortable when the provider exhibits off-stage behaviours or conversations. A provider is always on-stage, therefore should always exhibit on-stage behaviour. This provides consistency to a visitor, which builds rapport because it makes a visitor feel more relaxed always knowing what type of service s/he will receive, allowing him or her to avoid time spent on speculation or nervousness of what is to come. Also, utilizing tangible products in the performance ensures absolute consistency. For example, providing a burning fireplace in the lobby offers the visitor a physical feature that is the same throughout all performances no matter the provider.

On-stage behaviour makes a visitor feel important and valued. When s/he feels valued, s/he is more likely to return, and eventual loyalty leads to rapport. Taking all aspects of what goes into an on-stage performance, how well a provider performs contributes to the visitor's total impression of the service reality (Grove *et al.*, 1992). The combination of utilizing consistency throughout and valuing the visitor using the on-stage performance component leads to a positive impression, which leads to rapport.

Consequently, we offer the following proposition:

> P1: Firms that incorporate an on-stage/off-stage component in their service training for their frontline associates will achieve better rapport-building with visitors than firms that do not have an on-stage/off-stage training component.

The quality of a service interaction is judged, in part, on the quality of the verbal dialogue that characterizes the exchange (Noe *et al.*, 2010). Particular language and phrases serve to establish rapport, which yield co-creation (Noe *et al.*, 2010). This review contends, therefore, that verbal coaching should be incorporated into a service training system in order to enhance rapport-building at the frontline. Weak verbal communication habits should be identified and discussed – such as asking the customer 'Is everything OK?', because being 'OK' is a low bar to set in a service environment. On the flipside, strong verbal communication habits should also be identified and discussed – such as calling customers by their names and personalizing conversations whenever possible. As part of this verbal communication component, employees can be coached on some of the basic ways of remembering customers' faces and names (Magnini and Honeycutt, 2005).

Also regarding verbal communication, Hollman and Kleiner (1997) demonstrate that rapport can be fostered through empathetic listening and attentiveness. In spoken communication, empathetic listening is communicated when the service provider makes statements indicating that s/he can relate to the visitor (put him/herself in the visitor's shoes). Attentiveness is communicated verbally when the provider paraphrases segments of what the visitor has said. Both of these skills can be trained at the frontline. Based on these discussions, we offer the following proposition:

> P2: Firms that incorporate a verbal techniques component in their service training for their frontline associates will achieve better rapport-building with visitors than firms that do not have a verbal techniques training component.

While training pertaining to weak and strong verbal communication is quintessentially vital, it must also be recognized that most human communication transpires through non-verbal cues and gestures (Zaltman, 1997; Pease and Pease, 2004). Research dating back more than three decades finds that a service provider's non-verbal behaviours can have a significant influence on a customer's rapport perceptions (DiMatteo *et al.*, 1980). Knowing what kind of body language to use and not use is fundamental information that a service provider should internalize before engaging in interactions. As Smith (1995, p. 97) contends, people have certain expectations concerning specific non-verbal behaviours. Those gestures, expressions and intonations tending toward greater intimacy that can be used with care in a service situation include such behaviours as: (i) more smiling and positive facial expression; (ii) contact, including frequent and longer mutual gaze; (iii) more gesturing; (iv) forward body lean; (v) direct body orientation and more open body position; (vi) more head nods; (vii) closer distance or proximity; (viii) frequent touch (used with caution); (ix) moderate relaxation; (x) and less random body movement.

Research indicates that such non-verbal gestures play a significant role in rapport-building (Tickle-Degnen and Rosenthal, 1990). Tickle-Degnen and Rosenthal (1987) contend that rapport is highest when an encounter is characterized by a high level of mutual attentiveness between parties. Three non-verbal predictors of attentiveness include: eye contact, physical proximity and head nodding (Bernieri *et al.*, 1996). In a similar vein, smiling is perhaps one of the most significant non-verbal rapport builders (Duggan and Parrott, 2001). Dale Carnegie states it best: 'Actions speak louder than words, and a smile says, "I like you. You make me happy. I am glad to see you."' (1936, p. 63).

Based on these discussions, it is posited that customer service training that incorporates content on non-verbal communication is critical to service interaction success; consequently, we offer the following:

> P3: Firms that incorporate a non-verbal techniques component in their service training for their frontline associates will achieve better rapport-building with visitors than firms that do not have a non-verbal techniques training component.

This review goes on to contend that effective rapport-building training programmes should have an empowerment component. For instance, the training could stress that in the event of a service failure, the contact employee is fully empowered to make redress decisions. Such failure recovery empowerment expedites the failure resolution process and increases the likelihood that the contact employee will follow-through and take ownership of the situation (Magnini and Ford, 2004). Moreover, it is likely that empowered employees would be more likely to go the extra-mile in myriad customer service situations because empowered workers are more likely to be satisfied with their jobs (Liden *et al.*, 2000; Laschinger *et al.*, 2004; Gazzoli *et al.*, 2010). In fact, empowerment typically has a stronger influence on the job satisfaction of customer contact employees than on non-contact employees (Lee *et al.*, 2011). Empowerment is particularly vital to the co-creation process because if the provider is able to make decisions, then the visitor can better relate to and bond with the provider since they are both actively shaping the exchange. Based on these discussions, we offer the following proposition:

P4: Firms that incorporate an empowerment component in their service training for their frontline associates will achieve better rapport-building with visitors than firms that do not have an empowerment training component.

The quality of a service interaction is judged, in part, on the level of personalization that characterizes the exchange (Noe, 1999; Zeithaml and Bitner, 2000). As a result, customer rapport-building training should emphasize the skills necessary to provide personalization whenever possible. Such skills entail being attentive to the customer's verbal and non-verbal cues (Ford, 1998). Along these lines, empathetic listening skills are needed in which customers are encouraged to fully communicate their thoughts and feelings (Berry, 1999; Ciaramicoli and Ketcham, 2000). The Ritz-Carlton has drawn an understanding about customer engagement, the connection between the customer and the frontline associate, and found that analytically listening to and observing its customers has led to its global recognition through prestigious customer service awards (Michelli, 2008). Using this philosophy, if a frontline associate continually observes customers' impatience with a long check-in process, the hotel would implement a more prompt procedure. As customers begin to notice a firm's adaptation to their cues, the emotional bond of frontline associates and customers is enhanced. However, adaption to observations is contingent to what a firm is capable of offering.

Not only should it be stressed in training that personalized service can be delivered by paying attention to the customer (both verbal and non-verbal cues), personalized service can also be achieved in situations in which experienced workers share customer preference information with the novice workers. This information exchange among service workers should be encouraged so long as it pertains to the delivery of customized interactions.

To summarize, we offer the following proposition:

P5: Firms that incorporate a personalized attention component in their service training for their frontline associates will achieve better rapport-building with visitors than firms that do not have a personalized attention training component.

When designing a rapport-building training programme it should also be kept in mind that frontline roles in the service sector are more stressful and mentally taxing than many other lines of work (Furnham 2002; Netemeyer *et al.*, 2005). Due to this stress, training should incorporate content that provides guidance on how to keep composure while transacting at the frontline. Such composure, also termed emotional regulation, is a trainable skill (Bar-On, 2007; Lennick, 2007). Teaching employees to be more emotionally intelligent, for example, bolsters emotional regulation (Grandey, 2000; Totterdell and Holman, 2003). In addition, frontline providers well versed in the flows and paths of service in their respective areas of the servicescape and the proper pacing of these flows can also aid with composure and emotional regulation.

Composure is important for rapport-building because visitors want to be assured that providers are capable of performing their roles well. In other words, visitors want to be assured of employees' abilities to convey trust and confidence (Parasuraman *et al.*, 1988; Hinkin and Tracey, 2003). Including a composure component in the rapport-building training will aid this effort. Thus, proposition six states the following:

P6: Firms that incorporate a composure component in their service training for their frontline associates will achieve better rapport-building with visitors than firms that do not have a composure training component.

Finally, this review posits that customer service training should emphasize the notion that the happier the customer, the less strain s/he places on the frontline worker. In the literature, this logic is known as the satisfaction mirror that contends that customer satisfaction and employee satisfaction have a positive, reciprocating relationship in service firms (Heskett *et al.*, 1997). In extant literature, this mirror effect plays a key role in Normann and Ramirez's (1993) notion of 'value constellation' and in Liedtka *et al.*'s (1997) 'generative cycle' of mutually reinforcing employee–customer development.

Based on this logic, it should be emphasized to frontline employees that the better they establish rapport with the customer → the happier the customer → the happier they will be in their roles. More importantly, these relationships loop to form a recursive cycle of rapport and satisfied constituents (employees and customers). Highlighting this concept in training will serve to motivate the frontline provider to work to establish rapport with visitors. Hence, we propose the following:

P7: Firms that incorporate a satisfaction mirror component in their service training for their frontline associates will achieve better rapport-building with visitors than firms that do not have a satisfaction mirror training component.

Rapport-building Training: A Delivery Perspective

Despite the critical roles that frontline service workers serve representing their firms, coverage of how training programmes should be designed is scarce in the academic literature. There is pragmatic motivation to fill this gap for two reasons. First, poorly designed or poorly implemented training can evidently be counterproductive (Tan *et al.*, 2003). Second, frontline providers are the face of the service; consequently, those firms that work to 'get it right' should have a competitive advantage over others. This implications section, therefore, synthesizes findings from several streams of research to suggest how customer service training should be designed.

First, this research proposes that frontline service employees should receive rapport-building training as soon as possible following their hiring. In other words, the length of time that service workers are permitted to interact with customers without receiving the training is inversely related to the service performance of the firm. The basis for this logic lies with the concept of social proof, which contends that individuals look to others to determine how they should behave in a given situation (Cialdini, 2001). In accordance with this logic, this review posits that if frontline workers exhibit sub-par service habits in the servicescape, then it is possible (even likely) that these sub-par habits could be contagious to others transacting at the frontline. In fact, the theory of planned behaviour (TPB) goes further to suggest that these sub-par habits could be carried forward into future transactions. That is, TPB supports the notion that future behavioural intentions are, in part, driven by subjective norms (whether persons surrounding the decision-maker participate in the given behaviour) (Rhodes and Courneya, 2003; Ajzen, 2006). Thus, permitting frontline workers to transact at the frontline for an extended period of time without having received rapport-building training increases the likelihood that bad service habits can be exhibited and mimicked. Therefore, we offer the following proposition:

> P8: Firms that provide service training to their frontline associates at or near the beginning of their employment will achieve better rapport-building with visitors than firms that postpone the training.

Regarding training delivery mode, a number of technology-based training tools are available for purchase and use by firms, but this review contends that the use of a live customer service trainer is superior to the technology-based modes for a number of reasons. First, a live trainer can incorporate examples and scenarios germane to the business in which the training is being offered, thus making the training content more tangible for the trainees. Second, the trainer can be briefed *a priori* by management on any topics that need specific or in-depth coverage. Third, a live trainer has the ability to read the dynamics/energy of the attendees during the session to actively engage them more than is possible with a technology-based training mode. While the use of technology-based modes such as CD-ROMs is often associated with enhanced scheduling flexibility, this research contends that the use of a live facilitator is advantageous for customer service training. A meta-analysis of 1152 organizational training studies conducted by Arthur *et al.* (2003) echoes this sentiment. Specifically, Arthur *et al.* state:

> We highlight the effectiveness of lectures as an example because despite their widespread use (Van Buren and Erskine, 2002), they have a poor public image as a boring and ineffective training method (Carroll *et al.*, 1972). In contrast, a noteworthy finding in our meta-analysis was the robust effect obtained for lectures, which contrary to their poor public image, appeared to be quite effective in training several types of skills and tasks. (2003, p. 243)

Based on the above logic, we offer the following proposition:

> P9: Firms that provide service training to their frontline associates delivered live by a trainer will achieve better rapport-building with visitors than firms that use non-live training formats such as CD-ROM or online modes.

To extend the discussion in the previous section, this review moves forward to contend that a live trainer who actively engages the trainees with exercises that require the trainees to be verbally and physically active during the training will yield better results than a passive trainer. Extant research clearly indicates that active learning in which trainees participate in carefully constructed activities maintains trainees' attention spans better than passive instructional techniques such as lecturing (Middendorf and Kalish, 1996). Customer service skills, in particular, cannot be learned through rote, but are instead internalized through active engagement of the trainee (Burnard, 1989; Lin and Darling, 1997). Thus, a rapport-building training session should contain a combination of trainee participation exercises such as sentence completion and role-playing. In fact, role-playing in particular has been found to enhance the realism of training sessions (Nikendei *et al.*, 2005). Whether the trainer opts to utilize role-playing or other interactive and engaging exercises during the training session, we offer the following proposition:

P10: Firms that provide verbally and physically interactive service training to their frontline associates will achieve better rapport-building with visitors than firms that do not use interactive techniques during the training session.

Rapport-building Training: A Training Transfer Perspective

Contrary to research extolling the merits of employee training, studies have also found that training may not provide a significant benefit to firms. Select studies find that there is not much difference in the level of performance between those who receive training and those who do not (Hu *et al.*, 2002; Puck *et al.*, 2008). One study, in particular, found that 40% of trainees do not incorporate trained skills immediately after the training; 70% fail to do so one year after the training; and ultimately only 50% of training investments yield organizational improvements (Burke and Hutchins, 2007). Can these findings be accurate; is it possible that employee training might not be the optimum use of a firm's resources?

Simply offering training is not sufficient for amending employee behaviours in the area of rapport-building. Training transfer describes the degree to which trained skills actually get applied on the job (Burke and Hutchins, 2007). For training transfer to occur. 'learned behavior must be generalized to the job context and maintained over a period of time on the job' (Baldwin and Ford, 1988, p. 63). One variable found to be highly correlated with transfer is the content relevance of the training materials (Holton *et al.*, 2000; Rodriguez and Gregory, 2005; Lim and Morris, 2006). Thus, the more the firm can convince the trainee that the training is relevant to his/her job, the more training transfer will transpire. It should be stressed to the trainee that rapport that is established by applying the trained concepts in customer interactions will make his/her job more enjoyable by reducing the stress at the frontline. To summarize, the following proposition is offered:

P11: Training transfer will be maximized in firms that establish the content relevance of service training designed for rapport-building.

Research also indicates that training transfer is dependent on the trainee's peer support in implementing the trained skills (Facteau *et al.*, 1995). In hospitality and tourism settings there is often a large human component in service delivery; thus, it is not uncommon for frontline providers to work as teams within their respective work areas. As such, if some team members apply the trained rapport-building skills while other reject the content, this peer-pressure environment inhibits training transfer. In such a circumstance, training transfer is restricted for two reasons: (i) frontline providers deduce that if not all co-workers display the trained skills, then the skills must not be important; and/or (ii) even if a given employee knows that the skills are important, peer-pressure might restrict adherence if everyone is not on the same page.

With regard to peer support, a study conducted by Hawley and Barnard (2005) found that trainees who networked with peers and discussed training content experienced better training transfer (even six months after training) than those who did not. In fact, support from co-workers can have a more consistent influence on training transfer than support from supervisors (Facteau *et al.*, 1995). Based on this logic, we offer the following proposition:

P12: Training transfer will be maximized in firms that establish peer support of service training designed for rapport-building.

Training transfer is more likely to occur if the trainee senses that his/her supervisor is genuinely committed to the training content (Burke and Hutchins, 2007). The role of the supervisor in influencing training transfer has been demonstrated in a number of studies (Brinkerhoff and Montesino, 1995; Burke and Baldwin, 1999; Clarke, 2002). Organizations in which managers continuously signal to employees that they are committed to the given training content will witness a high level of training transfer. These signals can come in many forms, depending on the training content for which the commitment is being illustrated. In order for high levels of training transfer to take place it is vital that managers are not only committed to training content, but also that they take every opportunity to signal the commitment to the team. Based on these discussions, the following proposition is offered:

P13: Training transfer will be maximized in firms that establish supervisor support of service training designed for rapport-building.

Discussion

Recent research addresses the importance of rapport-building between the frontline provider and consumer within a service environment (Gremler and Gwinner, 2000; Noe *et al.*, 2010). The chapter contends that consumers' perceptions of rapport and co-creation are highly correlated at the frontline. In other words, co-creation is stimulated by a sense of rapport between the frontline provider and visitor. Therefore, this chapter synthesized existing studies within the marketing, psychology and service fields to derive a series of propositions pertaining to how rapport-building training should be designed to yield top-rate co-created experiences.

Since this chapter focuses on rapport-building training, it is prudent to note that there are three phases to any type of human resource training initiative: (i) needs assessment; (ii) development; and (iii) evaluation (Lin and Darling, 1997). In terms of needs assessment, we argue that all customer contact employees should be exposed to the same rapport-building training regardless of background. Those employees can be told that all new hires receive the same training content because the goal is to synchronize all those at the frontline to provide consistent-quality services and standards of delivery.

With regard to training development, it is hoped that the development of these propositions founded on existing research will aid training development and ultimate co-creation experiences. To summarize the propositions, it is posited that rapport-building training should be offered at or near the beginning of employment, in a live format (as opposed to technology-based) and by an interactive trainer. Further, the content should have an on-stage/off-stage component, verbal and non-verbal coverage, an empowerment facet, a personalized attention dimension, a composure component and satisfaction mirror coverage. While offering such training would not be a panacea for success, the synthesis of research summarized herein indicates that such a design should be useful in yielding rapport-filled interactions between providers and visitors that enhance the co-created experiences.

In terms of training evaluation, longitudinal data generated from firms that initiate the programme can be used to evaluate results (in essence, empirically testing the propositions). Dependent measures that could be used in such analyses may include:

- Customer satisfaction.
- Employee satisfaction.
- Employee turnover.
- Operational efficiency.
- Customer repurchase intent.
- Customer positive word-of-mouth.
- Customer negative word-of-mouth.
- Occurrences of service failures.
- Employee performance in failure recovery situations.
- Occurrences of customer delight.

While pinpointing cause and effect relationships with regard to the influence of training (or more specifically, particular training content) on one or more of these outcome variables can be nebulous, using longitudinal data, particularly across multiple firms, should yield reasonably valid and reliable findings. Gremler and Gwinner (2000) empirically demonstrate that rapport development at the frontline has a significant impact on customer satisfaction, loyalty and word-of-mouth communications, but future research is warranted that extends this knowledge domain to include the dependent measures listed above.

Regardless of training content and design, the effectiveness of a training programme hinges on employee reactions to the training (Tan *et al.*, 2003). Such reactions will largely be driven by whether the employees perceive that the key stakeholders and managers in the firm have a genuine commitment to the training and its content or whether a 'lip-service' climate prevails (Peccei and Rosenthal, 2000). Employee perceptions of this organizational commitment will moderate the proposed relationships between training mode/content and the outcome variables discussed above.

With regard to transfer, training is only useful if the trained skills are internalized and displayed by the frontline service providers. Both peer support and supervisor support are vital for transfer. Qualitative research approaches in which seasoned managers can share their experiences related to training transfer best practices would be useful in advancing this area of research. While it seems reasonable to presume that other constructs such as a training recipient's perceived utility of the training content and the training recipient's organizational commitment should influence rapport-building training transfer, empirical attention is warranted.

Although outside the scope of this review, research also indicates that various ambient variables in the service environment can also influence the level of rapport present between the service provider and customer. For example, research dating back more than 50 years finds that the presence of background music increases conversation and even the degree of smiling and eye contact between individuals (Dollins, 1956; Sommer, 1957; Dube *et al.*, 1995). In addition, the emerging research is finding that ambient scents can also increase interactional conversation between individuals (Zemke and Shoemaker, 2008). Thus, future research investigating how atmospheric cues influence co-creation through rapport development is ripe for consideration.

References

Ajzen, I. (2006) Constructing a TPB questionnaire: conceptual and methodological consideration. Available at: http://people.umass.edu/ajzen/pdf/tpb.measurement.pdf.

Arnould, E. and Thompson, C. (2005) Culture theory (CCT): twenty years of research. *Journal of Consumer Research* 31, 868–882.

Arthur, W. Jr, Bennet, W. Jr, Edens, P. and Bell, S. (2003) Effectiveness of training in organizations: a meta-analysis of design and evaluation features. *Journal of Applied Psychology* 88(2), 234–245.

Baldwin, T. and Ford, J. (1988) Transfer of training: a review and directions for future research. *Personnel Psychology* 41, 63–105.

Bar-On, R. (2007) How important is it to educate people to be emotionally intelligent, and can it be done? In: Bar-On, R., Maree, J. and Elias, M. (eds) *Educating People to be Emotionally Intelligent*. Praeger, Westport, Connecticut, pp. 1–35.

Bernieri, F., Gillis, J., Davis, J. and Grahe, J. (1996) Dyad rapport and the accuracy of its judgment across situations: a lens model analysis. *Journal of Personality and Social Psychology* 71(1), 110–129.

Berry, L.L. (1999) *Discovering the Soul of Service*. Free Press, New York.

Bolton, R. (2006) Forward. In: Lusch, R. and Vargo, S. (eds) *The Service Dominant Logic of Marketing: Dialog, Debate and Directions*. M.E. Sharpe, Armonk, New York, pp. ix–xi.

Brinkerhoff, R. and Montesino, M. (1995) Partnerships for training transfer: lessons from a corporate study. *Human Resource Development Quarterly* 6(3), 263–274.

Burke, L. and Baldwin, T. (1999) Workforce training transfer: a study of the effect of relapse prevention training and transfer. *Human Resource Management* 38(3), 227–243.

Burke, L. and Hutchins, H. (2007) Training transfer: an integrative literature review. *Human Resource Development Review* 6(3), 263–296.

Burnard, P. (1989) *Teaching Interpersonal Skills*. Chapman and Hall, London.

Carnegie, D. (1936) *How to Win Friends and Influence People*. Hutchinson, New York.

Carroll, S., Paine, F. and Ivancevich, J. (1972) The relative effectiveness of training methods – expert opinion and research. *Personnel Psychology* 25, 495–510.

Cialdini, R.B. (2001) *Influence: Science and Practice*, 4th edition. Allyn and Bacon, New York.

Ciaramicoli, A. and Ketcham, K. (2000) *The Power of Empathy*. Penguin, New York.

Clarke, N. (2002) Job/work environment factors influencing training effectiveness within a human service agency: some indicative support for Baldwin and Fords' transfer climate construct. *International Journal of Training and Development* 6(3), 146–162.

Deighton, J. (1994) Managing services when the service is a performance. In: Rust, R.T. and Oliver, R.L. (eds) *Service Quality*. Sage, Thousand Oaks, California.

DiMatteo, M., Taranta, A., Friedman, H. and Prince, L. (1980) Predicting patient satisfaction from physicians' nonverbal communication skills. *Medical Care* 18(4), 376–387.

Dollins, C. (1956) The use of background music in a psychiatric hospital to increase group conversational frequency. *Music Therapy* 6, 229–230.

Dube, L., Chebat, J.C. and Morin, S. (1995) The effects of background music on consumers' desire to affiliate in buyer–seller interactions. *Psychology and Marketing* 12(4), 305–319.

Duggan, A. and Parrott, R. (2001) Physicians' nonverbal rapport building and patients' talk about the subjective component of illness. *Human Communication Research* 27(2), 299–311.

Facteau, J., Dobbins, G., Russell, J., Ladd, R. and Kudisch, J. (1995) The influence of general perceptions of the training environment on pre-training motivation and perceived training transfer. *Journal of Management* 21, 1–25.

Ford, W. (1998) *Communicating with Customers*. Hampton Press, Cresskill, New Jersey.

Furnham, A. (2002) Happy staff is not the full answer: management style can be reflected in customer service – but the relationship is complex. *Financial Times* (accessed 5 February).

Gazzoli, G., Hancer, M. and Park, Y. (2010) The role and effect of job satisfaction and empowerment on customers' perception of service quality: a study in the restaurant industry. *Journal of Hospitality and Tourism Research* 34(1), 56–77.

Goffman, E. (1959) *The Presentation of Self in Everyday Life*. Doubleday, Garden City, New York.

Grandey, A. (2000) Emotion regulation in the workplace: a new way to conceptualize emotional labor. *Journal of Occupational Health Psychology* 5, 95–110.

Gremler, D. and Gwinner, K. (2000) Customer–employee rapport in service relationships. *Journal of Service Research* 3(1), 82–104.

Grönroos, C. and Voima, P. (2013) Critical service logic: making sense of value creation and co-creation. *Journal of the Academy of Marketing Science* 41, 133–150.

Grove, S. and Fiske, R. (1983) The dramaturgy of service exchange: analytical framework for services marketing. In: Berry, L.T., Shostack, G.L. and Upah, G.D. (eds) *Emerging Perspectives on Services Marketing*. American Marketing Association, Chicago, Illinois.

Grove, S., Fisk, R. and Bitner, M. (1992) Dramatizing the service experience: a managerial approach. In: Swartz, T.A., Brown, S. and Bowen, D. (eds) *Advances in Services Marketing and Management*. JAI Press, Greenwich, Connecticut, pp. 91–121.

Hawley, J. and Barnard, J. (2005) Work environment characteristics and implications for training transfer: a case study of the nuclear power industry. *Human Resource Development Quarterly* 8(1), 65–80.

Heskett, J.L., Sasser, E.W. and Schlesinger, L.A. (1997) *The Service Profit Chain*. Free Press, New York.

Hinkin, T. and Tracey, J. (2003) The service imperative: factors driving meeting effectiveness. *Cornell Hotel and Restaurant Administration Quarterly* 44(5/6), 17–26.

Hollman, W. and Kleiner, B. (1997) Establishing rapport: the secret business tool. *Managing Service Quality* 7(4), 194–197.

Holton, E., Bates, R. and Ruona, W. (2000) Development of a generalized learning transfer system inventory. *Human Resources Development Quarterly* 11(4), 333–360.

Hu, W., Martin, L. and Yeh, J. (2002) Cross-cultural impact and learning needs for expatriate hotel employees in Taiwan lodging industry. *Journal of Human Resources in Hospitality and Tourism* 1, 31–45.

Laschinger, H., Finegan, J., Shamian, J. and Wilk, P. (2004) A longitudinal analysis of the impact of workplace environment on work satisfaction. *Journal of Organizational Behavior* 25(4), 527–545.

Lee, G., Kim, B., Perdue, R. and Magnini, V. (2011) Time-varying effects of empowerment on job satisfaction for customer-contact versus non-customer-contact groups. *Proceeding of the 16th Annual Graduate Student Research Conference in Hospitality and Tourism*.

Lennick, D. (2007) Emotional competence development and the bottom line: lessons from American Express financial advisors. In: Bar-On, R., Maree, J. and Elias, M. (eds) *Educating People to be Emotionally Intelligent*. Praeger, Westport, Connecticut, pp. 199–210.

Liden, R., Wayne, S. and Sparrowe, R. (2000) An examination of the mediating role of psychological empowerment on the relations between job, interpersonal relationships and work outcomes. *Journal of Applied Psychology* 85(3), 407–417.

Liedtka, J., Haskins, M., Rosenblum, J. and Weber, J. (1997) The generative cycle: linking knowledge and relationships. *Sloan Management Review* 47–58.

Lim, D. and Morris, M. (2006) Influence of trainee characteristics, instructional satisfaction, and organizational climate on perceived learning and training transfer. *Human Resource Development Quarterly* 17, 85–115.

Lin, B. and Darling, J. (1997) A processual analysis of customer service training. *Journal of Services Marketing* 11(3), 193–205.

Magnini, V. and Ford, J. (2004) Service failure recovery in China. *International Journal of Contemporary Hospitality Management* 16(5), 279–286.

Magnini, V. and Honeycutt, E. (2005) Face recognition and name recall: training implications for the hospitality industry. *Cornell Hospitality Quarterly* 46(1), 69–78.

Michelli, J. (2008) *The New Gold Standard: 5 Leadership Principles for Creating a Legendary Customer Experience Courtesy of the Ritz-Carlton Hotel Company*. McGraw-Hill, New York.

Middendorf, J. and Kalish, A. (1996) The 'change up' in lectures. *Teaching Resources Center Newsletter* 5.

Netemeyer, R., Maxham, J. III and Pullig, C. (2005) Conflicts in the work–family interface: links to job stress, customer service employee performance, and customer repurchase intention. *Journal of Marketing* 69(2), 130–143.

Nikendei, C., Zeuch, A., Diekmann, P., Roth, C., Schafer, S., Volkl, M., Schellberg, D., Herzog, W. and Junger, J. (2005) Role-playing for more realistic technical skills training. *Medical Teacher* 27(2), 122–126.

Noe, F. (1999) *Tourist Service Satisfaction*. Sagamore, Champaign, Illinois.

Noe, F., Uysal, M. and Magnini, V. (2010) *Tourist Customer Satisfaction: An Encounter Approach*. Routledge, London.

Normann, R. and Ramirez, R. (1993) From value chain to value constellation: designing interactive strategy. *Harvard Business Review* 71, 65–77.

Parasuraman, A., Zeithaml, V. and Berry, L. (1988) SERVQUAL: a multiple-item scale for measuring customer perceptions of service quality. *Journal of Retailing* 64(1), 12–40.

Park, R. and Burgess, E. (1924) *Introduction to the Science of Sociology*. University of Chicago Press, Chicago, Illinois.

Payne, A., Storbacka, K. and Frow, P. (2008) Managing the co-creation of value. *Journal of the Academy of Marketing Science* 36, 83–96.

Pease, A. and Pease, B. (2004) *The Definitive Book of Body Language*. Bantam Dell, New York.

Peccei, R. and Rosenthal, P. (2000) Front-line responses to customer orientation programs: a theoretical and empirical analysis. *International Journal of Human Resource Management* 11(3), 562–590.

Prahalad, C. and Ramaswamy, V. (2000) Co-opting customer competence. *Harvard Business Review* 78, 79–90.

Puck, J.F., Kittler, M.G. and Wright, C. (2008) Does it really work? Re-assessing the impact of pre-departure cross-cultural training on expatriate adjustment. *International Journal of Human Resource Management* 19, 2182–2197.

Rhodes, R. and Courneya, K. (2003) Investigating multiple components of attitude, subjective norm, and perceived control: an examination of the theory of planned behaviour in the exercise domain. *British Journal of Social Psychology* 42, 129–146.

Rodriguez, C. and Gregory, S. (2005) Qualitative study of transfer of training of student employees in a service industry. *Journal of Hospitality and Tourism Research* 29, 42–66.

Smith, S. (1995) Perceptual processing of nonverbal-relational messages. In: Hewes, D.E. (ed.) *The Cognitive Bases of Interpersonal Communication*. LEA, Hillsdale, New Jersey.

Sommer, D. (1957) The effect of background music on verbal interaction in group psychotherapy. *Music Therapy* 7, 167–168.

Tan, J., Hall, R. and Boyce, C. (2003) The role of employee reactions in predicting training effectiveness. *Human Resource Development Quarterly* 14(4), 397–411.

Tickle-Degnen, L. and Rosenthal, R. (1987) Group rapport and non-verbal behavior. *Group Processes and Intergroup Relations: Review of Personality and Social Psychology* 9, 113–136.

Tickle-Degnen, L. and Rosenthal, R. (1990) The nature of rapport and nonverbal correlates. *Psychological Inquiry* 1(4), 285–293.

Totterdell, P. and Holman, D. (2003) Emotion regulation in customer service roles: testing a model of emotional labor. *Journal of Occupational Health Psychology* 8(1), 55–73.

Van Buren, M. and Erskine, W. (2002) *The 2002 ASTD State of the Industry Report*. American Society for Training and Development, Alexandria, Virginia.

Zaltman, G. (1997) Rethinking marketing research: putting people back in. *Journal of Marketing Research* 34(4), 424–437.

Zeithaml, V.A. and Bitner, M.J. (2000) *Services Marketing*. Irwin McGraw-Hill, Boston, Massachusetts.

Zemke, D. and Shoemaker, S. (2008) A sociable atmosphere: ambient scent's effect on social interaction. *Cornell Hospitality Quarterly* 49(3), 317–329.

11 Approaches for the Evaluation of Visitor Experiences at Tourist Attractions

ØYSTEIN JENSEN

University of Nordland, Bodø and University of Stavanger, Norway

Introduction

Tourist attractions have traditionally been regarded as the key element in the destination product (Middleton, 1988; Weidenfeldt *et al.*, 2010) and have been associated with the main reasons for visiting particular destinations. They have also been considered as arenas for unique experiences for travellers (Cohen, 1974) and tourist attractions are thus perfect, concentrated settings for studying tourist experiences. Because there are many approaches to understanding both tourist attractions and tourist experiences, there is obviously a need to clarify the different meanings of the concepts as used in various studies. This is of particular significance when comparing findings from different studies and evaluating their contributions to research and the practical field. Without attention to their points of departure and being able to categorize them along central common traits, such comparisons might lose some of their potential value for overall progress in this field, in an epistemological, ontological and methodological sense.

This chapter focuses on approaches to and challenges in the evaluation of visitor experiences at managed tourist attractions. The purpose is to uncover and to discuss critical aspects as demonstrated by this research, to identify some benefits and limitations in different approaches and to suggest some overall perspectives for the categorization of different studies. This is done by revealing and discussing various conceptual and methodological approaches for the evaluation of visitor experiences, first of all with reference to empirically based studies published in tourism research journals and textbooks. The empirical sources will primarily be linked to managed tourist attraction settings, but also some studies on destination level will be referred to. Finally arguments for the relevance of these types of studies for enhancing experience qualities of tourist attractions will be presented.

Delimiting the Tourist Attraction Setting

Tourist attractions have been defined with reference to the resources on which they are based, and/or the visitor experience they can or do offer. From a sociological perspective, they have also been described as symbols or signs (MacCannell, 1976) or as social constructs (Boorstin, 1964; Lash and Urry, 1994; Dann, 1996; Urry, 2002; Uriely, 2005b) experienced as mental states in time and space (Lash and Urry, 1994; Bauman, 2001). This chapter focuses on the evaluation of visitor experiences by managed (Middleton, 1988) or contrived (Cohen, 1995) tourist attractions. Basically the latter have many similarities with managed tourist events, such as hallmark events, despite their temporary character (Getz, 1997). As the terms 'visitor attractions' (Swarbrooke, 2002) and 'tourist attractions' are often used interchangeably in the tourism literature, the chapter will use the term tourist attractions to indicate that it is the experiences of the tourist segments that represent the main – though not the exclusive – target. Because there are many ways of identifying a prototypical tourist (Pearce, 2011), tourists will be described here quite simply as voluntary visitors from places outside the area of location of the attraction with recreational motives (compare Cohen, 1974). It is still acknowledged that many visitors at attractions represent segments with local origins or with other visitation motives, for example MICE (Meetings, Incentives, Conferences and Events) segments and local school classes visiting heritage attractions.

On a micro-level, a particular attraction can be understood as 'a single unit, an individual site or a clearly small-scale geographical area, based on a single feature and perceived by visitors as such' (Weidenfeld *et al.*, 2010, pp. 1–2). A particular group of attractions can be perceived as special agglomerations, clusters or systems frequently associated with specific themes linked to a wider geographical area (Gunn, 1979, 1988; Mill and Morrison, 1985; Weidenfeld *et al.*, 2010). Middleton and Clarke (2001) describe a visitor attraction more widely as a collection of permanent resources at a named site (Pearce, 1991), for example cultural and natural resources representing a basis for tourist experiences. However, Gunn (1988) directs the attention to the basic destination features that produce the *raison d'être* of the attraction. In managed tourist attractions the main focus is on the appealing visitor experiences (enjoyment, amusement, entertainment and/or education) created by the management of a set of permanent destination resources (Middleton and Clarke, 2001). Gunn, moreover, states that 'Attractions are physical place settings for experiences' (1979, p. 67). Because attractions are regarded here as separate units within the destinations they are located, it is recognized that they also 'present and deliver the particular sense of place' (Weidenfeld *et al.*, 2010, p. 2). This study is based on Gunn's (1979) understanding of attractions and also a main attention to contrived or managed attractions.

Conceptualizations of Tourist Experiences

The notion 'tourist experience' can obviously be understood in quite different ways (Quan and Wang, 2004; Uriely, 2005, Jennings and Nickerson, 2006, Jennings, 2006, Volo, 2009, Pearce, 2011; see also the special issue of *Scandinavian Journal of*

Hospitality and Tourism [2007, vol. 7, no. 1] on Tourist Experiences). While some of the dominant sociological structuralistic- and constructivistic-oriented conceptualizations of this social phenomenon have contributed to establishing a broad, culturally critical (Pearce, 2011) perspective on tourism and tourist experiences (MacCannell, 1976; Cohen, 1979, 1995; Urry, 2002; Bauman, 2001; Dann, 1996), efforts to operationalize and measure tourist experience concepts have to a greater extent been found in approaches from other disciplines, such as psychology or marketing. Recognizing that within consumer research, conceptualizations and typologies of consumption experiences have been under review for several years, for example with focus on emotions, fun and games (Holbrook and Hirschman, 1982; Holbrook *et al.*, 1984), hedonic consumption (Hirschman and Holbrook, 1982), extraordinary (Carù and Cova, 2003) or peak (Arnold and Price, 1993) experiences and wider classifications (Holt, 1995), including this array of research literature will exceed the limitations of this chapter.

Initially, a dominant view within tourism sociology is to look at tourist consumption as a de-differentiated experience from everyday life (Uriely, 2005) where the quest for strangeness and novelty (Cohen, 1974) can be experienced in different modes (Cohen, 1979). In linguistic terms one distinction in the understanding of experiences is expressed through the difference between the German notions 'Erlebnis' and 'Erfahrung', as discussed by Larsen (2007) and Boswijk *et al.* (2007). The first term relates to the immediate experience linked to a specific situation and the second is based on the result of an accumulation of experiences over time. From a dynamic or temporary perspective, tourism experiences can include dispositions and processes taking place before, during and after the tourist's exposure and interaction with the tourism setting (Jennings, 2006), for example as expressed through the notions of the anticipatory, the experiential and the reflective phase (Craigh-Smith and French, 1994) (compare also Chen *et al.*, Chapter 2, this volume). Larsen suggests that tourist experiences occur through individual mental, mainly memory processes and proposes that 'A tourist experience is a past personal travel-related event strong enough to have entered long-term memory' (2007, p. 15). Viewed as a post-experience attitude, it can also be affected by social representations formed through narratives with others (Pearce, 2011). Kim *et al.* (2012) present an overview of publications expressing different construct domains of 'Memorable Tourism Experiences'. Compared with Larsen (2007), they suggest focusing on the positively remembered experience. Furthermore, they state that 'relatively few studies have explored the components of the experience that are most likely to be recalled from tourists' memories' (Kim *et al.*, 2012, p. 13).

Boswijk *et al.* (2007) describe the wider generic term 'meaningful experiences' that assumes the satisfaction of a number of criteria linked to aspects of the immediate situation and the past. They also include several dimensions previously promoted by Pine and Gilmore (1999). Recently there has been growing attention to an even stronger widening of the perspective on tourist experiences by focusing on how they could contribute to the enhancement of quality of life or well-being (Neal *et al.*, 2007; Sirgy *et al.*, 2011).

Pearce (2011) parallels the development of the term behaviour in psychology to its use in the tourism context towards not just embracing what people do but also how people feel, think and react to tourism settings and states that the same aspects are in focus within research on tourist experiences. Furthermore, tourist experiences are 'an embodied process involving the physical world and the human body' (Pearce, 2011, p. 23). As stated by O'Dell (2007), these processes will have a material base anchored in space. Nevertheless, many authors hesitate to offer a particular, specified definition of quality tourist experiences and suggest that the understanding of this phenomenon needs to be examined through several theoretical approaches and agendas (see for example Jennings, 2006).

Approaches to the Measurement of Visitor Experiences of Attractions from Tourist Research Literature

Difficulties in evaluating tourist experiences by satisfaction and service quality measures

Perceived service quality, satisfaction and behavioural intention have frequently been used as operational concepts to evaluate visitors' experiences of tourist destinations, institutions and tourist activities (Crompton and Love, 1995; Baker and Crompton, 2000; Tomas et al., 2002; Yoon and Uysal, 2005; Meng et al., 2008; Hutchinson et al., 2009; Williams and Soutar, 2009; Alegre and Garau, 2010; McMullan and O'Neill, 2010; Zabkar et al., 2010). It can, however, on the one hand, be asked whether the preferred measurement scales on satisfaction assess all the critical dimensions needed for useful insights into visitors' behaviour and, on the other, how appropriate the perceived service quality and satisfaction constructs actually are for studies of visitor experiences.

Some of these issues have been addressed through the critics of the expectancy-disconfirmation logic (Oliver, 1997) such as expressed through the GAP model (Parasuraman et al., 1985, 1991; Zeithaml et al., 1996). Additional critical aspects are the lack of attention to the social dynamics of service encounters, the situational influence of experiences (Belk, 1975; Fournier and Mick, 1999), the narrow definition of expectations (Boulding et al., 1993; Buttle, 1996; Fournier and Mick, 1999), the occurrence of favourable surprises for the consumers and the corresponding affective reactions (Oliver, 1997) and, finally, the holistic aspects of service experiences (Buttle, 1996; Fournier and Mick, 1999; Vitterso et al., 2000; Maunier and Camelis, 2013). Related specifically to tourism, criticisms have been raised about failing to consider symbolic, emotional and existential values of tourism products (Vitterso et al., 2000) and the absence of dissonance-related items (McMullan and O'Neill, 2010), such as tourists' use of different cognitive dissonance strategies to reduce negative inconsistency between expectations and real events (Vitterso et al., 2000). Also issues linked to the influence of extraneous events and the state of the tourists (Maunier and Camelis, 2013) as well as international tourists' relatively limited access to information about tourist attractions restricting the possibilities of forming clear expectations of future site experiences at the site have been raised (Vitterso et al., 2000; Jensen, 2002; Jensen and Korneliussen, 2002) (though Yoon and Uysal (2005) found that pre-information of tourists did not have a significant effect on tourists' evaluation of their destination experiences). Moreover, it has also been asked whether perceived service quality understood as the result of a cumulative process of several service encounters with a service firm (Parasuraman *et al.*, 1985, 1991) is an appropriate construct for tourist attractions that frequently provide high proportions of one-time visits (Jensen, 2002).

Nowacki (2009) opposes the conviction that satisfaction represents an appropriate indicator of the successful/unsuccessful efforts of the service provider, such as an attraction, and argues that satisfaction is affected by several independent factors (compare Vitterø *et al.*, 2000). Examples of such factors would be the weather, the individual mood of the visitor or the mood in a group of visitors. As a consequence, many of the influencing factors on satisfaction are thus hard to control from the perspective of researchers as well as for managers (Tomas *et al.*, 2002). It has, for example, been found that mood moderates tourists' service quality evaluations and overall satisfaction level based on an empirical analysis of cruise tourists (Sirakaya *et al.*, 2004). de Rojas and Camarero (2008) found, based on a heritage context study, a significant relationship between quality and emotion and found that mood moderates the cognitive path that represents a central element within service quality and disconfirmation approaches. While MacMullan and O'Neill (2010) argue for the need of increased attention to the effects of emotions (compare Holbrook and Hirschman, 1982) and dissonance in relationship to satisfaction and future behavioural intentions, Nowacki (2009) claims that benefits have a significantly stronger effect on behavioural intentions as output of the visitor experience process than satisfaction. By paralleling attraction sites to other empirical contexts, such as adventure tourism, Williams and Soutar (2009) report in their participant study that value did not predict satisfaction and intentions and suggest, moreover, that despite difficulties in defining and measuring relevant constructs, such as risk and challenges, they occur as important components of adventure and should thus not be ignored. This example raises the question whether research frameworks frequently preferred within service or tourism contexts with a relatively modest 'excitement level' (in contrast to 'peak' experience situations (Arnold and Price, 1993)) or with a high proportion of standardized products, such as business hotels, actually cover some of the central issues when applied on more differentiated or extreme experiential contexts. As many such studies tend to be based on the use of 'traditional' questionnaires, primarily self-guided on-site, it could also be discussed how appropriate these data collection tools are for catching the nature of complex tourist experiences.

Alternative approaches to satisfaction and service quality by visitor experiences

There are several examples of alternative approaches to satisfaction and service quality as indicators for the character of visitor experiences at attractions. A few examples are presented for illustration.

Vitterø *et al.* (2000) focus on affective on-site experiences as caused by the process of cognitive information processing. They rely on the scheme theory of Eckblad (1981a, 1981b) explaining how affective experience are caused by the disposition of individuals to assimilate the world into structures of cognitive 'maps' or schemas (compare Gould and White, 1974). From this perspective, the process of assimilation takes place without resistance as long as a person's world perceptions accord with existing schemas; however, the assimilation resistance grows as the distance between an actual situation and this person's corresponding cognitive schemas expand (Vitterrø et al., 2000). For example, a small amount of assimilation resistance could cause just boredom, a larger amount could cause pleasantness and satisfaction, and a very large amount could cause frustration (compare the state of 'mindfulness' in a tourist attraction setting (Moscardo, 1996, 2003)). By the empirical study of six, mainly heritage-based, Norwegian attractions, Vitterrø et al. (2000) present a flow-simplex where each attraction is located on different specific positions based on affective visitor reactions. An important managerial implication of the results is that they indicate different types of challenges of each attraction in their efforts to move in the 'right' direction within the flow-simplex, still assuming that there might exist quite different types of goals of each attraction.

A more recent study based on a related theoretical point of departure is Dahl and Vitterrø (2010), who focused on interest, cognition and affect among young visitors (schoolchildren) at Svalbard Museum in Spitsbergen. They combined the use of several evaluation tools during and after the visit, including analyses of the respondents' own photographs at the site. The study relies on conceptual understandings of situational interest from psychology, such as Krapp (2002), Renninger et al. (2002) and Hidi (2006), and demonstrates how awareness and emotional reactions on different parts of the exhibits were influenced by the combination of affective and cognitive components of motivation (Hidi, 2006).

One conceptual basis for the evaluation of visitors' experiences of attractions known from consumer behaviour is behavioural intentions (Fischbein and Adjzen, 1975; Ajzen and Madden, 1986; Ajzen and Fischbein, 1980) that is demonstrated to be a good indicator of future behaviour of consumers, such as future intentions to revisit, willingness to pay a high price and to recommend a product or a site to others. Several destination-specific studies that have included behavioural intentions as one among several factors have produced diverging results, for example Crompton and Love (1995), Yoon and Uysal (2005), Chen and Tsai (2007), Meng et al. (2008), Zabkar et al. (2010), Bosnjak et al. (2011) as well as Baker and Crompton (2000); however, attraction studies with extensive focus on behavioural intentions are still scarce. Nowacki (2009) studied the relationships between a number of specific variables on behavioural intentions among visitors in four different types tourist attractions in Poland, including festivals. A main conclusion was that benefits (factors such as introspection, knowledge, spending time with family, escape, watching animals and spending time with friends) are more important for the influence on behavioural intentions than satisfaction. As satisfaction especially tends to be experienced during the visitation process (momentary satisfaction), benefits, however, are particularly linked to the results of the visit (compare Jensen and Hansen, 2007) and it reflected psychological long-term effects that remain remembered (compare Larsen, 2007). The study from adventure tourism of Williams and Soutar (2009) revealed that value-for-money and emotional value were significant predictors of both satisfaction and future intentions; however, functional value did not predict either of the two variables. Finally, Prebensen et al. (2013) demonstrate how both motivation and involvement (Kyle and Chick, 2004) occur as antecedents of the value of tourist experiences in destinations. The increasing research interest on the value of tourist experiences is generally also demonstrated through other contributions in this volume.

Several of the studies referred to in this chapter emphasize the service provider's performance or presentation form as most important for positive visitor experiences. For example, Nowacki's (2009) study demonstrated that the strongest load on behavioural intentions was on performance of service provider, including sources of information (information boards, panels and orientation signs) and exhibitions, and life exhibitions that allowed for interactions with the visitors were assessed the highest. The emphasis of assessing performance quality has earlier been promoted by Baker and Crompton (2000) and Tomas *et al.* (2002), who direct the attention to the advantage that this factor is under management control. As for cultural festivals, dramatized and interactive performances have been documented to have a positive effect on visitors' experience evaluations (Cole and Chancellor, 2009; Nowacki, 2009; Prebensen, 2010). In their study of downtown festival visitors, Cole and Chancellor (2009) found that entertainment quality had the most comprehensive effect on the participants' overall experience and their intentions to revisit and Prebensen (2010) identified the significance of participation for value creation in High North events.

Within the heritage sector some interpretive studies have been published, such as Beeho and Prentice (1997), Prentice *et al.* (1998), Tufts and Milne (1999), Poria *et al.* (2006) and Hertzman *et al.* (2008). Poria *et al.* stated that 'The more participants perceived the site as a part of their own heritage, the more they were interested in the visit' (2006, p. 171). This indicates a need to discriminate the interpretation approaches directed at different visitor segments based on their attachment to the sites and the associated themes. The study by Beeho and Prentice (1997) of a heritage village in Scotland concluded that the experiences gained by the visitors were emotional (such as provoking enjoyable educational experiences) and the main benefits were beneficial learning experiences. In the study of an industrial heritage park, Prentice *et al.* (1998) pointed at the need to focus on the experiential dimensions of tourism as perceived by visitors and to emphasize the multi-attribute nature of visitor experiences.

One approach that has been used to evaluate visitors' preferences with regard to attributes at heritage sites is Stated Preferences (Alexandros and Jaffry, 2005) combined with Choice Experiments (Willis, 2009), where the visitors are presented with alternative combinations of attributes and requested to indicate their highest ranked set of characteristics. This offers the opportunity of revealing status quo effects on uncertainties in preference with regard to alterations in the display of archaeological material (Willis, 2009). The results could thus be used as specific indicators for the management of where to do improvements. One observation within the context of an archaeological site is that visitors are obviously able to identify preferences for the future management of this site (Kinghorn and Willis, 2008). The fact that stated preferences of non-visitors also can be applied to detect critical attributes that could influence their decision to visit a heritage site can be regarded as an additional quality of this method. An alternative approach used by overall studies of heritage villages is the ASEB (activities, settings, experiences and benefits) grid analysis (Beeho and Prentice, 1997). This approach is claimed to be particularly developed for evaluating tourist attractions and can be combined with SWOT-analysis; the evaluation results are displayed in a matrix format. For detailed analysis of the encounter process between the visitor and the attraction, the critical incidents technique is an appropriate approach when focusing on possibilities of improvement of service failures and enforcement of positive elements (Gremler, 2004; Pritchard and Havitz, 2006). Maunier and Camelis (2013) made use of the critical incidents technique to investigate major driving factors determining tourists' satisfaction and dissatisfaction with destination and service firms. The main results offered support to a broader, holistic view on tourist experiences. For attractions, this method has been discussed by Lewis and Clacher (2001) with regard to UK theme parks.

A main finding of the interpretative study by Hertzman *et al.* (2008) of an 'edutainment heritage tourist attraction' (Storyeum in Vancouver) was that as visitors, on the one hand, appreciated the inherent educational and entertainment value of the historical representations they encountered, they were, on the other hand, also actively and critically engaged. The authors conclude that this critical engagement challenges the perception of tourist attraction audiences as predominantly passive and non-critical visitors primarily in search of entertainment and escapism. Moreover, Hertzman *et al.* (2008) argue for the need of increased knowledge on the nature of visitors' subjective critical criteria as well as of visitors' affective status and individual experiences. Volo suggests that 'unobstructive' methods, such as the use of diaries, videos, sensory devices and GPS-systems, 'appear to be promising in the search for emotions, moods and feelings of visitors' (2009, p. 115). Finally, there have also been studies trying to identify separate categories of factors with different types of effect on tourists (Swan and Combs, 1976; Noe, 1987; Uysal and Williams, 2004; Uysal and Noe, 2007).

Within ecotourism there has been an increased awareness of the synergic effects of combining approaches from mass tourism and environmental protection, as frequently demonstrated within 'soft' ecotourism (Newsome *et al.*, 2002; Weaver, 2008), for example within smaller dedicated sections of national parks and in interpretation centres. This also indicates a trend to adopt new and more advanced interpretation techniques within ecotourism-related sites. Reichel *et al.* (2008) provide an example of a study with a visitor experience focus, in a case study of visitors to an ecotourism site (World of Salt – a former salt mine in Canada) that offered interactive simulative mining experiences for visitors. The respondents in this study expressed preferences for an integrative approach combining concepts associated with both natural and artificial sites, including sites with themed simulations supporting the preservation of local nature and culture.

A variety of specific themes can be found in different types of parks (Wanhill, 2002), and they can also be classified in general categories, such as Wong and Cheung's (1999) systematic classification in seven categories: adventure, fantasy, futurism, history and culture, international, movie and nature. By matching the seven general theme categories with theme preferences in the market (derived from interviews with primarily Asians in Hong Kong), Wong and Cheung (1999) were able to set up a priority list of themes. Although the classification of the themes and the measurement of such priorities across contexts can be discussed, the study directs attention to the value of exploring the general aspects of the themes of attractions and theme priorities as predispositions among potential and/or actual tourists.

Finally, it should be added that the empirical studies previously referred to in no way claim to cover a representative selection of the research on attraction experiences. Additionally, there are obviously a number of methodological shortcomings that could be discussed of the approaches described. However, as the main purpose has been to offer some illustrative examples from various empirical studies of attraction, such a critical review will not be undertaken in this chapter.

Discussion

Overall considerations

The research literature on visitor experiences at managed attractions referred to generally demonstrates the complexity of the visitor experience epistemologically, ontologically and methodologically. It thus raises a number of questions for discussion, such as the conceptual approaches to visitor experiences, the choice of methods to actually measure the experiences, the nature of experiences within different categories of attraction and the influence of wider, embedding contextual factors.

One challenge when analysing visitor experiences is obviously to avoid the exclusion of too many aspects of the visitor experiences when limiting the analysis to on-site registrations. This potential loss includes, even by the use of retrospection, the antecedents of the experiences (pre-knowledge, prior attachment to the site or to the site-theme, pre-trial beliefs, expectations etc.) and post-reactions (memories (Larsen, 2007), social feedbacks and post-evaluations). As some of the research has indicated, the evaluation of goal attainment, benefits and the fulfilment of consumer values after the visit can contrast with the evaluation of momentary satisfaction measured on the site. Several studies of destination and attraction experiences have been based on satisfaction and service quality measures; however, arguments promoting a focus on behavioural intentions rather than on more 'traditional' satisfaction measures have been presented (Boulding et al., 1993; Nowacki, 2009). Also approaches taking the wider human experiences into account, for example the existential-encounter perspective (Lindberg, 2001), require an extended time frame for the evaluation of the experiences. The positioning of various attractions studies in accordance to their focus related to the time dimensions will thus be of relevance when considering limitations of the contributions.

There has been some evidence pointing out that it is first of all the quality of the presentation part or the performances of the attraction that produces the most positive experiences among visitors, such as the exhibits, the presentation process, as well as the involvement of the visitors in the performance process. The seemingly increased use and the corresponding growing appreciation of dramatized performances and modern presentation technology in managed heritage attraction demonstrate what has been denoted as the 'performance turn', characterized as an orientation towards 'embodied, collaborative and technologized doings and enactments' (Bærenholdt et al., 2008, p. 178). The 'performance turn' would imply a perception that 'Tourism is performed rather than preformed' (2008, p. 181) (compare Holbrook et al. (1984) and Holt (1995)). Furthermore, as exemplified by historic attractions, visitors are assumed to have the capacities to experience the connections between the past and the actual site, take possession of the past and make the connections as a part of their own lives, and it would thus be the connections that produce the specific experiences (Bærenholdt *et al.*, 2008). The existential-encounter approach (Jensen and Lindberg, 2000; Lindberg, 2001) has offered arguments for this view, still with even more emphasis on the lives of the visitors as the basic frame of reference for evaluating the experiences. The 'performance turn' perspective also represents a confronting view on MacCannell's (1976) critical concept of 'staged authenticity' and expresses the opinion that all cultures, in fact, are constructed. It also confronts Wang's (2000) concept of 'constructive authenticity' in arguing that the concept captures just a limited view of the authenticity phenomenon and is thus too simplistic to cover the wide range of processes involved in the encounters with the visitors at attraction sites (Bærenholdt *et al.*, 2008).

As for further research progress on the performance part of attraction, increased empirical focus should be directed at the significance of interactive involvement and co-production of attraction experiences between consumers and service producers, for example as demonstrated through the construct of extraordinary experiences (Arnold and Price, 1993; Quan and Wang, 2004; Mossberg, 2007, 2008; Prebensen and Foss, 2011, 2011) and as promoted within the evolving frameworks of the experience economy (Pine and Gilmore, 1999; Boswijk *et al.*, 2007) and the service-dominant logic (Li and Petrick, 2008; Vargo and Lush, 2008).

As demonstrated by Dahl and Vittersø (2010), interest can be an appropriate conceptual approach to measure experiences in historic attractions, but could basically be applicable to any theme-based attraction related to, for example, object of interest, epistemic interest or topic interest (Krapp, 2002). By the visit of attractions environmentally triggered 'situational interest' (involving affective reactions and focused attention), the way such interest is triggered and how it could lead to learning (Krapp, 2002; Hidi, 2006) would be of particular significance for capturing and maintaining the attention and involvement of visitors (compare 'mindfulness' (Moscardo, 1996, 2003)). Particularly important is the question of how to respond to visitors with less-developed interest (Renninger *et al.*, 2002) in the topics exposed in the attraction, as most 'typical' tourists tend to have limited pre-knowledge of the actual themes presented (compare Poria *et al.* (2003)) and frequently quite limited time available for the visit. However, as the visitors' attachments to the themes or the phenomena of the attraction can vary, there is a need to discriminate between the visitors relative to specific cues, such as ethnic origin or other characteristics that could influence their affective responses to various presentation approaches. The role of cognitive 'maps' or 'schemas' of the visitors before the visits has also proved to be of significance when evaluating their emotional responses on what they are exposed to at the site, such as demonstrated by the assimilation resistance approach (Vittersø *et al.*, 2000). Also the role of emotions or mood during the moment of visitation has been emphasized (de Rojas and Camarero, 2008) (compare circumstance-value of restaurant guests (Jensen and Hansen, 2007)).

An important step for progress in and for strengthening the applicability of the research on tourist experiences is also to be able to isolate sets of indicators with different types of effects on tourists in a tourism setting (Swan and Combs, 1976; Noe, 1987; Uysal and Williams, 2004; Uysal and Noe, 2007). The studies previously referred to present a set of discriminating indicators (linked to tourist destinations) distinguishing between expressive and instrumental indicators. Expressive indicators 'involve core experiences representing the major intent of an act' (Uysal and Noe,

2007, p. 144), that is personal experience as an end in itself, as 'instrumental indicators serve as actions or behaviours towards facilitating that desired end' (2007, p. 144), that is, as a means to an end. Uysal and Williams (2004) found partial support that expressive and instrumental factors might be predictors of overall satisfaction or dissatisfaction and that the travel type expressed by motivation ('novelty and fun and enjoyment seekers' vs 'familiarity and comfort seekers') moderate the importance of these factors. These indicators can also be compared with what is denoted as 'Plus' elements creating basic satisfaction and basic elements frequently causing dissatisfaction (Maunier and Camelis, 2013). Even though these set of factors initially are linked to the destination level, they can simultaneously also be associated with the micro level of attractions within which it can be assumed that the expressive indicators will be more important for the value of tourist experiences than functional indicators. Still a balanced handling of both sets of factors has to be catered for.

An attempt on general categorization of the research approaches

When comparing the studies referred to, some general categorizations along various dimensions can be done, as for example illustrated by Jennings (2006). One obvious distinction is between primarily object-oriented and subject-oriented approaches. Object-oriented approaches have a focus on visitor evaluations of specific aspects or elements by the attraction or the attraction-events and will thus have a predominantly extrovert direction. Evaluation of different attributes of the attraction, whether in pre-set or open-ended evaluation forms, will typically be of main concern. Subject-oriented approaches, on the other hand, have the primary focus on the visitor as such and the introvert visitor experience or perceptions. They will typically be based on overall psychological or/and existential aspects of the experience stimulated by an attraction visit, such as by the existential encounter approach (Lindberg, 2001), or simply by associations linked to existing attractions, such as by the assimilation resistance approach (Vittersø et al., 2000).

Beside the object–subject orientations, distinctions can be made between research foci on structures and processes. In structure orientations, the main attention is on fixed parts of the attraction, such as constructions, displays, artefacts, technology, available information, etc. These primarily have a static nature. Process orientations direct the attention to events, interactions, episodes, individual and social involvement, knowledge creations, emotions, etc. They are therefore of a dynamic nature.

Most approaches will be located on different positions along the object–subject and structure–process dimension continuums and they will rarely be positioned just at one end of a scale. In a simplified way, however, the various orientations have been located in a matrix, as demonstrated in Table 11.1.

Having a way to map the positions of different research approaches on visitor experiences offers an opportunity to see what aspects of this complex social phenomenon are widely or barely covered in different research contributions. This can be linked to specific contexts, such as type of attractions (museums, amusement parks, etc.), particular types of destinations and type of visitor category, and can also be related to the involvement of specific disciplines (psychology, sociology, geography, economics/marketing, etc.) and use of research designs (qualitative/quantitative or

Table 11.1. Categorization of main directions and dimensions in focus by research on visitor experiences at managed tourist attractions.

	Main direction of attention	
Dimensions in focus	Object orientation (properties/extrovert)	Subject orientation (introvert)
Structures (static)	A	B
Processes (dynamic)	C	D

explorative/descriptive/causal). Such distinctions are of significance for comparisons between studies, including estimations of strengths and limitations of their contributions, and spill-over possibilities. For example, there seem to be many descriptive studies on visitor evaluations on attraction attributes, especially linked to perceived service quality (position A in Table 11.1), as there are fewer studies on processes (C and D in Table 11.1), especially through subject-oriented approaches. As each of the approaches demonstrates different qualities regarding uncovering particular aspects of the visitor experience, it would furthermore be of importance for research progress to encourage more variations in the methodological approaches to encourage stronger complementarity between approaches in the elucidation of the field.

Implications and Concluding Remarks

Belonging to a 'special branch' within the tourism industry with the intention of creating exciting, entertaining, rewarding, knowledge-generating, meaningful and/or memorable experiences for national and international travellers, managers of tourist attractions face a great variety of challenges. Moreover, management capacities and access to financial means and specialized competence, as well as the basic purpose of the attractions, vary tremendously (Leask, 2010). Despite a wide range of differences between various types of attractions, many of the basic questions for how to create positive visitor experiences are generally still quite similar. At the level of application, the key question is how the knowledge from research on tourist experiences could contribute positively to efforts of enhancing experience quality of managed attractions and thereby creating value in tourism activities.

The first question to be raised is how to distinguish between main dimensions of experience quality to be able to identify what aspect or phase of the experience creation the attraction management needs to focus on in particular, for example constructions and displays, on the one hand, or human interactions, on the other, or what stage of the experience process critical incidents occur. This issue is also linked to the question of what actually causes positive or negative experience quality. 'From a management viewpoint, the main challenge is to understand the satisfactory and dissatisfactory elements of the tourism experience in order to design and deliver a memorable one likely to result in positive post-consumption reactions' (Maunier and Camelis, 2013, p. 19). For management and investors, the research overview can provide better underpinnings for deciding how to do improvements and even more to improve the right thing (Nowacki, 2009).

The second issue is to help sort out factors that have different and quite specific types of effects on the experience quality. An example would be the distinction between expressive and instrumental indicators of tourist experiences (Swan and Combs, 1976; Noe, 1987; Uysal and Williams, 2004; Uysal and Noe, 2007) and the different ways that each of these categories tends to influence experiences for different categories of tourists.

The third issue is helping to find research methods appropriate for the actual decision problem in question. As there is no method that covers all aspects of the factors influencing experience quality, it will be useful to access systematic overviews of different methods with specified strengths and weaknesses relative to purpose so that management does not waste capacity and attention on methods or results of applied methods that are unable to deliver the type of information needed for improvements. For example, instead of applying traditional service quality surveys when trying to find new and creative ways of presenting a phenomenon or theme, different identifiable qualitative techniques described in this chapter could be used with more success.

A critical issue is whether results from single studies on tourist experiences can be applied in different contexts, that is, to what degree are such research findings generic or contextualized? For example, comparing research findings and possible 'success factors' between different categories of attractions in destinations with heterogeneous structural characteristics and with varying basic mission statements is obviously a great challenge (Leask, 2010). As suggested by Uysal and Noe (2007) in their study of US national parks, the practical usefulness of the findings increases when relating to a specific programme that is closer to the particular substantive context (Blumer, 1954), rather than to global programmes or general issues. This is supported by Pearce (2011), emphasizing that 'context matters'. On the other hand, even within grounded theory (Strauss and Corbin, 1990), some degrees of generalization are 'allowed' between contexts with similar structural characteristics. It is thus assumed that comparisons and the application of results should first of all be made between groups of attractions or tourist settings with certain common characteristics, for example based on types of theme, mission and critical surrounding contextual conditions. However, a number of findings relative to effects of presentation tools at attraction settings and to tourist behaviour, for example based on psychology, are obviously still of generic nature. Their application should, however, be interpreted and adjusted relative to the actual contexts in question. Critical overview of different approaches to the measurement of tourist experiences as provided in this chapter could thus be of some guidance when trying to find how research on tourist experiences can be of use for increasing the value creation at managed tourist attractions.

For the progress of research, as well as for management purposes, more efforts are still needed to create a richer body of evidence that could contribute to identifying both generic and differentiated characteristics of visitor experiences within various contextual conditions. There is finally also a need for overall, simplified frameworks that facilitate comparisons and the positioning of the contributions from various studies.

References

Ajzen, I. and Fischbein, M. (1980) *Understanding Attitudes and Predicting Social Behavior*. Prentice-Hall, Englewood Cliffs, New Jersey.

Ajzen, I. and Madden, T.J. (1986) Prediction of goal-directed behavior: attitudes, intentions, and perceived behavioral control. *Journal of Experimental Social Psychology* 22, 453–474.

Alegre, J. and Garau, J. (2010) Tourist satisfaction and dissatisfaction. *Annals of Tourism Research* 37, 52–73.

Alexandros, A. and Jaffry, S. (2005) Stated preferences for two Cretan heritage attractions. *Annals of Tourism Research* 32, 985–1005.

Arnold, E.J. and Price, L.L. (1993) River magic: extraordinary experiences and the extended service encounter. *Journal of Consumer Research* 20, 24–45.

Bærenholdt, J.O., Haldrup, M. and Larsen, J. (2008) Performing cultural attractions. In: Sundbo, J. and Darmer, P. (eds) *Creating Experiences in the Experience Economy*. Edward Elgar, Cheltenham, UK.

Baker, D.A. and Crompton, J.L. (2000) Quality, satisfaction and behavioral intentions. *Annals of Tourism Research* 27, 785–804.

Bauman, Z. (2001) *Liquid Modernity*. Polity Press, Cambridge.

Beeho, A.J. and Prentice, R.C. (1997) Conceptualizing the experiences of heritage tourists: a case study of New Lanark World Heritage Village. *Tourism Management* 18, 75–87.

Belk, R. (1975) Situational variables and consumer behavior. *Journal of Consumer Research* 2, 157–164.

Blumer, H. (1954) What is wrong with the social theory? *American Sociological Review* 19, 3–10.

Boorstin, D.J. (1964) *The Image. A Guide to Pseudo-Events in America*. Athenaeum, New York.

Bosnjak, M., Sirgy, M.J., Hellriegel, S. and Maurer, O. (2011) Postvisit destination loyalty judgments: developing and testing a comprehensive congruity model. *Journal of Travel Research* 50, 496–508.

Boswijk, A., Thijssen, T. and Peelen, E. (2007) *The Experience Economy. A New Perspective*. Pearson Education Benelux, Amsterdam.

Boulding, W., Kalra, A., Staelin, R. and Zeithaml, V.A. (1993) A dynamic process model of service quality: from expectations to behavioural intentions. *Journal of Marketing Research* 30, 7–27.

Buttle, F. (1996) SERVQUAL: review, critique, research agenda. *European Journal of Marketing* 30, 8–32.

Carù, A. and Cova, B. (2003) Revisiting consumption experience: a more humble but complete view of the concept. *Marketing Theory* 3, 267.

Chen, C.F. and Tsai, D. (2007) How destination image and evaluative factors affect behavioral intentions? *Tourism Management* 28, 1115–1122.

Cohen, E. (1974) Who is a tourist? A conceptual clarification. *Sociological Review* 22, 527–553.

Cohen, E. (1979) A phenomenology of tourist experiences. *Sociology* 13, 179–201.

Cohen, E. (1995) Contemporary tourism – trends and challenges. Sustainable authenticity or contrived post-modernity? In: Butler, R.W. and Pearce, D. (eds) *Changes in Tourism. People, Places, Processes*. Routledge, London.

Cole, S. and Chancellor, H. (2009) Examining the festival attributes that impact visitor experience, satisfaction and re-visit intention. *Journal of Vacation Marketing* 15, 323.

Craigh-Smith, S. and French, C. (1994) *Learning to Live With Tourism*. Pitman, Melbourne, Australia.

Crompton, J.L. and Love, L.L. (1995) The predictive validity of alternative approaches to evaluating quality of a festival. *Journal of Travel Research* 34, 11.

Dahl, T.I. and Vittersø, J. (2010) What's cool about life in the Arctic? Situational interest, cognition, affect and teenagers. *Designs for Learning: 2nd International Conference – Towards a New Conceptualization of Learning*, Stockholm.

Dann, G.M.S. (1996) *The Language of Tourism. A Sociolinguistic Perspective*. CAB International, Wallingford, UK.

De Rojas, C. and Camarero, C. (2008) Visitors' experience, mood and satisfaction in a heritage context: evidence from an interpretation center. *Tourism Management* 29, 525–537.

Eckblad, G. (1981a) Assimilation resistance and affective responses in problem solving. *Scandinavian Journal of Psychology* 22, 1–16.

Eckblad, G. (1981b) *Scheme Theory. A Conceptual Framework for Cognitive-Motivational Processes.* Academic Press, London.

Fischbein, M. and Adjzen, I. (1975) *Belief, Attitude, Intention, and Behavior: An Introduction to Theory and Research.* Addison-Wesley, Reading, Massachusetts.

Fournier, S. and Mick, D. (1999) Rediscovering satisfaction. *Journal of Marketing* 63, 5–23.

Getz, D. (1997) *Event Management and Event Tourism.* Cognizant Communication Corporation, New York.

Gould, P. and White, R. (1974) *Mental Maps.* Penguin Books, Harmondsworth, UK.

Gremler, D.D. (2004) The critical incident technique in service research. *Journal of Service Research* 7, 65–89.

Gunn, C.A. (1979) *Tourism Planning.* Russak, Crane, New York.

Gunn, C.A. (1988) *Vacationscape: Designing Tourist Regions.* Van Nostrand Reinhold, New York.

Hertzman, E., Anderson, D. and Rowley, S. (2008) Edutainment heritage attractions: a portrait of visitors' experiences. *Museum Management and Curatorship* 23, 155–175.

Hidi, S. (2006) Interest: a unique motivational variable. *Educational Research Review* 1, 69–82.

Hirschman, E. and Holbrook, M. (1982) Hedonic consumption: emerging concepts, methods and propositions. *Journal of Marketing* 46, 92–101.

Holbrook, M.B. and Hirschman, E.C. (1982) The experiential aspects of consumption: consumer fantasies, feelings, and fun. *Journal of Consumer Research* 9, 132.

Holbrook, M.B., Chestnut, R.W., Oliva, T.A. and Greenleaf, E.A. (1984) Play as a consumption experience: the roles of emotions, performance, and personality in the enjoyment of games. *Journal of Consumer Research* 11, 728–739.

Holt, D.B. (1995) How consumers consume: a typology of consumption practices. *Journal of Consumer Research* 22, 1–16.

Hutchinson, J., Lai, F.J. and Wang, Y.C. (2009) Understanding the relationships of quality, value, equity, satisfaction, and behavioral intentions among golf travelers. *Tourism Management* 30, 298–308.

Jennings, G. (2006) Perspectives on quality tourism experiences: an introduction. In: Jennings, G. and Nickerson, N.P. (eds) *Quality Tourism Experiences.* Elsevier Butterworth-Heinemann, Oxford.

Jennings, G. and Nickerson, N.P.E. (2006) *Quality Tourism Experiences.* Elsevier Butterworth-Heinemann, Oxford.

Jensen, Ø. (2002) Service quality of managed tourist attractions: a conceptual discussion. In: Elliott, G. and Barnes, J. (eds) 2001 *ServSIG Services Research Conference: New Horizons in Service Marketing (Proceedings Series).* American Marketing Association, Chicago, Illinois.

Jensen, Ø. and Hansen, K.V. (2007) Consumer values among restaurant customers. *International Journal of Hospitality Management* 26, 603–622.

Jensen, Ø. and Korneliussen, T. (2002) Discriminating perceptions of a peripheral 'Nordic destination' among European tourists. *Tourism and Hospitality Research* 3, 319–330.

Jensen, Ø. and Lindberg, F. (2000) The consumption of a tourist attraction: a modern, postmodern, and an existential encounter perspective. In: Beckmann, S.C. and Elliott, R.H. (eds) *Interpretive Consumer Research: Paradigms, Methodologies and Applications.* Copenhagen Business School Press, Handelshøjskolens forlag, Copenhagen.

Kim, M.J., Chung, N., Lee, C.K. and Kim, J.M. (2012) Do loyalty groups differ in the role of trust in online tourism shopping? A process perspective. *Journal of Travel &Tourism Marketing* 29(4), 352–368.

Kinghorn, N. and Willis, K. (2008) Measuring museum visitor preferences towards opportunities for developing social capital: an application of a choice experiment to the discovery museum. *International Journal of Heritage Studies* 14(6), 555–572.

Krapp, A. (2002) Structural and dynamic aspects of interest development: theoretical considerations from an ontogenetic perspective. *Learning and Instruction* 12, 383–409.

Kyle, G. and Chick, G. (2004) Enduring leisure involvement: the importance of personal relationships. *Leisure Studies* 23, 243–266.

Larsen, S. (2007) Aspects of a psychology of the tourist experience. *Scandinavian Journal of Hospitality and Tourism* 7, 7–18.

Lash, S. and Urry, J. (1994) *Economies of Signs and Space*. Sage, London.

Leask, A. (2010) Progress in visitor attraction research: towards more effective management. *Tourism Management* 31, 155–166.

Lewis, B.R. and Clacher, E. (2001) Service failure and recovery in UK theme parks: the employees' perspective. *International Journal of Contemporary Hospitality Management* 13, 166–175.

Li, X.R. and Petrick, J.F. (2008) Tourism marketing in an era of paradigm shift. *Journal of Travel Research* 46, 235–244.

Lindberg, F. (2001) Ontological consumer research. Outline of the conceptual arguments illustrated through tourist experiences. PhD thesis. Copenhagen Business School, Copenhagen.

MacCannell, D. (1976) *The Tourist: A New Theory of the Leisure Class*. Schocken Books, New York.

Maunier, C. and Camelis, C. (2013) Towards an identification of elements contributing to satisfaction with the tourism experience. *Journal of Vacation Marketing* 19, 19–39.

McMullan, R. and O'Neill, M. (2010) Towards a valid and reliable measure of visitor satisfaction. *Journal of Vacation Marketing* 16, 29–44.

Meng, F., Tepanon, Y. and Uysal, M. (2008) Measuring tourist satisfaction by attribute and motivation: the case of a nature-based resort. *Journal of Vacation Marketing* 14, 41.

Middleton, V.T.C. (1988) *Marketing in Travel and Tourism*. Butterworth-Heinemann, Oxford.

Middleton, V.T.C. and Clarke, J. (2001) *Marketing in Travel and Tourism*. Butterworth-Heinemann, Amsterdam.

Mill, R.C. and Morrison, A. (1985) *The Tourism System: An Introductory Text*. Prentice Hall, Englewood Cliffs, New Jersey.

Moscardo, G. (1996) Mindful visitors. Heritage and tourism. *Annals of Tourism Research* 23, 376–397.

Moscardo, G. (2003) Interpretation and sustainable tourism: functions, examples and principles. *Journal of Tourism Studies* 14, 112–123.

Mossberg, L. (2007) A marketing approach to the tourist experience. *Scandinavian Journal of Hospitality and Tourism* 7, 59–74.

Mossberg, L. (2008) Extraordinary experiences through storytelling. *Scandinavian Journal of Hospitality and Tourism* 8, 195–210.

Neal, J.D., Uysal, M. and Sirgy, M.J. (2007) The effect of tourism services on travelers' quality of life. *Journal of Travel Research* 46, 154–163.

Newsome, D., Moore, S.A. and Dowling, R.K. (2002) *Natural Area Tourism. Ecology, Impacts and Management*. Channel View, Bristol, UK.

Noe, F.P. (1987) Measurement specification and leisure satisfaction. *Leisure Science* 9, 163–172.

Nowacki, M.M. (2009) Quality of visitor attractions, satisfaction, benefits and behavioural intentions of visitors: verification of a model. *International Journal of Tourism Research* 11, 297–309.

O'Dell, T. (2007) Tourist experiences and academic junctures. *Scandinavian Journal of Hospitality and Tourism* 7, 34–45.

Oliver, R.L. (1997) *Satisfaction. A Behavioral Perspective on the Consumer*. McGraw-Hill, New York.

Parasuraman, A., Zeithaml, V.A. and Berry, L.L. (1985) A conceptual model of service quality and its implications for future research. *Journal of Marketing* 49, 41–50.

Parasuraman, A., Berry, L.L. and Zeithaml, V.A. (1991) Understanding customer expectations of service. *Sloan Management Review* 32, 29–38.

Pearce, P. (1991) Analysing tourist attractions. *Journal of Tourism Studies* 2, 46–55.

Pearce, P.L. (2011) *Tourist Behaviour and the Contemporary World*. Channel View, Bristol, UK.

Pine, B.J. and Gilmore, J.H. (1999) *The Experience Economy. Work is Theater and Every Business a Stage.* Harvard Business School Press, Boston, Massachusetts.

Poria, Y., Butler, R. and Airey, D. (2003) The core of heritage tourism. *Annals of Tourism Research* 30, 238–254.

Poria, Y., Reichel, A. and Biran, A. (2006) Heritage site management: motivations and expectations. *Annals of Tourism Research* 33, 162–178.

Prebensen, N.K. (2010) Value creation through stakeholder participation: a case study of an event in the High North. *Event Management* 11, 99–108.

Prebensen, N.K. and Foss, L. (2011) Coping and co-creating in tourist experiences. *International Journal of Tourism Research* 13, 54–67.

Prebensen, N.K., Woo, E., Chen, J.S. and Uysal, M. (2013) Motivation and involvement as antecedents of the perceived value of the destination experience. *Journal of Travel Research* 52, 253–264.

Prentice, R.C., Witt, S.F. and Hamer, C. (1998) Tourism as experience: the case of heritage parks. *Annals of Tourism Research* 25, 1–24.

Pritchard, M.P. and Havitz, M.E. (2006) Destination appraisal: an analysis of critical incidents. *Annals of Tourism Research* 33, 25–46.

Quan, S. and Wang, N. (2004) Towards a structural model of the tourist experience: an illustration from food experiences in tourism. *Tourism Management* 25, 297–305.

Reichel, A., Uriely, N. and Shani, A. (2008) Ecotourism and simulated attractions: tourists' attitudes towards integrated sites in a desert area. *Journal of Sustainable Tourism* 16, 23–41.

Renninger, K.A., Ewen, L. and Lasher, A.K. (2002) Individual interest as context in expository text and mathematical word problems. *Learning and Instruction* 12, 467–490.

Sirakaya, E., Petrick, J. and Choi, H.S. (2004) The role of mood on tourism product evaluations. *Annals of Tourism Research* 31, 517–539.

Sirgy, M.J., Kruger, P.S., Lee, D.-J. and Grace, B.Y. (2011) How does a travel trip affect tourists' life satisfaction? *Journal of Travel Research* 50, 261–275.

Strauss, A. and Corbin, J. (1990) *Basics of Qualitative Research: Grounded Theory Procedures and Techniques.* Sage, Newbury Park, California.

Swan, J.E. and Combs, L.J. (1976) Product performance and consumer satisfaction: a new concept. *Journal of Marketing* 40, 25–33.

Swarbrooke, J. (2002) *The Development and Management of Visitor Attractions.* Butterworth-Heinemann, Oxford.

Tomas, S.R., Scott, D. and Crompton, J.L. (2002) An investigation of the relationships between quality of service performance, benefits sought, satisfaction and future intention to visit among visitors to a zoo. *Managing Leisure* 7, 239–250.

Tufts, S. and Milne, S. (1999) Museums: a supply-side perspective. *Annals of Tourism Research* 26, 613–631.

Uriely, N. (2005) The tourist experience: conceptual developments. *Annals of Tourism Research* 32, 199–216.

Urry, J. (2002) *The Tourist Gaze.* Sage, London.

Uysal, M. and Noe, F.P. (2007) Satisfaction in outdoor recreation and tourism settings. In: Laws, E. (ed.) *Tourism Marketing. Quality and Service Management Perspectives.* Thomson Learning, London.

Uysal, M. and Williams, J. (2004) The role of expressive and instrumental factors in measuring visitor satisfaction. In: Crouch, G.I., Perdue, R.R., Timmermans, H.J.P. and Uysal, M. (eds) *Consumer Psychology of Tourism, Hospitality and Leisure.* CAB International, Wallingford, UK.

Vargo, S.L. and Lush, R.F. (2008) Service-dominant logic: continuing the evolution. *Journal of the Academy of Marketing Science* 36, 1–14.

Vittersø, J., Vorkinn, M., Vistad, O.I. and Vaagland, J. (2000) Tourist experiences and attractions. *Annals of Tourism Research* 27, 432–450.

Volo, S. (2009) Conceptualizing experience: a tourist based approach. *Journal of Hospitality Marketing and Management* 18, 111–126.

Wang, N. (2000) *Tourism and Modernity: A Sociological Analysis.* Elsevier Science, Amsterdam.

Wanhill, S. (2002) Creating themed entertainment attractions: a Nordic perspective. *Scandinavian Journal of Hospitality and Tourism* 2, 123–144.

Weaver, D. (2008) *Ecotourism.* John Wiley, Sydney.

Weidenfeld, A., Butler, R.W. and Williams, A.M. (2010) Clustering and compatibility between tourism attractions. *International Journal of Tourism Research* 12(1), 1–16.

Williams, P. and Soutar, G.N. (2009) Value, satisfaction and behavioral intentions in an adventure tourism context. *Annals of Tourism Research* 36, 413–438.

Willis, K.G. (2009) Assessing visitor preferences in the management of archaeological and heritage attractions: a case study of Hadrian's Roman Wall. *International Journal of Tourism Research* 11, 487–505.

Wong, K.K.F. and Cheung, P.W. (1999) Strategic theming in theme park marketing. *Journal of Vacation Marketing* 5, 319–332.

Yoon, Y. and Uysal, M. (2005) An examination of the effects of motivation and satisfaction on destination loyalty: a structural model. *Tourism Management* 26, 45–56.

Zabkar, V., Brencic, M.M. and Dmitrovic, T. (2010) Modelling perceived quality, visitor satisfaction and behavioural intentions at the destination level. *Tourism Management* 31, 537–546.

Zeithaml, V.A., Berry, L.L. and Parasuraman, A. (1996) The behavioral consequences of service quality. *Journal of Marketing* 60, 31–46.

12 Storytelling in a Co-creation Perspective

LINE MATHISEN

Finnmark University College, Alta, Norway (currently at NORUT, Northern Research Institute, Alta, Norway)

Introduction

Stories have always been important for people and are increasingly being discussed in marketing and advertising literature as they are argued to impact on consumers' experience processes through emotions and comprehension (Mulvey and Medina, 2003; Escalas, 2004b; Fog *et al.*, 2005; Chronis, 2008; Lundqvist *et al.*, 2012). Stories that promote destinations communicate value propositions that engage tourists' imagination, and influence their expectations and attitudes about the destination and the upcoming experience through identification (Green and Brock, 2000; Oatley, 2002; Slater and Rouner, 2002; Kim and Richardson, 2003; Escalas, 2007; Tussyadiah *et al.*, 2011). As such, stories may be used by tourism firms in order to enhance the value for tourists by involving them in the value creation process, i.e. in co-creating experience value. The concept of co-creation of value is widely discussed in marketing and business strategy research and relates to how individual knowledge and skills are deployed during a tourist experience in order to influence behaviours that maximize the creation of participants' value (Prahalad and Ramaswamy, 2004; Vargo and Lusch, 2004; Madhavaram and Hunt, 2008; Prebensen *et al.*, 2013).

However, despite the relevance of storytelling in the design and promotion of experiential services, research on storytelling as firm-driven and thus a strategic resource for value co-creation is still limited (Padgett and Allen, 1997; Lundqvist *et al.*, 2012). The interest in and importance of storytelling as a resource rest in part in the belief that the particular qualities of storytelling may enhance the value of tourists' experiences. For instance, evocative stories capture participants because they influence emotions and cognitions, and subsequently value recognition. Further, value recognition helps participants in their construction of meaning, which is essential in order to inspire co-creation behaviours (Bruner, 1986; Polkinghorne, 1988; Adaval and Wyer, 1998; Mulvey and Medina, 2003; Porter, 2008; Vargo and Lusch, 2008). Hence, by using storytelling during host–guest interactions, important human values can be made salient, which facilitates identification with the elements in the story related to the self and the current situation (Mulvey and Medina, 2003; Green *et al.*, 2004; Escalas, 2007).

Indeed, communicative staging such as storytelling is described as essential in the determination of experience quality and value (Arnould and Price, 1993; Arnould *et al.*, 1998; Mossberg, 2008). This importance implies that stories may be used in order to enhance the value during host–guest interactions (Bruner, 1986; Polkinghorne, 1988; Slater and Rouner, 2002; Green *et al.*, 2004; Moisio and Arnould, 2005; Chronis *et al.*, 2012). Through story reconstruction and imagination, tourists engage with the stories to which they are exposed (Chronis, 2008). Stories with emotional appeal, that resonate with tourists' values and personal goal achievements, can help tourists to attach meaning to an experience, thus inspiring and motivating their behaviour (Babin *et al.*, 1994; Schwartz, 1994; Babin and Kim, 2001; Park and Rabolt, 2009; Lee *et al.*, 2010). Hence, storytelling is about telling stories with a message that is tuned to the values of the tourists, stories that can change the way they think and respond to tourist activities.

This chapter is a contribution to the understanding of the value-enhancing properties of storytelling, with a focus on co-creation. Moreover, it illustrates the importance of storytelling as a management operant resource that can be used in order to manage host–guest interaction in a way that enhances the value creation taking place during the interaction process. From a research perspective, this chapter adds to the body of knowledge about the qualities of communication in the form of stories and of storytelling as a value enhancer in a host–guest relationship. Also, from a managerial perspective it may serve as a starting point for resource planning, development and mobilization.

The Power of Storytelling (as a Resource)

Stories and storytelling are considered important within different research fields (Bruner, 1986; Polkinghorne, 1988; Green and Brock, 2000; McAdams, 2001; Green *et al.*, 2004; Denning, 2006; Moyer-Gusé, 2008; Schembri *et al.*, 2010; Tussyadiah *et al.*, 2011), thus, the power of stories is evident. The premise for using storytelling in order to enhance the value of the tourist experience is based on the belief that individuals listen to and create stories in order to understand the meanings of experiences. Further, stories are important in order to construct new stories with new meanings for the self and in order to momentarily escape from the routines and ordinary activities of life (Bruner, 1986; Polkinghorne, 1988). In a broad sense, stories can be used in order to manage the tourist experience through its entire lifespan.

Firstly, stories have entertainment value that attracts tourists' attention, and maintains their attention long enough for them to get engaged in the performance of the experience (Baumeister and Newman, 1994). This means that stories may serve as entrance points to an imagined reality in which an inner vision and outer reality interact with story characters' and interpreters' consciousness in order to create value (Bruner, 1986; Damasio, 1999; Schank and Berman, 2003). These imagined realities, or story frameworks, resemble tourists' life stories, in which emotions are connected to the knowledge of what arouses them, and in which action follows these feelings and subsequently the knowledge about the situation (Bruner, 1986). Viewing the tourist experience as a possibility for tourists to live out fantasies by imagining and appropriating experiences that satisfy a range of culturally constructed attitudes and values (Ateljevic, 2001; Carù and Cova, 2003; Holt and Thompson, 2004) means that the types of stories that draw on well-known master plots may prove to be fruitful avenues for tourism and destination marketing to explore. The reason for this may be that story genres, such as mysteries, myths and fairy tales, influence individual decontextualization readiness as these genres' pragmatic functions are learned through other stories (Polichak and Gerrig, 2002). Moreover, they are reflections of global value systems that are connected with local and personal values, in addition to desires and fears, which give them a rhetorical and emotional power (Bruner, 1986; Ateljevic, 2001; Taylor *et al.*, 2002; Porter, 2008; Curran Bernard, 2011). Hence, stories serve as a type of stimulus that has a significant influence on tourists' emotions, cognitions and subsequently action. In addition, stories provide individuals with direct and indirect experiences related to the self and that are to be understood and reflected on as they progress (Bruner, 1986; Polkinghorne, 1988; Schank and Berman, 2003).

Secondly, storytelling is suggested to be exceptional in communicating value and meaning as humans naturally process information in a story-like form (conceived in terms of settings, scenes, characters, plots, goals and themes) (Adaval and Wyer, 1998; Deighton *et al.*, 1989). Tourists perceive, interpret and match the elements and cues in the story with similar story elements stored in the memory, which facilitates understanding and the (re)creation of value (Baumeister and Newman, 1994; Adaval and Wyer, 1998; McAdams, 2001; Schank and Berman, 2003; Escalas, 2004b). Therefore, telling evocative stories can have a positive effect on the creation of meaning, determination of value and level of activity, resulting in recognition of self-identity claims and situational bonding (Polkinghorne, 1988; Deighton *et al.*, 1989; Arnould and Price, 1993; Arnould *et al.*, 1998; Mulvey and Medina, 2003; Escalas, 2004b; Carù and Cova, 2006; Denning, 2006; Mathisen, 2012). In particular, stories' emotional appeal is viewed as important for the level of engagement, immersion and imagination because emotions may induce empathy and/or sympathy with the stories' protagonists, which links the drama in the stories to emotional moments in their own lives (van Dijk, 1975; Taylor *et al.*, 2002; Escalas and Stern, 2003; Green *et al.*, 2004; Escalas, 2007; Chronis *et al.*, 2012). In addition, the emotional impact of stories is connected to transformation of the self, because stories give tourists a chance to relive emotions and thus reflect on personal values and meanings that add self-relevant knowledge (Oatley, 2002). This power of emotions in stories is linked to the creation of meaning in terms of cause, consequences and goal attainment that guides the priorities of the self (McAdams, 2001; Singer and Bluck, 2001). Thus, tourists actively participate in shaping their own versions of stories, as they interact with the story elements during the life of an experience (Merz *et al.*, 2009; Aitken and Campelo, 2011).

Before tourists decide to visit destinations, they are exposed to stories communicated through various media channels. These stories are argued to influence the tourists' perception of destination image (Kim and Richardson, 2003), and have an effect on pre-visit interaction between the host and the potential tourists. This may be viewed as a starting point for co-creation of the tourist experience, as potential tourists evaluate and decide on the importance of the offered service propositions portrayed through destination information (Ballantyne and Aitken, 2007; Merz *et al.*, 2009; Heinonen *et al.*, 2010). Communicative interaction moments like these offer value propositions that have to be supported by the actual experiences at the destination (Ballantyne and Aitken, 2007). Subsequently, the host–guest interaction processes taking place at the destination have to reflect these co-creation efforts in order to maintain the value enhancement (Arnould and Price, 1993; Arnould *et al.*, 1998; Prebensen and Foss, 2011), thus co-creation is most likely to continue if the value proposition represented by the destination brand is confirmed when tourists take part in experiences at the destination (Ballantyne and Aitken, 2007). Moreover, not only may storytelling enhance the value created in interaction processes, in addition the stories told during the life of the tourist experience have a greater chance of being remembered than listed facts or information (Graesser *et al.*, 2002). Tourists return with 'new' stories that they use both in the creation and maintenance of their own identity, and as input in their own storytelling and word of mouth (Fog *et al.*, 2005; Norris *et al.*, 2005; Lichrou *et al.*, 2008; Schembri *et al.*, 2010; Tussyadiah *et al.*, 2011). Hence, the value created during interaction may be maintained and shared between tourists and their networks.

Storytelling Management

Like service experiences, tourist experiences may be viewed as purposive performances, performed by those who participate and set in a particular context (Deighton, 1992; Arnould and Price, 1993; Arnould *et al.*, 1998; Grove *et al.*, 1998; Pine and Gilmore, 1999; Harris *et al.*, 2003). This view on performance reflects Schechner's (2003) and Goffman's (2006) thoughts on goal achievement, role performances and contextual influences. Adopting a drama metaphor can simplify the management of the tourist experience because it facilitates operationalization through intent and demands reflection on the elements needed in order to create desired effects (Grove *et al.*, 1998; Harris *et al.*, 2003; Schechner, 2003; Goffman, 2006). The dramatic form is made explicit through the story, in which the creation of characters, actions, language and symbols contributes to the intended dramatic meaning (Schechner, 2003; Porter, 2008). The purposiveness behind the story means that the type of story and story focus are essential when beginning to plan and create a tourist offer. With a tourism management focus on co-creation and value enhancement, the story creation and telling should reflect the spirit of the destination in terms of its history, culture and people (Aitken and Campelo, 2011). The reason for this is twofold. Firstly, stories central to the understanding of the destination's culture and values may be used in order to interest the right tourists: tourists that identify with the values communicated by the stories. Secondly, stories founded on the destination's communal values portray its assets more in line with how it is viewed by the locals, thus in a more 'genuine' way. This means that tourists perceive the destination, and subsequently their experience, as being more authentic (Olsen, 2002). Tourists' perception of authenticity may influence how they feel about the destination and their evaluation of value (Wang, 1999). In addition, stories have attraction power that influences tourists' involvement, which is especially important in the host–guest interaction taking place via different media channels (Havitz and Manell, 2005). Involvement is believed to be a state of motivation, arousal or interest, concepts of interest for tourism managers as they explain why tourists travel (Park and Yoon, 2009; Ritchie *et al.*, 2010). Further, involvement is influenced by various situational stimuli, which have consequences for how information is processed, decision-making and attitude formation and/or change (Havitz and Manell, 2005). In particular, enduring involvement is suggested to influence attitudes, while situational involvement acts as a mediator to increased involvement in particular situations (Havitz and Manell, 2005). Further, the strength of tourists' involvement in particular contexts depends on the object or activity's personal relevance (Havitz and Manell, 2005; Ritchie *et al.*, 2010). This indicates that stories, similar to other situational stimuli, may increase tourists' involvement and subsequent co-creation behaviours. Therefore, tourism managers have to pay attention to which stories to tell and manage during the lifespan of a tourist experience. For instance, the storytelling management process starts with promotional destination stories that are extended into tourists' on-site experience through interaction processes. Further, during interaction processes, tourists' involvement and co-creation behaviours influence their interpretation and reconstruction of the destination brand stories, and their creation of destination brand meaning, which enhances their experienced value (Green and Brock, 2000; Ballantyne and Aitken, 2007; Chronis *et al.*, 2012). The challenge is then to create stories that attract the right tourists, and to manage live versions of these stories in order to increase tourist involvement and degree of participation in tourist experiences, as this influences co-creation.

Performing a Story: The Mobilization of Storytelling Resources

Tourists have different reasons for being interested in a story and the story may also change in order to attract and interest potential tourists (Green *et al.*, 2002). Performing stories demands a focus on the stories' origins and their expressive components (Tumbat and Belk, 2013). As stories are a (re)presentation of events, situations and behaviours signified by words, images and gestures (Porter, 2008), the challenge for tourism managers (as storytellers) is both the construction of the story and how to mobilize the right resources (Porter, 2008). The construction of stories demands a focus on story structure. Stories have particular structures with a goal, a plot, causally connected events and characters, with the plot driving the audiences' emotions through a dramatization of cause and effect (Bruner, 1986; Polkinghorne, 1988; Stern, 1998; Gabriel, 2000; Kincaid, 2002; Porter, 2008). The structure of the events guides emotions and cognitions, while the performance is the transformation of this structure by using, for example, roles, language, metaphors and symbols (Oatley, 2002; Carlson, 2004). The characters act out their goal-oriented roles in relation to the story context and the other characters in the performance. The various roles inspire particular communications and creation of emotions (Stern, 1991; Kincaid, 2002; Krakowiak and Oliver, 2012). Hence, it is vital to pay attention to the characters, in terms of roles, during story creation and performance management. The importance of the characters can partly be explained in terms of their iconic power, as representations of characters with desired values and personalities (Porter, 2008; Woodside *et al.*, 2008). The characters' desires and values influence their role interpretation and their capacity to engage in co-creation behaviour (Carlson, 2004; Ritchie *et al.*, 2010). Further, their need for self-expression and the personal importance of the activity influence the vigour of their behaviour. In addition, in order for the story to be interesting, there has to be a gap between the characters and their goals, as this creates tension (Curran Bernard, 2011). This gap can be created in several ways, for example by characters having conflicting motivations, or it can be provided by unexpected events, quests and mysteries (O'Toole, 1992; Schechner, 2003). Tension and the story's presentation qualities add to a story's captivating power (Porter, 2008). Presentation quality is enhanced by an increased level of suggestiveness, created by tropes and metaphors that influence imagination (Polichak and Gerrig, 2002; Porter, 2008). Further communication details in the story provide information that influences tourists' expectations and increases the story's chance of being within the tourists' frame of reference (Green *et al.*, 2002). Such details may easily be changed in stories in order to resonate with tourists' attitudes and values.

In order to immerse tourists in the story, the context has to support the story in order for 'real life' to be suspended (O'Toole, 1992). This importance of the context is related to its dominant position that may constrain the effect of the performance and co-creation (O'Toole, 1992; Mathisen, 2012). It is the story context that provides the audience with an entry point they can use in order to follow and understand their experience (Porter, 2008; Curran Bernard, 2011). Therefore, story creation and management entails identification of contextualized core stories that represent themes and values embedded in destination images. Further, the position from which a story is told has implications for the perspective of values, needs, desires and trust contained in the message (Porter, 2008; Curran Bernard, 2011). This means that the characters in a story, or the storytellers themselves, have to fit the stories in terms of knowledge skills and personality. In terms of performing the story, this implies that the stories have to match tourists' ability to act (in terms of their personality, their resources such as knowledge and skills and their values). In order to match stories, particular sequences of actions can be forgone or their order switched to induce, for example, surprise, tempt curiosity or for learning purposes (Porter, 2008; Curran Bernard, 2011).

Discussion

The performance perspective of the co-creation of experience value in tourist experiences shows that tourism firms have to invest in the development of knowledge and skills related to the performance realm as these are resources that are important for how they will succeed with creating meaningful tourist experiences. Drawing on research on storytelling, co-creation and performance theory, this chapter extends and elaborates on how storytelling (as a resource) and performance (as a tool for operationalization of a tourist experience) may enhance value co-creation in tourist experiences. Indeed, operationalization of experiences by adopting theatre-like staging strategies is argued to be the best way to create a successful and transformational tourist experience that best meets tourists' experiential and personal needs (Pine and Gilmore, 1999; Gilmore and Pine, 2007). Moreover, communicative staging such as storytelling is described as essential in the determination of experience quality and value (Arnould *et al.*, 1998; Mossberg, 2008). This importance of stories implies that they may be used in order to enhance the value during host–guest interactions (Bruner, 1986; Polkinghorne, 1988; Slater and Rouner, 2002; Green *et al.*, 2004; Moisio and Arnould, 2005; Chronis *et al.*, 2012). Host–guest encounters provide tourism firms with an opportunity to directly influence tourists' perception of social and psychological experience value (Bitner, 1990; Williams and Soutar, 2009). During these interaction moments, tourists' level of interaction, and also the co-creation of value, might be low or high, mental or physical depending on contextual issues, the host and the tourist (O'Toole, 1992; Sandsröm *et al.*, 2008; Heinonen *et al.*, 2010).

The value embedded in interaction processes demands active participants in order for co-creation to take place (Vargo and Lusch, 2004). Research argues that storytelling engages individuals in, for example, story reconstruction and imagination (Chronis, 2008), thus inspires active participation from both the host and the tourist. In a co-creation perspective, the judgement of value is extended beyond merely exchange value, into value in use (Vargo and Lusch, 2004). Value in use is suggested to be 'a preferential judgement of the meaning of the service experience' (Ballantyne and Varey, 2006, p. 346). As such, value is a motivational construct, related to personal goal achievement, attitudes and life guidance (Babin *et al.*, 1994; Schwartz, 1994; Babin and Kim, 2001). In addition, the value-expressive attitudes and behaviour of individuals are likely to be influenced by the importance attached to a range of values (Schwartz, 1994; Park and Rabolt, 2009; Lee *et al.*, 2010). Some of these values carry similar meanings across cultures and indicate that tourists' personal values, emerging from their everyday life processes, may serve as a starting point in the creation of value-enhancing tourist experiences (Schwartz, 1994; Holbrook, 1999; Ateljevic, 2001; Arnould *et al.*, 2006; Gentile *et al.*, 2007; Heinonen *et al.*, 2010). Further, because co-creation of value is about enabling tourists to engage in co-creation behaviours, storytelling is not just about the telling of any story, but of telling stories that influence tourists' involvement and co-creation behaviours.

Hence, tourism managers have to identify and develop the stories that can be turned into performances that are most likely to impact on tourists' perceived value (see Prebensen *et al.*, 2012). The impact of storytelling varies during the life of a tourist experience, and depends on both the type and power of the story in terms of how it influences the tourist's engagement, and how it communicates destination culture and values, story management, story performance and interpretation and imagination (Bruner, 1986; Deighton, 1992; Mulvey and Medina, 2003; Schechner, 2003; Escalas, 2004a, 2004b; Lichrou *et al.*, 2008; Merz *et al.*, 2009; Chronis *et al.*, 2012). Embedded in destinations are multiple stories that may be developed and told in host–guest interactions in order to involve tourists in the present activity. The power of the story depends on whether it is the right story in terms of structure, its resonance with tourists' needs and values and its emotional power. Well-developed stories have emotional attraction power and may increase tourists' interest in the story through personal relevance (Ritchie *et al.*, 2010). Personal relevance facilitates transportation and imagination, and is also connected to the creation of attitudes and behaviour (Taylor *et al.*, 2002; Escalas, 2004a, 2007; Green *et al.*, 2004; Chronis *et al.*, 2012; Krakowiak and Oliver, 2012). Personal relevance may be further strengthened by performing the story – in particular through the interpretation of roles, as this guides interaction, through use of language and also body language (Schechner, 2003).

Conclusion/Future Research

The aim of this chapter is to add to the understanding of key resources that contribute to the co-creation of tourist value. Viewing the tourist experience as a performance illustrates the importance of storytelling as such a key resource that places it within a performance framework for operationalization of the tourist experience. It is suggested that key resources such as storytelling increase firms' competitiveness and this chapter indicates that storytelling can result in increased involvement and co-creation. Tourist engagement depends on their resources in terms of cultural experience, knowledge and skills, hence these differences result in higher or lower degrees of co-creation. For tourism managers, awareness of how the roles emerging in tourist groups reflect cultural and individual differences can indicate which types of actions and stories are to be performed. Creating and managing tourist experiences is about the creation and management of interactions. Further, host–guest interactions are about supporting tourists' individual performances by drawing on storytelling resources in order to support tourists' competence, and enable and facilitate their participation in the performance. Hence, creating value propositions is about providing opportunities for interaction, and the subsequent value co-creation, by creating stories that, first of all, attract the right tourists. The right tourists are the ones that take an interest in the stories portrayed through, for example, media or promotion. Further, tourism managers have to manage live versions of these stories in order to further increase tourists' engagement and degree of active participation shaping their own experiences. Hence, storytelling can facilitate the process of ongoing interaction that stretches from pre- to post-visit. Consequently tourism managers should consciously and continuously aim to identify and develop a typology of generic story themes that they can integrate into existing knowledge platforms in order to be adaptable to different tourists with a variety of attitudes and travel purposes. A typology of generic stories may also enable tourism managers to enhance co-creation when interacting with tourists from different cultural backgrounds as generic stories concern more common and maybe also global value conceptions. The reciprocity of such stories implies an exchange of information related to cultural values that facilitates involvement through increased understanding and interest. Hence, in a similar way, identification and development of a typology of more specific stories facilitates interactions on a more personal level, which may result in bonding or a feeling of communitas.

In order to gain more knowledge about the use and effect of storytelling, tourism marketing research could explore tourism firms' use and management of stories in terms of their marketing efforts and resource planning. In addition, more knowledge about how a performance view can facilitate the choice, staging and interpretation of stories when planning and creating tourist offers can broaden and refine strategy creation, resource planning and competence integration. Implications for future research also include which stories are suitable in the sense that they bring forth propositions that can be used in order to manage and enhance co-creation processes with tourists from different cultures and backgrounds.

References

Adaval, R. and Wyer, R.S.J. (1998) The role of narratives in consumer information processing. *Journal of Consumer Psychology* 7(3), 207–245.

Aitken, R. and Campelo, A. (2011) The four Rs of place branding. *Journal of Marketing Management* 27(9), 913–933.

Arnould, E.J. and Price, L.L. (1993) River magic: extraordinary experience and the extended service encounter. *Journal of Consumer Research* 20, 24–45.

Arnould, E.J., Price, L.L. and Tierney, P. (1998) Communicative staging of the wilderness servicescape. *Service Industries Journal* 18(3), 90–115.

Arnould, E.J., Price, L.L. and Malsche, A. (2006) Toward a cultural resource-based theory of the customer. In: Lusch, R.F. and Vargo, S.L. (eds) *The Service Dominant Logic of Marketing: Dialog, Debate and Directions*. M.E. Sharpe, New York.

Ateljevic, I. (2001) Searching for nature and imagining New Zealand. *Journal of Travel and Tourism Marketing* 10(1), 115–122.

Babin, B.J. and Kim, K. (2001) International students' travel behavior. *Journal of Travel and Tourism Marketing* 10(1), 93–106.

Babin, B.J., Darden, W.R. and Griffin, M. (1994) Work and/or fun: measuring hedonic and utilitarian shopping value. *Journal of Consumer Research* 20(4), 644–656.

Ballantyne, D. and Aitken, R. (2007) Branding in B2B markets: the service-dominant logic. *Journal of Business and Industrial Marketing* 22(6), 363–371.

Ballantyne, D. and Varey, R.J. (2006) Creating value-in-use through marketing interaction: the exchange logic of relating, communicating and knowing. *Marketing Theory* 6(3), 335–348.

Baumeister, R.F. and Newman, L.S. (1994) How stories make sense of personal experiences: motives that shape autobiographical narratives. *Personality and Social Psychology Bulletin* 20(6), 676–690.

Bitner, M.J. (1990) Evaluating service encounters: the effects of physical surroundings and employee responses. *Journal of Marketing* 54(2), 69–82.

Bruner, J.S. (1986) *Actual Minds, Possible Worlds*. Harvard University Press, Cambridge, Massachusetts.

Carlson, M. (2004) *Performance: A Critical Introduction*, 2nd edn. Routledge, New York.

Carù, A. and Cova, B. (2003) Revisiting consumption experience: a more humble but complete view of the concept. *Marketing Theory* 3(2), 267–286.

Carù, A. and Cova, B. (2006) How to facilitate immersion in a consumption experience: appropriation operations and service elements. *Journal of Consumer Behaviour* 5, 4–14.

Chronis, A. (2008) Co-constructing the narrative experience: staging and consuming the American Civil War at Gettysburg. *Journal of Marketing Management* 24(1/2), 5–27.

Chronis, A., Arnould, E.J. and Hampton, R.D. (2012) Gettysburg re-imagined: the role of narrative imagination in consumption experience. *Consumption Markets and Culture* 15, 261–286.

Curran Bernard, S. (2011) *Documentary Storytelling: Creative Non-Fiction on Screen*. Elsevier, Oxford.

Damasio, A.R. (1999) *The Feeling of What Happens: Body and Emotion in the Making of Consciousness*. Harcourt Brace, New York.

Deighton, J. (1992) The consumption of performance. *Journal of Consumer Research* 19(3), 362–372.

Deighton, J., Romer, D. and McQueen, J. (1989) Using drama to persuade. *Journal of Consumer Research* 16(3), 335–343.

Denning, S. (2006) Effective storytelling: strategic business narrative techniques. *Strategy and Leadership* 34(1), 42–48.

Escalas, J.E. (2004a) Imagine yourself in the product: mental simulation, narrative transportation, and persuasion. *Journal of Advertising* 33(2), 37–48.

Escalas, J.E. (2004b) Narrative processing: building consumer connections to brands. *Journal of Consumer Psychology* 14(1/2), 168–180.

Escalas, J.E. (2007) Self-referencing and persuasion: narrative transportation versus analytical elaboration. *Journal of Consumer Research* 33(4), 421–429.

Escalas, J.E. and Stern, B.B. (2003) Sympathy and empathy: emotional responses to advertising dramas. *Journal of Consumer Research* 29(4), 566–578.

Fog, K., Budtz, C. and Yakaboylu, B. (2005) *Storytelling: Branding in Practice*. Springer, Berlin.

Gabriel, Y. (2000) *Storytelling in Organizations: Facts, Fictions, and Fantasies*. Oxford University Press, Oxford.

Gentile, C., Spiller, N. and Noci, G. (2007) How to sustain the customer experience: an overview of experience components that co-create value with the customer. *European Management Journal* 25(5), 395–410.

Gilmore, J.H. and Pine, B.J. (2007) *Authenticity: What Consumers Really Want*. Harvard Business School Press, Boston, Massachusetts.

Goffman, E. (2006) The presentation of self. In Brissett, D. and Edgley, C. (eds) *Life As Theater: A Dramaturgical Sourcebook*, 2nd edn. Transaction, New Brunswick, New Jersey.

Graesser, A.C., Olde, B. and Klettke, B. (2002) How does the mind construct and represent stories? In: Green, M., Strange, J.J. and Brock, T.C. (eds) *Narrative Impact: Social and Cognitive Foundations*. Lawrence Erlbaum, Mahwah, New Jersey, pp. 231–263.

Green, M.C. and Brock, T.C. (2000) The role of transportation in the persuasiveness of public narratives. *Journal of Personality and Social Psychology* 79(5), 701–721.

Green, M.C., Strange, J.J. and Brock, T.C. (eds) (2002) *Narrative Impact: Social and Cognitive Foundations*. Lawrence Erlbaum, Mahwah, New Jersey.

Green, M.C., Brock, T.C. and Kaufman, G.F. (2004) Understanding media enjoyment: the role of transportation into narrative worlds. *Communication Theory* 14(4), 311–327.

Grove, S.J., Fisk, R.P. and Dorsch, M.J. (1998) Assessing the theatrical components of the service encounter: a cluster analysis examination. *Service Industries Journal* 18(3), 116–134.

Harris, R., Harris, K. and Baron, S. (2003) Theatrical service experiences: dramatic script development with employees. *International Journal of Service Industry Management* 14(2), 184–199.

Havitz, M.E. and Manell, R.C. (2005) Enduring involvement, situational involvement, and flow in leisure and non-leisure activities. *Journal of Leisure Research* 37(2), 152–177.

Heinonen, K., Strandvik, T., Mickelsson, K.J., Edvardsson, B., Sundström, E. and Andersson, P. (2010) A customer-dominant logic of service. *Journal of Service Management* 21(4), 531–548.

Holbrook, M. B. (1999) *Consumer Value: A Framework for Analysis and Research*. Routledge, London.

Holt, D.B. and Thompson, C.J. (2004) Man of action heroes: the pursuit of heroic masculinity in everyday consumption. *Journal of Consumer Research* 31(2), 425–440.

Kim, H. and Richardson, S.L. (2003) Motion picture impacts on destination images. *Annals of Tourism Research* 30(1), 216–237.

Kincaid, L.D. (2002) Drama, emotion, and cultural convergence. *Communication Theory* 12(2), 136–152.

Krakowiak, K.M. and Oliver, M.B. (2012) When good characters do bad things: examining the effect of moral ambiguity on enjoyment. *Journal of Communication* 62(1), 117–135.

Lee, J.A., Soutar, G.N. and Sneddon, J. (2010) Personal values and social marketing: some research suggestions. *Journal of Research for Consumers* 18, 1–4.

Lichrou, M., O'Malley, L. and Patterson, M. (2008) Place-product or place narrative(s)? Perspectives in the marketing of tourism destinations. *Journal of Strategic Marketing* 16(1), 23–39.

Lundqvist, A., Liljander, V., Gummerus, J. and van Riel, A. (2012) The impact of storytelling on the consumer brand experience: the case of a firm-originated story. *Journal of Brand Management* 19(5), 1–15.

Madhavaram, S. and Hunt, S.D. (2008) The service-dominant logic and a hierarchy of operant resources: developing masterful operant resources and implications for marketing strategy. *Journal of the Academy of Marketing Science* 36(1), 67–82.

Mathisen, L. (2012) The exploration of the memorable tourist experience. In Chen, J.S. (ed.) *Advances in Hospitality and Leisure*, vol. 8. Emerald, Bingley, UK.

McAdams, D.P. (2001) The psychology of life stories. *Review of General Psychology* 5(2), 100–122.

Merz, M.A., He, Y. and Vargo, S.L. (2009) The evolving brand logic: a service-dominant logic perspective. *Journal of the Academy of Marketing Science* 37(3), 328–344.

Moisio, R. and Arnould, E.J. (2005) Extending the dramaturgical framework in marketing: drama structure, drama interaction and drama content in shopping experiences. *Journal of Consumer Behaviour* 4(4), 246–256.

Mossberg, L. (2008) Extraordinary experiences through storytelling. *Scandinavian Journal of Hospitality and Tourism* 8(3), 195–210.

Moyer-Gusé, E. (2008) Toward a theory of entertainment persuasion: explaining the persuasive effects of entertainment-education messages. *Communication Theory* 18, 407–425.

Mulvey, M.S. and Medina, C. (2003) Invoking the rhetorical power of character to create identification. In: Scott, L.M. and Batra, R. (eds) *Persuasive Imagery: A Consumer Response Perspective*. Lawrence Erlbaum, London, pp. 223–245.

Norris, S.P., Guilbert, S.M., Smith, M.L., Hakimelahi, S. and Phillips, L.M. (2005) A theoretical framework for narrative explanation in science. *Science Education* 89, 535–563.

Oatley, K. (2002) Emotions and the story worlds of fiction. In: Green, M.C., Strange, J.J. and Brock, T.C. (eds) *Narrative Impact: Social and Cognitive Foundations*. Lawrence Erlbaum, Mahwah, New Jersey.

Olsen, K. (2002) Authenticity as a concept in tourism research: the social organization of the experience of authenticity. *Tourist Studies* 2(2), 159–182.

O'Toole, J. (1992) *The Process of Drama: Negotiating Art and Meaning*. Routledge, London.

Padgett, D. and Allen, D. (1997) Communicating experiences: a narrative approach to creating service brand image. *Journal of Advertising* 26(4), 49–62.

Park, D.B. and Yoon, Y.S. (2009) Segmentation by motivation in rural tourism: a Korean case study. *Tourism Management* 30(1), 99–108.

Park, H.-J. and Rabolt, N.J. (2009) Cultural value, consumption value, and global brand image: a cross-national study. *Psychology and Marketing* 26(8), 714–735.

Pine, J. and Gilmore, J.H. (1999) *The Experience Economy: Work is Theater and Every Business a Stage*. HBS Press, Boston, Massachusetts.

Polichak, J.W. and Gerrig, R.J. (2002) 'Get up and win!' Participatory responses to narrative. In: Green, M.C., Strange, J.J. and Brock, T.C. (eds) *Narrative Impact: Social and Cognitive Foundations*. Lawrence Erlbaum, Mahwah, New Jersey.

Polkinghorne, D.E. (1988) *Narrative Knowing and the Human Sciences*. State University of New York Press, Albany, New York.

Porter, H. (2008) *The Cambridge Introduction to Narrative*, 2nd edn. Cambridge University Press, New York.

Prahalad, C.K. and Ramaswamy, V. (2004) Co-creating unique value with customers. *Strategy and Leadership* 32(3), 4–9.

Prebensen, N.K. and Foss, L. (2011) Coping and co-creating in tourist experiences. *International Journal of Tourism Research* 13(1), 54–67.

Prebensen, N.K., Woo, E., Chen, J.S. and Uysal, M. (2013) Motivation and involvement as antecedents of the perceived value of the destination experience. *Journal of Travel Research* 52(2), 253–264.

Ritchie, B.W., Tkaczynski, A. and Faulks, P. (2010) Understanding the motivation and travel behavior of cycle tourists using involvement profiles. *Journal of Travel and Tourism Marketing* 27(4), 409–425.

Sandsröm, S., Edvardsson, B., Kristensson, P. and Magnusson, P. (2008) Value in use through service experience. *Managing Service Quality* 18(2), 112–126.

Schank, R.C. and Berman, T.R. (2003) *The Pervasive Role of Stories in Knowledge and Action*. Lawrence Erlbaum, Mahwah, New Jersey.

Schechner, R. (2003) *Performance Theory*. Routledge, London.

Schembri, S., Merrilees, B. and Kristiansen, S. (2010) Brand consumption and narrative of the self. *Psychology and Marketing* 27(6), 623–638.

Schwartz, S.H. (1994) Are there universal aspects in the structure and contents of human values? *Journal of Social Issues* 55(4), 19–45.

Singer, J.A. and Bluck, S. (2001) New perspectives on autobiographical memory: the integration of narrative processing and autobiographical reasoning. *Review of General Psychology* 5(2), 91–99.

Slater, M.D. and Rouner, D. (2002) Entertainment – education and elaboration likelihood: understanding the processing of narrative persuasion. *Communication Theory* 12(2), 173–191.

Stern, B.B. (1991) Who talks advertising? Literary theory and narrative 'point of view'. *Journal of Advertising* 20(3), 9–22.

Stern, B.B. (1998) *Representing Consumers: Voices, Views and Visions*. Routledge Press, New York.

Taylor, S.S., Fisher, D. and Dufresne, R.L. (2002) The aesthetics of management storytelling: a key to organizational learning. *Management Learning* 33(3), 313–330.

Tumbat, G. and Belk, R.W. (2013) Co-construction and performancescapes. *Journal of Consumer Behaviour* 12(1), 49–59.

Tussyadiah, I.P., Park, S. and Fesenmaier, D.R. (2011) Assessing the effectiveness of consumer narratives for destination marketing. *Journal of Hospitality and Tourism Research* 35(1), 64–78.

Van Dijk, T.A. (1975) Action, action description, and narrative. *New Literary History* 6(2), 273–294.

Vargo, S.L. and Lusch, R.F. (2004) Evolving to a new dominant logic for marketing. *Journal of Marketing* 68(1), 1–17.

Vargo, S.L. and Lusch, R.F. (2008) Service-dominant logic: continuing the evolution. *Journal of the Academy of Marketing Science* 36(1), 1–10.

Wang, N. (1999) Rethinking authenticity in tourism experience. *Annals of Tourism Research* 26(2), 349–370.

Williams, P. and Soutar, G.N. (2009) Value, satisfaction and behavioral intentions in an adventure tourism context. *Annals of Tourism Research* 36(3), 413–438.

Woodside, A.G., Sood, S. and Miller, K.E. (2008) When consumers and brands talk: storytelling theory and research in psychology and marketing. *Psychology and Marketing* 25(2), 97–145.

13 Tourist Information Search: A DIY Approach to Creating Experience Value

TOR KORNELIUSSEN

University of Nordland, Bodø, Norway

Introduction

The search for information is a key factor in tourists' decision-making processes regarding where and how to spend a vacation (Gursoy and Umbreit, 2004). This information acquisition provides good opportunities for tourism marketers to influence tourists' decisions (Schmidt and Spreng, 1996). Any marketing strategy designed to attract tourists should carefully consider the ways tourists search for information (McGuire *et al.*, 1988). There is therefore much interest among tour operators, tourism providers and tourist destination managers in how tourists search for information.

When we think back to as recently as a decade ago, tourists used to acquire information from family and friends, destination-specific literature, media and travel consultants (Snepenger and Snepenger, 1993). But that was then, and this is now. Restricting oneself to using only these information sources may today be considered a rather cookie-cutter approach to gathering information. All of this changed with the internet. Searching for information on the internet provides a gold mine of colourful photos, pictures that move, animations, videos, sound, music … everything a person would need to patch together the perfect, tailor-made vacation – in short, a do-it-yourself (DIY) approach to designing one's own perfect vacation.

This chapter explores the many ways in which tourists use a DIY approach to look for information on the internet. The information search creates affective (Vogt and Stewart, 1998), cognitive and sensory stimulation (Vogt and Fesenmaier, 1998) and provides experience value. A by-product of this search is that it may allow tourists to become co-producers of their own vacation.

There are two major theoretical approaches to information searching that can help us decide how a DIY searching method can provide a richer and more nuanced experience value. These are the psychological/motivational approach (e.g. Beatty and Smith, 1987; Gursoy, 2011) and the economics approach (e.g. Avery, 1996). The psychological/motivational approach suggests several factors that motivate tourists to search for information (Schmidt and Spreng, 1996) so that they may have a successful vacation. One shortcoming of this approach is that it gives only limited weight to the actual experience value of searching the internet for vacation information. By ignoring the experience value of the information search, one does not really take into account the strong motivation at least some tourists will have for a DIY approach to vacation planning.

The economics approach tends to use a cost–benefit framework to determine the extent of the information search. This approach sees the information search as a cost the tourist must incur in order to reap the benefits of travel. The cost–benefit framework does not usually include experience value as a benefit. By not including experience value as a motivational force and as a benefit, the two approaches do not predict well enough how much information tourists search for. This leads to an underestimation of tourists' willingness to spend time, money and cognitive effort on information searches (Prebensen et al., 2013).

There are several studies of information searches before travel (e.g. Gursoy and Chen, 2000; Jun et al., 2007; Wong and Lieu, 2011). There is, however, less research investigating information searches during travel (DiPietro et al., 2007) and very little research studying information searches after travel.

This research contributes to the information search literature by arguing that due to the various types of needs satisfied and the experience value created on the internet, tourists search much more for information than was previously thought. Including experience value in the psychological/motivational approach and in the economics approach helps users of these two approaches to develop more realistic predictions of how much information tourists search for.

The next section investigates the various needs that information searching helps satisfy. This is followed by reviews of the psychological/motivational approach and the economics approach to information searching. It is shown that the internet provides experience value by stimulating tourists in various ways before, during, after (and sometimes also instead of) their travel. Finally, conclusions, limitations and topics for future research are proposed.

Tourists' Information Search and the Creation of Experience Value

Information search

The search for information is generally considered an early step in a tourist's decision-making process (Gursoy and Umbreit, 2004). The information search has been defined as 'the motivated activation of knowledge stored in memory or acquisition of information from the environment' (Engel et al., 1995, p. 182). Information searching can be both internal and external. Internal search means that tourists' previous experience and knowledge is retrieved from memory (Fodness and Murray, 1997). If the internal search turns out to be inadequate (Beatty and Smith, 1987) or the information is not up-to-date, then tourists will move to an external search for information (Gursoy and Umbreit, 2004). External information searching implies that information sources outside of personal experience are employed (Fodness and

Murray, 1998). The internet is a particularly important source of external information and is the focus here.

The internet is available in many homes and can be accessed from almost everywhere. People are spending more time online and more tasks are performed on the internet (MacKay and Vogt, 2012). It is now fully integrated into work life. Spillover theory suggests that the internet would therefore influence other domains of life, such as tourism (MacKay and Vogt, 2012). As expected, individuals, to an increasing degree, use the internet for information searching both at work and at home, and for many purposes including planning vacations.

The internet is one of the most effective means of searching for information. The volume of information available on the internet is, however, so vast that it is impossible to process it (Pan and Fesenmaier, 2006) given people's limited capacity for information processing (Simon, 1955). Information searching may therefore be both rewarding and frustrating.

Creation of experience value

According to Vogt and Fesenmaier (1998), tourists' information searching helps satisfy five types of needs: functional, hedonic, innovation, aesthetic and social. Functional needs have to do with identifying choices and making product-related decisions. Hedonic needs are related to searching information as a way of achieving entertainment (Hirschman and Holbrook, 1982) and pleasure – activities that produce sensory stimulation. Innovation needs are related to having a large likelihood for adopting novel products and information (Hirschman, 1980) through novelty seeking, variety seeking, and creativity. Aesthetic needs have to do with seeing information as a stimulus for visual thinking and for fantasizing (Vogt and Fesenmaier, 1998). The above four needs (functional, hedonic, innovation and aesthetic) are individual-based needs, while social needs are interpersonal needs. Social needs relate to 'sign' aspects of the information search, such as symbolic expression and social interaction.

One main reason that a consumer is doing an information search is to satisfy functional needs (Hwang et al., 2013), but tourism is also about satisfying hedonic needs (Hirschman and Holbrook, 1982), innovation needs (Hirschman, 1980), aesthetic needs (Hirschman, 1983) and social needs (Mick, 1986). The internet's ability to help the tourist use multiple senses makes it a particularly good vehicle for satisfying hedonic and aesthetic needs.

Many tourists want to experience something new and unexpected on vacation, though there are people who enjoy returning to the same travel destination year after year. Experience is a function of individual psychological processes (Larsen, 2007). 'An experience is made up inside a person and the outcome depends on how an individual, in a specific mood and state of mind, reacts to the interaction with the staged event' (Mossberg, 2007, p. 60). Since tourists have different interests and different backgrounds, they may be inclined to interpret a single tourist product in various ways (Kim et al., 2012). It may therefore be appropriate to focus on tourists' subjective meaning of their experiences (Uriel, 2005).

Prahalad and Ramaswamy suggest that 'a new point of view is required; one that allows individual customers to actively construct their own consumption experiences through personalized interaction, thereby co-creating unique values for themselves' (2003, p. 12).

There are several views on what experience value is (Uriely, 2005), what co-creation means (Ind and Coates, 2013) and how experience value is co-created. Prahalad and Ramaswamy (2004a, 2004b) suggest that dialogue, access, risk assessment and transparency are key concepts in co-creation. Dialogue means creating opportunities for interaction, a set of conversations between firm and consumer (Prahalad and Ramaswamy, 2004b). Dialogue requires engagement and ability to act from both parties. Interaction is the basis for co-creation and allows a consumer to influence what experiences and experience value will be achieved.

It is difficult to have a fruitful dialogue if both parties do not have access to transparent information. The internet can provide access to such information and has tools that let a consumer interact with providers of tourism products. Risk assessment has to do with making sure that both the firm and the consumer have a good understanding of whether the co-creation of experience can harm the consumer. In the case of tourism, this will mostly relate to whether the consumer achieves the expected vacation experience or not. Transparency is provided to the degree that the internet allows the consumer to find the necessary information regarding providers of tourism products and services. This lets the consumer compare the various attributes of offerings and serves as a basis for comparison, dialogue and experience development.

All forms of interaction between firm(s) and consumer(s) are opportunities to create value, and experience value can be co-created at several points of interaction (Prahalad and Ramaswamy, 2004b). The consumers govern the creation of experience value in their consumption context (Vargo and Lusch, 2004), but this co-creation partly depends on the 'experience environment' providers of tourism products build up. The co-creation depends much on the consumer and what operant resources the consumer has (Saarijärvi et al., 2013). Since operant resources are individual and heterogeneous, a consumer's knowledge, skills, needs and information affect what type of experience value is being created. The internet facilitates the dynamic combination of capabilities, competencies and knowledge that allow co-creation of value in collaborative relations (Cabiddu et al., 2013), whether it is created between a firm and a consumer or between a network of firms and a consumer.

Experience value can be created in several domains (i.e. functional, hedonic, innovation, aesthetic and social) and in several configurations of firm(s) and consumer(s) (consumer and experience environment, consumer and firm, consumer and network of firms). The easiest way to co-create experience value may possibly be the one created through a consumer's interaction with experience environments on the internet during an information search. Slightly more complex forms of experience value, related to aspects of the vacation, such as accommodation, dining and activities, can be co-created during interactions between consumers and individual firms. Even more complex experience value can be created when '(a) IT value is increasingly being created and realized through actions of multiple parties, (b) value emanates from robust collaborative relationships among firms, and (c) structures and incentives for parties to partake in and equitably share emergent value are necessary to sustain co-creation' (Kohli and Grower, 2008, p. 28). The internet allows for collaboration that can make the creation of experience value possible (Payne et al., 2008).

Theoretical Approaches to Information Search

There are many factors that may influence an information search. Information search is, for example, influenced by characteristics of the environment (e.g. Schmidt and Spreng, 1996), situational variables (e.g. Fodness and Murray, 1999), characteristics of the tourist (e.g. Chen, 2000a, 2000b), characteristics of the holiday (e.g. Fodness and Murray, 1999), the availability of well-produced content to create experience value for the consumer, and the consumer's DIY approach to information searching.

According to Gursoy (2011) there are three major theoretical approaches influencing consumers' information search strategy: the psychological/motivational approach, the economics approach and the consumer information processing approach. The first two approaches are relevant here. Both the psychological/ motivational approach and the economics approach are flexible approaches that allow for the inclusion of experience value. This has consequences in that tourists' information searching becomes more motivating and has larger benefits than previously assumed by users of these approaches.

The psychological/motivational approach

Consumers' motivations influence their information searching as well as the information sources they use (Gursoy, 2011; Tan and Chen, 2012). There are potentially many important motivational factors. Some of the more important ones may be prior knowledge (Brucks, 1985) and previous experience (Chen and Gursoy, 2000), perceived risk and uncertainty (Schmidt and Spreng, 1996) and involvement (Beatty and Smith, 1987). Other motivators can be personal factors such as needs, interests and values (Huang *et al.*, 2010).

Prior knowledge and previous experience are important motivating factors, as the internal search starts by retrieving this information. Perceived risk is important for consumers' evaluation and purchasing behaviour (Laroche *et al.*, 2010). A vacation trip is often a high-risk purchase (Reisinger and Mavondo, 2005), because of uncertainty related to accommodation, transportation and activities (Fodness and Murray, 1998, Snepenger *et al.*, 1990). Involvement is an important predictor of information searching. Havitz and Dimanche (1997) analysed 52 studies of involvement in the leisure industry. They found strong support for the proposition that involvement leads to more information searching.

The internet's ability to support creation of experience value in the various domains (i.e. functional, hedonic, innovation, aesthetic and social) and the opportunity for consumers to be part of the co-creation (Prahalad and Ramaswamy, 2004b) of experience value are important motivators for their information search.

The economics approach

The economics approach tends to use a cost–benefit framework and the economics of information theory (Stiegler, 1961) to determine the extent of information searching.

A vacation trip is often a high-risk purchase (Reisinger and Mavondo, 2005). An active use of information sources makes a vacation trip appear less risky by reducing the perceived risk of the trip. The perceived costs and the perceived benefits of information searching are important predictors of how much information tourists search (Vogt and Fesenmaier, 1989; Gursoy and McCleary, 2004).

The costs of information searching include the time spent, the financial costs (Gursoy and McCleary, 2004) and the cognitive effort made to collect and evaluate information. The internet lowers the cost of the information search (Gursoy and McCleary, 2004), helps satisfy multiple needs and increases the experience value gained from the search. Including the additional benefit of experience value into the cost–benefit analysis of information searching changes the cost:benefit ratio, and shows that the benefits of the information search are considerably larger, at least for some tourists, than previously thought.

Let us take the old adage 'time is money'. Some features of the information search that are generally considered to be costs also provide new experiences and added experience value. For example, let us consider that you are planning a trip to Paris – a destination you have never visited before. There are literally hundreds of web sites that will guide you through specific areas of your own interest, whether it is bookshops, cinema, food, fashion or architecture. Searching these web sites is time-consuming and requires cognitive effort. Some may consider the inspiration that is planted during the search to be a waste of one's time, while others may see it as beneficial and leading towards a more nuanced vacation. Many internet surfers/users find that just the search for travel information alone is worth the time and cognitive effort – without having to leave the comforts of home.

Information Search: Before, During, After and Instead of Travel

A vacation comprises multiple goals (Sirakaya and Woodside, 2005) and it may therefore be an oversimplification to assume that all information searching is done before travelling. The internet makes it convenient to search information and make decisions at any stage of the trip – before, during and after. Searching for information is therefore an ongoing process (Jun *et al.*, 2007). It may still be useful to consider the information search by travel stage (pre-travel, at destination, post-travel) as there is a tendency for certain forms of search to take place during a specific stage. For example, information about travel and lodging tends to be searched during the pre-travel stage (DiPietro *et al.*, 2007), whereas information about dining, restaurants and activities tends to be searched at the destination (DiPietro *et al.*, 2007).

The pre-travel information search helps consumers to reduce uncertainty by providing knowledge about the various aspects of the vacation (Fodness and Murray, 1997) and enhances the quality of the trip (Wong and Liu, 2011). Information searches are often done to plan a vacation and for functional needs related to identifying choices and making product-related decisions (Vogt and Fesenmaier, 1998). Needs related to knowledge, risk and efficiency may be particularly important (Hwang *et al.*, 2013).

The internet makes it easy to use a large amount of information (Jun *et al.*, 2007) and will perhaps create a tendency to over-plan one's vacation (Stewart and Vogt,

1999). Choice of activities is the part of the plan that is most often changed (Jun *et al.*, 2007) due to frequent updates of information and options. Travellers make decisions at different times during the trip. Decisions related to dining, entertainment and recreation activities tend to be made at the destination (Gursoy and Chen, 2000; DiPietro *et al.*, 2007). The most important influences on information searching at the destination are friends, relatives, hotel staff and visitor centres (Fodness and Murray, 1999), but the internet also plays a role. Romf *et al.* (2005) show that tourists often rely on local 'experts' for advice about issues related to dining, lodging and recreational referrals. Advice from local experts is a type of context-specific word-of-mouth and a broad range of residents within a community give this type of expert advice (Wang *et al.*, 2005).

User-generated content such as blogs (Schmallegger and Carson, 2008), online reviews (Litwin *et al.*, 2008) and product recommendation (Senecal and Nantel, 2004) are growing in popularity (Pan *et al.*, 2007). One now has access to electronic word-of-mouth (Litwin *et al.*, 2008) via internet 'friends', comprising many more points of view than just those of friends, family, co-workers and the local travel agency. Many tourists create travel diaries online, where they tell about their travels and experiences (Schmallegger and Carson, 2008). Some do it to maintain social relationships at home and 'promote a sense of being present while absent' (White and White, 2006, p. 101), but self-expression and social interaction are the most important motivations for bloggers (Pan *et al.*, 2007). Many blogs are interactive and allow readers to post comments (Schmallegger and Carson, 2008). The internet is really an interactive medium (Tjostheim *et al.*, 2007). User-generated content is perceived to have higher credibility than more commercial information sources (Senecal and Nantal, 2004; Mack *et al.*, 2008).

Tourists also search information after the travel/vacation. Part of the satisfaction of a vacation is the recollection phase where one, for example, looks at pictures and old blogs. Post-trip sharing by word-of-mouth is one of the joys of tourism (Litwin *et al.*, 2008). Many people who search information about a tourist destination do not actually visit it, or even intend to (Vogt and Fesenmaier, 1998). They may for example be satisfying hedonic or aesthetic desires. Many people just like to stay at home. With the richness of content to be discovered on the internet, a 'traveller' need not leave the comforts of home to enjoy the thrills of new destinations. One just clicks a button and then one has access to the world.

Providers of products and services that have high inventory costs and high distribution costs can only afford to sell products and services that are high in demand. The internet decreases the costs of inventory, distribution and communication and allows sales of less popular products. If you, for example, go to a travel agent to get advice for a forthcoming vacation, you will be given only a limited number of options, or in other words, options known to have a rather mass market appeal. Similarly, a search in a brochure or travel guide will provide only information about the more popular offerings that may be of interest to the general public. However, the internet is able to offer information about less mainstream products. Here you will get access to a large and varied offering of tourism products. This allows tourists the opportunities to search, find and tailor-make tourism experiences according to individual preference.

For many, a vacation in a mid-priced hotel with quick access to a beach is the ideal getaway, but what if your travel goals are a bit on the obscure side? Consider the travel needs of an antiquarian bookseller whose sole desire is to discover a musty, underground bookshop filled with rare books that is open to only a few chosen experts of the field. What about the animal behaviourist in search of the elusive Costa Rican one-toed sloth? It is hard to imagine a shopping mall travel agent who can offer travel advice to such special-needs customers. This is where the 'long tail' attributes (Anderson, 2006) of the internet search come in handy.

Another interesting phenomenon related to searching out information on the internet is the 'birds-of-a-feather' experience. In all societies, it is possible for various 'types' of individuals to find kindred spirits who share similar interests. Since the internet is representative of a world containing societies of all types, it is therefore possible for individuals seeking travel information to link up with other, like-minded people by narrowing their search terminology/words in a very fine-tuned way. This 'birds-of-a-feather' approach to vacation search on the internet can yield a very finely edited travel file for those who have interests outside of what is generally considered mass market.

Conclusions and Implications

This chapter explores tourists' use of a DIY approach to information searching on the internet. This information search satisfies functional, hedonic, innovation, aesthetic and social needs and provides, to an increasing degree, new experiences and experience value.

Experience value is on the rise for several reasons. First, the time use, the financial costs and the cognitive efforts of looking for information are decreasing due to the general availability of the internet. The use of the internet is an integrated part of work life. This frequent use of the internet for work purposes spills over into tourists' information search behaviour and increases the use of the internet as a source of information.

Second, the motivation to access information and the benefits of searching the internet increase as the producers of information provide more affective, cognitive and sensory stimulation and in this way help create entertainment, pleasure and experience value for the tourist. As more content is being made available on the internet by providers of products and services and by tourists and tourist destinations, the experience value of the information search is enhanced.

Third, more experience environments are being created to facilitate co-creation of experience value. Similarly, more forms of interaction between firms and consumers are being used to co-create experience value in ever more varied configurations. Information searching on the internet will therefore continue to increase before, during, and after travel … not to mention instead of travel.

This chapter has implications for tourists and for providers of tourism experiences. Vacation planning on the internet is a complex and dynamic process (Pan and Fesenmaier, 2006). The information search depends on technology skills, technology use and ownership adoption (MacKay and Vogt, 2012). Consumers require dependable internet access and need to develop appropriate searching skills in order to maximize the need fulfilment and experience value that information searching provides. Similarly, they should try to eliminate environmental factors that may be barriers to internet searching. By understanding the internet's possibility to satisfy multiple needs and to provide experience value, consumers will, to an increasing degree, use the internet as a source of information. Some consumers may also become active providers of content. By providing content, such as reviews of destinations, hotels and restaurants on blogs and online videos, tourists will actively increase the diversity and value of information searches on the internet.

If you are the type of consumer who only wants your basic vacation needs to be met or if you are a time-is-money 'type', beware of the internet-based information search because it leads individuals to become engrossed in affective, cognitive and sensory stimulation. If, however, you are a person who enjoys diversions, serendipity and unexpected findings, then the internet search will offer a richness of choice.

This chapter also has implications for providers of tourist experiences. By considering the internet's potential for helping to satisfy needs and creating experience value in the information search, providers of tourism experiences (e.g. tour operators and managers of tourist destinations) may put increasing emphasis on providing experience environments consisting of web pages and content that balances tourists' various needs with their search for experience value. As more nuanced quality content is made available on the internet, the higher the use and experience value becomes.

Producers should take the opportunity to use the benefits of the internet's ability to exploit the long tail by introducing more products in niche categories and use the rich possibilities to produce more content to interact and communicate with consumers. Making use of the wide range of viewer using tools, such as YouTube and user-generated reviews, allows for creative, flexible and inexpensive ways to interact with consumers and to use affective, cognitive and sensory stimulations to engage consumers in order to provide experience value for them and to promote tourism products.

Providers of tourism experience should do their utmost to try to avoid intrusive and irritating web advertisements, or at least try to provide advertising value and to be skilled in advertising placement and advertising execution (Ying *et al.*, 2009) in order to make the internet experience as pleasurable as possible. This will have positive consequences in that tourist destinations may come closer to reaching their potential when it comes to attracting tourists and achieving financial success.

Future research

The internet develops rapidly and in unexpected ways. Few of us are able to conceive of what the new developments will be. It is therefore not easy to give guidance for future research. Clearly, more work is needed to explore the various ways in which tourists use the internet to help satisfy their needs and wants for the perfect vacation.

Further research should investigate ways to satisfy the functional, hedonic, innovation, aesthetic and social needs by designing more experience value into particular aspects of the internet. This will help increase the experience value of the information search and lead to additional use. There is need for more research on the volume and types of content that producers of tourist information provide. How much content should a producer of tourism product provide? How often should it be updated? How is content related to experience value?

One weakness of this chapter is that it treats the internet as one single information source. It is time to subdivide the internet into categories of information sources and to determine what the strengths and weaknesses of the various information sources are. Tjostheim *et al.* (2007) classify information into the subcategories of editorial, marketing, social and personal. A new typology of information on the internet would be helpful. There is a need for more research on tourist attitudes about the information search. What are the characteristics of tourists who primarily see the information search as a cost, as opposed to those who primarily see it as an experience? Which groups of tourists focus on functional, hedonic, innovation, aesthetic or social needs?

The internet allows tourists to activate their senses of sight and hearing. Future research should investigate whether it also is possible to use smell, taste and touch to further increase tourists' experience value. The internet provides affective, cognitive and sensory stimulations. Further research should investigate whether the types of stimulation can be made more fine-grained. Does the internet provide other types of stimulation? Another potential area of new research is to investigate consumer culture around particular types of information sources, such as Facebook and blogs. In addition, it would be useful to widen the research done on how particular social/cultural factions of societies connect to each other via the internet and how they exchange information of a more obscure nature.

The internet is an amazing source of information for tourists. Information searches on the internet will therefore continue to increase before, during, after and also instead of travel. Modern tourism is really an information-intensive business.

References

Anderson, C. (2006) *The Long Tail: Why the Future of Business is Selling Less of More*. Hyperion, New York.

Avery, R.J. (1996) Determinants of search for nondurable goods: an empirical assessment of the economics of information theory. *Journal of Consumer Affairs* 30(2), 390–420.

Beatty, S.E. and Smith, S.M. (1987) External search effort: an investigation across several product categories. *Journal of Consumer Research* 14(1), 83–95.

Brucks, M. (1985) The effects of product class knowledge on information search behavior. *Journal of Consumer Research* 12(1), 1–16.

Cabiddu, F., Lui, T.W. and Piccoli, G. (2013) Managing value co-creation in the tourism industry. *Annals of Tourism Research* 42, 86–107.

Chen, J.S. (2000a) A comparison of information usage between business and leisure travelers. *Journal of Hospitality and Leisure Marketing* 7(2), 65–76.

Chen, J.S. (2000b) Cross-cultural differences in travel acquisition among tourists from three Pacific-Rim countries. *Journal of Hospitality and Tourism Research* 24(2), 239–251.

Chen, J.S. and Gursoy, D. (2000) Cross-cultural comparison of information sources used by first-time and repeat travelers and its marketing implications. *International Journal of Hospitality Management* 19(2), 191–203.

DiPietro, R.B., Wang, Y., Rompf, P. and Severt, D. (2007) At-destination visitor information search and venue decision strategies. *International Journal of Tourism Research* 9(3), 175–188.

Engel, J., Blackwell, R.D. and Miniard, P. (1995) *Consumer Behavior*, 8th edn. Dryden Press, Forth Worth, Texas.

Fodness, D. and Murray, B. (1997) Tourist information search. *Annals of Tourism Research* 24(3), 503–523.

Fodness, D. and Murray, B. (1998) A typology for tourist information search strategies. *Journal of Travel Research* 37(2), 108–120.

Fodness, D. and Murray, B. (1999) A model of tourist information search behaviour. *Journal of Travel Research* 37(3), 220–230.

Gursoy, D. (2011) Destination information search strategies. In: Wang, Y. and Pizam, A. (eds) *Destination Marketing and Management. Theories and Applications*. CAB International, Wallingford, UK, pp. 67–81.

Gursoy, D. and Chen, J. (2000) Competitive analysis of cross cultural information search behavior. *Tourism Management* 21(6), 583–590.

Gursoy, D. and McCleary, K.W. (2004) An integrative model of tourists' information search behaviour. *Annals of Tourism Research* 31(2), 353–373.

Gursoy, D. and Umbreit, W.T. (2004) Tourist information source behaviour: cross-cultural comparison of European Union member states. *International Journal of Hospitality Management* 23(1), 55–70.

Havitz, M. and Dimanche, F. (1997) Leisure involvement revisited: conceptual conundrums and measurement advances. *Journal of Leisure Research* 29(3), 245–278.

Hirschman, E.C. (1980) Innovativeness, novelty seeking and consumer creativity. *Journal of Consumer Research* 7(3), 283–295.

Hirschman, E.C. (1983) Aesthetics, ideologies and the limits of the marketing concept. *Journal of Marketing* 47(3), 45–55.

Hirschman, E.C. and Holbrook, M.B. (1982) Hedonic consumption: emerging concepts, methods and propositions. *Journal of Marketing* 46(3), 92–101.

Huang, C.Y., Chou, C.J. and Lin, P.C. (2010) Involvement theory in constructing bloggers' intention to purchase travel products. *Tourism Management* 31(4), 513–526.

Hwang, Y.H., Jani, D. and Jeong, H.K. (2013) Analyzing international tourists' functional information needs: a comparative analysis of inquiries in an online travel forum. *Journal of Business Research* 66(6), 700–705.

Ind, N. and Coates, N. (2013) The meanings of co-creation. *European Business Research* 25(1), 86–95.

Jun, S.H., Vogt, C.A. and Mackay, K.J. (2007) Relationship between travel information search and travel product purchase in pre-trip context. *Journal of Travel Research* 45(3), 266–274.

Kim, J.H., Ritchie, J.R.B. and McCormick, B. (2012) Development of a scale to measure memorable tourism experiences. *Journal of Tourism Research* 51(1), 12–25.

Kohli, R. and Grower, V. (2008) Business value of IT: an essay on expanding research directions to keep up with the times. *Journal of the Association of Information Systems* 9(1), 23–39.

Laroche, M., Nepomuceno, M.V. and Richard, M.O. (2010) How do involvement and product knowledge affect the relationship between intangibility and perceived risk for brands and product categories. *Journal of Consumer Marketing* 17(3), 197–210.

Larsen, S. (2007) Aspects of a psychology of the tourist experience. *Scandinavian Journal of Hospitality and Tourism* 7(1), 7–18.

Litwin, S.W., Goldsmith, R.E. and Pan, B. (2008) Electronic word-of-mouth in hospitality and tourism management. *Tourism Management* 29(3), 458–468.

Mack, R.W., Blose, J. and Pan, B. (2008) Believe it or not: credibility of blogs in tourism. *Journal of Vacation Marketing* 14(2), 133–144.

MacKay, K. and Vogt, C. (2012) Information technology in everyday and vacation contexts. *Annals of Tourism Research* 39(3), 1380–1401.

McGuire, F.A., Uysal, M. and McDonald, C.D. (1988) Attracting the older traveler. *Tourism Management* 9(2), 161–164.

Mick, D.G. (1986) Consumer research and semiotic: exploring the morphology of signs, symbols and significance. *Journal of Consumer Research* 13(2), 196–213.

Mossberg, L. (2007) A marketing approach to the tourist experience. *Scandinavian Journal of Hospitality and Tourism* 7(1), 59–74.

Pan, B. and Fesenmaier, D.R. (2006) Online information search: vacation planning process. *Annals of Tourism Research* 33(3), 809–832.

Pan, B., MacLaurin, T. and Crotts, J. (2007) Travel blogs and their implications for destination marketing. *Journal of Travel Research* 46(1), 35–45.

Payne, A.F., Storbacka, K. and Frow, F. (2008) Managing the co-creation of value. *Journal of the Academy of Marketing Science* 36(1), 83–96.

Prahalad, C.K. and Ramaswamy, V. (2003) The new frontier of experience innovation. *MIT Sloan Management Review* 44(4), 12–18.

Prahalad, C.K. and Ramaswamy, V. (2004a) Co-creating unique value with customers. *Strategy and Leadership* 32(3), 4–9.

Prahalad, C.K. and Ramaswamy, V. (2004b) Co-creation experiences: the next practice in value creation. *Journal of Interactive Marketing* 18(3), 5–14.

Prebensen, N.K., Vittersø, J. and Dahl, T.I. (2013) Value co-creation significance of tourist resources. *Annals of Tourism Research* 42, 240–261.

Reisinger, Y. and Mavondo, F. (2005) Travel anxiety and intentions to travel internationally: implications of travel risk perceptions. *Journal of Travel Research* 43(3), 212–225.

Rompf, P., DiPietro, R.B. and Ricci, P. (2005) Locals' involvement in travellers' information search and venue decision strategies while at destination. *Journal of Travel and Tourism Marketing* 18(3), 11–22.

Saarijärvi, H., Kannan, P.K. and Kuusela, H. (2013) Value co-creation: theoretical approaches and practical implications. *European Business Review* 25(1), 6–19.

Schmallegger, D. and Carson, D. (2008) Blogs in tourism: changing approaches to information exchange. *Journal of Vacation Marketing* 14(2), 99–110.

Schmidt, J.B. and Spreng, R.A. (1996) A proposed model of external consumer information search. *Journal of the Academy of Marketing Science* 24(3), 246–256.

Senecal, S. and Nantal, A. (2004) The influence of online product recommendations on consumers' online choices. *Journal of Retailing* 80(3), 159–169.

Simon, H. (1955) A behavioral model of rational choice. *Quarterly Journal of Economics* 69(1), 99–118.

Sirakaya, E. and Woodside, A.G. (2005) Building and testing theories of decision making by travelers. *Tourism Management* 26(6), 815–832.

Snepenger, D. and Snepenger, M. (1993) Information search by pleasure travelers. In: Kahn, M.A., Olsen, M.D. and Var, T. (eds) *Encyclopedia of Hospitality and Tourism*. Van Nostrand Reinhold, New York, pp. 830–835.

Snepenger, D., Meged, K., Snelling, M. and Worall, K. (1990) Information source strategies by destination-naive tourists. *Journal of Travel Research* 29(1), 13–16.

Stewart, S. and Vogt, C. (1999) A case-based approach to understanding vacation planning. *Leisure Sciences* 21(2), 79–95.

Stiegler, G. (1961) The economics of information. *Journal of Political Economy* 19(3), 213–225.

Tan, W.K. and Chen, T.H. (2012) The usage of online tourist information sources in tourist information search: an exploratory study. *Service Industries Journal* 32(3), 451–467.

Tjostheim, I., Tussyadiah, I. and Heom, S. (2007) Combination of information sources in travel planning a cross national study. *Information and Communication Technologies in Tourism* 4, 153–162.

Uriel, N. (2005) The tourist experience: conceptual developments. *Annals of Tourism Research* 32(1), 199–216.

Vargo, S.L. and Lusch, R.F. (2004) Evolving to a new dominant logic for marketing. *Journal of Marketing* 68(1), 1–17.

Vogt, C.A. and Fesenmaier, D.R. (1998) Expanding the functional information search model. *Annals of Tourism Research* 25(3), 551–578.

Vogt, C.A. and Stewart, S.I. (1998) Affective and cognitive effects of information use on the course of a vacation. *Journal of Leisure Research* 30(4), 498–520.

Wang, Y., Severt, D. and Rompf, P. (2005) Examining the nature and dynamic of at-destination recommendations: the local experts' perspective. *Journal of Hospitality and Leisure Marketing* 13(3/4), 139–160.

White, N. and White, P. (2006) Home and away in a connected world. *Annals of Tourism Research* 34(1), 88–104.

Wong, C.K.S. and Liu, F.C.G. (2011) A study of pre-trip use of travel guidebooks by leisure travelers. *Tourism Management* 32(3), 616–628.

Ying, L., Korneliussen, T. and Grønhaug, K. (2009) The effect of ad value, ad placement and ad execution on the perceived intrusiveness of web advertisements. *International Journal of Advertising* 28(4), 623–638.

14 Co-creation of Value and Social Media: How?

ATILA YÜKSEL AND AKAN YANIK

University of Adnan Menderes, Aydın, Turkey

Introduction

Consumers in the tourism business are demanding greater levels of personalization in their consumption experience and also placing tourism business under increasing pressure to create value with them. Considering the rise in the 'individuality' and the recent changes in the way tourism business is executed, thanks to the advent of the internet, it is reasonable to claim that markets have become more fragmented than they used to be and consumers have exceptional access to information and networks. This challenges the conventional wisdom about the concept of consumer behaviour, since such consumer behaviours as loyalty have become highly fragile in a world where customers are only a mouse click away from a better deal. Consequently, today's consumers have become 'change agents' as well as 'resources' of destinations, and they are no longer seen as simply buying goods or services but products that provide a service and value that depends on the customer experience. Tourism business has to continuously reinvent itself in order to adapt to these increasingly complex and dynamic market realities.

Co-creation, a new approach to innovation and customer involvement, offers destination managers an avenue for soliciting input, ideas and viewpoints from customers, with the intent of integrating some of this input into a new, improved product or service, or to provide more lifetime value to customers. In other words, co-creation is considered as the customers' 'seal of approval'. The benefits of co-creation for consumers and destination authorities are numerous. It enables the destination to talk with real customers who feel a connection with the destination and its products/services. Talking to real customers is a perspective that's often missed in many destination organizations. The conventional methods, such as focus groups, may produce some insights on customer behaviour and attitudes, but are more of a 'snapshot in time'. Since the final product has a part of 'them' involved, the customers involved in co-creation are more likely to be loyal to the destination and positively influence others on behalf of the destination. Under the right conditions, co-creation would help destination authorities build value and reduce risks, in areas including strategy, innovation and new product/service development.

Collaborating with customers for the purpose of innovation, entitled value co-creation, requires focusing on the process of 'the change in competitive environment', as mentioned in Prahalad and Ramaswamy's (2002) study, 'The Co-creation Connection'. The change of the competitive manners in the market and the direction of this change eventually force the practices of value co-creation. Rather than functional possession of goods or services, contemporary customers are more interested in the hedonic (delight, status, etc.) value of the experienced possession. Businesses create experiential contexts in which they can serve the joy and status in the nature of the product or service, since the concept of value in the market sphere has changed from rational and functional use to experiential and status value. In such experiential contexts as tourism destinations, contemporary customer groups whose levels of satisfaction rise, along with their growing knowledge, are incorporated into the co-production. The aim of co-creation is to let the customers choose what they actually desire and share information while engaging them with experiences in an interactive manner. Sharing is both a natural and an obligatory extension of value co-creation.

Social networks and preliminary users and opinion leaders called social-lites play a crucial role in co-creation endeavours that can be summarized as the transfer of the very best characteristics of the virtual world to the real world. Social-liters, being the opinion headers of online social networks with their exegetic power, share the information overload within the market pandemonium experienced by the customers. Social-lite groups are followed in social networks, whereas the ideas of family and friends are more important in the classical context. Moreover, nowadays, along with the improving technology, products and services that are to be purchased in retail stores outside the e-market environment are simultaneously shared and discussed via mobile systems.

Destinations support social sharing by using this attitude of customers to their advantage. For instance, within the concept of the project 'I AMSTERDAM', in order to promote touristic experience, suggestions are asked for and feedback is received from friends on social networks in many Facebook connected kiosks around the Netherlands. Cities like New York, Paris, and Amsterdam reward the changes that their virtual residents in the Second Life website make, and create the opportunities to be put into practice in real life. Using 'ngConnect' technology, L'Oreal created online environments in offline contexts by producing cabins at the airports where its customers can create 3D avatars of themselves and apply the products on these avatars and share their experiences in the social networks. In our age, in which internet technologies are on the rise, it is observed that classical market environments called offline will not disappear, on the contrary, through the technology-driven social media where another renaissance is in progress, the customers are willing to be the creators of the process in all the products and services generated.

The chapter will begin by outlining how co-creation offers a new paradigm that fosters growth, innovation and competitive advantage for companies and destination authorities. It then draws attention to the renaissance presently occurring in the market, and how conditions and dimensions of this renaissance will shape our understanding of consumer behaviour. Stages of co-creation are explicated to develop a better understanding of what the co-creator experiences during a single co-creation activity. Co-creation campaigns that tourism services and destinations do by using social media tools are highlighted next. Along with the evaluations about the benefits of the transfer of the best features in a virtual world to the real world in co-creation campaigns, the ethical aspects of creation endeavour and futuristic foresights in the light of Web 3.0 technology are then reviewed. Overall, the chapter aims to help comprehend the reasons for the rise of co-creation through social media by asking 'how?'

Co-creation of Value and Social Media

> Tell me and I forget. Teach me and I remember. Involve me and I learn. (Benjamin Franklin)

Technological developments and the wind of social networks entirely shape the world of tourism, as they do everything. All procedures from passports to visas are now being carried out in the virtual media; bookings are made via the internet; all destinations suitable for the holiday are three-dimensionally visited beforehand; and all processes can be discussed virtually. Tens of social networks such as Facebook, Twitter, YouTube and Flickr involve many processes, including perceiving, learning, decision-making and sharing with broad convergence without any restrictions of time and space by being backed up by technological tools. Establishments have integrated their corporate websites into professional social sharing networks (Facebook, Foursquare, Gogobot, etc.) and now leave their space-based campaigns and announcements to the social network societies.

'Co-creation' is a fantastic starting point for the concept of marketing. Drucker interprets this as the materialization of the fantastic dreams of the human mind. Basically, co-creation has become possible together with a service-dominant logic approach. The new service-dominant logic of marketing acknowledges the consumer, i.e. the tourist role in value creation and co-creation. This logic includes the idea that in the process of value co-creation, the consumers – in addition to firms and organizations – act as resource integrators (Prebensen and Dahl, 2013). Likewise, value is centred in the experiences of consumers (Prahalad and Ramaswamy, 2004; Richards and Wilson, 2006; Prebensen and Foss, 2011). This idea has been fostered by Prahalad and Ramaswamy (2004), who argue that instead of consuming staged experiences, consumers now seek more authenticity and expect a balance between the experience stager and their role as co-creators of experiences and value (Binkhorst, 2006; Ramaswamy and Gouillart, 2010). In addition, there is evidence that tourism experiences are not only co-created but increasingly technology-enabled (Tussyadiah and Fesenmaier, 2007, 2009; Tussyadiah and Zach, 2011).

Travelling involves encountering unfamiliar scenes and people, rendering coping and co-creating valuable experiences as situational and dependent on the skills and knowledge of the tourist (such as socializing, discussing, receiving information, re-scheduling planned activities) (Prebensen and Foss, 2011). Co-creation tourism experiences can be considered as experiences that are not only passively staged but rather actively shaped and created by the tourist consumer in conjunction with the company. With the increasing intensification of co-creation, the tourism experience becomes more consumer-oriented and interactive, resulting in a higher level of value being obtained (Neuhofer *et al.*, 2013). However, in the current understanding of co-creation experiences, as defined in the literature (Prahalad and Ramaswamy, 2004; Boswijk *et al.*, 2007; Ramaswamy and Gouillart, 2008; Binkhorst and Den Dekker, 2009; Ramaswamy, 2009), co-creation lacks the integration of technology.

Through co-creation, companies enter a new paradigm of value creation that fosters growth, innovation and competitive advantage (Shaw *et al.*, 2011). Co-creation of value can occur anywhere throughout the service chain. With the availability of new tools, this process is reinforced, as consumers are more involved in every part of the system to proactively co-create experiences and value in every step of the consumption (Prahalad and Ramaswamy, 2004). In this vein, information and communication play a particularly crucial role by facilitating co-creation (Prahalad and Ramaswamy, 2004) and mediating the overall tourism experience (Tussyadiah and Fesenmaier, 2007, 2009).

In the market environment, where the concept of value has shifted from functional benefit to the value of experience and status (Schmitt, 1998), the present profile of customers whose level of satisfaction rises as their knowledge level increases is made the subject of marketing, especially with the creation of value. The main goal of the systems of co-creation of value also taking place in the social media is to allow the customer to exactly determine his/her wishes while being busy with the experiences within an interactive structure and finally to ensure the sharing of the information desired. The social media services should be designed very carefully, since sharing is a natural and an indispensable extension of the process of co-creation of value (Prahalad and Ramaswamy, 2002).

The relationship between technology and social media should not be ignored to provide the desired impact and create networks of experience. In the world where all technologies unite through convergence and form some integrated power, with systems like Second Life, cities and the restaurants, hotels and entertainment centres serving in cities, historical spaces, universities and many commercial establishments can co-create value beyond interaction with their target masses through three-dimensionally augmented reality media.

It is necessary to focus in detail on 'The Change in the Competitive Environment' in Prahalad and Ramaswamy (2002) in order to understand the impact of social media on tourism. In his studies *Competing for the Future*, *The New Age of Innovation* and *The Future of Competition*, Prahalad focuses on the rapid and continuous change in the forms of competition and suggests that studies of co-creation of value are going to become an imperative marketing strategy in the near future (Hamel and Prahalad, 1996; Prahalad and Ramaswamy, 2004; Prahalad and Krishnan 2008). In his work *The Gutenberg Galaxy* (2001), focusing on the change in the competitive environment, the famous futurist Marshall McLuhan suggests that not every change in the market should be regarded as a revolution and that every change must be perceived as a 'renaissance' that nourishes the next change. The latest trend, which McLuhan calls 'the market renaissance', is experience-oriented co-creation of value programmes.

While dealing with co-creation of values and the concept of social media, in this section of the book we aim to introduce the reasons for co-creation of values by asking the 'how' question, moving from 'creating values for the customer' to 'creating values with the customer', rather than just presenting the marketing practices of the companies.

The Market Renaissance: Change in the Competitive Environment

In their study entitled 'The Co-creation Connection', Prahalad and Ramaswamy (2002) emphasize that one must focus strongly on 'the change in the competitive environment' in order to assimilate the concept of co-creation of value and to develop sound applications. Today the competitive environment is continually changing, and an electronic age in which the non-transparent and dull areas of the past have become evident with technological developments and at which all lines defining the present can easily be tracked is being experienced. With the question 'what changes have taken place in attitudes, beliefs and values so that technological innovations are able to progress in such a free and extensive area?', in his work entitled *Technology and Culture*, Peter Drucker (1977) emphasized how important a past-oriented perspective of the features of technological innovations is. The famous futurist Marshall McLuhan also tells that when technology is the case, both the past and the present of technological developments must be evaluated together. In his work entitled *The Gutenberg Galaxy*, McLuhan tries to form a perspective for the future by providing an opportunity of comparing the impacts the present technological innovations will create with the technological developments of centuries ago and the changes afterwards. McLuhan suggests that not every change in the market should be regarded as a revolution and that every change must be perceived as a 'renaissance' that nourishes the next change. Describing the future in the language of the past, McLuhan particularly describes the impacts of electronic technology considering the printing press technology and the processes afterwards. Although the printing press is regarded as a simple and old character when compared with the present technology, the revealing of the virtues of some technology which created the information leaps that gave rise to the Renaissance and the French Revolution will provide a deep prediction of comprehending the present technology. *The Great Transformation* by Karl Polanyi (1944) on the economic origins of the change resulting from technological developments is directly connected with the mosaic of *The Gutenberg Galaxy*. The concepts of social media and co-creation of value will be clarified by considering all developments in the social media and technology, which we will try to describe as the Gutenberg Galaxy 2.0, as 'the market renaissance'.

'Market renaissance' comes into existence after many transformations, as shown in Fig. 14.1. 'Co-creation of value' activities, taking place in social media, are not the outcomes of a short-run perception like fashion; it is a long-term trend called market renaissance that is a combination of many transformations and that has its own reasons, conditions and results.

Market renaissance spectrum presents all the transformations in the world and the market environment that will constantly develop, as the world changes over time. Just like Renaissance developments that resulted in the French Revolution, market

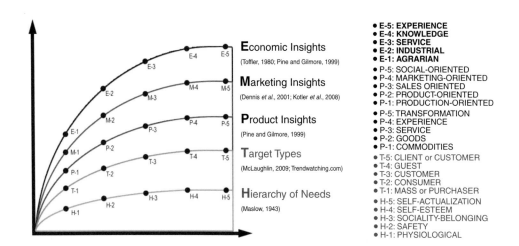

Economic Insights

(Toffler, 1980; Pine and Gilmore, 1999)

Marketing Insights

(Dennis *et al.*, 2001; Kotler *et al.*, 2008)

Product Insights

(Pine and Gilmore, 1999)

Target Types

(McLaughlin, 2009; Trendwatching.com)

Hierarchy of Needs

(Maslow, 1943)

- E-5: EXPERIENCE
- E-4: KNOWLEDGE
- E-3: SERVICE
- E-2: INDUSTRIAL
- E-1: AGRARIAN
- P-5: SOCIAL-ORIENTED
- P-4: MARKETING-ORIENTED
- P-3: SALES ORIENTED
- P-2: PRODUCT-ORIENTED
- P-1: PRODUCTION-ORIENTED
- P-5: TRANSFORMATION
- P-4: EXPERIENCE
- P-3: SERVICE
- P-2: GOODS
- P-1: COMMODITIES
- T-5: CLIENT or CUSTOMER
- T-4: GUEST
- T-3: CUSTOMER
- T-2: CONSUMER
- T-1: MASS or PURCHASER
- H-5: SELF-ACTUALIZATION
- H-4: SELF-ESTEEM
- H-3: SOCIALITY-BELONGING
- H-2: SAFETY
- H-1: PHYSIOLOGICAL

Fig. 14.1. Spectrum of the market renaissance. (From Authors.)

renaissance also feeds on many transformations, each of which has different effects. The wider the wavelengths of the transformations (in other words, their effects), the higher their rate of influence on other transformations. The best definition to explain the relationship between market renaissance and co-creation of values is Swedish historian Jacob Burckhardt's statement that Renaissance is the exploration of human being. In an atmosphere where human profiles change along with the change in needs, where the profit expectations from products and services transform, where the marketing approaches and strategies become broader, and thus where the economic system changes its shell, market renaissance is the re-exploration of consumer as human being.

The concepts of co-creation of value and the social media denote a peak where consumers have got rid of the passive market conditions. In agreement with the expression 'Aren't my consumers my producers?', in *Finnegans Wake* by James Joyce (2012), the internet and especially social media in the twenty-first century reversed the passive conditions of the Gutenberg Galaxy and paved the way for a new galaxy. The replacement of asymmetric means of communication, such as the printing press that initiated the dissemination of information, and television, radio and newspapers, with symmetrical means such as social media enabled the passive air over consumers to clear away.

Particularly with social media, the communication and message ownership of the means of information began to be controlled by consumers for the first time in history. The information that had flowed asymmetrically and unilaterally to consumers until the twenty-first century has now been reversed under the influence of the channels of social media and the developments in the electronic technology. In conclusion, millions of messages, such as promotional messages sent either via advertisements or in other ways, are sent from consumers to producers today. The initial impacts of the market renaissance that began with the wave of information created by Internet 1.0 were seen with the transformation of the structure of customer behaviour from a passive structure into an active structure. With Internet 2.0, active customer behaviour was transformed into a proactive structure on the interactive power of the systems of social media and under the influence of convergence of technological tools. Customers' reaching a proactive behaviour level is both the most important result of the market renaissance and the most important starting point of the studies of co-creation of value. Many causes and processes that enable customers to become proactive and that make value co-creation practices almost imperative for competition will be presented under the dimensions of 'Gutenberg Holistic View'.

For this purpose, considering the work *The Gutenberg Galaxy* by McLuhan, it is suggested that there are four dimensions that created the market renaissance (see Fig. 14.2).

The four important dimensions that created 'the market renaissance', depicted in *The Gutenberg Galaxy*, will be reviewed holistically. The authors' purpose in calling the figure 'Gutenberg's holistic view' is to emphasize the work *The Gutenberg Galaxy* – the source of inspiration for the study – and to commemorate M. McLuhan, the owner of the work, for the ideas that he provided the world of science.

Technological dimension

Co-creation is an emerging phenomenon and technology makes this phenomenon possible. The initiating and driving impacts of technology appear irrefutable,

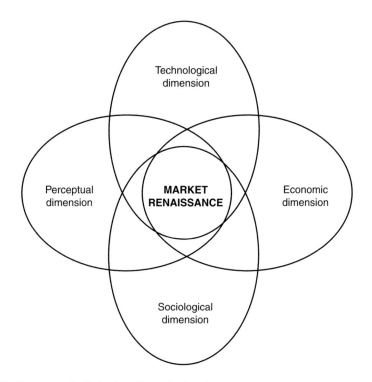

Fig. 14.2. The Gutenberg holistic view. (From Authors.)

regardless of the detail, considered in the fact that social media created a proactive customer profile and in which the market underwent a metamorphosis and became much stronger. Even though technology – a manifestation of the miracle of the human brain – is a significant virtue at every age, considering the impact of social media systems, its meaning in and its impact on the current age are much greater. Today the speed and the impact of technology have gone beyond pushing the limits of the human biology that we describe as a 'perfect structure' and of the cultural structure that is a century-old social brain.

Technology and especially social media systems are influencing and altering not only people's or establishments' ways of doing physical work, but also the decision support systems and their ways of doing logical work through databases and software. Those signals that used to be impossible to turn into data can be turned into data by electronic technology; they can be processed with data processing systems, in which the channels of social media are also included; and instant value added can be created. For example, Starwood, owner of the chic W brand as well as the Westin and Sheraton chains, is the first real-world hospitality company to open in Second Life, and joins a growing list of other companies who are using the online world to build their brand name, test products and co-creation. For Starwood, opening in Second Life is a way to test-market the hotel's design and rapidly prototype the evolving concept. For instance, staffers will observe how people move through the space, what areas and types of furniture they gravitate towards, and what they ignore. The project is also an effort to tap customers for ideas. They're encouraged to post on a blog, started in 2008 and that features steady updates on the virtual hotel's design, along with detailed screenshots. The ultimate goal is, of course, to attract hip, youthful, tech-savvy customers to the brand. For that reason, the virtual hotel will remain online, as an interactive marketing tool, even after the real-world buildings open (*Businessweek*, 2013). The number of other hotels using social media is increasing by the day. That is not surprising, since social media can easily be applied for customer service with little to no costs. Qbic Hotels Amsterdam, part of La Bergère Group, is another example of a hotel group that offers customer services through social media. Qbic Hotels' guests can pose their questions both in Dutch and English. They can ask for specific information about reservations, room preferences and cancellations, but they can also ask about the best restaurants in Amsterdam.

The fact that the boundaries of technological developments crossed logical boundaries and that they have now reached as far as the mythical worlds called the logos will enable the emergence of new unlimited needs and opportunities in the market system in the near future. With the convergence of three-dimensional virtual world software, petaflop[1] computer technology, GPS 2 and 3, LTE, Web 4.0 and screen technology in the near future, it is no more a dream for utopian and dystopian scientists that the 'logos' in our subconscious perform an explosion just like that in the Big Bang Theory. The value of this technological prediction in terms of the science of marketing will be regarded as the emergence of new needs and opportunities; furthermore, it might also manifest itself as the problem of analysing the customer with a multidimensional perspective crossing the boundaries of marketing research. We interpret the situation as the materialization of the fantastic dreams of the human mind.

Perceptual dimension

In his book entitled *Value-based Marketing*, Peter Doyle stresses the strategic importance of creation of experiential value and focuses on the fact that a customer's perspective of the product significantly changed on the developments in technology (Doyle, 2000). Blake, who focused on the perceptual dimension of the market renaissance, sets forth that perception objects will also change when the perception organs have changed and puts forward that human beings also change with the change in the rates of use of the sense organs (Huxley, 1954). According to Blake, the technological externalization of any of the physical and mental functions underlies the change in the impulses that stimulate the human being. In his work, entitled *The Science of Culture*, Leslie A. White (2005) proposes that, thanks to technology, an individual creates a new lifestyle via digital extensions.

Asserting that products need organic packaging with the concept of experiential marketing, Schmitt (1999) also suggests that on the change in the customer's perspective, products now have a multidimensional meaning beyond their functional benefit. Pine and Gilmore (1999) explained the changes in the market and the processes of transformation in a detailed manner in their economic differences table (Figure 14.3). The reason for the typology and perceptual motivation lying behind co-creation of values idea are these changes and transformations. Indeed, the process called co-creation of values is creating a value-added experience by co-designing experiences. Experience design is not only aesthetic, but also the process of creating an interactive sphere where social media systems are very active, and feedback resulting from the change in perception is conveyed. By designing interactive experience situations, global companies like Apple, Ikea, Victoria's Secret, Nike Town, Museum of Modern Art (New York) and Disneyland construct value co-creation platforms where the visitors can create their own ever-changing expectations and fantasies.

Separation of competences or externalization of one of the senses causes the services to be seen as 'stage' and the products as 'decoration'. This condition brings to mind the sentence 'not sensory phenomena but the ideas with validity' (Wölfflin, 1915, p. 22). The replacement of sensory phenomena by instant validity, trends, fashion or phenomena created in the social media and their becoming the origin of behaviours verify the ideas with validity against the reality of sensory phenomena.

Sociological dimension

Particularly with the social media, we have sensory extensions that might live pluralistically in many cultures today. The social media recreated the concept of 'sphere' in all social relationships. We are no more dependent on a single culture, a single book, a single language or a single technology than we were. The global village that McLuhan conceptualized on the sociological impact of technological developments is mentioned as 'noosphere' or 'cosmic membrane' in the book *The Phenomenon of Man* by De Chardin (2003). Social media expanded the sensing and perceiving sphere of the human being with the new communicative extensions they particularly offered for social life, thereby creating a sociological cosmic membrane on the earth. The cosmic membrane, called 'noosphere' by De Chardin, denotes a social brain in which communication and perception are accumulated.

Today the social media play an efficient role in the expansion of a sociological cosmic membrane. With the studies of co-creation of value, establishments wish to get firmly established in the market environment by using the social brain inside the cosmic membrane in a world that has become a global village. Although Jacques Barzun (2002), who calls himself a fearless and wild Luddite,[2] approaches the matter critically in his book entitled *The House of the Intellect*, he holds that the new communicative extensions resulting from technological developments create a sociological impact starting with people's senses and perception. The expansion, in a universal dimension, of one or several of our senses with the extensions offered by a new technological tool within the cosmic membrane of De Chardin will give rise to the emergence of new ratios among all senses. This can be compared with the case when a new note is added to a melody. When the ratios among the senses change, those phenomena that belong to cultures and that used to be seen clearly will suddenly become dull, while those phenomena that used to appear vague and dull will become transparent.

Economic dimension

Technology created significant changes in the economic system in the early twentieth century and ensured the rapid development of the technological management understandings and the capitalist production system. When the examples in Pine and Gilmore's study, *The Experience Economy* (1999), are carefully examined, it is clearly seen that technology has a principle effect on the developmental stages of the economic system. Prahalad and Ramaswamy's work 'The Co-creation Connection' (2002), also emphasizes that the economic function, demand factors and product presentation have become different, and economic system has changed along with co-creation of values. Summary of this change is clearly depicted in Pine and Gilmore's (1999) table (Table 14.1).

Table 14.1. Economic distinctions. (cf. Pine and Gilmore, 1999; Maslow, 1943; Dennis *et al.*, 2001; Kotler *et al.*, 2008; McLaughlin, 2009; Trendwatching.com, 2013.)

	Economic distinction			
Economic offering	Commodities	Goods	Services	Experiences
Economy	Agrarian	Industrial	Service	Experience
Economic function	Extract	Make	Deliver	Stage
Nature of offering	Fungible	Tangible	Intangible	Memorable
Key attribute	Natural	Standardized	Customized	Personal
Method of supply	Stored in bulk	Inventoried after production	Delivered on demand	Revealed over a duration
Seller	Trader	Manufacturer	Provider	Stager
Buyer	Market	User	Client	Guest
Factors of demand	Characteristic	Features	Benefits	Sensations

In the marketing environment, elasticized by technology, social media totally change the classical production model by enabling co-creation of interactive situations and experience values. Along with the change in perceptions and the spread of social sphere accelerated by social media, economic structure has reached the point of experience design in which the customers are also included in the process of commodity production. As a result, in the new economic system, companies are redefined as 'stage', commodities as 'decoration', products as 'experience' and consumers as 'guests', and thus guests are enabled to put their signs on the values being sold. The following section outlines experiences that a co-creator, as the guest, is likely to experience during a course of co-creation activity that aims to produce unique and memorable products and services.

The Co-creation Tourism Experience

Imagine that a hotel company in destination X wants to benefit from social media and calls for volunteers to help design a high-tech hotel room. The possible and multiple stages that a co-creator goes through in such a co-creation activity are outlined in Figure 14.3.

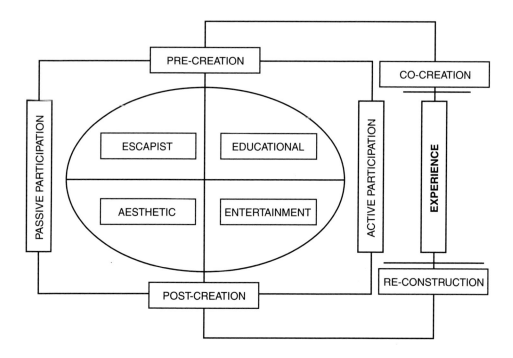

Fig. 14.3. The anatomy of co-creation. (From Authors.)

Pre-creation (motivation and personalization) stage

The concept of 'prosumers' was coined by futurologist Alvin Toffler (1980) when he predicted that the role of producers and consumers would begin to blur and merge. Toffler's 'producer consumer' or prosumers were common consumers who were predicted to each become active to help personally improve or design the goods and services of the marketplace, transforming it and their roles as consumers. From the consumers' perspective, co-creation entails monetary and non-monetary costs of time, resources, physical and psychological effort to learn and participate in the co-creation process. It is likely that potential co-creators would compare benefits of engaging in co-creation activities against its costs, and then choose to behave accordingly (Etgar, 2008; O'Hern and Rindfleisch, 2009). To manage co-creation through social media, companies need first to understand why some consumers are willing and able to take part in the co-creation process. We think that prosumers of co-created products, varying in their degree of interest and ability in co-creation, have a variety of motives, ranging from financial rewards to psychological benefits. This may shape their willingness and their level of participation intensity in co-creation activities. Consumers as co-creators may reap such cognitive and emotional benefits as increased status, self-esteem, recognition through visibility, increased knowledge, a sense of pride, self-expression opportunity, etc. The call from the company, the stager, should entice the co-creator that by involvement in the activity she can fulfil her holiday need(s). We must note that not all prosumers will respond to the call of the company. Only a relatively small number of consumers may fully take part in co-creation of product development and launch processes due to their appropriate skills, though the number of such skilled consumers appears to grow steadily.[3]

Browsing stage

A potential co-creator may find 'a creation call' from a company by coincidence or his/her internal urge to 'create/transform' may drive her intentionally to search such creation opportunities by 'browsing' suitable places (e.g. travel blogs of socialites). Browsing involves both delving into the details of the desired experience by visiting the social media sites and gaining status through being visible in the network of the social media. We need to reiterate that social media browsing is not just done for gaining information but also for increasing one's status and fame. Social media browsing is rather different from browsing the internet. It is like catwalk; the more you are seen, the higher fame you gain. A co-creator at the browsing stage, charged with a motive to create in general, is likely to be alert to innovation opportunities. Depending on her previous experiences, however, she will also be sensitive to the genuineness of the call (i.e. if felt necessary, she will need to assess transparency of the company, reputation of the company, informational quality and check out the intellectual property rights accompanying the offer).

Transformation stage

Every human being born with a need for transformation and the social media paves the way for its fulfilment. Once the co-creator has identified a suitable habitat for her co-creation needs (i.e. the needs, and how and where they can be satisfied should be identified up until this stage) and locates ways to overcome possible impediments on the path of co-creation, the creation circle begins. At this stage, the co-creator actively interacts with others, including the company, online and offline, to determine and best exploit available resources (e.g. information, intellectual ability and skills, social network) that would help fulfil initially identified co-creation needs. She starts converging personal inputs (holiday need, knowledge, ability and skills), as well as necessary external inputs, and transforms them into a personal, consumable and memorable product. During this process, she may capitalize on either self-generated idea sets or already-existing sets of ideas that can be collated from such available external sources as blogs of socialites. 'Imagination' acts as the vital fuel of the co-creator. Only through this ability can she envisage an otherwise utopian product as an integrated bundle of consumable experience. The co-creator may opt to take already existing 'available offers' (scanning through customer reviews about high tech hotel rooms, etc.) from diverse interactive resources and merge these independent pieces to mould the 'imagined product'. Alternative product propositions are also made by a series of alterations in the design of the product.

An intensive interaction takes place between the co-creator and others. At this stage, she acts both as a resource (input provider) and a change agent (transformer) on behalf of the hotel company. When the abstract product and its alternatives start taking shape, she may act as the 'communicator' and share the early form of the product details with others. As a result of the curiosity about what others think about the proposed product, she may seek feedback from her social media connections (e.g. clicks on the 'Like' box). Based on the feedback's quantity and quality, she may finalize and reshape the proposition in accordance with the feedback to strengthen its value.

Mental and actual experience stages

Up until now, creation of a product that is going to be offered by the company to the market is achieved through an active participation of the consumer. While this consumer-driven 'to-be-experienced' product could be put on sale for other potential consumers by the company, its creation process already encompasses several experiences on the co-creator's part. Departing from Pine and Gilmore's argument, one may claim that prosumers of co-creation may encounter different types and intensity of experiences during a single co-creation activity. When the co-creator is faced with a challenge of creation, she may need to build up her knowledge to a certain extent and this learning experience may lead to an educational satisfaction with the creation experience. Similarly, she may escape from every day hustle and bustle while searching and thinking for the best 'creation' on social media. And this escapist experience may contain value and hence satisfaction. The creation 'involves' aesthetics, another innate need, as a series of decisions have to be made about 'hows' of the proposition (e.g. colour, size, shape, location, etc.). Finally, the creation process may bring about entertainment through learning new information, building new skills, socializing and connecting with others. Thus, a co-creation experience itself represents a bundle of experiences of escape, entertainment, education and aesthetics.

Reconstruction stage

We have reason to believe that 'creation' does not end when the product is developed and transferred to the company. Not only experience during product development but also actual consumption of the innovated product by self or others is thought to be part of the co-creation circle. Assuming that the creator becomes the actual consumer of the product (e.g. one who has designed a new high-tech hotel room is actually staying in that room), she would incline to share the 'experience' with others who are in her social-media circle. Here the participation in social-media circulation is comparatively passive for the co-creator, as opposed to the active participation at the early mental creation stage. The motive sought here is to receive comments from the others in the circle that would add value to the consumption experience and hence the co-created product. While experiencing the self-developed high-tech room, she will be able to 'sense' the ability of the product in terms of its performance in delivering the four forms of experiences, namely education, entertainment, escape and aesthetics. Once the experience is 'sensed' and the customer returns home with first-hand information, she will be able to reflect both about the created and the lived experience. This comparison eventually may lead to reconstruction of the product, as some experience dimensions may (or not) be able to live up to the expected level. The reconstructed product is expected to be shared with others in detail, particularly with those in the social media. Thus feedback governs the reality. We therefore propose naming co-creation through social media 'creperience (creation + experience)' to better describe the concept.

The Co-creation Strategies over Social Media

The process of co-creation of values – with its power acquired from social media and technology – has been proceeding towards a fantastic market structure in which the best properties of a virtual world are transferred to the real world by making radical changes in a wide range of factors varying from market structure to communication systems, from behavioural patterns to production models. Nowadays, the services provided by social media and technological devices' creation of an integrated power using protocols and algorithms consistent with the idea of convergence have created a wide strategic field ranging from media-integrated feedback systems known simply as 'feedback' to Co-creation Laboratories that we call 'Made in Customer'.

F-EEDBACK

Social-lites vs market pandemonium

The lexical meanings of 'pandemonium' that the Wachowski siblings, the scenarists of the world-famous film *The Matrix,* used to describe the chaotic environment are chaos, hubbub and the moment of hell. Particularly the information overload the internet has recently created constitutes some chaos and hubbub for marketing management. In his book *Future Shock,* Alvin Toffler (1970) suggested that the ability of external sources to meet the needs in the solution of a problem provides the creation of a decision. Nevertheless, when the dimension of the external source and the alternatives it has created exceed the operation capacity of an individual, the quality of the decision is damaged (Gross, 1964) and the need is not solved. Summarized as information overload, this is suggested in the book *The Managing of Organizations* (Gross, 1964) as the fact that decision-makers approach products or services with a limited cognitive operation capacity. The information that arrives in such a dimension that exceeds the cognitive operation capacity creates indecision and shock – called information anxiety – in the decision-maker. The problem of access to information, regarded as a serious problem until the early 21st century, was particularly reversed following Web 2.0 and transformed into the processes of filtering of information and sorting of alternatives. This environment, where no early warning systems in terms of marketing have been constructed and where temporary trends predominate, denotes the chaotic environment and hubbub that the Wachowski siblings described.

Using the social network websites and integrated applications, the customer is able to share the heavy burden of information with the social groups he belongs to, he can discuss issues with opinion leading social-lites, and he receives recommendations to solve market pandemonium. Customers are increasingly tapping into their networks of friends, fans and followers to discover, discuss and purchase goods and services, in ever-more sophisticated ways. As a result, it's never been more important for brands to make sure they too have the F-EEDBACK.

FOURSQUARE: Foursquare is a location-based social networking website for mobile devices, such as smart phones. Users 'check in' at venues using a mobile website, text messaging or a device-specific application by selecting from a list of venues the application locates nearby. Location is based on GPS hardware in the mobile device or network location provided by the application. Foursquare is a web and mobile application that allows registered users to post their location at a venue ('check-in') and connect with friends. Check-in requires active user selection and points are awarded at check-in. By April 2012, there had been more than 2 billion check-ins with Foursquare. Users are encouraged to be hyper-local and hyper-specific with their check-ins – one can check into a certain floor/area of a building, or indicate a specific activity while at a venue. Users can choose to have their check-ins posted on their accounts on Twitter, Facebook, or both. The service provides three levels of 'Superuser status' (which is not to be confused with the 'Super User' badge). Superuser status is conferred on users who have been selected by Foursquare staff for their helpful contributions to the community.

Foursquare brands allow companies to create pages of tips and allow users to 'follow' the company and receive special, expert tips from them when they check-in at certain locations. Some of the companies even allow users to unlock special badges with enough check-ins. On most company's pages, their Facebook, Twitter and company website links are displayed as well as tips and lists generated by the company. Foursquare specials are intended for businesses to use to persuade new customers and regular customers to visit their venue. Some businesses now display a Foursquare sign on their door or window, letting users know that there is a 'Special' at that particular venue. http://www.youtube.com/watch?v=YPyJsPdHX_c

POGOSEAT AND SPORT TOURISM: Pogoseat also is an app that enables audience members at live sports events to identify and purchase upgrades to better seats via their smartphone. The app identifies empty seats with the best views, and once users have selected their new seats they are able to enter payment details, purchase and move. http://www.pogoseat.com/

BISTIP: Bistip is a peer-to-peer courier service from Indonesia that helps travellers to discover (and negotiate a fee with) an individual who needs something delivered to their end destination. http://www.bistip.com/

COACHELLA FESTIVAL AND NFC: Guests of the 2012 Coachella festival in California were given encrypted NFC (near field communication) enabled wristbands instead of tickets. Those wearing the wristbands could wave them at various stations around the grounds and their Facebook status would automatically notify their friends which stage they were at, and which band they were watching at that moment. In another example, The STRP Art and Technology Festival, in Eindhoven, the Netherlands 18–28 November 2010, employed the use of RFID in museums and galleries that allow guests to rate art via RFID wristbands. Visitors used RFID wristbands and 'dashes' (which represent how much they liked something) to tag art, with the results collated to create a visible 'tag cloud' showing the most popular exhibits, and where they were located. http://www.coachella.com/festival-passes/about-wristbands

WALIBI'S RFID BRACELETS: Several theme parks, including Walibi in Belgium, Luna Park in Australia, and a temporary space set-up by Coca-Cola in Israel, have introduced RFID bracelets that let visitors update their Facebook status while on the move. By swiping their wrists over sensors before going on rides, participants can 'Like' features, notify friends about their activities, and have their pictures captured and tagged. http://www.walibiconnect.be/

HOLIDAYCROWD: Launched in beta during March 2011, HolidayCrowd invites travellers to list a trip they'd like to take, specifying details such as destination and

budget. Participating travel agents then assess the request and build an itinerary, resulting in competing offers for the traveller. http://www.trendwatching.com/trends/innovationextravaganza/

TRIPADVISOR AND OTHERS: The TripAdvisor tie in, launched in December 2010, means that visitors to the travel site who are logged into Facebook see their friends' reviews first, as well as being able to quickly view which of their friends have been to particular sites. Friends can also message each other quickly for additional travel tips. In other examples, Travel Q&A sites Gogobot and Hotel Me are trying to bridge the gap between known friends (who are trusted but may not have the answer) and wider audiences. Gogobot is an online travel community with a social lens. Users ask questions about destinations (think 'Where's a fun restaurant in Paris?'), not just to the Gogobot community but also to their Facebook and Twitter networks. Gogobot collates the answers, and includes pictures and links to all of the places mentioned. Finally, British Airways' Metrotwin is an online portal that compares and contrasts city 'twins', and is a social utility for time-starved, novelty-seeking urbanites living or travelling between the two cities. The site currently features London, New York and Mumbai, providing recommendations for the best neighbourhoods, businesses, attractions and places to visit. http://www.tripadvisor.com/instantpersonalization

Online to Offline and Gamification

Bringing the best of online to the real world

Consumers love online because when it comes to online consumption, they can act (participate, talk, create, adjust) to get what they want. Now, they expect the same from 'offline' consumption. Thanks to social media and co-creation, customers don't just buy a product or service: they also buy an experience and into a two-way relationship in which they get to express their desires, and brands get valuable. The most important motivation of co-creation of values and social media is to attain platforms where millions of people all around the world can share and discuss opinions about the products and services. These digital platforms within the frame of co-creation enable the experience designs to be viewed, discussed, revised through virtual reality systems, and thus to be turned into services and experiences with high added-value which are called 'know-how'. Expectations and gains, which are have not yet been affected by economy and which are still intact, are made closer to the real world by being integrated ('gamification') with virtual reality game systems and social-media systems; and create new opportunities economy needs. Along with social media and other value creation concepts, when marketing exceeds the logical borders called 'logic' and reaches mythic worlds called 'logos', new needs and opportunities will arise in the near future.

We believe that the steps in tourism marketing need to gain speed as suggested in the examples given within the perspective of a famous automotive brand's 'the future has already come' motto and subsequently within the strategy of 'online to offline gamification'.

VIRTUAL HILTON SANYA RESORT and SPA: A virtual replica of the Hilton Sanya Resort and Spa is to be built in the video game and social media Hot Dance Party following a deal between the hotel operator and Perfect World Technology. 'Hot Dance Party' was released by PW Network in 2008 as their first 3D online game. The virtual five-star hotel will be constructed by the developer as Hilton seeks to maintain its position as an industry leader on the internet. Timothy Soper, vice president of hotel operations from Hilton in Greater China explained the new hotel would 'increase our influence among younger generations and further strengthen our leading position in the global hospitality industry' (breakingtravelnews.com, 2013). http://www.breakingtravelnews.com/news/article/hilton-to-build-virtual-hotel/

HILTON – ULTIMATE TEAM PLAY: Hilton Garden Inn® became the world's first hotel brand to offer an intensive, interactive employee training programme designed and created specifically for use on Sony Computer Entertainment Inc.'s PSP® (PlayStation® Portable) handheld entertainment system and its vibrant widescreen LCD. The game is a benchmark in interactive training in the hospitality industry created especially for Hilton Garden Inn by Virtual Heroes, Inc. – a graphically-intense, 3-D, first-person video game built featuring an immersive player experience. In addition to providing employees with one of the most realistic guest simulation experiences in the industry, Hilton Garden Inn will use the new program to aggressively recruit next-generation team members grounded in technology, the internet, entertainment and video games. David Kervella, head of Hilton Garden Inn training for spearheading the enhanced program, stated 'Ultimate Team Play is part of our ongoing commitment to making employee training compelling and relevant, which are our two most important criteria for ensuring long-term customer service success.'

The overall goal of the new program, titled HGI Ultimate Team Play for PSP®, is to show hotel team members how their actions have an impact on the hotel and on the guest's mood, which in turn drives the brand's Satisfaction and Loyalty Tracking (SALT) scores higher or lower. The game puts team members in a 3-D, graphically-intensive virtual Hilton Garden Inn hotel where they must respond to a number of different guest-related requests by a specific deadline. The appropriateness, level and speed of their response directly affect the simulated guest's satisfaction as well as the hotel's SALT scores. The full interactive game version was launched at all Hilton Garden Inn locations in January 2009 and included training content for positions in housekeeping, food and beverage, engineering/maintenance and front desk customer service. http://virtualheroes.com/projects/hilton-ultimate-team-play

PLAYSTATION + LONELY PLANET GUIDE= GAMIFICATION MASHUP: International travel content business Lonely Planet and software publisher Sony Computer Entertainment Europe (SCEE) have announced a major new commercial partnership to develop a series of fully interactive, portable and up-to-the-minute city guides for use on the PSP® (PlayStation®Portable). The partnership sees the next step in the evolution of the travel guide, creating an immediate and accessible travel resource with a dynamic mix of film-, audio-, photography- and copy-based content. A dedicated website www.PSPpassport.com will offer further content to be downloaded, ensuring the guides are continually relevant and up-to-date. Helen Hewitt, Product Marketing Manager, Lonely Planet commented: 'Lonely Planet leads the market in delivering stylish and reliable destination guides developed with the city traveller in mind. Our partnership with Sony allows us to extend our product range by offering a new type of interactive guidebook; designed to meet the evolving needs of the technology-savvy traveller. We're working with local networks in each territory to ensure this is a really high impact and integrated campaign to engage the consumer. Development has been a joint effort – Lonely Planet shared our insights into traveller types, the different stages of the travel cycle, provided destination advice and generated content for the guides. This was a collaborative effort.' http://www.lonelyplanet.com/press-centre/press-release.cfm?press_release_id=246

Made in Customer

Customer as a designer of innovation and co-creation lab

In today's 'experience economy', consumers want the best, they want it now and first, and they want real, human connection, too. In fact, they demand all that. Thanks to social media and co-creation platforms and new manufacturing technologies that are finally tipping into the mainstream, the market becomes an increasingly 'Made in Customer' structure.

Obviously consumer involvement in products and services pre-launch has been building for years. Think crowdsourcing, which is still an active trend. But a consumer engaging in crowdsourcing is often looking to showcase his or her own design or marketing talent, while co-creations are primarily about getting what they want – ideally a great product and an amazing status story – by getting involved early.

Status has always been the driver deep at the heart of all consumer behaviour. When customers, thanks to the co-creation, connect with a pre-launch product or service, and support that project towards launch, it makes for a great status story to tell, tweet, post and otherwise share.

TIERRA PATAGONIA HOTEL and SPA-TRACKABLE SEEDS: Co-creations are even more potent if they're not simply about a great product or service, but about a broader movement or cause that the consumer believes in, providing a sense of belonging that goes beyond the thrill of possession. Chile's Tierra Patagonia Hotel and Spa has launched an initiative to give each of its guests a trackable virtual tree seed. Every guest is given a code and can choose where in the relevant protected area they would like their tree to be planted. Once planted, guests receive a geo-referenced Google Maps link to track their tree. http://www.springwise.com/eco_sustaineility/chilean-hotel-guest-virtual-trackable-tree-seed-reforest-patagonia/

DINE WITH THE DUTCH: Dine with the Dutch is a unique way that guests get to know Dutch culture. Dine with the Dutch matches visitors with one of their specially selected hosts for a home dinner. Guests can listen to stories about Dutch culture, find out more about Holland and enjoy a three-course dinner. http://www.dinewiththedutch.com/

FINAIR – QUALITY HUNTERS: An interesting example of co-creation in the tourism sector is Finnair's campaign 'Quality Hunters'. Finnair has created a forum called 'Rethink quality' to define what people expect in terms of service quality. Then the company selected four people whose mission was to travel around the world for two months and share their experiences through the Finnair blog. The purpose was to know what the company can propose as the best experience for future travellers in each city. This is a perfect example of a travel company listening to its customers' needs. http://media.finnair.com/Rethink/quality/

Conclusion

The 'desire of transformation' has become an important agent for both customers and companies, in a business world where competition has become fierce. The tourism business is no exception. The changing realities in the market demonstrate that consumers have started to lead a far different life than conventionally described in books. Failure to adequately understand consumers in a market where renaissance has begun will result in withering of once strong companies. With the rise of social media, the classical view, regarding the consumer as a highly rational entity who tries to obtain a hedonic and/or functional benefit begs for a substantial re-assessment. Users joining social media, a different universe, are gradually increasing day by day. This increase in the use of the social media provokes one to think that 'transformation' has become the initiator of other needs. Transformative experiences, through social-media involvement, resemble charging with new form of energy. Each energy intake will leave a trace for others and this trace will become more evident as it is tracked by followers. Conventionally, experiences taking place in the social media have been taken as virtual. Co-creation endeavours through social media however involve 'real experiences'. This chapter attempts to outline how co-creation offers a new paradigm that fosters growth, innovation and competitive advantage for companies and destination authorities, by drawing attention to the renaissance presently occurring in the market, and how conditions and dimensions of this renaissance will shape our understanding of consumer behaviour. Stages of co-creation, explicated in the chapter, call for more research to better understand what the co-creator experiences during a single co-creation activity.

Notes

[1] Petaflop Computer: A computer system that surpasses human intelligence with some power of a quadrillion operations per second.

[2] Luddite: Ned Ludd was a person who broke the windows of a shop in Leicestershire in a moment of insanity in 1779. The Luddites, who took their name from Ludd, were a group organized in England in 1811 that aimed to break manufacturing machines.

[3] More research is needed to understand which type of consumer has the highest potential for co-creation via social media.

Further Reading on F-EEDBACK Insights

http://www.technologyreview.com/tomarket/415858/annotated-areas/
http://www.imaginews.com/archives/706#more-706
http://storytelling.concordia.ca/oralhistorianstoolbox/pop_up_pages/wikitude_pop_up.html
http://www.michelintravel.com/

Further Reading on PSP Passport

http://www.youtube.com/watch?v=ti1OZV5vrEc
http://mt.playstation.com/psp/news/lonely-planet-s-tom-hall-on-passport-to-.html
http://www.youtube.com/watch?v=BRqIBNnXTZw
http://www.youtube.com/watch?NR=1&feature=endscreen&v=qts0ZB2ML0E

References

Barzun, J. (2002) *The House of Intellect*. Harper Perennial, New York.

Binkhorst, E. (2006) Creativity in the experience economy, towards the co-creation tourism experience? Presentation at the annual *ATLAS Conference on Tourism, Creativity and Development*, Barcelona, Spain.

Binkhorst, E. and Den Dekker, T. (2009) Agenda for co-creation tourism experience research. *Journal of Hospitality Marketing and Management* 18, 311–327.

Blake, W. (1975) *The Marriage of Heaven and Hell*. Oxford University Press, Oxford.

Boswijk, A., Thijssen, T. and Peelen, E. (2007) *The Experience Economy: A New Perspective*. Pearson Education Benelux, Amsterdam.

Breakingtravelnews.com (2013) Hilton to build virtual hotel. Available at: http://www.breakingtravelnews.com/news/article/hilton-to-build-virtual-hotel/ (accessed 5 March 2013).

Businessweek (2013) Starwood hotels explore second life first. Available at: http://www.businessweek.com/stories/2006-08-22/starwood-hotels-explore-second-life-first/ (accessed 5 March 2013).

De Chardin, T. (2003) *The Phenomenon of Man*. (Originally published as 'Le phenomena humain' Editions du Seuil, 1955.) HarperCollins, New York.

Dennis, J.L., Lamomthe, L. and Langley, A. (2001) The dynamics of collective leadership and strategic change in pluralistic organizations. *Academy of Management Journal* 44, 809–837.

Doyle, P. (2000) *Value-Based Marketing*. Wiley, Oxford.

Drucker, P.F. (1977) *Technology and Culture* (first published in 1966). University of Chicago Press, Chicago, Illinois.

Etgar, M. (2008) A descriptive model of the consumer co-production process. *Journal of the Academy of Marketing Science* 36(1), 97–108.

Gross, B.M. (1964) *The Managing of Organizations: The Administrative Struggle.* Free Press of Glencoe, New York.

Hamel, G. and Prahalad, C.K. (1996) *Competing for the Future.* Harvard Business School Press, Boston, Massachusetts.

Huxley, A. (1954) *The Doors of Perception.* Chatto and Windus, London.

Joyce, J. (2012) *Finnegans Wake.* Wordsworth, Ware, UK.

Kotler, P., Armstrong, G., Harris, L. and Piercy, N.F. (2008) *Principles of Marketing.* Pearson, Harlow, UK.

Maslow, A.H. (1943) Hierarchy of needs. *Psychological Review* 50, 370–396.

McLaughlin, H. (2009) What's in a name: 'client', 'patient', 'customer', 'consumer', 'expert by experience', 'service user' – what's next? *British Journal of Social Work* 39, 1101–1117.

McLuhan, M. (2001) *The Gutenberg Galaxy.* University of Toronto Press, Toronto, Canada.

Neuhofer, B., Buhalis, D. and Ladkin, A. (2013) Experiences, co-creation and technology: a conceptual approach to enhance tourism experiences, Cauthe Conference. Available at: http://www.academia.edu/2703085/Neuhofer_B._Buhalis_D._and_Ladkin_A._2013._Experiences_Co-creation_and_Technology_A_conceptual_approach_to_enhance_tourism_experiences (accessed 9 March 2013).

O'Hern, M.S. and Rindfleisch, A. (2009) Customer co-creation: a typology and research agenda. *Review of Marketing Research* 6, 84–106.

Pine, B.J. and Gilmore, J.H. (1999) *The Experience Economy.* Harvard Business School Press, Boston, Massachusetts.

Polanyi, K. (1944) *The Great Transformation.* Rinehart, New York.

Prahalad, C.K. and Krishnan, M.S. (2008) *The New Age of Innovation.* McGraw-Hill, New York.

Prahalad, C.K. and Ramaswamy, V. (2002) The co-creation connection. Available at: http://www.tantum.com/tantum/pdfs/2009/2_the_co_creation_connection.pdf (accessed 12 March 2013).

Prahalad, C.K. and Ramaswamy, V. (2004) *The Future of Competition: Co-creating Unique Value with Customers.* Harvard Business School Press, Boston, Massachusetts.

Prebensen, N.K. and Dahl, T. (2013) Value co-creation: significance of tourist. *Annals of Tourism Research* 42, 240–261.

Prebensen, N.K. and Foss, L. (2011) Coping and co-creation in tourist experiences. *International Journal of Tourism Research* 13, 54–57.

Ramaswamy, V. (2009) Leading the transformation to co-creation of value. *Strategy and Leadership* 37(2), 32–37.

Ramaswamy, V. and Gouillart, F. (2010) Building the co-creative enterprise. *Harvard Business Review* (October), 100–109.

Richards, G. and Wilson, J. (2006) Developing creativity in tourist experiences: a solution to the serial reproduction of culture? *Tourism Management* 27, 1209–1223.

Schmitt, B.H. (1998) *Experiential Marketing: How to Get Customers to Sense, Feel, Think, Act and Relate to Your Company and Brands.* Free Press, New York.

Schmitt, B.H. (1999) Experiential marketing. *Journal of Marketing Management* 15, 53–67.

Shaw, G., Bailey, A. and Williams, A. (2011) Aspects of service dominant logic and its implications for tourism management: examples from the hotel industry. *Tourism Management* 32, 207–214.

Toffler, A. (1970) *Future Shock.* Random House, New York.

Toffler, A. (1980) *The Third Wave.* Bantam Books, New York.

Trendwatching.com (2013) Presumers and custowners. Available at: http://www.trendwatching.com/tr/trends/10trends2013/?presumers/ (accessed 10 March 2013).

Tussyadiah, I.P. and Fesenmaier, D.R. (2007) Interpreting tourist experiences from first-person stories: a foundation for mobile guides. *Proceedings of the 15th European Conference on Information Systems*, St Gallen, Switzerland, pp. 2259–2270.

Tussyadiah, I.P. and Fesenmaier, D.R. (2009) Mediating tourism experiences: access to places via shared videos. *Annals of Tourism Research* 36, 24–40.

Tussyadiah, I.P. and Zach, J.F. (2011) The role of geo-based technology in place experiences. *Annals of Tourism Research* 39(2), 780–800.

White, L.A. (2005) *The Science of Culture: A Study of Man and Civilization*. Percheron Press, Canada.

Wölfflin, H. (1915) *Principles of Art History. The Problem of the Development of Style in Later Art*. Translated from 7th German edition (1929) into English by M.D. Hottinger (Dover Publications, New York 1932 and reprints).

15 Prices and Value in Co-produced Hospitality and Tourism Experiences

Xiaojuan (Jady) Yu[1] and Zvi Schwartz[2]

[1]Sun Yat-Sen University, Guangzhou, China; [2]Virginia Tech, Blacksburg, USA

Consumer Involvement: Co-creation vs Co-production

This chapter explores the role of pricing when the consumed product is co-produced in the context of tourism and hospitality experiences. The traditional approach of associating the tourist's experience with the tourism product and the service provider has been replaced in recent years with the recognition that the tourists themselves have considerable impact on the tourism experience by investing their time, effort and skills in their experience (Prebensen *et al.*, 2013). Some scholars refer to this phenomenon as 'co-creation', while others prefer the term 'co-production'. The distinction between the two terms is not clear though, and sometimes the two are used interchangeably, or in different ways by different authors. Following the service-dominant logic (Vargo and Lusch, 2004), it is suggested that the 'co-creation of value' and 'co-production' are two components of the value co-creation (Lusch and Vargo, 2006; Lusch *et al.*, 2007). The 'co-creation of value' means that 'value can only be created with and determined by the user in the "consumption" process and through use or what is referred to as value-in-use' (Lusch and Vargo, 2006, p. 284). This view is in opposition to the view of the goods-dominant logic, in which value is 'something that is added to products in the production process and at point of exchange is captured in value-in-exchange (i.e., price)' (Lusch and Vargo, 2006, p. 284). Co-production 'involves the participation in the creation of the core offering itself' (Lusch and Vargo, 2006, p. 284). The former is the most encompassing one and is superordinate to the latter. In a somewhat different way, Chathoth *et al.* (2013) conceptualize co-production and co-creation as two ends of a continuum indexed by the degree of customer involvement.

This confusion is not surprising since the 'co-creation'/'co-production' concept is a rather new one, and is yet to be constructed and defined through individual contemplations, and through social interactions. This phenomenon is quite salient in the discussions on the lexicon issue in the development of the service-dominant logic (Vargo and Lusch, 2004, 2008; Kohli, 2006; Lusch and Vargo, 2006; Rust, 2006).

Our current view is largely consistent with Lusch and Vargo (2006), and, as explained below, the term 'co-production' is viewed as being more suitable for our scope of discussion.

'Co-creation' appears to be a wider and somewhat vaguer construct to which more meanings can be attached. When an audience member is watching a performance, she is 'co-creating' her experience: she involves her attention, perception and memory, and she engages her imagination. Despite being passive and simply sitting in her chair, her involvement shapes her experience. Obviously, this happens in conjunction with the players' performance on stage. The involvement of such cognitive and emotional processes is on the fundamental level of a person's interaction with an object or with her environment. It is, perhaps, the minimum required from a person who is consuming an experience. In other words, it is the minimum one can 'do' to contribute to her experience. Contribution here means that these personal processes affect the nature of the consumed experience. We think that it is in this sense that 'the customer is always a co-creator of value' (Vargo and Lusch, 2008, p. 7). Customer contribution may also include communication and interaction with the product/service provider, and increasing levels of involvement in the form of physical activity, time, effort and skills. The more involvement, the more impact on the experience, and thus the more co-created the outcome/experience.

In this regard, the term 'co-creation' is too broad for our discussion. Instead, we opt for the term 'co-production' to describe what happens when customers participate in the creation of the core offering itself (Lusch and Vargo, 2006). Production is an economic term in which the input, the output and the process can be more clearly defined with regard to a particular product or service, most often in monetary terms. Accordingly, co-production here describes a situation in which part of the traditional production/service function is shifted to, and performed by, the consumer. For example, the customers of the Culinary Arts Theatre in Tromsø, Norway, perform the function of a cook when they learn how to make a meal. Their labour is an input into the production function of the meal they consume. As an increasing number of contemporary tourists wish to experience 'more', one way to achieve this goal is for the tourists to become a 'productive' part of the production function of the tourism products and services. It is in this specific goal of experiencing the co-production process that our discussion context may differ from other possibilities of co-production (e.g. co-production for the purpose of a more customized end product while the co-production process itself may not be the goal for enjoyment). When such a production function, including its inputs, outputs and processes, is reshuffled, many interesting pricing and value-related questions arise.

Accordingly, the goal of this chapter is to explore some possible implications of the tourism experience co-production phenomenon on the pricing of products and services. The discussion covers three phases of tourism consumption/transaction: advanced booking, production/service and payment, which all have implications on pricing and revenue, but in different ways. The chapter continues as follows. We first focus on the production/service phase. The basic analytical framework in microeconomics is reviewed, in which price is seen as a trade regulator. Drawing on this framework, we analyse the impact of co-production on demand, supply, prices, revenues and profits. Then the assumption of perfect information in the microeconomic analysis is relaxed, and the informational value of price in purchases with uncertainty and how it may be influenced by co-production are discussed. We propose that tipping may be a desirable payment method associated with co-production. We also pay attention to the economic and socio-cultural experiences of the Chinese, which may be different from the western normality in the related sections. Last we turn to the co-creation of prices in the advanced booking context (here we use the broader term 'co-creation' as pricing is not part of the more narrowly defined 'co-production' process). We summarize our conclusions and provide suggestions for future investigations.

Prices as Trade Regulators

Price plays a central role in microeconomics, the sub-area in economics that describes the behaviour of individuals, households, firms and markets (Samuelson and Nordhaus, 2009). In a market economy, individuals and firms' decisions about the allocation of their scarce resources are guided by an informal system of prices and profits. Prices are the means to 'regulate' the trade in an economy with scarce resources in that they provide an incentive for sellers to reduce production, and for buyers to reduce consumption.

Specifically, for any given good or service, consumers are willing to pay less when their consumption of that good or service increases, due to their diminishing marginal utility. In the demand–price relationship framework, consumer demand decreases when the price rises. The decrease is due to two effects: (1) the substitution effect, which occurs when a higher price leads to the substitution of other products or services to meet satisfaction; and (2) the income effect, which occurs when the higher price lowers real income and thereby reduces the desired consumption of most products and services. In a typical supply-and-demand analysis diagram, the relationship described above is represented by a downward-sloping demand curve, and the influence of price on demand is shown as a movement along the curve.

Market demand, i.e. the aggregation of individual demands, is influenced by factors beyond the price. These additional factors include income, population, the prices of related products and services, tastes or preferences, and special influences. These influences shift the demand curve to the left or to the right. In other words, these factors can either increase or decrease the quantity demanded for a good or service for any given price per unit. Among those influences, consumer tastes or preferences are more relevant to our discussion and their role in the co-produced environment will be explored.

Price also plays a pivotal role in the behaviour of firms. In a perfectly competitive market, a firm sells a homogeneous product and is too small to influence the market price, i.e. it faces a horizontal demand curve. With rising marginal cost of production, the firm will choose the output level at which price equals its marginal cost. However, perfect competition rarely exists in the real world. The more realistic market includes various forms of imperfect competition, i.e. monopoly, oligopoly and monopolistic competition, which is also true for the diverse tourism goods and services markets. Here, a firm has some control over its price and faces a downward-sloping demand curve (as shown in Fig. 15.1, the d curve). In this case, in order to sell more, the firm has to lower its price. Hence the marginal revenue (the MR curve in Fig. 15.1) it gets

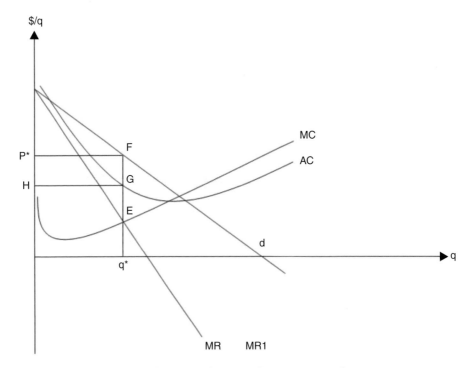

Fig. 15.1. Supply-and-demand analysis of an imperfect competitive firm.

from selling an additional unit of product is lower than the price it charges for the product. It can be shown that if the demand curve is a straight line, $p = a^*q + b$, then $MR = 2^*a^*q + b$. Since $a < 0$, $MR < p$. The MR curve is twice as steep as the d curve here. To maximize its profit (the difference between the revenue and the cost), the firm will also consider its production cost structure. Usually, after an initial phase of decrease, the marginal cost (the MC curve in Fig. 15.1) will rise with the increase of production. The intersection of MR and MC determines the firm's profit-maximizing production level, q^*. At this quantity, consumers are willing to pay – and the supplier will charge – a price of p^*. But here, the average cost (AC) is lower than the price, and the firm earns extra economic profit[1] represented by the rectangle FGHp*.

In this chapter we will utilize the framework outlined above to explore possible shifts of the demand and the cost curves caused by co-production, and the likely impact on relevant factors such as price, demand and profits.

The Impact of Co-production on Prices, Costs, Revenues and Profits

As explained at the beginning, in this chapter co-production means that tourists perform one or more of the roles that are traditionally performed by the seller of the tourism good or service. It may influence both the demand side and the supply side, which will be analysed in the following subsections respectively. We then also analyse the tourist's non-monetary price or costs in marketing terms and how they may be incorporated in the co-production framework.

The influence of co-production on utility and the demand curve

In the context of tourism and hospitality, the co-production phenomenon is associated mainly with creating a better experience for the tourist. The prevailing view is that by actively participating in the creation of the tourism experiences, the tourists become more involved and invested, develop a sense of ownership and consequently are more satisfied with the consumed tourism experience. This increase in perceived value of the tourism activity or in the tourist utility from consuming a certain co-produced amount at a certain price represents a change in the so-called 'consumers' taste' or the set of variables whose change shifts the demand curve in the imperfect competition market framework depicted in Fig. 15.2. Specifically, the expectation is that as the tourism service is viewed more favourably (because of the co-production nature of the experience), the demand curve shifts up and to the right. As the demand curve moves, so does the derived marginal revenue line: it also shifts up and to the right. The outcome of this shift is rather clear (if the seller's cost remains unchanged). Since the new equilibrium (the point at which the demand line intersects the marginal revenue one) is at a higher price and a higher quantity, it follows that the revenue must be higher.

Hence, the trivial/fundamental impact of an increase in co-production is higher revenues for the producer of the tourism experience because of the increase in quality/value perception and the tourism actual and expected satisfaction. It can be shown (though beyond the scope of this chapter) that the new maximal profit, due to the shift of the demand curve and the new equilibrium, will be higher as well.

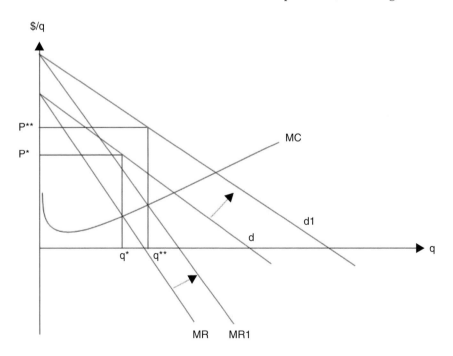

Fig. 15.2. Shift of the demand curve due to increased value.

The impact of co-production on the seller's offering and cost structure

The analysis above ignores the possible impact of co-production, that is, the increase in the co-produced portion of the tourism service, on the offering and cost structure of the tourism provider. There are two conceivable opposing impacts in this regard. On one side, if a substantial portion of the production responsibilities are effectively shifted from the service provider to the tourists, then the average cost per unit produced should decrease as well. For example, if the participants of a multi-week rafting expedition on the Columbia River row, cook, clean and perform other tasks, then the tour operator saves considerably by not having to pay tour guides for these services. In other words, by engaging in self-service, those tourists are competing with tourism service providers and substituting for exchange in the marketplace (Lusch *et al.*, 1992; Prahalad and Ramaswamy, 2000; Vargo and Lusch, 2004). Hence while costs are decreased, it is possible that tourists' willingness to pay may also be reduced for the part of the self-service.

On the other side, co-production might have a negative impact on the cost structure, that is, it might increase the average cost per tourism service unit produced, because of two main reasons. First, training might be needed as some of the tourists might not be qualified for the 'job'. The more complex and critical to the success of the experience the function they perform, the more costly the training and supervision are likely to be. Consider, for example, an adventure tourism vendor who elects to delegate the responsibility of belaying to the participants when they rock climb in the Mojave Desert. In this case, the company is likely to spend considerable time teaching and testing the clients' proficiency in performing this life-supporting task. That is, while the tourists engage in co-production and providing self-service, they need to develop requisite knowledge and skills. For the tourism provider, this is an opportunity to develop new offerings that enable their customers' self-service (Vargo and Lusch, 2004). Delegating life-supporting tasks to customers will most likely incur higher insurance need and cost because of the high risk involved in placing such a responsibility in the hands of the novice. Second, given that the tourists might not perform well, and given that training and careful supervision is sometimes needed while the experience is being consumed, as is the case with typical high-risk adventure tourism activities, the cost of delivering the tourism experience could increase due to direct monetary expenses associated with on-the-job training and supervision, and due to indirect expenses such as decreased productivity of the trained staff, inefficient operation due to mistakes of the participants, etc.

With the two opposing potential impacts of the 'co' element on the production's offering and cost, the question is what the net impact is. If positive, in the sense that the overall impact is to reduce the average cost per unit produced, then when combined with the expected increase in revenue and profit (due to the shift of the demand curve) it is clear that the net result is even higher profitability for the tourism experience provider. However, if the net impact on the cost structure is to increase costs then again the question is what is higher, the increase in profitability due to the shift of the demand curve or the decrease due to the shift of the cost curve?

Non-monetary price

Additional complications are the notion of non-monetary elements of price and related customers' price-fairness perceptions. The marketing literature emphasizes that from the customer point of view cost often includes non-monetary elements. Typically, these elements include time, inconvenience, risk and loss of dignity. So while these elements are not reflected in the cost function depicted in Figs 15.1 and 15.2 above, they seem 'real' to the consumer in the sense that they impact the tourists' perception of the overall price, that is, what they need to 'give up' in order to purchase, and consume, the product. We can now return to the framework of demand/supply. When the tourism provider sets a price of P*, which reflects that optimal point at which the marginal revenue equals marginal costs, the tourist perceives the 'total' price to be: P*+Ψ where Ψ represents the non-monetary elements of the cost to the tourist. This means that the quantity at that equilibrium will be somewhat lower than q*, say q*-β where β denotes the drop in quantity demanded per given price due to the increase in the perceived cost (Ψ). The connection to co-producing the tourism experience is rather simple. If indeed the co-produced elements are substantial, and if indeed they require considerable investment of the consumer's resources, then the tourists might modify their perception about the price. The more co-production, the more likely the tourist will view each quoted price as being higher than its mere monetary level. The impact on the expected revenues is also straightforward: it will be lower. Interestingly, the price demand elasticity, the tool used to estimate whether a price change will generate an increased or decreased stream or revenues, is irrelevant in this case. This is because the 'price increase' is due to an increase in non-monetary cost to the tourist and is not reflecting higher monetary compensation per unit to the tourism provider. Based on the above, it is argued that with lower marginal revenues the impact of the co-production due to potentially higher non-monetary cost is to lower profits.

To summarize, the analysis discussed above suggests that co-production will impact both the demand and supply curves. Whether these moves will result in higher profits depends on the relative magnitude as well as the direction in which the costs and the perceived non-monetary costs are impacted.

Co-production and the Informational Value of Price

Traditional economic modelling is based on an unrealistic assumption of perfect information. This common assumption means that the consumers and producers know all there is to know about all products they consider. In other words, both sides of the market, buyers as well as sellers, have complete information as to prices and quality of the products. In reality though, a market with perfect information is a rare if non-existent phenomenon. Facing incomplete information, asymmetric information and uncertainty, consumers often rely on visible elements as signals of hidden, or hard-to-observe, attributes of a product (Solomon, 2010) and price is one of these elements often used as a signal of quality in tourism and hospitality management (Schwartz, 2006). Consumers tend to infer high quality from high prices and according to economic theory there is a good reason for this apparent association. The theory stipulates that sellers of goods and services send a reliable signal about the quality of their product by charging a premium. The reliability of the price quality signal stems from the notion that in the long run cheating (that is, charging high premium for a low quality product) is not a sustainable strategy. There is ample empirical evidence and theoretical support for the price quality signalling mechanism in general and within the tourism industry in particular. A multitude of studies show that consumers are accustomed to associating price with quality. Moreover, recent research demonstrated that there is an increase in activity in areas of the brain that are associated with pleasure when people are shown high prices. Specifically to tourism, it was argued that from the tourist perspective the 'reputation mechanism' (a competing explanation as to how quality is 'enforced' in imperfect information markets) is insufficient to ensure quality, hence the 'need' for the price quality signalling mechanism in the tourism domain.

An immediate implication of the price quality signalling mechanism to the topic at hand is that instead of causing a move along the slope of the demand curve, a change in price might signal a change in the product's quality, thus affecting willingness to pay, causing instead a move of the demand curve rather than along it (Schwartz and Chen, 2010). In this regard, it is interesting to explore how the notion of 'co-production' within the tourism experience (that is, mixing or substituting the tourists/providers roles) fits within this price/quality signalling framework. First to consider is the impact of an increase in the perceived price due to the 'co' element of the production discussed earlier in this chapter. Given that this increase has to do with non-monetary (time, inconvenience, etc.) aspects of the perceived price, it is very unlikely that it will have an impact in terms of affecting quality perception. Research suggests that consumers are conditioned to associate the monetary price with quality, and there are no indications that producers can use non-monetary price elements to reliably signal quality. However, as discussed above, under certain situations the monetary price in equilibrium might be higher due to a move of the demand curve (higher satisfaction with the product due to co-production) and move of the production cost curve due to the cost associated with training and maintaining the co-production system. In this case a higher equilibrium price might trigger a further move of the demand curve as this higher price might signal a higher product quality to prospective tourists, boosting their willingness to pay. This resulting secondary move will generate a new equilibrium with a higher price.

There are, however, additional potential impacts of co-production on the notion of price/quality signalling that are somewhat less trivial. Consider, for example, the issue of information asymmetry. Prices have informational value, that is, they signal quality, when there is a gap between what the tourism experience provider knows about the product and what the tourist knows. This is true for 'experience products', that is, products where the tourists can assess the quality only after consumption, and even more so, for the 'credence products', where it is difficult or even impossible to assess the quality even after the tourism product was consumed. One potential outcome is that by actively participating in the process of producing the tourism experience, the tourist becomes more intimately acquainted with the process and the product. As a result the information gap between the provider and the tourists shrinks, reducing the need for quality signalling, that is, reducing the informational value of the price. A possible counter-argument is that in some co-production circumstances, confusion and uncertainty might be higher because the 'experts' (that is, the trained professional tourism experience providers) are not present to provide valuable information, because they are replaced by the novice tourists who are performing the tasks for the first time.[2]

Another potential non-trivial impact has to do with the tourists' sense of self-esteem and their level of well-being, and consequently, their reaction to price increases. If the act of co-production is associated with higher level of involvement, and intensified sense of ownership, then it is reasonable to assume that some tourists will feel increasingly better as the perceived quality of the experience improves, not just because they just consumed a better product, but because they produced, or helped produce, a better product. Interestingly this might lead to a peculiar situation if we re-consider the price/quality signalling mechanism. An increasingly higher price represents an increasingly higher perceived quality, and in turn, this higher perceived quality results in higher self-esteem. It means that a higher price might increase the tourists' utility from the product. If the impact is strong enough, it turns the co-produced tourism product into a Veblen one. A Veblen product is a peculiar and rare case where the quantity demanded increases with higher prices, that is, the slope of the demand curve is positive, rather than negative, at least within that price range where a normal price–quantity relation exists. Here the argument is that the tourist's self-esteem (generated by the co-production process) is equivalent in terms of impact to the consumer's self-esteem or utility generated by conspicuous consumption as described in Veblen's classic book on the theory of the leisure class (Veblen, 1899).

The discussion so far assumed that price is used as a reliable signal of quality. However, what if it cannot function as a reliable signal? For the Chinese, price is a doubtful indicator of real quality or value. As China is still developing a market economy, characterized by pursuit of profits, institutions and mechanisms to ensure quality and fair trade are not yet fully established or enforced. Furthermore, given the enormous size of the Chinese market, cheating in the short run can quickly generate a sizeable fortune (though this is probably unsustainable in the long run). Hence high prices are often quoted for low-quality or even fake products. For example, a tourist may pay US$10,000 for an antique souvenir that may turn out to be a modern replica. The unreliability of price as a quality signal has three apparent implications. The first is that the Chinese may turn to other more reliable signals, for example, brand and place of production. This may be one reason behind the international shopping tours of many Chinese. The second is that the Chinese have to develop skills to directly evaluate the quality of products, to bargain and to seek deals. In this case, they are 'co-creating' a fair price with the sellers; in a way, this is similar to the deal-seeking behaviour in advanced booking discussed later.

Interestingly, the third implication of the unreliability of price as a quality signal is that it may lead to co-production. For example, some Chinese diners may go into the kitchen to make sure that the live fish they have chosen is not replaced by other types of fish or dead fish. In this situation the diner may be viewed as playing the role of a quality inspector in the production process. A greater extent of co-production exists in Hot Pot restaurants, where restaurants prepare the materials and guests are responsible for cooking (though they may ask for help). The transparency of co-production may be one reason for the popularity of those restaurants – an upward shift of the demand curve in Fig. 15.2. As discussed before, another impact of the co-production could be to lower the provider's costs (a downward shift of the cost curve in Fig. 15.2). The two shifts lead to lower price but larger quantity, and very likely higher revenues and profits.

In summary, it appears that the impact of co-production within the price/quality signalling framework might take various forms, and further theoretical modelling and empirical investigations are needed.

Tipping and Co-production

The custom of tipping is a strong social norm in many societies, though it varies considerably in what occupations are being tipped, who is being tipped, how tips are distributed among the service providers and the size of the tip. From an economics perspective, tipping is considered a mechanism that helps to motivate employees to provide good service. Specifically, the microeconomics explanation argues that customers monitor the service quality more efficiently than the firm. Since the service quality determines the amount tipped, management view tipping as a less expensive service-quality monitoring mechanism. It is also argued that some of the savings in the 'production' costs are passed on to the customers. Sellers and buyers both benefit from tipping as a quality control mechanism. In addition it was shown that tipping can explain higher profitability when the tipping crowed is heterogeneous in its willingness to pay and propensity to tip (Schwartz, 1997), and that tipping is associated with motivation to evade taxation and levels of tax burden (Schwartz and Cohen, 2000).

We speculate here that when it comes to co-production of the tourism experience, tipping might prove to provide another function. We discussed above the notion of on-the-job training and supervision, that is, the need of the tourism service provider to invest in training and monitoring the performance of the tourists while they co-produce their tourism experience, especially in environments where their role is critical to the success of the experience, and might involve physical danger. Now consider a situation where the tourists are heterogeneous in their level of competency, that is, not all customers are the same in how well they can perform the task or tasks on hand. This heterogeneity means that how much training and supervision is needed for each tourist, and consequently how expensive each customer is to the tourism service provider, varies. In other words, demand and hence the responsive supply is contextual (Prahalad and Ramaswamy, 2004). Since it is often impractical to verify this information ahead of the production/consumption of the tourism experience, and since it might be also impractical to charge customers differently to better reflect the fact that due to their level of competency it costs more or less to serve them, it follows that tipping could 'bridge' that gap. If indeed people tip based on the perceived quality and value of the service they consumed, it might be that tourists who 'sense' that they had to consume more training and supervision while co-producing the tourism experience will also tip more. In other words, tipping might serve as an equalizer in the sense that high maintenance/expensive to seller co-producing tourists will tip more. By tipping more, they pay more to the seller, thus covering more of the seller's cost of providing the service to them. Hence, tipping may be a response to Lusch *et al.*'s (2007) proposition that price should also be co-produced.

However, it is recognized that at times tipping may be practised by default. That is, for some customers a tip is a social norm and the size of a tip is a fixed portion of the payment or some other amount unrelated to the quality of the service. Direct adoption in the co-production environment in these circumstances might mean that tipping fails to play the role of differentiating the experience value received. Hence, we propose that a tip-like payment method, instead of a direct application of the traditional tipping practice, may be developed for the evaluation of provider's contribution to co-production. As co-production of the tourism experience is a relatively new concept compared with services such as dining, how a more appropriate tipping practice may be established and accepted is left open. However, Vargo and Lusch see distinct roles for the service provider and the customer: 'The enterprise cannot deliver value, but only offer value propositions' and 'Value is always uniquely and phenomenologically determined by the beneficiary' (2004, 2008, p. 7). If a tourist is asked to tip, how much would a tourist tip? How does the tourist 'calculate' the amount? What factors would affect the amount in a co-produced environment? These questions may be best explored by looking at the interaction between tourism service providers and customers.

The discussion above pertains to cultures where tipping is customary. How should heterogeneous services (which may or may not result from the functional heterogeneity of tourists as co-producers) be priced in non-tipping societies? For example, consider the Chinese, who do not have a tipping culture. Some international guests in Hai Di Lao, the most successful and popular hotpot restaurant chain in China, attempt to tip waiters/waitresses as a reward for their exceptional service (Huang, 2011). The waiters/waitresses refuse those tips, as the act of refusing the tips is deemed laudable. Huang (2011) suggests that tips may be an appropriate compensation for their service, but is also concerned that the tipping practice may distain the spontaneity or authenticity of their efforts to serve their guests. It seems that tipping is viewed as necessary, but factors that impede or facilitate the establishment of this practice should be explored in non-tipping societies. Further, an interesting question is what other mechanisms may compensate for the tourists' functional heterogeneity in co-production and service heterogeneity in general.

Co-creation of Revenue-management Pricing and Customers' Hedonic Motivations

Besides co-producing tourism products and services, tourists may also influence and co-create their prices in more direct ways as they become more informed, connected, empowered and active, and learn that 'they too can extract value at the traditional point of exchange' (Prahalad and Ramaswamy, 2004, p. 6). Specifically, we refer here to deal-seeking activities, such as those related to services offered by opaque online travel agencies (OTA), e.g. Priceline and Hotwire. The travel booking services offered by these opaque OTAs typically include bidding and game-like processes and elements. The uncertain risky elements these OTAs infuse into the booking process are designed to help in achieving the two basic elements of efficient price discrimination: namely identification of the market segments (with various levels of willingness to pay) and ensuring enforcement, that is, preventing leakage of customers from higher willingness to pay segments into the lower price tiers. A game-like atmosphere seems to have emerged in recent years in conjunction with pre-travel deal-seeking activities to the point that it was recently suggested there is a process of 'gamification', where customers are learning how revenue management systems work and attempt to 'play the system' in the sense that they adjust their pre-travel behaviour and action in order to get the best deal. Mostly it has to do with ideal timing for reserving the tourism services, selecting where to book (distribution channels) in a strategic manner, and developing sophisticated search practices as well as ways to handle these systems, such as multiple logins using various IPs etc.

The more intense these pre-travel tourists' efforts, the more they are associated with tourists' high involvement. Furthermore, anecdotal evidence suggests that for these customers, this search and the 'game-like' activity is enjoyable and is becoming an integral part of their trip, something they even brag about to fellow travellers. It could be argued that these pre-travel activities become part of the co-production as the traveller affects the price in a substantial way: the discount for the same travel product could go up to 70% for the seasoned/lucky deal seeker. Since the overall perception about the quality of the tourism experience and the resulting satisfaction is affected by all facets and phases of the trip, it follows that an enjoyment from participation in that phase might increase the tourists' perception of the overall value of the tourism experience. Moreover, as travellers and providers seem to agree that the process is (or should be viewed as) enjoyable to the customers, it was argued that there is hedonic motivation involved in the process of searching for the best travel deal. In this regards hedonic motivation means that the tourists enjoy the process and game-like aspects of the deal-seeking activity, and this is on top of the lower price that is the utilitarian motivation or outcome of a successful deal-seeking activity. Schwartz and Chen (2012) showed that the hedonic motivation must be considered by travel providers who attempt to curtail deal-seeking behaviour and increase the propensity to purchase their products and services. Their model demonstrated that because of the enjoyment or the hedonic motivation, a deal seeker might respond in an undesirable way to the measures put in place by the providers to curtail deal-seeking behaviour. In other words, the hedonic motivation is likely to negatively impact the identification and enforcement elements of the price discrimination policy we discussed above. It was shown that deal-seeking activity could increase instead of decline.

To summarize, it is argued that certain kinds of co-production activities (that is, the active deal-seeking searches) are 'co-producing' the price and more interestingly, due to the hedonic motivation nature of the 'game' activity, this co-production is counterproductive for the service providers because it generates some level of immunity to the 'anti-deal-seeking' measures put in place by the industry.

Conclusion

As 'co-creation of value fundamentally challenges the traditional distinction between supply and demand' (Prahalad and Ramaswamy, 2004, p. 12), pricing, as the final measurement of the value exchanged between the two sides, has to disentangle this entanglement. This is arguably a great challenge as the phenomenon of, and the views on, the co-creation of value and co-production are still evolving (Vargo and Lusch, 2008). Overall, in the face of this challenge, we have discussed some possibilities, proposed some solutions, raised more questions, and even more is left to be explored.

In this chapter, we discussed the phenomenon of co-production/co-creation and its implications on pricing in three tourism and hospitality production/consumption phases: the production process, payment and advanced-booking. On the demand side, co-production may lead to higher satisfaction and utility, and increase willingness to pay. The impact of co-production on the supply side in terms of the cost structure may turn out in opposite ways, that is, it may increase or decrease the supplier's cost, depending on whether the tourist needs to be trained and monitored as the co-producer. The resulting combination of shifts in the demand curve and in the cost curve hence determines profitability. Higher willingness to pay coupled with lower costs will lead to higher revenue and profits. When higher willingness to pay is coupled with increased costs, revenue and profits depend on the relative size of the two.

Besides price as a trade regulator, we discussed its informational role as a quality signal and how it may be influenced by co-production. Co-production might expose the tourist to more information about the seller, the tourism product or service. As a result the tourist has more information about the quality of the tourism experience and therefore his need to use the price as an indicator of quality diminishes.

We also argued that due to the heterogeneity of tourists' competence and their functional co-production independence, tourism providers have to customize their offerings. Hence *a priori* uniform pricing seems difficult. Tipping may be a mechanism that compensates the provider appropriately. The questions remain for future research is (1) how do tourists make the tipping 'decision' in the relatively new co-production context, with no socio-cultural standards to rely on; and (2) how may non-tipping cultures develop tipping, or in the absence of tipping, what other pricing mechanisms that compensate for tourist and service heterogeneity could be used?

Tourists may also 'co-create' prices with revenue managers in advanced booking contexts by their deal-seeking behaviour and the gamification of this process with hedonic motivation. This is found to be detrimental to revenue management and further research is needed on this issue.

Notes

[1] In the long run, the extra economic profits will attract more supply from competitors into this market, reducing the demand for the producer in this analysis (the demand curve shifts to the left until the extra economic profits are reduced to zero). For the simplicity of analysis, we focus on the short run.

[2] We thank Mehmet Altin for this idea.

References

Chathoth, P.K., Altinay, L., Harrington, R.J., Okumus, F. and Chan, E.S.W. (2013) Co-production versus co-creation: a process based continuum in the hotel service contest. *International Journal of Hospitality Management* 32(1), 11–20.

Huang, T. (2011) *Hai Di Lao, You Can Not Copy It*. China CITIC Press, Beijing.

Kohli, A.K. (2006) Dynamic integration: extending the concept of resource integration. *Marketing Theory* 6(3), 290–291.

Lusch, R.F. and Vargo, S.L. (2006) Service-dominant logic: reactions, reflections and refinements. *Marketing Theory* 6(3), 281–288.

Lusch, R.F, Brown, S.W. and Brunswick, G.J. (1992) A general framework for explaining internal vs. external exchange. *Journal of the Academy of Marketing Science* 20(2), 119–134.

Lusch, R.F., Vargo, S.L. and O'Brien, M. (2007) Competing through service: insights from service-dominant logic. *Journal of Retailing* 83(1), 5–18.

Prahalad, C.K. and Ramaswamy, V. (2000) Co-opting customer competence. *Harvard Business Review* 78(1), 79–87.

Prahalad, C.K. and Ramaswamy, V. (2004) Co-creation experiences: the next practice in value creation. *Journal of Interactive Marketing* 18(3), 5–14.

Prebensen, N.K., Vittersø, J. and Dahl, T.I. (2013) Value co-creation: significance of tourist resources. *Annals of Tourism Research* 42, 240–261.

Rust, R.T. (2006) Does the service-dominant logic need to go further? *Marketing Theory* 6(3), 289–290.

Samuelsson, P.A. and Nordhaus, W.D. (2009) *Economics*, 19th edn. McGraw-Hill/Irwin, New York.

Schwartz, Z. (1997) The economics of tipping: tips, profits and the market's demand–supply equilibrium. *Tourism Economics* 3(3), 265–279.

Schwartz, Z. (2006) Revenues and asymmetric information: how uncertainty about service quality and capacity management affect optimal advanced booking pricing. *Journal of Quality Assurance in Hospitality and Tourism* 7(4), 1–22.

Schwartz, Z. and Chen, C. (2010) The peculiar impact of higher room rates on customers' propensity to book. *International Journal of Contemporary Hospitality Management* 22(1), 41–55.

Schwartz, Z. and Chen, C. (2012) Hedonic motivations and the effectiveness of risk perceptions oriented revenue management policies. *Journal of Hospitality and Tourism Research* 36(2), 232–250.

Schwartz, Z. and Cohen, E. (2000) Tipping and the nation's tax burden: a cross-country study. *Anatolia, an International Journal of Tourism and Hospitality Research* 10(2), 135–147.

Solomon, M.R. (2010) *Consumer Behavior*, 9th edn. Pearson Prentice Hall, Upper Saddle River, New Jersey.

Vargo, S.L. and Lusch, R.F. (2004) Evolving to a new dominant logic for marketing. *Journal of Marketing* 68, 1–17.

Vargo, S.L. and Lusch, R.F. (2008) Service-dominant logic: continuing the evolution. *Journal of the Academy of Marketing Science* 36(1), 1–10.

Veblen, T.B. (1899) *The Theory of the Leisure Class: An Economic Study of Institutions*. Macmillan, London.

16 Value Creation: A Tourism Mobilities Perspective

BRUCE PRIDEAUX

James Cook University, Brisbane, Australia

Introduction

This chapter explores issues relating to value creation and co-creation during the tourism mobilities component of holiday travel. In a tourism context, value may be created in several ways, by firms supplying goods and services to tourists, and by tourists creating value through the experiences they encounter during travel. Looking first at value creation by firms, the traditional approach based on firms acting autonomously to design products and production processes with little or no input from customers (Prahalad and Ramaswamy, 2004a) is beginning to shift to a new approach where the customer is now included in the production process, leading to the co-creation of value by the firm and the customer.

The rapid growth of customer-to-customer communications networks via platforms such as YouTube, Facebook and TripAdvisor provides customers with alternative information sources from those provided by firms helping to overcome the prevailing information asymmetry that has been the norm for customer–firm interaction in the past. Acting as a 'disruptive' technology, these platforms are beginning to force firms to reconsider the traditional customer–firm encounter and move tourism consumption beyond the production economy into the experience economy (Andersson, 2007). Aware of the growing power of consumers, firms are now beginning to understand the need to 'negotiate' with customers in the value creation process and move away from past value creation models to new value creation models that provide customers with opportunities to co-create unique experiences and through this process generate new avenues for developing competitive advantage (Prahalad and Ramaswamy, 2004b). The rapid adoption of IT has aided this process (Cabiddu *et al.*, 2013).

In a recent paper, Zhang *et al.* (2011) listed a range of strategies that firms may consider if they wish to explore avenues for value co-creation, including flexibility, customer feedback and customerization of product design and delivery based on an enhanced ability to meet changes in customer demands. Although there is mounting evidence of the opportunities that co-creation can confer, many firms in the transport sector have failed to adopt this approach, either because of inertia within the firm or because the perceived nature of their relationship with their customers does not appear to lend itself to co-creation. Seen within the context of innovation theory (Rogers, 1995; Hjalager, 2010), early adopters of the co-creation approach to value creation who adopt strategies of the nature suggested by Zhang *et al.* (2011) are likely to gain a competitive advantage over firms that are slow to adopt the new approach. The tourism mobilities sector has in the past shown an aptitude for adopting new technologies that have led to faster, cheaper and safer transport but in many areas still lags in its adoption of strategies that facilitate value co-creation with their customers.

According to Prahalad and Ramaswamy, 'co-creation is about joint creation of value by the company and the customer' (2004b, p. 8), where dialogue, access and transparency have become the new benchmarks for interaction. Commenting on this view of co-creation, Cabiddu *et al.* observed 'firms can only provide services as value propositions, which become an input into value realisation' (2013, p. 88). Cabiddu *et al.* further state that 'no value exists without the customers' incorporation [of] the firm's offering into their own lives' (2013, p. 88). In terms of the travel component of holiday travel, this view appears overly narrow in that it suggests that the creation of value is entirely tied to the interaction between firms and their customers.

Apart from the value created by transport providers, tourists also gain value from interaction with other tourists, events they experience and the landscapes through which they pass. Value in this sense is created as the result of the tourists' own experiences and reflection on these experiences. The end result of this process is the individuals' acquisition of a set of unique experiences and impressions that may be stored or shared and used to evaluate their own and others' experiences of travel. While the opportunities for customer interaction and landscape observations are indirect results of the services provided by companies, they are not directly governed by the service provider and instead may be viewed as incidental to the services paid for. From a tourism perspective, this creation of additional value, separate to that provided by firms, is able to provide an increase in the overall enjoyment of the journey.

Tourism mobilities, described as temporary travel for leisure and recreation in both time and space (Sofield, 2006) is a key, although often overlooked, element of all holiday travel. From a tourism mobilities perspective, the profile of the journey between home and the holiday location is governed by customer requirements based on time, cost, comfort and the mode of travel selected. In the 20th century, new mobility technologies such as the car, fast train and air travel radically changed the manner in which travel was organized (Williams, 2013). This change has significant implications for tourism and, as Haldrup (2004, p. 441) has argued, changed the manner in which 'people sense and make sense of landscapes', with mobility speeds both creating and destroying opportunities for interaction with the landscape and fellow tourists.

New transport technologies have given tourists the opportunity to maximize the time available at destinations by minimizing the time spent travelling (Page, 2005). For some this has added value to the holiday experience by, as Halsall (1992) observed, reducing the time wasted in that part of the journey between home and destination. For others the ability to create value through opportunities to meet fellow tourists has been significantly reduced and from this perspective has reduced the overall enjoyment of the holiday experience. It is the latter group for whom the growing popularity of slow travel (Dickinson *et al.*, 2010) offers some hope to create value by reclaiming the ability to encounter new landscapes and other tourists.

Firms operating in the tourism mobilities sector have to navigate a pathway between customer's desires for low-price, high-speed travel with their demands for service, while at the same time adhering to the plethora of regulations that now govern mobility operations. Security, for example, adds costs and procedures that cannot be circumvented and must therefore be built into costs and operating procedures. Security concerns may also restrict the ability of firms to co-create value, at least in some aspects of the travel process. The solutions are likely to range from high cost–high service to low cost–low service models, or some position in between, and will influence the ability of firms to engage in genuine co-creation of value activities.

As this chapter will demonstrate, while the mobilities phase of a tourism journey offers scope for both value creation by the tourist as well as co-creation by firms, the highly organized nature of contemporary mass travel places many limits on opportunities for passengers (tourists) to interact with other passengers, staff and the landscapes through which they pass. Indeed, the pressure to lower costs may lead to firms outsourcing services to the customer, self-service check-in for example, making it difficult, though not impossible, to generate opportunities for genuine value co-creation.

In his assessment of the role of tourism mobilities in the tourist experience, Haldrup (2004) pointed out that tourism mobility, movement, dwelling and experience intersect to create the tourism experience. Yet while occupying a pivotal role in the tourism experience, mobility has often been treated as 'a mere precondition for performing tourism, a practical problem related to the act of "getting there and about"' (Haldrup, 2004, p. 434). The view is also supported by Lofgren, who argued that there is a need to examine different modes according to 'the ways movement, non-movement, and experience go together' (1999, p. 69). Going even further, Haldrup stated that 'mobilities has been mainly treated as a mere precondition for performing tourism … rather than a phenomenon in its own right' (2004, p. 434). Similar observations may be made about the level of research into co-creation of value in the mobilities sector.

In the last 80 years the transport system has developed new mechanisms and structures to deal with the rapid growth in leisure and business travel. Mechanisms in the sense used here refer to the processes and architecture that have been designed to streamline the flow of tourists through transport terminals as they board and disembark from public transport modes such as trains, ferries, planes and coaches. The drive to lower costs has been met with the introduction of high-volume processing systems such as online and self-service check-ins that, while reducing the time spent queuing and administrative costs, have also depersonalized this element of the travel experience. One of the costs of reducing the time spent travelling has been the loss of opportunities to interact in a meaningful manner with fellow tourists and the staff of service providers. It has also created barriers that limit the ability of firms to move from value creation to co-creation.

The following discussion first suggests a number of factors that influence the value creation process in the tourism mobilities sector. The chapter then decomposes the typical tourist journey into the stages of travel and identifies the opportunities that may occur for value creation and co-creation during each stage. This is followed by an analysis of several actual encounters to explore how individual stages of travel generate opportunities for value creation.

Factors that Influence Value Creation

In an insightful assessment of the travel experience, de Botton observed 'the pleasure we derive from a journey may be depending more on the mind-set we travel with than the destination we travel to' (2002, p. 242). During each stage of the journey, a range of factors govern the opportunity for value creation and co-creation. These factors may be categorized as:

- The stranger syndrome. Except for one's immediate travel party, other passengers are often seen as strangers and for this reason communication barriers may be present. It is often difficult for firms to create opportunities for meaningful interaction with other passengers in these circumstances. New technology such as MP3 players, iPads and smart phones have provided an attractive alternative to striking up conversations with other passengers and in this way reinforced the stranger syndrome.
- Richness of experiences – The standardization of air travel has all but eliminated the opportunities for new experiences, creating an experience desert. Even the view from windows is restricted to a small percentage of passengers who even then have only an aperture view of the world below them. A road trip on the other hand offers the opportunity for a rich variety of experiences. As Larsen wrote 'trains and especially cars are not the only machines for transporting tourists to particular destinations, they are also technologies for visually experiencing or consuming those very places through mobile sightseeing' (2010, p. 81).
- Architecture – The design of transport facilities and of specific modes influences opportunities for interaction with other passengers. In mass mobilities such as air and to some extent coaches, the structure of the vehicle restricts the freedom of passengers to move about the cabin and engage with fellow passengers. A cruise ship on the other hand offers numerous opportunities for value creation by tourists and co-creation by cruise companies.

Journey Stages from a Tourism Mobilities Perspective

To understand the opportunities that travel can offer for value creation, it is useful to subdivide the tourist journey into stages. Using a psychological perspective, Fridgen (1984) identified five stages. However, in the following discussion, which looks at the journey from a mobilities perspective, Fridgen's 'return travel' and 'recollection' stages are compressed into a single stage titled 'the return home'. The stages discussed in this chapter are: journey preparation; the journey from origin to the destination; travel within the destination; and the return home. The decomposition of the journey into stages facilities a greater understanding of the role that the various elements of the journey may play in value creation. In the past, when speed was governed by wind or the speed an animal or person could walk, travel was measured on an ordinal scale based on distance as well as speed. In the contemporary world of high-speed mobility, time has become at least as important as distance in travel decisions.

The following discussion departs from the widely accepted view of travel as being little more than a necessity in the task of relocating from home to the destination (Haldrup, 2004) and opens the journey to becoming a more central part of the tourism experience (Larsen, 2008; Dickinson *et al.*, 2010), where opportunities for co-creation exist through the action of firms and where further value creation by the tourist can occur through interaction with other passengers, the landscape and the unexpected. At the core of modern travel lies the technology that governs the cost and time of travel, the architecture of terminals and individual transport modes, safety, comfort provided and the resulting opportunities for value co-creation. An understanding of the factors that collectively shape each stage of a journey is a useful start point for developing an understanding of the opportunities for value creation.

Journey preparation

In this stage of the journey the attention of the prospective tourist is focused on information gathering, assessment of the various destination options and identifying the most appropriate form of transport based on cost and time factors (Prideaux, 2000). The first act that sets the scene for future value creation occurs in the mental processes that lead to destination selection. If a boat cruise is selected, it can be expected there will be numerous opportunities for the service provider to build a platform that invites co-creation of value; however, if air is selected there may be fewer opportunities for co-creation. During this stage there is opportunity for significant discourse between the intending tourist and others in their social, family and work networks as questions about prospective destinations are asked, opinions sought and given, and secondary sources evaluated. In this sense travel preparation is a social event and, as Fridgen (1984) observed, often takes place in the home.

The journey from origin to destination

This stage offers a range of opportunities for firms to co-create value with passengers, although the level will depend on the type of transport used, time factors, class of travel, security concerns and so on. However, the monopoly-like advantage that airport companies and many of the firms supplying services enjoy removes many of the incentives that the unfettered marketplace offers firms wishing to look for opportunities for co-creation. This stage may be either a single or multi-sector journey.

In the contemporary world, the transport element of a holiday is often seen as a tiresome yet necessary part of travel to be endured but rarely enjoyed, to be forgotten rather than remembered fondly, and counted in hours and perhaps in movies watched rather than counted by days spent on a leisurely sea voyage or a train journey. It is worth briefly exploring some of the travel options available during this part of the journey to identify opportunities for value creation. Three contrasting journey profiles are explored, the long-haul air journey, the long-haul rail journey and the multiday road journey.

The typical profile of a long-haul air trip provides modest opportunities for co-creation of value and limited value creation through interaction with fellow passengers, in part because the opportunities for interacting are limited by boarding/ exit procedures and the architecture of aircraft to produce what Larsen (2010) describes as 'non-places' that exist only to facilitate mobility. Sommer adds to this dark view of aviation, describing an airport as 'socially destructive building' (1974, cited in Fridgen, 1984, p. 28). This element of the journey starts at an airport check-in. Between check-in and finding their seat, the passenger may have to progress through a security check point, customs, possibly an airline lounge, service encounters at commercial outlets within the airport, staff at the boarding gate and finally an aircraft crew member who directs the passenger to his/her allocated seat. During this process the passenger may interact with a large number of people, but only within the confines of a depersonalized process where the passenger is no more than a nameless face in a crowd. Airport staff providing these services rarely have time for conversation that goes beyond the required formalities. In circumstances of this nature it is difficult for firms to implement strategies that co-create value, but not impossible. The airport operator, for example, has ample opportunities for co-creation of value through the amenities provided within the airport terminal and the manner in which airport management chooses to interact with its customers. Airlines also have scope for co-creation through membership of airline lounges and the range of services lounges are able to provide. The challenge for firms seeking to co-create value with customers in this stage of the journey is to search for opportunities to transform Larsen's (2010) view of aircraft, and by inference airport terminals, from 'non-places' into 'engaging-places'.

Once on the plane, the passenger becomes a seat number who has to be managed in a manner prescribed by the airline. Many airlines have realized the need to engage in strategies for co-creation in business class, but in economy the opportunities are more limited, particularly where cost is an issue. Because of the nature of the typical airline cabin, the passenger is in effect confined to a seat with limited opportunities to interact with fellow passengers. In full service airlines, this may be offset by in-flight entertainment systems and regular meals. In low-cost carriers even these elements of the trip may be forfeited unless the passenger is willing to pay an added fee for service. Figure 16.1 illustrates five opportunities for interaction between fellow passengers, airline crew and entertainment systems (if available) on a typical flight. Each of these opportunities has the potential to generate positive or negative impressions, but in general only provide limited opportunities for interaction with other passengers. Because of the nature of modern air travel, the in-cabin environment offers a standardized experience which, while shared with all passengers on the flight, offers little opportunity to break through the barriers of the stranger syndrome. On occasions new, generally unwanted opportunities for conversation occur when an unanticipated incident upsets the usual rhythm of a flight. This may include a

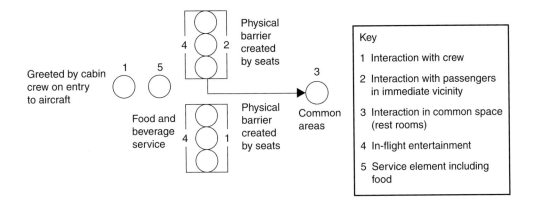

Fig. 16.1. Opportunities and barriers for interaction between passengers on an aircraft.

disagreement between passengers or an incident that threatens the safety of the aircraft and its occupants. Incidents of this nature and their impact have been explored by Berkley and Ala (2001).

Reflecting on the airline experience, several issues stand out because of the standardization of the experience, the architecture of the aircraft cabin and the mass nature of air travel. The first is the straightjacketing of movement enforced by the need for passengers to have safety belts engaged at all times. A second is the desert of opportunities for engaging in new memorable experiences, a result of the standardized nature of air transport. While the preceding narrative paints a rather dark picture of the aviation experience, there are opportunities for firms in each area of the process to seek ways of interacting with customers and mitigate the most depersonalizing aspects of the process. This may be as simple as offering passengers a wider selection of in-flight entertainment, the opportunity to preselect menu items or order duty free items they wish to purchase.

The long-haul rail journey provides a useful example of how it is possible to enjoy the benefits of modern technology yet retain a level of personalized service and opportunities for interaction with fellow passengers in a manner that is not possible with air travel. Two elements of the rail trip provide opportunities for value creation: encounters with fellow travellers and opportunities for co-creation between the passenger and the firm. The less restricted architecture of rail carriages offers opportunities for passengers to meet total strangers in a range of relatively safe settings, including dining areas. Long-distance train travel may also offer a much richer opportunity to experience the panorama of landscapes through which the train travels.

The third opportunity for co-creation activities is provided by the overnight road trip. Car ownership offers opportunities for exploration and indulging in new experiences in a manner not possible by rail or air travel (Hoyer, 2000). Tourists have greater control over the journey, who they meet and under what circumstances. The less structured more informal nature of car travel offers participants many points of contact with other people, including at facilities that sell fuel, commercial outlets for food, accommodation, roadside tourist experiences, information services, road-related services such as enforcement and breakdown, and fellow tourists who may be encountered along the way (Prideaux *et al.*, 2001). Compared with air travel, however, the road trip consumes a greater proportion of holiday time and may cost significantly more than mass transport once the cost of fuel, accommodation and wear and tear on the vehicle are taken into account. The higher level of control passengers are able to exercise over their journey offers significant opportunities for value creation. There are also greater opportunities for co-creation, particularly where services that are offered by commercial chains such as accommodation, food and beverage and fuel can be brought together via an IT platform to assist the tourist to pre-plan their route, select their accommodation and access other information. Compared with the relative desert of experiences available during air travel, the road journey offers a feast of opportunities to meet new people, engage in a variety of novel experiences to create tourist value and co-create value with firms.

Travel within the destination

Travel within a destination offers considerable scope for interaction with firms, other tourists and the host population, and opportunities to seek out new experiences. The scope for travel in the destination is largely a function of the location of attractions relative to accommodation, time budgets and the types of transport available. Organized coach tours, for example, offer another set of opportunities for interactions with other tourists and co-creation between the tourist and the firm. The scale of opportunities is governed by a number of factors, including opportunities built into the itinerary (a communal meal, for example), the propensity for individuals on the tour to look for opportunities to engage in conversations with other passengers and the driver/guides' inclination to act as an 'ice breaker' to encourage passenger interaction. Co-creation may, for example, allow passengers to exercise control over elements of the trip including sites visited, length of stay at various sites and selection of special interest commentaries.

In other forms of inter-destination travel there may be little opportunity for interaction with other tourists or with the host population. In large cities, Paris, Tokyo and New York for example, public transport offers an efficient method for visiting major attraction but fewer opportunities to interact, either because of the architecture of public transport or because of language issues. However co-creation opportunities do exist if destination marketing organizations provide IT platforms that enable tourists to have greater control over itinerary design and scheduling.

The return home

This final part of the journey has two major components, the return home from the destination and recounting experiences with family, friends and colleagues. The first component is governed by the mode of travel and in many cases will be a repeat of the experiences encountered during the journey from the origin to the destination. The second component, during which the tourist may boast, perhaps grieve at the end of the experience, relive the experience with others and savour the activities just experienced, is an important part of the journey that has been investigated through research into intention to return, the role of social media in recommendations and the impact of word of mouth on the receiving destination. From a destination perspective, this is an important aspect of any holiday because the recounting may be either positive or negative and will in the tourists' minds confirm the value they derive from travel.

Case Studies

The following short case studies of actual tourism mobilities-related situations illustrate the positive and negative elements of value creation that typically occur during the various stages of travel. Ethnographic research, described by Botterill and Platenkamp as '"engagement with" and "participation in" everyday situations of social life' (2012, p. 83), was utilized to investigate the type of value creation opportunities that occur during the various stages of travel and involved the author reflecting on events that occurred while writing this chapter. Two journey stages (the origin to destination stage and the travel within destination stage) are examined in the following discussion. This approach enabled the author to be fully immersed in the range of events that occurred in each journey stage. To have adopted an alternative approach based on a survey, for example, would have yielded a plethora of data on statistical relationships, but very little understanding of their actual meaning or the causality of the range of factors identified in this chapter. The first case study is based on an overnight road trip undertaken by the author and his son. The second describes opportunities for interacting with other passengers during a day tour in Helsinki.

Case one: the road trip

During a typical road trip, the individual tourist can create significant value for his/herself and other passengers because of the opportunity to meet and engage in casual conversations with a range of people, including fellow travellers, staff at commercial facilities and in some cases with personnel who attend breakdowns and accidents that are occasionally a feature of road trips. Value may also be created through enjoyment of views and other activities experienced during the trip. In some cases the driver and/or passengers may also create unanticipated value for the people they encounter along the way. The value created for both the tourist and the people they encounter may be positive or in some cases negative, depending on the circumstance of the interaction. Co-creation is largely determined by the willingness of service providers to engage with customers.

The author and his youngest son decided to travel from their origin city to attend a family function in another city. The decision to drive was taken on cost grounds and because access to a car was essential in the destination given its poor public transport system. The decision to drive also allowed the author to give his son an opportunity to acquire additional hours of supervised driving instruction. As occasionally occurs on road trips, the car was involved in an accident that caused extensive damage to the author's car but not to the other vehicle involved, a solidly built four-wheel-drive light truck.

As a result of the accident the local police were called. Because battery acid spilt onto the road the local fire and rescue service also attended. The driver of the other vehicle reported a stiff neck, so the attending police officer called the paramedic service. As the driver of the other vehicle left before the paramedics arrived, they soon left the scene, there being no other injuries. As the accident occurred in the vicinity of road works, the onsite staff provided traffic control while the accident was investigated by the police. Recovery of the damaged car was undertaken by a local tow truck firm. Because the car was not driveable, the local taxi service, which also operated a hire-car service, was called and a car rented to continue the journey. During the period of the accident (no charges were laid), the author engaged in numerous conversations with attending personnel (14 in total, including the off-site representative of the insurance company that was notified of the accident by phone). Despite the obvious negative emotions associated with the accident and the damage to the car, the author left the scene with a set of mostly positive feelings, in part because there were no injuries and in part because of the very friendly and professional assistance that was provided by all attending emergency personnel.

The accident also seemed to offer a source of amusement for children at a day care centre on the opposite side of the road to the accident. As they watched the unfolding of events as various emergency services arrived at the scene, a number of the children called out a reminder to those in attendance of the need to wear a hat, the day being a hot midsummer day. It was apparent that the children had taken notice of the frequent public health warnings that people should avoid sun damage by wearing hats and sun cream.

In past decades recounting the incident would have occurred some time after the incident and generally after returning to the origin. The widespread adoption of social media and smartphone technology has now added a new dimension to trip story-telling. Within 30 minutes of the accident, the author's son had posted a photo of the accident on his Facebook site. On a wider scale, the rapid dissemination of experiences, positive and negative, has added a new dimension to travel, including the mobilities components. The impact of this has yet to be widely explored in the literature.

The story did not end at the scene of the accident. The damage to the car was so extensive that it was written off by the insurance company. During the period that the accident occurred, most vehicle manufacturers were offering very attractive deals on new cars. The author spent most of the following day test-driving a range of new vehicles, in itself a rather pleasant experience. Once a decision was made, negotiations were undertaken and a deal struck.

In terms of value creation, the overall journey generated a rich range of positive and negative experiences, many of which were recounted to friends and colleagues. Apart from the motor vehicle dealership where the replacement vehicle was purchased, there was no evidence of other firms and organizations making serious attempts to engage in value co-creation. Given the nature of the services offered, this is not surprising; however, as Zhang *et al.* (2011) suggest, there are strategies that are available that would allow each of the firms and service providers involved to create information exchange with customers/patients that can lead to value co-creation. This may be as simple as asking customers to connect with a social media site to respond to a short questionnaire on their experiences.

Case two: the tour bus trip

During a trip to Helsinki, the author and his daughter purchased tickets on a 2-hour sightseeing trip around the city's central business district. The trip had two main components, an on-board commentary delivered in eight languages via a plug-in headset on the tour coach and three 5-minute stops to walk around major sites. The on-coach experience presented almost no opportunity to talk to other passengers, but did give an excellent commentary of the city, including tips on places to visit that were later taken advantage of by the author and his daughter. The three short stops in general failed to provide sufficient time to strike up casual conversations and overcome even in a small way the stranger syndrome. However, on one stop at a park the author was asked by of one of the other passengers if he would take a photo of her beside a monument. This request provided a brief opportunity to engage in a conversation that, as one would expect, covered just basic information such as origin and a little about the other's trip to date. While fleeting, the conversation did create some value on a trip that could otherwise be described as a one-way flow of information from the tour operator to the participant. Analysed in terms of its value creation, the architecture of the trip (itinerary and coach layout) provided only a small window of opportunity to interact with other passengers, but from an experience perspective provided a rich opportunity to learn about Helsinki. The set nature of the itinerary and the limited time available offered opportunities for value creation, but little opportunity for co-creation.

Implications and Conclusion

The objective of this chapter was to examine the opportunities that arise for value creation during the mobilities stage of a holiday journey. To facilitate analysis of this aspect of the tourist experience, the chapter examined the manner in which value may be created during the various stages of the holiday journey, taking the approach that value may be created by the tourist through the various experiences they encounter, as well as from the value provided by the firms from which they purchased goods and services. It is apparent that some forms of the holiday journey provide a greater opportunity than others for value creation both by the individual tourist and firms. For example, the restricted cabin environment of a passenger aircraft and the mass processing approach used in airports provides fewer opportunities for value creation by the tourist or co-creation of value by firms than is possible on a cruise ship.

It is apparent that the desire by many tourists to minimize travel time has reduced the opportunities for value creation through interaction with fellow tourists, gazing on the landscape or participation in activities during the journey. From the firms' perspective, the value-sensitive nature of many of the tourists they serve is seen as a limitation to value co-creation, particularly where tourists are willing to trade all manner of services for a lower cost. In the airline sector the growing popularity of low cost carriers illustrates the willingness of many tourists to trade service for a lower price. This creates a difficult operating environment for firms, but given the range of communications platforms that now enable customers to connect with the firms this should not be seen as a reason for not actively seeking ways to co-create value with customers. Many firms trading in the tourism mobilities sector have yet to switch from the traditional firm-centric model of value creation to the customer-centric model of co-creation of value, either because they do not see any tangible benefits or find it difficult to develop processes that facilitate engagement with customers.

The situation in the tourism mobilities sector is probably little different from most sectors of the economy where firms are being forced to reconsider their approach to value creation. If the concept of co-creation is treated as an innovation, it is apparent that in the mobilities sector, in parallel with all other sectors, there will be innovator firms that see the opportunity offered by co-creation, seize it and gain a competitive advantage over rivals. Others, particularly where the market is not open or where monopolies exist, will be much slower and in terms of the innovation process most likely be characterized as late adopters.

From a tourism mobilities perspective, the concept of co-creation offers scope to transform Larsen's (2010) 'non-places' into 'engaging-places' where customers have the opportunity to directly engage with firms and influence the value that firms can offer customers. The reengineering of firms to place co-creating at the heart of their relationship with customers also offers considerable scope to elevate tourism mobilities from merely a means of performing Haldrup's (2004) 'getting there and about' role into a role where customers both create their own value from the experiences they engage in and co-create value with the firms they interact with.

References

Andersson, T. (2007) The tourist in the experience economy. *Scandinavian Journal of Hospitality and Tourism* 7, 46–58.

Berkley, B.J. and Ala, M. (2001) Identifying and controlling threatening airline passengers. *Cornell Hospitality Quarterly* 42, 6–23.

Botterill, D. and Platenkamp, V. (2012) *Key Concepts in Tourism Research*. Sage, Thousand Oaks, California.

Cabiddu, F., Lui, T.W. and Piccoli, G. (2013) Managing value co-creation in the tourism industry. *Annals of Tourism Research* 42, 86–107.

De Botton, A. (2002) *The Art of Travel*. Pantheon Books, New York.

Dickinson, J., Robbins, D. and Lumsdon, L. (2010) Holiday travel discourses and climate change. *Journal of Transport Geography* 18, 482–489.

Fridgen, J. (1984) Environmental psychology and tourism. *Annals of Tourism Research* 11, 19–39.

Haldrup, M. (2004) Laid-back mobilities: second-home holidays in time and space. *Tourism Geographies: An International Journal of Tourism Space, Place and Environment* 6, 434–454.

Halsall, D. (1992) Transport for tourism and recreation. In: Hoyle, B.S. and Knowles, R.D. (eds) *Modern Transport Geography*. Belhaven, London, pp. 155–177.

Hjalager, A.M. (2010) A review of innovation research in tourism. *Tourism Management* 31, 1–12.

Hoyer, K. (2000) Sustainable tourism or sustainable mobility? The Norwegian case. *Journal of Sustainable Tourism* 8, 147–160.

Larsen, J. (2008) De-exoticizing tourist travel: everyday life and sociality on the move. *Leisure Studies* 27, 21–34.

Larsen, J. (2010) Tourism mobilities and the travel gaze, tourism mobilities and the travel glance: experiences of being on the move. *Scandinavian Journal of Hospitality and Tourism* 1, 80–98.

Lofgren, O. (1999) *On Holiday: A History of Vacationing*. University of California Press, Berkeley, California.

Page, S. (2005) *Tourism and Transport Global Perspectives*, 2nd edn. Pearson, Harlow, UK.

Prahalad, C. and Ramaswamy, V. (2004a) Co-creating unique value with customers. *Strategy and Leadership* 32, 4–9.

Prahalad, C. and Ramaswamy, V. (2004b) Co-creation experiences: the next practice in value creation. *Journal of Interactive Marketing* 18, 5–14.

Prideaux, B. (2000) The role of transport in destination development. *Tourism Management* 21, 53–64.

Prideaux, B., Wei, S. and Ruys, H. (2001) The senior drive tour market in Australia. *Journal of Vacation Marketing* 7, 209–219.

Rogers, E.M. (1995) Diffusion of Innovations, 4th edn. Free Press, New York.

Sofield, T. (2006) Border tourism and border communities: an overview. *Tourism Geographies: An International Journal of Tourism Space, Place and Environment* 8, 102–121.

Sommer, R. (1974) *Tight Spaces*. Prentice-Hall, San Francisco, California.

Williams, A. (2013) Mobilities and sustainable tourism: path-creating or path-dependent relationships. *Journal of Sustainable Tourism* 21, 511–531.

Zhang, X., Chen, Y., Chen, R. and Wang, Z. (2011) Multi-focused strategy in value co-creation with customers: examining cumulative development pattern with new capabilities. *International Journal of Production Economics* 132, 122–130.

17 Guide Performance: Co-created Experiences for Tourist Immersion

Lena Mossberg,[1] Monica Hanefors and Ann Heidi Hansen[2]

[1]University of Gothenburg, Sweden; [2]University of Nordland, Bodø, Norway

Introduction

This chapter concerns the co-creation of experience during the consumption stage of the tourist trip. It deals with face-to-face meetings where the guides perform their activities. The tour guides' roles and performances are crucial for tourists' creation of value during extraordinary experiences. The extraordinary state of the trip is characterized by tourist immersion. The tourists are so deeply involved in the moment and activity that they lose track of time. The development of the concept of immersion linked to various consumption experiences has been a matter for experiential marketing and it has also been used in tourism research. Immersion is also often used in connection to extraordinary experiences (Arnould and Price, 1993). For comparison see also Privette's discussion (1983) concerning peak performance, Csíkszentmihályi (1990) on flow and Lipscombe (1999) on peak experiences.

Immersion is a subjective occurrence that implies a spatio-temporal belonging to the world that is characterized by deep involvement in the here and now (Hansen and Mossberg, 2013). Immersion has characteristics, such as intensive, positive and enjoyable hedonic consumption activities and letting-go processes where action and awareness are merged.

According to Carù and Cova (2007), three interrelated qualities constitute the underlying foundations in order for consumers to become immersed. The first quality, the enclavized context, implies that the guides act within the same space as tourists, and that all experiences occur outside everyday life. Security is the second quality. It concerns the tour guides' various roles, and relevance for the tourists' feelings of safety and control. The third quality of the context refers to how guides act according to a theme. The theme communicates content and value in an understandable, meaningful and memorable way to the tourists. Through using a theme, tour operators and tour guides can create meaning to what is communicated.

The specific objectives with this chapter are first to explore the guides' basic roles and then their performances in enclavized, secure and thematized contexts and second to discuss if there are specific performances that have potential for co-creation of extraordinary experiences and for facilitation of tourists' immersion.

Tour Guides Roles and Performances

Interest in tour guides, their roles and skills has increased over the years in industry and academia alike. Tour guides contribute to company image, word-of-mouth and customer loyalty, as well as to successful tours. In a number of studies on tour guides, several guide role types appear. Tour guides have been discussed as being, for example, indigenous or local guides, tourist guides, tour coordinators or informal street guides, depending on their performance in various tourism circumstances and settings (Pearce, 1982; Guildin, 1989; Crick, 1992; Poynter, 1993; Wong *et al.*, 1998; Howard *et al.*, 2001; Salazar, 2008). Mancini (2001) argued that tour guides at the same time are psychologists, diplomats, entertainers and miracle workers. In another study, 16 roles were listed (Zhang and Chow, 2004). Holloway (1981), Hughes (1991) and later McDonnell (2001) chose to use six role types: ambassador, missionary, teacher, instructor, knowledge fount and information giver. Pond (1993) added to the list, and argued that the guides often performed as educators, and metaphors like host and window have been used (Salazar, 2005). Cohen *et al.* (2002) discussed tour guides' educational responsibility, as did Pearce (1982), Fine and Speer (1985), Weiler and Davis (1993) and Mancini (2001). The guides can also act as counsellor guides or driver-couriers (Cohen *et al.*, 2002).

Other studies have dealt specifically with different aspects of tourists' satisfaction related to tour guides (e.g. Lopez, 1980; Pearce, 1982; Whipple and Thach, 1988; Quiroga, 1990; Geva and Goldman, 1991; Hughes, 1991; Crick, 1992; Mossberg, 1995; Duke and Persia, 1996; Ap and Wong, 2001; Wong, 2001; Bowie and Chang, 2005; Chang, 2006; Heung, 2007; Peake *et al.*, 2009).

Crang (1997) discussed performance and tourism employment. Edensor (2000) focused on tourists as performers, while Zhang and Chow (2004) and Bowie and Chang (2005) argued the importance of tour guides' performances. In this chapter we will follow these leads.

Tour Guides in the Co-creating Process

Both the tourist and the guide co-create meaningful experiences through personal interaction and involvement. Co-creation is a joint process of creation of value where all kinds of interactions are critical touch points (Prahalad and Ramaswamy, 2003; Shaw and Williams, 2009). The experience of co-creation itself is the basis of a unique value for each individual. Prahalad and Ramaswamy write about co-creation in experience environments: 'In the experience space, the individual consumer is central and an event triggers a co-creation experience. The events have a context in space and time, and the involvement of the individual influences that experience. The personal meaning derived from the co-creation experience is what determines the value to the individual' (2003, p. 14). Cohen (1982) discussed the interactional character of the guide role. A few years later his seminal work on tour guides contributed much to the understanding of tour guides' roles and role components (Cohen, 1985). He claimed that the roles of contemporary guides resembled the status of original professional guides – the main difference being 'the transition of emphasis from the instrumental to the communicative component' (1985, p. 5). The original guides were either pathfinders, who provided access to otherwise non-public geographic or social territory, or mentors, who served as gurus. Cohen (1985) also introduced two new role types – the tour leader and the animator. The first type emphasized the interactional character of the guide role that included a safe and secure context for tourists, while the involved animators used necessary social skills in order to satisfy tourists.

Price et al. (1995) tried to understand what happens between guides and tourists when they discuss temporal duration, emotional content and intimacy in service encounters. They pointed out that 'when encounters become long and outcomes less predictable, service providers must do more' (1995, p. 95). If the tour guides spend their time with tourists on a package tour of several days, we can talk about an extended service encounter. By contrast, if the encounter is shorter we talk either about tour guides during one-day excursions or about the guides who perform their guiding along an attraction. Their guiding can take place within different tourism contexts: attractions (e.g. Pearce, 1984), excursions (e.g. Holloway, 1981; Edensor, 2000; Momchedjikova, 2002; Gentry, 2007) and package tours (e.g. Enoch, 1996; Wang et al., 2000; Bowie and Chang, 2005).

Guiding within these three contexts is either personal or impersonal, and the tour guides can perform either in a standardized or non-standardized way. Both ways imply low or high level of interaction between guides and tourists, and, hence, vary in intimacy. Emotional content refers to the 'arousal associated with the encounter' (Price et al., 1995, p. 86). However, any encounters that are standardized or routine for the organization are often exceptional for the customer (Price et al., 1995). Most of the time tour guides perform near the tourists, that is, proximate spatially. For example, on bus tours the tour guides and the tourists interact closely, and both can act spontaneously.

Enclavized Context

Several studies suggest that the tourists' part of the destination seems to be an extension of the tourists' home culture, instead of a specific place located outside the well-known everyday life; right along with the thrill of going away tourists look for, and find, the familiar and known. Shaw and Williams (1994) argued that this is a scene of their dreams, and Theroux (1986) discussed the same phenomenon when he said that many people travel in order to experience 'home plus'. Much earlier than this, Knebel (1960) wrote about the 'touristische Eigenwelt', that is the tourists' own world. Dumazedier (1967) similarly argued that this world was cooked up solely for the benefits of tourists. Sampson (1968) noted the cruise liner effect of that world.

The concept 'parenthesis' was introduced by UNESCO in 1976, while Smith (1978) labelled the phenomenon a 'tourist bubble'. She defined it as being physically in a foreign culture, but socially outside that culture. Her understanding of the bubble included tourists who congregated with their co-tourists in bars and hotel lobbies, creating their own reality. After having called the bubble environmental in 1972, Cohen discussed 'tourist space', and said that 'the tourist is caught in a covert, but all embracing "tourist space", constructed by the tourist establishment' (1979, p. 20). An 'enclave of familiarity' is Farrell's suggestion (1979), which resembles what Cohen and Taylor called an 'activity enclave', 'where you literally create a new landscape' (1992, p. 131). Others that also discuss the bubble or activity enclave are, for example, Graburn (1978), Jafari (1987), Garcia (1988), Hanefors (1994, 2001) and Selänniemi (1993).

Research in this area generally agrees that a tourist bubble exists; however, Crouch et al. (2001) say that tourism overflows any boundaries of tight contexts. Jacobsen (2003) identifies the weakening of the bubble, and Richards and Wilson (2006) prefer to discuss creative space instead of a bubble. Nevertheless, an all-inclusive hotel constitutes a perfect example of an enclaved space, argues Edensor (2000). It is a highly controlled and managed environment characterized by Western standards, such as air conditioning, cleanliness, particular décor and quality control. Also the standards of appearance are Western, i.e. dress code or general behaviour (e.g. Adib and Guerrier, 2001). Carù and Cova suggest that the enclave has specific boundaries that let the consumer 'break with (and step outside of) their daily lives (…) into a separate world of enchantment where all the worries and hardships that they face in their ordinary lives disappear' (2007, p. 41). Edensor (2002) argues that the tour groups move around in a safe enclave away from intrusions and disruptions (cf. Adib and Guerrier, 2001, p. 342).

The enclave limits the intrusion of elements that do not belong to the theme and, thereby, enhances the intensity of the experience (Firat and Dholakia, 1998, p. 107). Jackson et al. (1996) speculate that tourists give up some control over their lives during a holiday and expect the industry to take control instead. 'The moment we develop and discover new relationships and explore new territories, we remove ourselves from the existing familiar environment and we lose control' (Boswijk et al., 2007, p. 26). Despite the inherent freedom of the tour, tourists willingly act according to the programme and to the strict time schedules that are offered by tour guides.

Within the enclavized context the tour guides have certain roles that help tourists. Holloway (1981) argued that those guides are group leaders who can act as shepherds or ministering angels in order to support the tourists within the enclave. Whipple and Thach (1998) used the role-type tour escort instead, while Cohen (1985) preferred to talk about pathfinders, gurus or tour managers (McKean, 1976; Hughes, 1991; Poynter, 1993). Others used the term tour organizer (Pearce, 1982; Schuchat, 1983) or discussed tour guides as salespersons (Fine and Speer, 1985; Bras, 2000). Tour guides act as bridge builders (Gurung et al., 1996; Xin et al., 2001) – perhaps among those with different cultural backgrounds, i.e. culture broker (McKean, 1976; Holloway, 1981; Katz 1985; Timothy, 1995, 1998; Smith, 2001), sometimes among people with agendas that dramatically differ from each other. Then they can also be called middlemen (van den Berghe, 1980), intermediaries (Schmidt, 1979; Pearce, 1982; Ryan and Dewar, 1995), interpreters (Almagor, 1985; Cohen, 1984, 1985; Katz, 1985; Ryan and Dewar, 1995) or cultural mediators (Taft, 1977; de Kadt, 1979; Nettekoven, 1979; Schmidt, 1979; Holloway, 1981; Cohen, 1985; Katz, 1985; Gelbman and Maoz, 2012).

Secure Context

Schuchat (1983, p. 472) supported the idea of a bubble or an enclave that provided tourists' safety in a strange place. The enclave is often thought of as risk-free because it is contrasting sharply with the pressures often faced in everyday life (Goulding *et al.*, 2002, p. 281). Prior to this, however, Schmidt argued that tourists perceive the tourism environment as a 'complex and potentially dangerous place' (1979, p. 458). Pizam *et al.* (1997) reported that from many parts of the world there is evidence that security and safety constitute necessary conditions for prosperous tourist venues.

There are several authors that have addressed tourists' perceptions of risk, and tourists' fear for tourism as such and for specific destinations (typically Cohen, 1985; Larsen, 2011). Roehl and Fesenmaier (1987) categorized tourists into three groups based on their respective perception of risk. Risk-neutral tourists do not consider either tourism or destination as risky, while tourists in the functional risk group associate risk with mechanical or organizational problems. The suggested last group of tourists is categorized based on place risk; these tourists perceive their holidays and the visited destinations as rather risky. Fear, on the other hand, can be related to oneself (such as not being able to cope physically, or falling behind in a tourist group), to other people and to the natural environment. Ladwein (2007) argues that there is a close relationship between the three, and that most fears are connected to a tourist group's human environment.

Wong and Kwong (2004) say that personal safety concerns are a major reason for taking package tours. Scandinavian package tourists seek security (Roper *et al.*, 2005) and they demonstrate feelings of safety due to the tourist group and their holiday situation – along with the thrill of going away, they also look for, and find, safety of the already familiar and known (Hanefors, 2001). Gorman argued along the same lines that 'the group provides safety in strange places' (1979, p. 472; also e.g. Crompton, 1981; Quiroga, 1990; Pizam *et al.*, 1997; Adib and Guerrier, 2001). It must be noted here, however, that the behaviour of package tourists may be unique and does not necessarily spillover to all other types of tourists (e.g. Cohen, 1972; Smith, 1978). Safety, security and fear are particularly important concerns among tourists who travel abroad. Tourists' personality is important, and avoiding risks is crucial to tourists and guides alike.

Certain authors have discussed the importance and influence of other customers – 'simply being with other people generally improves a person's mood significantly, regardless of what else is happening' (Csíkszentmihályi, 1990, p. 251; for social benefits in co-production see also e.g. Gainer, 1995; Pizam, 1999; Wang *et al.*, 2000; Etgar, 2008). Schuchat said, for example, that the Americans she studied joined tours to meet 'safe strangers' (1983, p. 465) – strangers in a safe environment, whether the strangers are tourists or locals. She referred to anonymous industry experts who 'agree that people move in groups for safety' (1983, p. 472). Schmidt argued that if the tourists 'follow the norms (the tour guide's advice)' (1979, p. 458), they will remain safe.

In natural circumstances the presence of a guide or a nature broker (e.g. Almagor, 1985; Weiler and Ham, 2001) is compulsory due to the dangers of the environment, for instance, while in a game reserve. In other cases, the use of tour guides is required but not obligatory. In Nepal, for example, one reason for hiring a guide is to secure personal safety (Gurung *et al.*, 1996). Other hazards that tourists may detect in the natural environment are, for example, bad weather, rock falls or dangerous animals (Ladwein, 2007). Noteworthy here is that all risks do not have to be as overwhelming as weather catastrophes. Just as problematic for tourists may be, for instance, unhealthy industry practices, disruptive sights, unreliable infrastructure, bad smells, or offensive sales.

Solving problems is included among tour guides' responsibilities, according to Reisinger and Waryszak (1994), and so is protecting tourists from hardships encountered during the holiday (Taft, 1977). Ryan (2002) shows, with the help of flow theory (Csíkszentmihályi, 1990), how tourists can avoid feelings of misadventure and get a peak adventure when helped by a guide. For the tour guide, it is an investment in trust (Jonasson and Scherle, 2012), and in many instances, the tour guides can act as peers, or become trusted friends of the visiting tourists (McKean, 1976; Holloway, 1981; Cohen, 1985; Wong and Wang, 2009) – relationships also described as parent–child relations (Cohen, 1985). Schuchat (1983) identified guides as surrogate parents, while Hanefors and Wong (2007) talked about nannies that take care of problems, i.e. problem solver, disciplinarian, caretaker (Grönroos, 1978; Schmidt, 1979; Holloway, 1981; Fine and Speer, 1985). Moreover, the friendly guides may act as buffers, within the tourist groups, or between one group and its outside (Gorman, 1979; Schmidt, 1979; Pearce, 1982; Zhang and Chow, 2004). Pearce (1984) argued that a good guide, working in the correct context, might provide a relatively safe and secure context for the tourists (see also e.g. Buckley, 2010).

Thematized Context

Research emphasizes the re-enchantment of consumption by thematizing the context (Firat *et al.*, 1995a, 1995b). For consumers, the consumption experiences in themed environments are interesting because they represent something different from their everyday life. The thematized context is designed to stimulate the consumers' senses, to help consumers escape and to help them meet other consumers. For comparison, see Holt (1995) regarding communing and socializing during a baseball game. The context is symbolically packed (Carù and Cova, 2007, p. 41). Alternatively, it can be a (re)(constructed) symbolic site or a dramaturgical space, as Edensor (2000) called it. Tour guides are trained to enact roles on-stage that fit with the appropriate thematized context.

Tourists consume with the help of tourism employees, including tour guides (Crang, 1997) in thematized contexts. When the guides perform, the theme is reflected, for example, in stories, songs, dresses, equipment, printed material and other paraphernalia. The importance of dramaturgical skills and performance competence has been highlighted (Schmidt, 1979; Holloway, 1981) as well as the guides' way of speaking (Fine and Speer, 1985). The guides' performances are only enacted for tourists who normally have to accept and adapt 'to the "touristified" identities and cultural views that are created for them' (Salazar, 2006, p. 836). Tour guides weave together an array of fantasy and facts in order to reproduce local history (Wynn, 2005, p. 399). How guides convey narratives varies, ranging from impersonal selling of commercial tourism imaginaries and telling of tourism facts to a more intimate sharing of personal tales (Bryon, 2012). Tour guides were described by Schmidt (1979) as shamans, while Holloway (1981) preferred to call them actors, entertainers or catalysts. They were named storytellers and entertainers by Dahles (2002), imagemakers by Zhang and Chow (2004) and animators by Hanefors and Wong (2007).

Mossberg (2008) recognizes the importance of involvement in the experience, that is, the type and strength of someone's involvement in a particular experience. Many tourists like to be highly involved and be part of the ongoing creative process – they like to co-create their experience. They sometimes become tourism storytellers themselves (Bryon, 2012). The result is a value unique to every individual (Prahalad and Ramaswamy, 2004). The creative process may include anything from creating an own ghost experience in a castle with a guide dressed up as a ghost to experiencing a particular identity or playing someone else in a medieval event. The individual can be anonymous, but the new status may be accepted and legalized with different symbols, such as a costume with a sword and a helmet at the medieval event. These experiences are interesting to tourists due to their difference from everyday life. 'Therefore, they give consumers a chance to experience different lifestyles that provide excursions into production or "customizing" of alternative selves and self-images, experiences that allow playful experimentation, and the fulfilment of various human dimensions' (Firat and Dholakia, 1998, p. 97).

Discussion and Implications

The relationship between tourists and tour guides entails mutual trust and agreement (Heung, 2007). The interaction process helps the respective tourists and tour guides to co-create the experience that provides best value for each participant. Beside the guides' necessary professional skills there are a number of guide performances that are basic for all guides in all situations. Regardless of the situation, the context must be enclavized, secure and thematized. We argue that these underlying foundations are the prerequisites for immersion.

It is known that for tourists in the non-ordinary to get immersed and to experience something extraordinary, interactions between people are vital and the tourists should have a perception of control (Arnould and Price, 1993; Mossberg, 2008). It is difficult for any consumers to get immersed if they are unfamiliar with the situation, particularly first-time visitors or novel tourists. To them immersion is problematic unless they are assisted in some way. Various situations can be perceived differently by various tourists, depending on their cultural and personal background. For example, sense of safety and risk perception are such features that may vary between tourists. Prahalad and Ramaswamy (2004) speak of the dark principle, where risk assessment is one of four building blocks of co-creation. Risks can be more or less eliminated with the help of tour guides. The guides are possible risk eliminators because they are expected to present interesting and involving programmes to the tourists, and also to handle arrangements in a way that reduces viable risks.

A themed context contributes to tourists' involvement during a tour, which increases the likelihood of becoming immersed. Edensor (2000) argues that the reflexive awareness experienced during the guide's performance influences tourists' involvement. He suggests that total immersion in a performance includes a critical reflection, depending on the conditions, such as repertoire, degree of improvization and tourists' expectations, under which it is performed. Tour guides during bus tours, walking tours, package tours, river rafting or gaming are all examples of when and where guides can facilitate tourists' immersion into stories if the guides are good actors and animators (e.g. Leclerc and Martin, 2004).

We suggest that there are guide 'plus' performances. Extra efforts from the tour guides, for example, thorough caretaking, exquisite storytelling, entertaining or animation can facilitate immersion. Basic performances of the guides have to be fulfilled in order for the tourists to feel 'plunged in this thematized and secure spatial enclave where they can let themselves go' (Carù and Cova, 2007, p. 31). The tourists' ability to become immersed hence depends on their relationships, interactions and interpretations of the situation, and a good guide can enhance a dynamic process. If the tour guide is not able to establish an enclavized, thematized and secure context, it is hard for the tourist to get an extraordinary experience and become immersed. One example could be that the tour guides are not able to tell stories according to any theme or provide enough trust and safety during the tour, depending on the tourists' respective cultural background.

The following model separates guide performances: below basic, basic and plus. If the guide's performance is below basic, they are probably not willing, or only to a certain level willing, to co-create. They might feel scared or uncomfortable in the situation, and prefer to sit in the bus instead of going to a site or to take part in activities, for example fishing, walking or shopping at a local market. The guides might have failed in, for example, place selection, information-giving, language and security, or any other basic performances. If the guides perform 'plus', i.e. above the basic, the individual tourist can get into a letting-go-process, enjoyment and co-creation.

In Fig. 17.1 there is a relationship between the performance of the guide, co-creation and tourist immersion. The tourist's willingness to co-create depends on the guide performance. If the degree of co-creation is high there is a better chance for the tourist to become immersed under the condition that the prerequisites are met.

There is no doubt that tour operators must emphasize their recruiting and training if they want to satisfy tourists, and also be successful in the competitive leisure and vacation market. The same was suggested by Ap and Wong (2001) in their study on tour guiding and professionalism. They stated that tour guides are key front-line players in the tourism industry. Through the guides' knowledge and interpretation of a destination's attractions and culture, and through their own communication and service skills, they have the ability to transform the tourist's visit from being just any tour into an experience. Also Lopez (1981) put forward that training of tour guides, including effective communication, problem solving method, and leadership patterns, have a positive effect on tourists' experiences.

If anything goes wrong during tourists' tour, the tour guides must solve the problems, no matter if it is a question about complaining about hotel, restaurant or tour members. The training should include an understanding of guide performances related to various situations. The tour guides have to handle tourists' behaviour in the 'bubble' and they should be trained to enact roles on-stage that fit with the appropriate

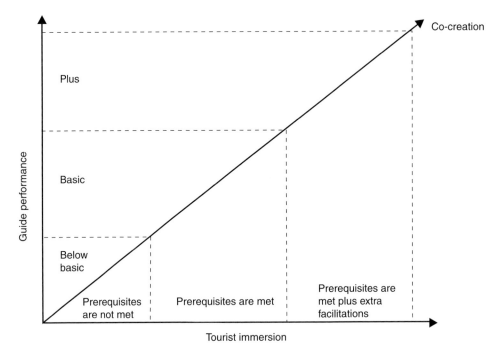

Fig. 17.1. Tour guide performance, co-creating process and tourist immersion.

tourism context. The roles are sometimes difficult to grasp and manage for the operator, but all, whether basic or guide 'plus' performances, are essential. It is true that tour guides often are members of the tourists' home society; therefore, they can convey specialized information that can be used for service improvements. However, that information is not enough to give them the ability to transform tourists' visits from being just any regular tours into becoming extraordinary experiences. A deeper insight is necessary to be able to understand the tourists need to be highly involved, and feel both comfort and familiarity in tourist groups in various safe, thematized and acceptable contexts. Also knowledge is necessary concerning tourists' cultural backgrounds and demographic profiles in the fast-changing and fragile world, and regarding the suggested new understanding of tourists' immersion during consumption.

Concluding Remarks

Much attention has been directed towards tour guides' performance and customer satisfaction and this research shows what factors influence tourists' satisfaction and dissatisfaction on guided tours. In general, tourists are satisfied if the guides perform just their basic performances, such as professional skills, customer relationship/

empathy and communication (e.g. Wong, 2001). Our chapter has tried to go beyond the previous research and focused on the prerequisites for immersion by investigating the guides' performances in establishing enclavized, thematized and secure contexts. To our knowledge there have been no studies directed towards tour guides and tourists' immersion. This is surprising because all tour operators must dream of creating products for tourists to experience something extraordinary. As immersion is seen as a process of accessing an experience where the tourist becomes one with the experience (Carù and Cova, 2007), it certainly needs more focus. Also, the context can be described as happening outside tourists' everyday lives, where a well-known and discussed implication of perceived freedom associated with the 'tourist bubble' adds an additional ingredient in tourists' immersion.

The present study is explorative and extended empirical research is required to understand the importance of the guides' roles and performances for tourists' immersion related to different travel arrangements in various situations.

References

Adib, A. and Guerrier, Y. (2001) The experience of holiday reps in maintaining and losing control of holidaymakers. *International Journal of Hospitality Management* 20(4), 339–352.

Almagor, U. (1985) A tourist's 'Vision Quest' in an African game reserve. *Annals of Tourism Research* 12(1), 31–47.

Ap, J. and Wong, K.K.F. (2001) Case study on tour guiding: professionalism, issues and problems. *Tourism Management* 22(6), 551–563.

Arnould, E. and Price, L. (1993) River rafting: extraordinary experience and the extended service encounter. *Journal of Consumer Research* 20(1), 24–45.

Boswijk, A., Thijssen, T. and Peelen, E. (2007) *The Experience Economy. A New Perspective*. Pearson Prentice Hall, Amsterdam.

Bowie, D. and Chang, J.C. (2005) Tourist satisfaction: a view from a mixed international package tour. *Journal of Vacation Marketing* 11(4), 303–322.

Bras, K. (2000) *Image-Building and Guiding on Lombok: The Social Construction of a Tourist Destination*. Department of Leisure Studies, Tilburg University, Tilburg, the Netherlands.

Bryon, J. (2012) Tour guides as storytellers – from selling to sharing. *Scandinavian Journal of Hospitality and Tourism* 12(1), 27–43.

Buckley, R. (2010) Communications in adventure tour products. Health and safety in rafting and kayaking. *Annals of Tourism Research* 37(2), 315–332.

Carù, A. and Cova, B. (2007) Consumer immersion in an experiential context. In: Carù, A and Cova, B. (eds) *Consuming Experience*. Routledge, London, pp. 34–47.

Chang, J.C. (2006) Customer satisfaction with tour leaders' performance: a study of Taiwan's package tours. *Asia Pacific Journal of Tourism Research* 11(1), 97–116.

Cohen, E. (1972) Towards a sociology of international tourism. *Social Research* 39(1), 164–182.

Cohen, E. (1979) Rethinking the sociology of tourism. *Annals of Tourism Research* 6(1), 18–35.

Cohen, E. (1982) Jungle guides in Northern Thailand – the dynamics of a marginal occupational role. *Sociological Review* 30(2), 234–266.

Cohen, E. (1984) The sociology of tourism. *Annual Reviews in Anthropology* 10, 373–392.

Cohen, E. (1985) The tourist guide: the origins, structure and dynamics of a role. *Annals of Tourism Research* 12(1), 5–29.

Cohen, E.H., Ifergan, M. and Cohen, E. (2002) A new paradigm in guiding: the madrich as a role model. *Annals of Tourism Research* 29(4), 919–932.

Cohen, S. and Taylor, L. (1992) *Escape Attempts: The Theory and Practice of Resistance to Everyday Life*, 2nd edn. Routledge, London.

Crang, P. (1997) Performing the tourist product. In: Rojek, C. and Urry, J (eds) *Touring Cultures: Transformation of Travel and Theory*. Routledge, London, pp. 137–154.

Crick, M. (1992) Life in the informal sector: street guides in Kandy, Sri Lanka. In: Harrison, D. (ed.) *Tourism in the Less Developed Countries*. Belhaven Press, London, pp. 135–147.

Crompton, J.L. (1981) Dimensions of the social group role in pleasure vacations. *Annals of Tourism Research* 8(4), 550–568.

Crouch, D., Aronsson, L. and Wahlstrom, L. (2001) The tourist encounter. *Tourist Studies* 1(3), 253–270.

Csíkszentmihályi, M. (1990) *Flow: The Psychology of Optimal Experience*. Harper and Row, New York.

Dahles, H. (2002) The politics of tour guiding. Image management in Indonesia. *Annals of Tourism Research* 29(3), 783–800.

Duke, C.R. and Persia, M.A. (1996) Performance-importance analysis of escorted tour evaluations. *Journal of Travel and Tourism Marketing* 5(3), 207–223.

Dumazedier, J. (1967) *Toward a Society of Leisure*. Free Press, New York.

Edensor, T. (2000) Staging tourism. Tourists as performers. *Annals of Tourism Research* 27(2), 322–344.

Enoch, Y. (1996) Contents of tour packages: a cross-cultural comparison. *Annals of Tourism Research* 23(3), 599–616.

Etgar, M. (2008) A descriptive model of the consumer co-production process. *Journal of the Academy of Marketing Science* 36, 97–108.

Farrell, B.H. (1979) Tourism's human conflicts. Cases from the Pacific. *Annals of Tourism Research* 6(2), 122–136.

Fine, E.C. and Speer, J.H. (1985) Tour guide performances as sight sacralization. *Annals of Tourism Research* 12(1), 73–95.

Firat, A.F. and Dholakia, N. (1998) *Consuming People: From Political Economy to Theaters of Consumption*. Routledge, London.

Firat, A.F., Dholakia, N. and Venkatech, A. (1995a) Marketing in a postmodern world. *European Journal of Marketing* 29(1), 40–56.

Firat, A.F., Fuat, A. and Venkatech, A. (1995b) Liberatory postmodernism and the reenchantment of consumption. *Journal of Consumer Research* 22(3), 239–267.

Gainer, B. (1995) Ritual and relationships: interpersonal influences on shared consumption. *Journal of Business Research* 32(3), 253–260.

Garcia, A. (1988) And why don't you go to the Seychelles? In: Rossell, P. (ed.) *Tourism: Manufacturing the Exotic*. IWGIA, Copenhagen, pp. 93–116.

Gelbman, A. and Maoz, D. (2012) Island of peace and island of war: tourist guiding. *Annals of Tourism Research* 39(1), 108–133.

Gentry, G.W. (2007) Walking the dead. The place of ghost walk tourism in Savannah, Georgia. *Southeastern Geographer* 47(2), 222–238.

Geva, A. and Goldman, A. (1991) Satisfaction measurement in guided tours. *Annals of Tourism Research* 18(2), 177–185.

Gorman, B. (1979) Seven days, five countries. The makings of a group. *Urban Life* 7(4), 469–491.

Goulding, C., Shankar, A. and Elliot, R. (2002) Working weeks, rave weekends: identity fragmentation and the emergence of new communities. *Consumption, Markets and Culture* 5(4), 261–284.

Graburn, N.H.H. (1978) Tourism: the sacred journey. In: Smith, V.L. (ed.) *Host and Guests. The Anthropology of Tourism*. Basil Blackwell, Oxford, pp. 17–31.

Grönroos, C. (1978) A service oriented approach to marketing of services. *European Journal of Marketing* 12(3), 588–601.

Guildin, G.E. (1989) The anthropological study tour in China: a call for cultural guides. *Human Organization* 48(2), 126–134.

Gurung, G., Simmons, D. and Devlin, P. (1996) The evolving role of tourist guides: the Nepali experience. In: Butler, R. and Hinch, T. (eds) *Tourism and Indigenous People*. International Thomson Business Press, London, pp. 107–128.

Hanefors, M. (1994) Travelling in the periphery of culture. *3rd Annual International Seminar on Tourism Development* 29 May–4 June, pp. 166–171.

Hanefors, M. (2001) *Paradise Regained. Swedish Charter Tourists Visiting the 'Non-Ordinary'*. North London University, London.

Hanefors, M. and Wong, A. (2007) Tourist guides – from cross-cultural understanding to animation. *The 5th APac-CHRIE and 13th APTA Joint Conference*, 24–27 May. Beijing, PR China.

Hansen, A.H. and Mossberg, L. (2013) Consumer immersion: a key to extraordinary experiences. In: Sundbo, J. and Sörensen, F. (eds) *Handbook on the Experience Economy*. Edward Elgar, Cheltenham, UK, pp. 209–227.

Heung, V.C.S. (2007) Effect of tour leader's quality on agency's reputation and customers' word-of-mouth. *Journal of Vacation Marketing* 14(4), 305–315.

Holloway, J.C. (1981) The guided tour. A sociological approach. *Annals of Tourism Research* 8(3), 377–402.

Holt, D.B. (1995) How consumers consume: a typology of consumption practices. *Journal of Consumer Research* 22(1), 1–16.

Howard, J., Thwaites, R. and Smith, B. (2001) Investigating the roles of the indigenous tour guides. *Journal of Tourism Studies* 12(2), 32–39.

Hughes, K. (1991) Tourist satisfaction: a guided 'cultural' tour in North Queensland. *Australian Psychologist* 26(3), 166–134.

Jackson, M., White, G. and Schmierer, C. (1996) Tourism experiences within an attributional framework. *Annals of Tourism Research* 23(4), 798–810.

Jacobsen, J.K.S. (2003) The tourist bubble and the Europeanisation of holiday travel. *Journal of Tourism and Cultural Change* 1(1), 71–87.

Jafari, J. (1987) Tourism models. The socio-cultural aspects. *Tourism Management* 8(2), 151–159.

Jonasson, M. and Scherle, N. (2012) Performing co-produced guided tours. *Scandinavian Journal of Hospitality and Tourism* 12(1), 55–73.

de Kadt, E. (ed.) (1979) *Tourism. Passport to Development*. Oxford University Press, Oxford.

Katz, S. (1985) The Israeli teacher-guide. The emergence and perpetuation of a role. *Annals of Tourism Research* 12(1), 49–72.

Knebel, H.J. (1960) *Soziologische Strukturwandlungen im Modernen Tourismus*. Ferdinand Enke, Stuttgart, Germany.

Ladwein, R. (2007) Consumption experience, self-narrative, and self-identity: the example of trekking. In: Carù, A. and Cova, B. (eds) *Consuming Experience*. Routledge, London, pp. 95–108.

Larsen, S. (2011) Tourism in a decade of terrorism, disasters and threats – some lessons learned. Special issue. *Scandinavian Journal of Hospitality and Tourism* 11(3), 215–394.

Leclerc, D. and Martin, J.N. (2004) Tour guide communication competence: French, German and American tourists' perceptions. *International Journal of Intercultural Relations* 28(3/4), 181–200.

Lipscombe, N. (1999) The relevance of the peak experience to continued skydiving participation: a qualitative approach to assessing motivations. *Leisure Studies* 18(4), 267–288.

Lopez, E.M. (1981) The effect of leadership style on satisfaction levels of tour quality. *Journal of Travel Research* 18(4), 20–23.

Mancini, M. (2001) *Conducting Tours*, 3rd edn. Delmar Thomson Learning, Clifton Park, New York.

McDonnell, I. (2001) *The Role of the Tour Guide in Transferring Cultural Understanding*. School of Leisure, Sport and Tourism, University of Technology, Sydney.

McKean, P.F. (1976) An anthropological analysis of the culture brokers of Bali: guides, tourists and Balinese. *UNESCO/IBDR Seminar on the social and cultural impact of tourism*, 8–10 December, Washington, DC.

Momchedjikova, B. (2002) My heart in the small lands. Touring the miniature city in the museum. *Tourist Studies* 2(3), 267–281.

Mossberg, L. (1995) Tour leaders and their importance in charter tours. *Tourism Management* 16(6), 437–445.

Mossberg. L. (2008) Extraordinary experiences through storytelling. *Scandinavian Journal of Hospitality and Tourism* 8(3), 195–210.

Nettekoven, L. (1979) Mechanism of cultural interaction. In: de Kadt, E. (ed.) *Tourism: Passport to Development*. Oxford University Press, New York, pp. 135–145.

Peake, S., Innes, P. and Dyer, P. (2009) Ecotourism and conversation: factors influencing effective conversation messages. *Journal of Sustainable Tourism* 17(1), 107–129.

Pearce, P.L. (1982) *The Social Psychology of Tourist Behaviour*. Pergamon Press, Oxford.

Pearce, P.L. (1984) Tourist–guide interaction. *Annals of Tourism Research* 11(1), 129–146.

Pizam, A. (1999) The American group tourists as viewed by British, Israeli, Korean and Dutch tour guides. *Journal of Travel Research* 38(2), 119–126.

Pizam, A., Tarlow, P.E. and Bloom, J. (1997) Making tourists feel safe: whose responsibility is it? *Journal of Travel Research* 36(1), 23–28.

Pond, K. (1993) *The Professional Guide: Dynamics of Tour Guiding*. Van Nostrand Reinhold, New York.

Poynter, J.M. (1993) *Tour Design, Marketing and Management*. Regents/Prentice Hall, Upper Saddle River, New Jersey.

Prahalad, C.K. and Ramaswamy, V. (2003) The new frontier of experience innovation. *MIT Sloan Management Review* 44(4), 12–18.

Prahalad, C.K. and Ramaswamy, V. (2004) *The Future of Competition: Co-Creating Unique Value with Customers*. Harvard Business School Press, Boston, Massachusetts.

Price, L., Arnould, E.J. and Tierney, P. (1995) Going to extremes: managing service encounters and assessing provider performance. *Journal of Marketing* 59(1), 83–97.

Privette, G. (1983) Peak experience, peak performance, and flow: a comparative analysis of positive human experiences. *Journal of Personality and Social Psychology* 45(6), 1361–1368.

Quiroga, I. (1990) Characteristics of package tours in Europe. *Annals of Tourism Research* 17(2), 185–207.

Reisinger, Y. and Waryszak, R. (1994) Japanese tourists' perceptions of their tour guides: Australian experiences. *Journal of Vacation Marketing* 1(1), 28–40.

Richards, G. and Wilson, J. (2006) Developing creativity in tourist experiences: a solution to serial reproduction of culture? *Tourism Management* 27(6), 1209–1223.

Roehl, W.S. and Fesenmaier, D.R. (1987) Tourism land use in the United States. *Annals of Tourism Research* 14(4), 471–485.

Roper, A., Jensen, Ø. and Jegervatn, R.-H. (2005) The dynamics of the Norwegian package tour industry. *Scandinavian Journal of Hospitality and Tourism* 5(3), 193–211.

Ryan, C. (2002) From motivation to assessment. In Ryan, C. (ed.) *The Tourist Experience*, 2nd edn. Cassell, London, pp. 58–77.

Ryan, C. and Dewar, K. (1995) Evaluating the communication process between interpreter and visitor. *Tourism Management* 16(4), 295–303.

Salazar, N.B. (2005) Tourism and glocalization. 'Local' tour guiding. *Annals of Tourism Research* 32(3), 628–646.

Salazar, N.B. (2006) Touristifying Tanzania: local guides, global discourse. *Annals of Tourism Research* 33(3), 833–852.

Salazar, N.B. (2008) 'Enough stories'. Asian tourism redefining the roles of Asian tour guides. *Civilisations* 57(1/2), 207–222.

Sampson, A. (1968) *The New Europeans*. Hodder and Stoughton, London.

Schmidt, C.J. (1979) The guided tour. Insulated adventure. *Urban Life* 7(4), 441–467.

Schuchat, M.G. (1983) Comfort of group tours. *Annals of Tourism Research* 10(4), 465–477.

Selänniemi, T. (1993) Secular pilgrims and holiday makers: Finnish tourists in Athens. Paper presented at the 13th *International Congress of Anthropological and Ethnological Sciences*. Symposium on 'Tourism as a Determinant of Culture Change', 29 July–4 August, Mexico City.

Shaw, G. and Williams, A.M. (1994) *Critical Issues in Tourism. A Geographical Perspective*. Routledge, London.

Shaw, G. and Williams, A.M. (2009) Knowledge transfer and management in tourism organizations: an emerging research agenda. *Tourism Management* 30, 325–335.

Smith, V.L. (ed.) (1978) *Hosts and Guests. The Anthropology of Tourism*. Basil Blackwell, Oxford.

Smith, V.L. (2001) The culture brokers. In: Smith, V.L. and Brent, M. (eds) *Hosts and Guests Revisited: Tourism Issues of the 21st Century*. Cognizant, New York, pp. 275–282.

Taft, R. (1977) Coping with unfamiliar culture. In: Warren, N. (ed.) *Studies in Cross-Cultural Psychology*. Academic Press, London.

Theroux, P. (1986) *Sunrise with Seamonsters, Travels and Discoveries 1964–1984*. Penguin, Harmondsworth, UK.

Timothy, D.J. (1995) Political boundaries and tourism: borders as tourist attractions. *Tourism Management* 16(2), 525–532.

Timothy, D.J. (1998) Collecting places: geodetic lines in tourist space. *Journal of Travel and Tourism Marketing* 7(4), 123–129.

UNESCO (1976) The effects of tourism on socio-cultural values. *Annals of Tourism Research* 4(1), 74–105.

van den Berghe, P.L. (1980) Tourism as ethnic relation. A case study of Cusco, Peru. *Ethnic and Racial Studies* 3(4), 375–371.

Wang, K.-C., Hsieh, A.T. and Huan, T.C. (2000) Critical service features in group package tour: an exploratory research. *Tourism Management* 21(2), 177–189.

Weiler, B. and Davis, D. (1993) An exploratory investigation into the roles of the nature based tour leader. *Tourism Management* 14(2), 91–98.

Weiler, B. and Ham, S. (2001) Tour guides and interpretation in ecotourism. In: Weaver, E. (ed.) *Encyclopedia of Ecotourism*. CAB International, Wallingford, UK, pp. 549–563.

Whipple, T.W. and Thach, S.V. (1988) Group tour management: does good service produce satisfied customers? *Journal of Travel Research* 27(1), 16–21.

Wong, A. (2001) Satisfaction with tour guides in Hong Kong. *Pacific Tourist Review* 5(1), 59–67.

Wong, C.-K.S. and Kwong, W.Y.Y. (2004) Outbound tourists' selection for choosing all-inclusive package tours. *Tourism Management* 25(5), 581–592.

Wong, J.-Y. and Wang, C.-H. (2009) Emotional labor of the tour leaders: an exploratory study. *Tourism Management* 30(2), 249–259.

Wong, K., Ap, J., Yeung, K.K.F. and Sandiford, P. (1998) *An Evaluation of the Need to Upgrade the Service Professionalism of Hong Kong's Tour Co-ordinators*. Hong Kong Polytechnic University, Hong Kong, PR China.

Wynn, J.R. (2005) Guiding practices: storytelling tricks for reproducing the urban landscape. *Qualitative Sociology* 28(4), 399–417.

Xin, Y., Weiler, B. and Ham, S.H. (2001) Intercultural communication and mediation: a framework for analyzing the intercultural competence of Chinese tour guides. *Journal of Vacation Marketing* 8(1), 75–87.

Zhang, H.Q. and Chow, I. (2004) Application of importance-performance model in tour guides' performance: evidence from mainland Chinese outbound visitors in Hong Kong. *Tourism Management* 25(1), 81–91.

18 Value Creation and Co-creation in Tourist Experiences: An East Asian Cultural Knowledge Framework Approach

Young-Sook Lee[1] and Nina K. Prebensen[2]

[1]Griffith University, Southport, Australia; [2]School of Business and Economics, UiT, Norway

Introduction

The outlook of international tourism has significantly changed today from the early mass tourism era at the end of the Second World War. One of the most distinctive traits in current international tourism is the diverse composition of tourists as well as types of products offered. For tourism researchers studying tourists' experience value creations and co-creations, these changing trends are highly significant (Ryan, 2002). The late 20th century witnessed a growing number of non-Euro/Western tourists. In particular, China is forecast to produce nearly 100 million tourists by the year 2020 (World Tourism Organization, 1999). Asia Pacific as a tourist-generating region has been growing at the rate of 5.6% per annum between 2000 and 2010 (UNWTO, 2011). With this growing number of East Asian outbound tourists, it is imperative that research has a fundamental understanding of these tourists in the 'new tourism' era where holiday is consumed on a large scale, yet, more flexibly and more individually focused than some decades ago (Poon, 1993, p. 18). A fundamental understanding of East Asian tourists may come from an insight into the region's cultural philosophies. In this chapter, Taoism, Confucianism and Zen Buddhism, constituting the underlying philosophical and cultural backbones of East Asia (Hahm, 2004; Schirokauer and Clark, 2004), are studied in relation to East Asian tourists' experience value creations and co-creations.

Tourism is about visiting other places, attractions, people and nature. The significance of nature – the scenery, the smell, touch and sounds of various natural scenes – is described as a fundamental aspect of tourism (Kaplan and Kaplan, 1989). Nature is thus often focused on in tourism promotion materials. Despite the awareness of the importance of the customers partaking in co-creating value for her- or himself, and for others including the company (Prahalad and Ramaswamy, 2004), few have actually studied the operant resources the customer provides to enhance consumption value (Claycomb et al., 2001; Baron and Harris, 2008) and there is a total lack in acknowledging learning regarding nature in a cultural framework.

Tourism professionals and market researchers are eager to study the variations and similarities of tourist behaviour to become competitive in the marketplace. Acknowledging that people have different attitudes and behavioural patterns depending on their cultural background is vital from two points of view. First, it will allow the tourism firms to focus and develop their offerings in line with the tourists' needs and wants. Second, it will attract tourists to participate in value creation and co-creation processes and subsequently enhance the experience value for tourists with different cultural backgrounds. As such, by acknowledging tourists' cultural backgrounds, the tourism providers will receive new knowledge in terms of how to develop and promote their amenities in order to increase tourist satisfaction and loyalty.

The aim of the present chapter is thus to propose an East Asian cultural knowledge framework based on the main East Asian cultural philosophies and revisit some previous study findings in order to facilitate a deeper understanding of East Asian tourist behaviours. In the eye of current tourism research focusing on the tourist as a key actor in creation experience value, the study aims to discuss relationships between cultural backgrounds, i.e. East Asian, and tourist attitude towards and learning regarding nature-based tourism. Based on a review of the literature on East Asian cultural philosophies, the chapter establishes a departure point to enhance East Asian tourists' experience value creation and co-creation. The proposed East Asian cultural knowledge framework is expected to inform researchers, at fundamental level, on tourists' value creation and co-creation, East Asian tourists' enduring motivations for seeking tourism experiences and their attitudes towards nature experiences and learning.

Organized into two main sections, the first part of the chapter reviews key cultural traits of Zen Buddhism, Confucianism and Taoism, specifically focused on the meanings of nature and learning. An East Asian cultural knowledge framework relevant to tourists' value creations and co-creations is proposed at the end of the first section. The second part of the chapter applies the concepts drawn from the framework in order to better understand East Asian tourists' attitudes and learning orientations regarding nature-based experiences.

Tourist as a Value Creator

Creating and co-creating experiences, as a theoretical construct, reflects the consumer as an active part in consuming and producing values (Dabholkar, 1990). It is about involving the customer to partake in defining, designing and performing various aspects of the experience (Meuter *et al.*, 2000; Bendapudi and Leone, 2003; Vargo and Lusch, 2004). The process of experiencing a vacation is an 'interactive, relativistic, preference experience' (Holbrook, 2006, p. 715) and it involves an interaction between people and/or between products and people (Gummeson, 2008; cf. Vargo and Lusch, 2008). Within these perspectives the customer is depicted as a resource integrator in the process of value co-creation (Arnould *et al.*, 2006; Baron and Harris, 2010) and value of consumption is in the use of a product or the experience created through the consumption process rather in the product itself (Lancaster, 1971; Sandström *et al.*, 2008). Knowledge and learning, i.e. operant resources, are subsequently imperative constructs in the new service-dominant logic (Vargo and Lusch, 2008). Operant resources in research are also depicted as a core imperative in order to gain competitive advantages (Shaw and Ivins, 2002). Given the significance of recognizing tourists as value creators and the increasing number of East Asian tourists in the global tourism sector, it is imperative that tourism planner product providers are competently equipped with East Asian cultural constructs that have profound influences on tourists' value creation. The following section provides detailed explanations on Zen Buddhist, Confucian and Taoist meaning of nature and learning.

Meaning of Nature and Learning in Zen Buddhism, Confucianism and Taoism

An essential qualification needs to be given when discussing the meaning of nature and learning from Zen Buddhist, Confucian and Taoist cultural values in this chapter. When we refer to Buddhist, Confucian and Taoist ideologies of East Asian societies in the current chapter, we primarily refer to the societies' cultural backgrounds rather than their religious values *per se*. For example, not dissimilar to the other East Asian nations, Christianity has been accepted with zeal in South Korea since its introduction in 1884 and it has become the second largest religious group in the country after Buddhism. By 1989, about a quarter of the 40 million population were Protestant Christians (Kim, 2000). Therefore, the Buddhist, Confucian and Taoist values on nature and learning and their principles used in this chapter primarily refer to the cultural heritage of East Asia.

It should also be noted that only English-language publications on Buddhism, Confucianism and Taoism have been the sources for the current chapter. We acknowledge that literature in other languages may strengthen the proposed East Asian cultural knowledge framework.

Meaning of nature and learning in Zen Buddhist cultural values

Discussions on Buddhist meaning of nature have been active in Western academia. One of the pioneering studies highlighting the meaning of nature from a Zen Buddhist perspective is by Lynn White (1967). Arguing that the origin of the current environmental crisis in the West is attributed to the Judaeo-Christian attitude towards the human and nature relationship where humans are perceived superior to nature, he suggests that the Zen Buddhist meaning of nature of East Asia should be considered by the West (White, 1967). Zen Buddhism is the Buddhist branch prevalent in East Asia (Eckel, 1997) and nature and humanity are perceived as one entity rather than one being superior to the other (James, 2003).

It should be noted that Zen is a Japanese word and other East Asian nations have different names for this school of Buddhism. In Chinese, it is *Ch'an* and in Korean *i Sŏn*. For the sake of simplicity, the English translation of this school of Buddhism, derived from the Japanese word, is used in this chapter. Since White's study, there have been other scholars in environmental or religious studies who argue that Buddhism is environmentally friendly (Schmithausen, 2000), as it respects nature by placing its value for its own existence.

Three Zen Buddhist principles of nature are drawn from the literature research. First is the relational dimension, which is often discussed as a trait that makes Zen Buddhism environmentally friendly (Sponberg, 1997, p. 353; Zimmerman, 1993). The relational dimension is attributed to the emptiness teaching in the Zen tradition, which has its root in Mahāyāna Buddhism (McFarlan, 1990). Emptiness teaching entails that all properties are interrelated, hence relational. A prominent Zen Buddhist scholar Thich Nhat Hanh explains the notion this way:

> When we look at a chair, we see the wood, but we fail to observe the trees, the forest, the carpenter, or our own mind. When we meditate on it, we can see the entire universe in all its interwoven and interdependent relations in the chair. The presence of the wood reveals the presence of the tree. The presence of the leaf reveals the presence of the sun. The presence of the apple blossoms reveals the presence of the apple. Meditators can see one in many, and the many in the one. (Hanh, 1992, cited by James, 2003, p. 153)

The second principle is non-instrumental value, which is described as the value that 'a being has an end in itself rather than as a means to an end' (James, 2004, p. 87). That is to say, within a Zen Buddhist worldview, nature does not exist as an instrument for the life and existence of humanity (for a detailed explanation, see Green, 1996). This chapter may benefit from recognizing non-instrument value as one of Zen's principles of nature.

The last principle of nature from the Zen Buddhist tradition is Zen Buddhist tendency to include plants or seemingly non-sentient beings such as mountains, rivers or even pebbles on the beach as part of natural beings that can be enlightened. The inclusion of these non-sentient beings within the realm of nature, or things that can have enlightened 'Buddhahood', is uniquely a Zen trait and not found in the Indian tradition of Buddhism (Lafleur, 2000). This notion to include seemingly lifeless beings in the realm of nature is taken as a trait in Zen's principle of nature in this study.

Following the three principles of nature from Zen Buddhism, one principle relating to the concept of learning can be drawn. In the Zen Buddhist notion of learning, all aspects of events or contexts are valued and these include some things that are normally not adequate to learn from (Johansen and Gopalakrishna, 2006, p. 340). This view to learning demonstrates the embedded Zen Buddhist philosophy that espouses the heuristic nature of the world. This principle, termed 'learning from mundane everyday life', could also be related at a fundamental level to non-sentient beings as nature, where seemingly insignificant things in the world are just as important as other, bigger things in the universe (Lee *et al.*, 2013).

To summarize, three Zen Buddhist traits regarding its meanings of nature are: (i) relatedness; (ii) non-instrumental value; and (iii) non-sentient beings as nature; and one trait on learning being learning from mundane life. In this chapter, relatedness is defined as any action or belief that regards human and nature as a related being. Non-instrumental value is defined as any act or belief that treats nature as an end in itself rather than as a means to another end. Non-sentient beings as nature refer to any act or belief that includes seemingly lifeless things or non-animal species in the realm of nature. Learning from mundane life as the principle of Zen

Buddhist learning is defined as the belief that even things seemingly non-educative or too small to learn from can be a source of learning. A summary table of Zen Buddhism's meaning of nature and learning and its relevance in tourism operation is presented in Table 18.1.

With this defined set of Zen Buddhist meaning of nature and learning, we now turn to Confucian meaning of nature and learning.

Meaning of nature and learning in Confucian cultural values

Founded by the sage teacher K'ung Fu-tzu (551–479 BCE), classic Confucianism has five constant regulations, including: ren (benevolence, humaneness); yi (righteousness); li (propriety or rites, rules of proper conduct); zhi (wisdom); and xin (sincerity or trustworthiness) (Yao, 2000; Tamney and Chiang, 2002). It emphasizes the practice of moral virtue in order to become a righteous man who always acts according to justice through the notion of yi (Zhang, 2000). In their efforts to realize the yi state, people should employ the correct ways of doing things or li. These instructive methods are in the pursuit to be in harmony with the universe according to Confucian philosophy. Confucius' followers had nurtured the teaching of the sage for centuries and neo-Confucianism was developed around 11th and 12th centuries. The leading neo-Confucian scholar Chu His (1130–1200) elevated the neo-Confucian ideology to one superior to classic Confucianism. His philosophy was worldly spirited, emphasizing the balance of religious reverence, ethical practice, scholarly investigation and political participation (Tucker, 1991, p. 61). From both classic and neo-Confucianism, a person's moral virtue to reach yi is regarded with the utmost importance and this can be realized by observing li. Reaching the righteous state through the acts of proper conduct is deemed particularly significant in the Confucian tradition, as the ones who reach this state of yi can then govern the nation with an accomplished high moral virtue (Haynes, 2009). Such governance can then bring harmony to a nation, the ultimate reason for the Confucian teaching of yi, li and ren.

With this philosophical ground, Confucian scholars view the universe with three main elements in mind: heaven, earth and human. In this triadic relationship,

Table 18.1. Meaning of nature and learning in Zen Buddhism and implications for tourism practice.

	Zen Buddhism
Meaning of nature	Relational dimension
	Non-instrumental value
	Non-sentient beings as nature
Meaning of learning	Learning from everyday mundane life
Managerial implications for tourism practice	Tourism products should emphasize that physical nature and humanity are interrelated
	Nature should not be treated as a tool for human use
	Small and/or not living things are part of nature
	Learning, as part of touristic experience, can be created from everything, even from small/insignificant things

human is perceived as the child of father heaven and mother earth. Tu quotes Chang Ysai to highlight the neo-Confucian view of the universe:

> Heaven is my father and Earth is my mother, and even such a small being as I finds an intimate place in their midst. Therefore that which fills the universe I regard as my body and that which directs the universe I consider as my nature. All people are my brothers and sisters, and all things are my companions. (1985, p. 157)

Mote described this view of the universe as '[everything] belonging to one organic whole and that they all interact as participants in one spontaneously self-generating life process' (1971, p. 19). With critical analysis of Mote's view of an East Asian model of the universe, there is no distinction between energy and matter or spirit and matter (Chan cited in Tu, 1985, p. 36). As reviewed, organismic relation in Confucian philosophy of universe and nature is recognized as a significant trait, thus the first Confucian principle of nature identified in this study is organismic relation.

Extending from the organismic relation of the universe, the 'all-enfolding harmony of impersonal cosmic function' as a continuing being (Mote cited in Tu, 1985, p. 40) subsequently requires humans to be in harmony with the universe.

Harmony cannot be said to be a unique Confucian value. The notion of harmony existed in East Asia for a long time before the beginning of the Confucian thought. From the Confucian five constant regulations, three of them: yi (righteousness), li (propriety or rites, rules of proper conduct) and ren (benevolence, humaneness) fundamentally place high importance on harmony, as the teaching's aim is to reach the state of harmony (Yao, 2000, pp. 77–78). Subsequently, this underlying cultural notion gives the rationale for Confucian thought of self-cultivation. Self-cultivation (Tucker, 1998; Cua, 2007; Shusterman, 2009) is a way to bring humans in harmony with nature (Yao, 2000). Being in harmony with nature relates closely to the search for knowledge and action by humans, or creative transformation. Referring to Tu's seminar work, Tucker argues:

> Confucian humanism is fundamentally different from anthropocentrism because it professes the unity of man and heaven rather than the imposition of the human will on nature. In fact, the anthropocentric assumption that man is put on earth to pursue knowledge and, as knowledge expands, so does man's dominion over earth is quite different from the Confucian perception of the pursuit of knowledge as an integral part of one's self-cultivation. … The human transformation of nature, therefore, means as much an integrative effort to learn to live harmoniously in one's natural environment as a modest attempt to use the environment to sustain basic livelihood. The idea of exploiting nature is rejected because it is incompatible with the Confucian concern for moral self-development. (1991, p. 65)

Interpreted from the Confucian fundamental perspective of the universe where humans, heaven and earth form one entity, the notion of 'creative transformation' has been discussed as a significant point when it comes to Confucian self-cultivation ethics. Interpreting the concept of li from the Analects as a guide for one's moral structure, Lai (2006) argues that when one's moral building matures, the concept of li becomes something beyond a mere guideline to follow. Indeed it becomes 'a channel for meaningful self-expression' (p. 69), which highlights creative transformation. Critically comparing the pragmatist and Confucian aesthetics, Shusterman argues that the cultivating and perfecting human life is the central philosophy in both of the traditions and this philosophy is aimed to improve our humanism (2009, p. 19). It should be noted here that in an aesthetic sense, clearly making creative transformation is to improve humans, so that humans can be in harmony with nature but not to enhance nature.

As mentioned above, Confucius was an educator who taught many students to succeed in national examinations, enabling them to become high officials in the country. Confucian philosophy for learning emphasized acquisition and under-standing with the aim of being successful in nation-wide examinations (Pratt *et al.*, 1999). Accordingly, Confucianism holds that only when the students learn classical works by heart and are able to reproduce them would they then be able to question and try to be an independent, critical thinker. For this reason, reproducing the classical works was a main part of the national examination. Within this context of learning for succeeding in the examination, learning was viewed as an instrumental entity for a worldly success (Yang *et al.*, 2006, p. 348). Thus, one principle on learning identified for this chapter is 'learning for worldly development'.

In summary, Confucian principles of nature extracted from literature are: (i) organismic relation and (ii) creative transformation. For the purpose of this chapter, organismic relation is defined as any belief or action that regards nature and human as an inherently related single organism. Creative transformation is defined in the chapter as the changes made to nature by humans in an integrative effort to learn to live harmoniously in one's natural environment or as an attempt to use the environment to sustain basic livelihood. Confucian principle of learning distilled for this chapter is learning for worldly connection and development. A summary of Confucian meaning of nature and learning along with managerial implications is presented in Table 18.2.

Meaning of nature and learning in Taoist cultural values

Sharing essential philosophical grounds with Zen Buddhism and Confucianism, Taoism is a major cultural philosophy in contemporary East Asia. Since its inception in China, long before Confucianism and Zen Buddhism, Taoism has influenced the development of Confucianism and Zen Buddhism. While sharing an underlying

Table 18.2. Meaning of nature and learning in Confucianism and implications for tourism practice.

	Confucianism
Meaning of nature	Organismic relations
	Creative transformation
Meaning of learning	Learning for worldly development
Managerial implications for tourism practice	Tourism products should emphasize that physical nature and humanity are interrelated
	Changes made to physical environment/nature are regarded as an integrated effort for human and physical environments by Confucian heritage tourists
	Learning, as part of touristic experience, should bring some tangible/practical outcome

philosophical view of the universe that all things are related or a 'oneness' trait, as identified, a unique Taoist view of the world consists of ying and yang, the opposite elements of the universe. Yang is the positive element of beings and often described as masculinity, strength, brightness and so forth. Ying is the negative element of beings and can be described as femininity, weakness and darkness. Nature in Taoism is a construct of yin and yang, signifying a unity between humanity and physical environment (Lao Zi, cited in Lee, 2010).

Taoist meaning of learning may be described as a constant work of the two opposing forces, yin and yang. Referring to beauty, goodness, teaching and creation, Tao Te Ching states:

> Under heaven all can see beauty as beauty only because there is ugliness
> All can know good as good only because there is evil.
>
> Therefore having and not having arise together;
> Difficulty and easy complement each other;
> Long and short contrast each other;
> High and low rest upon each other;
> Voice and sound harmonize each other;
> Front and back follow one another.
>
> Therefore the sage goes about doing nothing, teaching no-talking,
> The ten thousand things rise and fall without cease,
> Creating, yet not possessing,
> Working, yet not taking credit.
> Work is done, then forgotten.
> Therefore it lasts forever. (Lao, 1972, Chapter 2)

Espousing the work of yin and yang, the Taoist meaning of learning reflects two opposite sides of wisdom and creativity. The opposing sides of all things in the universe are not to be taken as a conflict but a method to improve the quality of learning (Glanz, 1997).

In summary, Taoist meaning of nature identified in this chapter is oneness, having profoundly influenced the development of Zen Buddhism and Confucianism. Taoist meaning of learning is a 'unity through paradox' trait, where opposing forces of the universe are the leading forces for unity, the perfection. A summary of Taoist meaning of nature and learning, along with managerial implications for tourism operations, is presented in Table 18.3.

The three major cultural philosophies of East Asia share the most central idea of 'harmony' related to both nature and learning. For the meaning of nature, Zen

Table 18.3. Meaning of nature and learning in Taoism and implications for tourism practice.

	Taoism
Meaning of nature	Oneness
Meaning of learning	Unity through paradox
Managerial implications for tourism practice	Tourism products should emphasize that physical nature and humanity are interrelated
	Learning, as part of touristic experience, can incorporate opposite sides of things

Buddhism and Confucianism share the notion that all entities in the world are related (related dimension from Zen Buddhism and organismic relation from Confucianism). Both of these ideas are also shared with Taoism's oneness view of nature. Zen Buddhism also has a unique view on nature: 'non-instrumental value' and 'non-sentient being as nature' as explained above. Similarly Confucianism has its distinctive meaning of nature: creative transformation.

On learning, the three cultural philosophies represent their unique traits most distinctively. For Zen Buddhism, learning is from everyday mundane life; for Confucianism, learning is for worldly development; and Taoism views learning as unity through paradox. The following section further explicates how the extracted cultural knowledge framework can be applied to facilitate East Asian tourists' value creation and co-creation recognizing the tourists as active participants. Following the identification of the cultural traits on nature and learning, Fig. 18.1 presents the Zen Buddhist, Confucian and Taoist meaning of nature and learning.

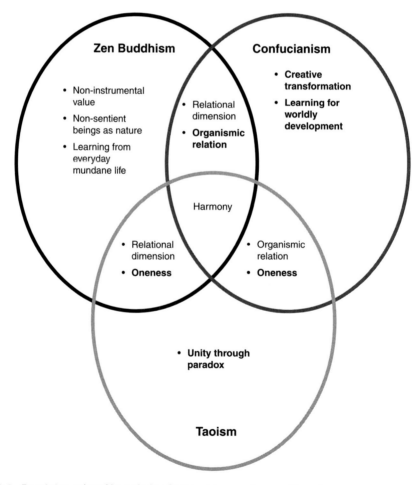

Fig. 18.1. East Asian cultural knowledge framework on nature and learning.

Application of the Framework

As Fig. 18.1 illustrates, there are certain shared cultural values among Zen Buddhism, Confucianism and Taoism, constituting the meanings of nature and learning. These shared cultural traits include 'relational dimension', 'organismic relation' and 'oneness', leading to the overall harmony of everything in the universe (between individual persons as well as between nature and humanity). When planning, developing and providing tourist experiences, destination management organizations and personnel need to possess an advanced level of cultural knowledge. This is particularly so for a successful tourism business when the creation and co-creation of tourist experience values concerns East Asian tourists – the fastest growing outbound tourist market in the world, according to UNWTO.

The meanings of learning from the perspectives of the three main cultural philosophies of East Asia reflect their unique traits. The Zen Buddhist meaning of learning recognizes learning from mundane everyday life – no matter how small or insignificant things might appear to be, there is something to be learnt from them. The Confucian meaning of learning is more practical than the Zen Buddhist approach. Learning is very much related to individuals' worldly connection and development, which may bring personal career achievements and/or economic success. Learning in this Confucian sense is, one might say, a tool for a psychologically and/or economically successful life. The Taoist meaning of learning clearly reflects its unique worldview of yin and yang and emphasizes unity through paradox. As the opposing side exists, the true quality and existence of the other side can be appreciated in the most paradoxical yet revealing way.

With the shared meaning of nature as well as comparable meanings of learning established from Zen Buddhist, Confucian and Taoist values, the following section recounts the application of the developed cultural knowledge framework to tourism research. The application is essayed in this chapter by re-evaluating some research findings on East Asian tourists' experience creations and co-creations.

Re-evaluating research on East Asians' tourism experience

The East Asian cultural meanings of nature and learning, presented in the East Asian cultural knowledge framework, contribute to deepening the level of cultural analysis in tourist experience value creations and co-creations. First part of this section is on the meaning of nature and re-evaluates South Korean ecotourists' value creation and consumption in a recent study. Following the re-evaluation of the South Korean ecotourism experiences, two other earlier findings on Asian backpackers and special interest tourists are revisited in relation to the East Asian cultural meanings of learning.

A recent study presents an analysis on a South Korean form of ecotourism that is influenced by Taoist, Confucian and Zen Buddhist cultural values (Lee *et al.*, 2013). This study highlights the significant contribution of the developed cultural knowledge framework in an effort to better understand East Asian ecotourists' experience creation. Studies have argued that East Asian, more specifically, Chinese, meaning of nature views nature and humanity as a united single entity (Sofield and

Li, 2007; Wen and Ximing, 2008). Affirming these earlier studies, the recent study illustrates a South Korean form of ecotourism, which regards nature and humanity as an inseparable entity.

This in turn brings out a particular attitude towards human changes of nature – as human and nature are one entity, changes in nature in accordance with the changing human society are a way of showing harmony between human and nature and hence are not considered negative, let alone disturbing (Lee *et al.*, 2013). Reflected through the proposed East Asian cultural knowledge framework of this chapter, East Asian ecotourists' experience value creations are expected to be influenced by the meaning of nature – that humanity and nature are one entity. That is, when planning and marketing tourism experiences for East Asian markets, namely Chinese, Japanese, Korean and Taiwanese, who seek nature or ecotourism experiences, their value creations can be further facilitated by recognizing the East Asian cultural meaning of nature rather than reviewing the market as those who are in pursuit of 'catching up' Western tourists. This cultural sensitivity may lead to developing particular tourism products that could include certain sites and/or activities involving natural settings as well as other tourists on sites, integrating humanity and physical nature as a related single entity seeking an overall harmony. This, in turn, could lead to enhanced tourist experiences of the fastest growing international tourist market.

The East Asian meanings of learning presented in the framework include: learning from mundane everyday life of Zen Buddhist tradition; learning for worldly connection and development distilled from Confucianism; and unity through paradox from Taoist philosophy. Studies of Asian backpackers identified that young travellers are highly motivated to learn English, because having proficiency in English would equip them to become more competitive in their search for jobs and subsequent success in their careers, as well as create cultural capital (Prideaux and Shiga, 2007; Maksay, 2007; Kawashima, 2010). This finding can be clearly explained by the identified Confucian meaning of learning. Similarly, in a study of South Korean golf tourists in Queensland, Australia, the special interest tourists consider whether the golf courses have any associations with well-known golf celebrities such as Greg Norman, Arnold Palmer or Adam Scott when choosing their destinations (Kim and Lee, 2009). These findings on the young Asian backpackers and the South Korean special interest tourists can be understood at a more fundamental level with the use of the developed framework of the current chapter. In other words, the cultural meaning of learning shapes the East Asian tourists' experience value co-creation. Interestingly, the findings point to one singular trait of cultural meaning of learning – Confucian learning for worldly connection and development. Tourism planners, marketers and service providers need to recognize the East Asian cultural meanings of learning influencing contemporary tourists at a fundamental level. And this can lead to the satisfaction of enduring motivations to learn/improve English in the case of Asian backpackers and playing rounds of golf at world-recognized golf courses in the case of South Korean golf tourists. Similarly, other niche market tourists such as adventure travellers from East Asia may be motivated by their cultural trait to be connected to the world and develop themselves rather than blindly trying to catch up the Western adventure tourists. The recognition in turn would be able to provide more focused marketing strategies to the tourism experience providers, who target the growing East Asian market in the international tourism sector.

Concluding Remarks

As tourist experience is becoming more and more service-dominant and tourists are being viewed as the co-creator of the overall tourism experience, tourists' value positions towards important elements in tourism experiences prove to be a significant area of attention for both researchers and practitioners. Recognizing the current state of international tourism, where East Asian tourists are the fastest growing international outbound tourist market, and yet little is understood about the market at a fundamental level, this chapter proposed an East Asian cultural knowledge framework on nature and learning – two main elements in tourism experiences.

Three East Asian cultural philosophies, Zen Buddhism, Confucianism and Taoism, have defined meanings for nature and learning. One shared meaning of nature is that all elements in the universe are related to one another. While this meaning of nature is represented in all three tenets of the East Asian cultural philosophies, each has their unique cultural traits in nature and learning. A clear understanding of the fundamental cultural traits of the East Asian tourist market would help practitioners to enhance value creation and co-creation.

The current chapter recommends further research on this fast-growing market in international tourism at fundamental level. In particular, future study may investigate the dynamic trend of the dominant East Asian cultural philosophies in light of the region's political and economic developments. Indeed, despite the diverse trajectories of contemporary East Asian, where Communism, democracy, capitalism and socialism have been leading socio-political and economic developments, traditional philosophical cultural values and their modification and adjustment could provide the enduring yet dynamic nature of the cultural forces that shape today's East Asian market.

References

Arnould, E.J., Price, L.L. and Malshe, A. (2006) Toward a cultural resource-based theory of the customer. In: Lusch, R.F. and Vargo, S.L. (eds) *The New Dominant Logic in Marketing*. M.E. Sharpe, Armonk, New York, pp. 91–104.

Baron, S. and Harris, K. (2008) Consumers as resource integrators. *Journal of Marketing Management* 24(1–2), 113–130.

Baron, S. and Harris, K. (2010) Toward an understanding of consumer perspectives on experiences. *Journal of Services Marketing* 24(7), 518–531.

Bendapudi, N. and Leone, R.P. (2003) Psychological implications of customer participation in co-production. *Journal of Marketing* 67(1), 14–28.

Claycomb, C., Lengnick-Hall, C.A. and Inks, L.W. (2001) The customer as a productive resource: a pilot study and strategic implications. *Journal of Business Strategy* 18(1), 47–69.

Cua, A.S. (2007) Virtues of Junzi. *Journal of Chinese Philosophy* 34(1), 125–142.

Dabholkar, P.A. (1996) Consumer evaluations of new technology-based self-service options: an investigation of alternative models of service quality. *International Journal of Research in Marketing* 13(1), 29–51.

Eckel, M. (1997) Is there a Buddhist philosophy of nature? In: Tucker, M.E. and Williams, D.E. (eds) *Buddhism and Ecology: The Interconnection of Dharma and Deeds*. Harvard University Press, Cambridge, Massachusetts, pp. 327–349.

Glanz, J. (1997) The Tao of supervision: Taoist insights into the theory and practice of educational supervision. *Journal of Curriculum and Supervision* 12, 193–211.

Green, K. (1996) Two distinctions in environmental goodness. *Environmental Values* 5, 31–46.

Gummesson, E. (2008) Extending the service-dominant logic: from customer centricity to balanced centricity. *Journal of the Academy of Marketing Science* 36(1), 15–17.

Hahm, C. (2004) The ironies of Confucianism. *Journal of Democracy* 15(3), 93–107.

Haynes, J. (2009) *Routledge Handbook of Religion and Politics*. Routledge, London.

Holbrook, B.M. (2006) Consumption experience, customer value, and subjective personal introspection: an illustrative photographic essay. *Journal of Business Research* 59, 714–725.

James, S.P. (2003) Zen Buddhism and the intrinsic value of nature. *Contemporary Buddhism* 4(2), 143–157.

James, S.P. (2004) *Zen Buddhism and Environmental Ethics*. Ashgate, Aldershot, UK.

Johansen, B.C. and Gopalakrishna, D. (2006) A Buddhist view of adult learning in the workplace. *Advances in Developing Human Resources* 8, 337–435.

Kaplan, R. and Kaplan, K. (1989) *The Experience of Nature: A Psychological Perspective*. Cambridge University Press, Cambridge.

Kawashima, K. (2010) Japanese working holiday makers in Australia and their relationship to the Japanese labour market: before and after. *Asian Studies Review* 34(3), 267–286.

Kim, A.E. (2000) Korean religious culture and its affinity to Christianity: the rise of Protestant Christianity in South Korea. *Sociology of Religion* 61(2), 117–133.

Kim, A. and Lee, Y.S. (2009) Queensland as a golf tourism destination: from South Korean market perspective. *International Journal of Tourism Policy* 2(1/2), 124–137.

Lafleur, W. (2000) Enlightenment for plants and trees. In: Kaza, S. and Kraft, K. (eds) *Dharma Rain*. Shambhala, Boston, Massachusetts, pp. 109–116.

Lai, K. (2006) Li in the analects: training in moral competence and the question of flexibility. *Philosophy East and West* 56(1), 69–83.

Lancaster, K. (1971) Consumer demand: a new approach. *Journal of International Economics* 10, 151–175.

Lao, T. (1972) *Tao Te Ching* (G.F. Feng and J. English, Trans.). Vintage Press, New York.

Lee, Y.S. (2010) Nature as unity between humanity and environment in Korean travel literature from the late Goryeo to Joseon Dynasties. *Literature and Aesthetics* 22(1), 198–214.

Lee, Y.-S., Lawton, L. and Weaver, D. (2013) Evidence for a South Korean model of ecotourism. *Journal of Travel Research* 52(4), 520–533.

Maksay, A. (2007) Japanese working holiday makers in Australia: subculture and resistance. *Tourism Review International* 11, 33–43.

McFarlan, S. (1990) Mushin, morals, and martial arts: a discussion of Keenan's YogZicara critique. *Japanese Journal of Religious Studies* 17(4), 397–420.

Meuter, M.L., Ostrom, A.L., Bitner, M.J. and Roundtree, R. (2003) The influence of technology anxiety on consumer use and experiences with self-service technologies. *Journal of Business Research* 56(11), 899–906.

Mote, F. (1971) *Intellectual Foundations of China*. Knopf, New York.

Poon, A. (1993) *Tourism, Technology and Competitive Strategies*. CAB International, Wallingford, UK.

Prahalad, C.K. and Ramaswamy, V. (2004) Co-creation experiences: the next practice in value creation. *Journal of Interactive Marketing* 18(3), 5–14.

Pratt, D.D., Kelly, M. and Wong, W.S. (1999) Chinese conceptions of effective teaching in Hong Kong: towards culturally sensitive evaluation of teaching. *International Journal of Lifelong Education* 18, 121–134.

Prideaux, B. and Shiga, H. (2007) Japanese backpacking: the emergence of a new market sector: a Queensland case study. *Tourism Review International* 11, 45–56.

Ryan, C. (2002) Motives, behaviours, body and mind. In: Ryan, C. (ed.) *The Tourist Experience*, 2nd edn. Continuum, London.

Sandström, S., Edvardsson, B., Kristensson, P. and Magnusson, P. (2008) Value-in-use through service experience. *Managing Service Quality* 18(2), 112–126.

Schirokauer, C. and Clark, D.N. (2004) *Modern East Asia: A Brief History.* Thomson/Wadsworth, Belmont, California.

Schmithausen, L. (2000) Buddhism and the ethics of nature: some remarks. *Eastern Buddhism* 32(2), 26–78.

Shaw, C. and Ivins, J. (2002) *Building Great Customer Experiences.* Palgrave, London.

Shusterman, R. (2009) Pragmatist aesthetics and Confucianism. *Journal of Aesthetic Education* 43(1), 18–29.

Sofield, T. and Li, F.M.S. (2007) China: ecotourism and cultural tourism, harmony or dissonance? In: Highham, J. (ed.) *Critical Issues in Ecotourism: Understanding a Complex Tourism Phenomenon.* Elsevier, Amsterdam, pp. 368–385.

Sponberg, A. (1997) Green Buddhism and the hierarchy of compassion. In: Tucker, M.E. and Williams, D.R. (eds) *Buddhism and Ecology: The Interconnection of Dharma and Deeds.* Harvard University Center for the Study of World Religions, Cambridge, Massachusetts.

Tamney, J.B. and Chiang, L.H.L. (2002) *Modernisation, Globalisation and Confucianism in Chinese Societies.* Praeger, Westport, Connecticut.

Tu, W.M. (1985) *Confucian Thought: Selfhood as Creative Transformation.* State University of New York Press, Albany, New York.

Tucker, M.E. (1991) The relevance of Chinese neo-Confucianism for the reverence of nature. *Environmental History Review* 15(2), 55–69.

Tucker, M.E. (1998) Religious dimensions of Confucianism: cosmology and cultivation. *Philosophy East and West* 48(1), 5–45.

UNWTO (2011) *UNWTO Tourism Highlights.* Available from http://mkt.unwto.org/sites/all/files/docpdf/unwtohighlights11enlr.pdf (accessed 18 October 2012).

Vargo, S.L. and Lusch, R.F. (2004) Evolving to a new dominant logic for marketing. *Journal of Marketing* 68(1), 1–17.

Vargo, S.L. and Lusch, R.F. (2008) Why 'service'? *Journal of the Academy of Marketing Science* 36(1), 25–38.

Wen, Y. and Ximing, X. (2008) The differences in ecotourism between China and the West. *Current Issues in Tourism* 11(6), 567–586.

White, L. (1967) The historic roots of our ecological crisis. *Science* 155(3767), 1203–1027.

World Tourism Organization (1999) *Tourism: 2020 Vision – Executive Summary.* World Tourism Organization, Madrid.

Yang, B., Zheng, W. and Li, M. (2006) Confucian view of learning and implications for developing human resources. *Advances in Developing Human Resources* 8(3), 346–354.

Yao, X.Z. (2000) *An Introduction to Confucianism.* Cambridge University Press, Cambridge.

Zhang, Q. (2000) The idea of human dignity in classical Chinese philosophy: a reconstruction of Confucianism. *Journal of Chinese Philosophy* 27(3), 299–330.

Zimmerman, M. (1993) Heidegger, Buddhism and deep ecology. In: Guignon, C. (ed.) *The Cambridge Companion to Heidegger.* Cambridge University Press, Cambridge, pp. 240–268.

19 Challenges and Future Research Directions

Nina K. Prebensen,[1] Muzaffer Uysal[2] and Joseph S. Chen[3]

[1]School of Business and Economics, UiT, Norway; [2]Pamplin College of Business, Virginia Tech, Blacksburg, USA; [3]Indiana University at Bloomington, USA

Introduction

In this book we took the position that creating value, no matter how it is contextualized, is naturally nested in the nature of tourism experiences. A careful review of the current literature and the chapters in this book point to the fact that a common feature of the most current approaches to value creation and co-creation is the shift toward a broader perspective; including the tourist as imperative in the value creation processes. The experience setting within which both the tourist and provider interact is also of immense importance in this process of value creation. In tourism experiences, where the tourist moves in time and space and leaves his/her home to be present and partaking in the making of holiday, the tourist has to some extent be motivated, involved and active in producing and consuming the experience. Consequently, a new and open perspective on how to acknowledge and facilitate value creation processes in experience-based consumption is needed. Previous research in the related area is mostly focused on antecedents and outcomes; there is ample opportunity for researchers to also focus on understanding and facilitating the nature of the value creation processes in hedonistic consumption of goods and services.

Experience Value and Creating Experiential Value

Creation and co-creation of experiences, as theoretical constructs, contemplate the consumer as an active part in consuming and producing value (Dabholkar et al., 2000), and deals with customer participation in defining and designing the experience. This description of the phenomenon is named prosumtion by Toffler (1980). Prosumption includes both production and consumption rather than focusing on either one (production) or the other (consumption), which is consistent with the analogy that tourism experiences, to a large extent, are produced and consumed simultaneously. In addition to participation, creating and co-creating experiences during a vacation include interaction with other people (e.g. host and/or guests) and with products and services in various experience settings (Prebensen and Foss, 2011), which results in increased (or decreased) value for themselves and others, in that it is an 'interactive, relativistic, preference experience' (Holbrook, 2006, p. 715). Throughout the book the common thread subsequently asserts that experience value comes from the creation and co-creation processes. Borrowing from Dabholkar, tourist participation may be defined as 'the degree to which the customer is involved and partakes in producing and delivering the service' (1990, p. 484). Based on this fundamental perspective of an active, willing and present consumer, this final chapter outlines challenges and future research directions in terms of value creation in tourist experiences and integrates the previous chapters to further delineate research directions. The first two chapters 'Co-creation of Tourist Experience: Scope, Definition and Structure' by Nina Prebensen, Joseph Chen and Muzaffer Uysal and 'Dynamic Drivers of Tourist Experiences' by Joseph Chen, Nina Prebensen and Muzaffer Uysal provide a general overview of the tourist experience and how this experience may be shaped and created throughout the duration of the different phases of a journey; each phase possessing the potential to create value not only for the participant but also for the provider of goods and services. If any, there has been very limited research on examining how different phases of a journey may create value in different experience settings and spheres. We wholeheartedly encourage researchers to conduct research in these aspects of vacation journeys. By the same token, a tourist experience driver model as presented in Chapter 2 (this volume) is also salient in advancing theory development and business practices in relation to tourist experience creation so as to recognize its associated challenges and limitations.

The three drivers of value creation – personal, environmental and interactive – in tourist experiences could not only produce a long-term, latent influence on experience creation but also render a short-term effect to moderate tourist experiences. Every possible driver of value creation under each category certainly requires a new and in-depth examination of their role in co-creating vacation experiences and contributing to value creation. In Chapter 3, 'Tourist Experience Value: Tourist Experience and Life Satisfaction', after presenting a tripartite view of people, service and places as the dimensionality of tourist experiences, Peter Björk establishes a theoretical link from the relationships that exist between tourist experiences and life satisfaction mediated through quality-of-life measures such as happiness and well-being, implying that creating value in experiences could also have different outcomes through spillover effects of the process. The chapter further argues that considering tourist experience as a process has the potential to enhance life satisfaction and subjective well-being of tourists as consumers. Consequently, it is important that destination marketing managers assess the portfolio of tourist well-being and value-enhancing service offerings, and guarantee quality assurance that may resonate better with the requirements of postmodern and transmodern travellers. We invite researchers to further delve into these areas of research in different experience settings using case studies and cross-sectional and longitudinal data.

It is argued that, from a tourism context, the tourist interacts with the destination's products and services leading to a higher level of engagement and tourist experiences. Chapter 4, 'Conceptualization of Value Co-creation in the

Tourism Context' by Prakash Chathoth, Gerardo Ungson, Robert Harrington, Levent Altinay, Fevzi Okumus and Eric Chan, suggests that a continuum from co-production to co-creation may be a way of capturing the essence of what tourism organizations and destinations offer. The level of tourist involvement in the value creation process and the modality of production/consumption-usage would guide and influence where firms as destinations and destination marketing organizations (DMOs) would lie on the continuum and how they would move within it. The chapter presents tourism destinations as moving towards a co-creation modality to attract and satisfy their current and future visitor markets. There is ample opportunity to conduct research in the area of building deeper customer engagement, appropriate engagement platforms, monitoring engagement and measuring outcomes of engagement platforms.

Different Behavioural Constructs and their Roles

A fundamental issue in order to comprehend the concept of value creation in tourism is about acknowledging why tourists travel during their spare time and understanding the natural link that exists between motivation and experience, between personal drive and what derives experiential value. There is limited research in this area. One rare study in this area was conducted by Prebensen *et al.* (2013a), which examined motivation as an antecedent in creating the perceived value of a destination, and this in turn is empirically linked as an antecedent to outcome measures such as satisfaction and loyalty. Chapter 5, 'Why, Oh Why, Oh Why Do People Travel Abroad?' by Graham Dann, provides a comprehensive review of different approaches to motivation and identifies further theoretical and methodological issues and encourages us to further empirically establish suggested links between motivation and experience and how motivation as personal driver may influence experimental value as antecedent, mediating or moderating variable in the process of creating experiential value. One of the important behavioural constructs as part of the process of creating experiential mental value is the notion of self-congruity. Chapter 6, 'Revisiting Self-congruity Theory in Travel and Tourism' by M. Joseph Sirgy, provides a state-of-the-art review of self-congruity research and presents several areas of future research with delineated propositions. There may be a reciprocal interaction and influence between self-congruity and travel behaviour. The chapter argues that self-congruity plays an important role in behavioural constructs such as motivation, loyalty, satisfaction and tourist attitude through perceived value. This implies that increased self-congruity could serve to increase the perception of value. Again, we invite researchers to engage in furthering the link between different types of congruity in different settings and its role in creating experiential value and predicting future behaviour.

There is no question that tourists' motivations and interests determine their involvement, if the ultimate goal of tourism is to 'move people'. How we get people to our destinations and how we get them to return later is fundamentally affected by how visitors are psychologically moved by their experiences and the value they may derive from their experiences. Chapter 7, 'Moving People: A Conceptual Framework for Understanding How Visitor Experiences can be Enhanced by Mindful Attention to Interest' by Tove Dahl, proposes that we are perhaps moved most by experiences that capture our interest. Interest is a key for focusing attention and giving us a reason to engage. Experiences can be deliberately structured to foster interest development. By so doing, hosts can make investments that can increase the chance of turning fleeting experiences into lasting ones by: (i) linking those powerful experiences to visitor knowledge, emotions and feelings of meaningfulness or (ii) using experiences to arouse interest in something new that can, with proper attention and care, evolve from a fleeting interest into something lasting and personal, thus creating value and enhancing one's self being. This chapter presents an interest-based working model that defines the concepts and mechanisms behind interest development that can be used to thoughtfully create visitor experiences that we hope move people for life. There is much room here for research in empirically understanding the role that the construct of differing levels of interest may take on in creating vacation experiences. 'Co-creation of Experience Value: A Tourist Behaviour Approach', by Lidia Andrades and Frédéric Dimanche (Chapter 8), provides a comprehensive treatment of the construct of involvement and interest in leisure and travel behaviour and further emphasizes the notion that in order to reinforce destination competitiveness, one approach would be to involve the visitor/tourist in taking an active role together with service providers in the process of creating rewarding and memorable experiences. In this context, the construct of involvement may be employed both as a moderating and mediating variable in the process of creating experimental value. It is important that we as researchers examine how the level of involvement of individuals in the process of value creation and also the degree of interactions with the spheres of tourism experience settings along with the type of tourism products may moderate the existing relationship between co-creation and possible outcome measures of creating value such as satisfaction, loyalty and subjective well-being of tourists as consumers. We encourage researchers to bring possible moderators into the examination of co-creation and creating value in tourism experiences and the effect of co-creation on the outcome variables of tourism experiences. One of the most recent studies, a thesis by Mathis (2013), demonstrated a significant relationship exists between co-creation and satisfaction with both the activity level and vacation in general, and involvement serving a significant role as a moderating variable between co-creation and satisfaction. Furthermore, her study established an empirical connection of co-creation to the enhancement of the subjective well-being of the tourist as a consumer, signifying that we have ample opportunity to connect creating value to several consumer constructs and decision-making in the tourism and hospitality field.

In tourism settings, epistemic value is of extreme importance. A significant number of studies show that even though people are satisfied and intend to recommend the destination or firm to others, the intention to return is relatively low compared with similar results tested in other consumption settings (buying a car or electric device, or in services such as banking, insurance and hair salons). Tourists want to experience something new, novel and exciting, and might not return, not because the previous experience was dissatisfying, but because they want to learn and experience something different and authentic. Chapter 9, 'Authenticity as a Value Co-creator of Tourism Experiences' by Haywantee Ramkissoon and Muzaffer Uysal, explores authenticity as a value co-creator of tourism experiences using the island of

Mauritius as a case study. The aim is to broaden the understanding of authenticity's various interpretations and its role as a value co-creator of tourism experiences in a cultural tourism context. Authenticated objects at cultural tourism sites often depict appreciation and tend to be conducive to personal experiences of object authenticity. The tourist is viewed as part of the authentication process rather than as a passive observer. Through a range of examples, implications for the future discourse of authenticity in tourism scholarship are presented, showing that there is tremendous potential in this area to explore and substantiate the dynamics of authenticity as a value co-creator of tourism experiences in different cultural settings.

In order to facilitate an environment that is conducive to creating satisfying and rewarding experiences with a high level of perceived authenticity, one could not overlook the importance of rapport-building between the frontline provider and consumer within a service environment. Chapter 10, 'Experience Co-creation Depends on Rapport-building: Training Implications for the Service Frontline' by Vincent Magnini and Kasey Roach, contends that consumers' perceptions of rapport and co-creation are highly correlated at the frontline. In other words, co-creation is stimulated by a sense of rapport between the frontline provider and visitor. Therefore, drivers of rapport building such as general training, training recovery and training transfer need to be identified, contextualized and linked to rapport in visitor–provider interactions and thus their effects on experience co-creation as an outcome variable. We concur with their research propositions that we urgently need solid research on how rapport-building training should be designed to yield top-rate co-created experiences.

Tourist firms and destinations ought to address and understand not only tourist needs and behaviour but also gain knowledge about the tourist evaluation of attractions and their role in contributing to creating experience value in order to facilitate for positive value creation situations. Chapter 11, 'Approaches for the Evaluation of Visitor Experiences at Tourist Attractions' by Øystein Jensen, discusses performance presentation strategies in managed tourist attractions and what type of consumer experience such strategies will produce. The chapter presents different perspectives on the evaluation of the quality of customer experiences and how different contexts will influence the role of the visitors as participants, further stressing the urgency to conduct research in critical aspects of the involvement of visitors in the consumption processes and the antecedents for this involvement. Thus, it is implied that much research is also needed focusing on the understanding of managed attractions from a marketing and an experience production point of view and how managed attractions may be positioned to create tourist experiences. From the perspective of managed attractions, we still need to identify not only generic but also unique features of visitor experiences within various contextual settings and conditions. For example, 'Storytelling in a Co-creation Perspective' by Line Mathisen (Chapter 12) points out that stories have always been important for people and are increasingly being discussed in marketing and advertising literature as they are argued to impact consumers' experience processes through emotions and comprehension. Stories that promote destinations communicate value propositions that engage tourists' imagination, and influence their expectations and attitudes about the destination and the upcoming experience through identification. The chapter demonstrates how stories may be used by tourism firms and destinations in order to enhance the value for tourists by involving them to partake in the value creation process, i.e. in co-creating experience value. How destinations may facilitate the choice of storytelling, staging and interpretation of stories when planning and creating tourist offerings for the appropriate setting would be a challenge and offer great opportunities for us as researchers. Also, exploring the role of social media and tourist information search to augment the art of destination management and the setting in which experiences are created would be of immense value to researchers and practitioners.

The literature is replete with studies that have examined the role of information search in decision-making. We do have a good understanding of how the search for information is structured and how this acquisition process works. Furthermore, we also have plenty of studies that demonstrate the value of obtaining and generating information in terms of cost, time and effort. However, there are very few empirical studies that specifically focus on creating experience value in tourism activities. For example, Prebensen *et al.* (2013) revealed a significant relationship between tourist information and perceived experience value. The effect of tourist operant resources on experience value should as such be further explored and tested, as enhanced experience value is an important key in order to shed light on outcome measures such as loyalty in tourism. Chapter 13, 'Tourist Information Search: A DIY Approach to Creating Experience Value' by Tor Korneliussen, makes a convincing argument for using a do-it-yourself (DIY) approach to creating experience value and suggests that attempts should also be linked to internet use and social media platforms.

Chapter 14, 'Co-creation of Value and Social Media: How?' by Atila Yüksel and Akan Yanık, provides an extensive discussion on how co-creation may offer a new paradigm that can foster growth, innovation and competitive advantage for destinations and marketing managers, thus creating value not only for users as tourists but also for providers in terms of visibility, competitive advantage and sustained business activities. It is argued that co-creating campaigns and strategies, intended to be shared and communicated, can easily find their way into social media tools such as Facebook, Twitter, YouTube and Flickr. In the context of this chapter, one can easily ask the question, 'How co-creation or creating value in experiences via social media may improve destination image, reduce risks in areas of strategy, innovation and new product development and contribute to the sustainability of business activities in general?' The area certainly begs for more research.

Experience value and creating value by definition invoke costs and benefits that would accrue from engagement in leisure and travel activities, search behaviour and budget constraints. For example, a recent study of costs and benefits in a tourist setting reveals a positive relationship between time, effort and the overall evaluation of a tourist trip (Prebensen *et al.*, 2013b), calling for new knowledge in terms of consumers' perceptions of costs and benefits in settings where the customer wants to be present and enjoy the moment of whatever being consumed, i.e. tourism experience setting, cultural arrangements and events or special interest events. Chapter 15, 'Prices and Value in Co-produced Hospitality and Tourism Experiences' by Xiaojuan (Jady) Yu and Zvi Schwartz, first presents the functions of pricing and then focuses on the informational role of pricing in a co-created tourism experience. Recently, researchers have tested the extended value scale in tourism settings (e.g. Prebensen *et al.*, 2013a, 2013b). Although value and quality are linked to price, there is ample opportunity to further explore the role of pricing and pricing strategies as antecedent or mediating/moderating variables in influencing creating value in experiences.

It is clear from most of the chapters that tourists also gain value from interactions with different stakeholders of the production and consumption of tourism experiences. Value in this sense may be created as the results of the tourists' own experiences and reflection on these experiences as tourists go through different phases of their journeys. Chapter 16, 'Value Creation: A Tourism Mobilities Perspective' by Bruce Prideaux, argues that tourism mobility, movement, dwelling and experience surely intersect to create the tourism experience. The chapter examines the manner in which value can be created during the various stages of the holiday journey. That is, the value may be created by the tourist through a host of experiences they may encounter, as well from the added value provided by the stakeholders and firms from which they obtain goods and services. We encourage researchers to further examine the nature of value that may be created both by the tourist and the provider in each phase of the vacation experience and the value that may be created at the intersection of the encounter process of co-creation. Chapter 17, 'Guide Performance: Co-created Experiences for Tourist Immersion' by Lena Mossberg, Monica Hanefors and Ann Heidi Hansen, provides a great example of how the interaction of the guides and the tourists co-create experiences for tourist immersion. The chapter discusses co-creation as a dynamic process in which tour guides and tourists interact. The chapter first explores the guides' basic roles and then their performances in enclavized, secure and thematized contexts and identifies specific performances that may have potential for co-creation of extraordinary experiences and for facilitation of tourists' immersion. It is important that we also understand the process of co-creating value in experiences as much as understand outcomes of the value creation process. We believe that there is ample opportunity for researchers to empirically examine the creation process using both qualitative and quantitative approaches.

Chapter 18, 'Value Creation and Co-creation in Tourist Experiences: An East Asian Cultural Knowledge Framework Approach' by Young-Sook Lee and Nina Prebensen, brings a cultural context into the discussion of value creations and co-creation by, first, reviewing key cultural traits of Zen Buddhism, Confucianism and Taoism, specifically focusing on the meanings of nature and learning, and then applying the concepts drawn from the framework in order to shed light on East Asian tourists' attitudes and learning orientations regarding nature-based experiences. It is argued that a clear understanding of the fundamental cultural traits of a given market would help practitioners and researchers to enhance value creation in different aspects of marketing and management strategies.

Further Research Areas

We have spent and continue to spend an enormous amount of time and money to understand the antecedents of behaviour and the consequences of behaviour; we have little research on the process of experiences that resulted in certain outcomes. We believe that the process that is creating the outcomes and consequences of behaviour needs to be paid more attention by researchers. What is the effect of that process on experience and value creation? To what extent can providers play a role in getting individuals to become part of the process of co-creation?

Destinations have tremendous pressure in facilitating value creation and co-creation in tourist experiences. We need to generate information and build knowledge systematically that could help decision-makers and destination planners to move forward with their value creation and co-creation efforts in appropriate settings. We have a host of challenges here. We need to develop appropriate scales and value scales unique to tourism experience settings that can be used not only for examining antecedents of creating value but also understanding the process and possible outcome measures that are not necessarily traditional.

It is given that the experience providers, the business and the destination actors plan, facilitate and partake in value creation and co-creation processes. Based on a perception of what tourists value before, during and after a vacation trip, tourist firms and facilitators may enhance the value creation process by implementing and staging service encounters and by appealing to the customer to partake in the value creation process. Appealing in this context is to start the process of motivating, involving and teaching tourists to partake and enjoy various dimensions of making a tourist journey; a key in value creation processes in tourist experiences. As such, the level of providing novel and exciting scenes and stories for the tourists through innovative practices is a core strategy in tourism, where the customer may switch despite previous satisfying experiences.

As service is delineated as the application of competences (knowledge and skills) by one entity for the benefit of another (Vargo and Lusch, 2006, 2008), we as tourism researchers and practitioners need to recognize how experience value is created as a result of mutual exchange throughout the whole experience process. The tourist firms reside in a continuous mode of transformation in order to meet the changing needs of their customers (Stamboulis and Skayannis, 2003). Hence, resources and the making of experience value is a key to acknowledging innovation potentials in service systems (Spohrer *et al.*, 2007). The designation of innovation as a capability that embraces learning dynamics endorsing the customer value and thus supporting renewal of the competitive advantage should also be adopted in tourism settings. Tourist firms need to address and understand tourist needs and wants in order to facilitate positive value creation situations.

As intangible aspects of tourism products through innovative technology are made tangible and automated, standardized and delivered, providers have to become more innovative in the way they provide experiences for future travellers. Providers need to act as facilitators and agents of the tourist in order to continue to sustain their financial viability and expand their market base. This trend certainly would require more in-depth understanding of how tourists as individuals interact with both the provider and the experience setting. Although we have seen a plethora of both qualitative and quantitative studies that have examined the effect of ambience on consumption and customer satisfaction, there is not much research in the context of the process of co-creation and creating value in tourism experiences. We challenge researchers to do research in this area.

References

Dabholkar, P. (1990) How to improve perceived service quality by improving customer participation. In: Dunlap, B.J. (ed.) *Developments in Marketing Science*. Academy of Marketing Science, Cullowhee, North Carolina, pp. 483–487.

Dabholkar, P.A., Shepherd, C.D. and Thorpe, D.I. (2000) A comprehensive framework for service quality: an investigation of critical conceptual and measurement issues through a longitudinal study. *Journal of Retailing* 76(2), 139–173.

Holbrook, B.M. (2006) Consumption experience, customer value, and subjective personal introspection: an illustrative photographic essay. *Journal of Business Research* 59, 714–725.

Mathis, E. (2013) The effects of co-creation and satisfaction on subjective well-being. Unpublished Master's thesis, Virginia Tech, Blacksburg, USA.

Prebensen, N.K. and Foss, L. (2011) Coping and co-creation in tourist experiences. *International Journal of Tourism Research* 13(1), 54–57.

Prebensen, N.K., Woo, E., Chen, J.S. and Uysal, M. (2013a) Motivation and involvement as antecedents of the perceived value of the destination experience. *Journal of Travel Research* 52(2), 253–264.

Prebensen, N.K., Dahl, T. and Vittersø, J. (2013b) Value co-creation: significance of tourist resources. *Annals of Tourism Research* 42, 240–261.

Spohrer, J., Maglio, P.P., Bailey, J. and Gruhl, D. (2007) Steps toward a science of service systems. *Computer* 40, 71–77.

Stamboulis, Y. and Skayannis, P. (2003) Innovation strategies and technology for experience-based tourism. *Tourism Management* 24, 35–43.

Toffler, A. (1980) *The Third Wave*. Bantam Books, New York.

Vargo, S.L. and Lusch, R.F. (2006) Service-dominant logic: what it is, what it is not, what it might be. In: Lusch, R.F. and Vargo, S.L. (eds) *The Service-Dominant Logic of Marketing: Dialog, Debate and Directions*. M.E. Sharpe, Armonk, New York, pp. 43–56.

Vargo, S.L. and Lusch, R.F. (2008) Service dominant logic: continuing the evolution. *Journal of the Academy of Marketing Science* 36, 42–53.

Index